Advanced Turbo C

Advanced Turbo C

Dr. James T. Smith

Intertext Publications
McGraw-Hill Book Company

New York St. Louis San Francisco Auckland Bogotá
Hamburg London Madrid Mexico Milan Montreal
New Delhi Panama Paris São Paulo
Singapore Sidney Tokyo Toronto

Library of Congress Catalog Card Number 88-82422

ISBN 0-07-058708-6 (Hardcover)
ISBN 0-07-058707-8 (Paperback)

10 9 8 7 6 5 4 3 2 1

Intertext Publications/Multiscience Press, Inc.
One Lincoln Plaza
New York, NY 10023

McGraw-Hill Publishing Company
1221 Avenue of the Americas
New York, NY 10020

Turbo C is a registered trademark of Borland International
Turbo C TOOLS is a registered trademark of Blaise Computing Inc.

Composed by Castle Productions, Limited

Table of Contents

Preface

This book is an introduction to systems programming concepts and techniques for the IBM PC family. Its language is Turbo C, one of the most popular for PC software development, developed by Borland International Inc. The book will show you how to use Turbo C for many systems programming tasks commonly encountered in applications software development. These range from mundane but tricky string processing problems, screen handling with windows and menus, through directory searches and execution of other programs, and finally to arcane techniques for constructing keyboard and timer interrupt service routines. Heavily documented programming examples are provided throughout, and their source code is also available to you on an optional diskette. A special feature of the book is its detailed description of one of the most complete systems programming tool tool kits for Turbo C, the Blaise Computing Inc. product Turbo C TOOLS.

The core of the book, which shows how most of the Turbo C Library and Turbo C TOOLS routines are constructed, is its chapter on interrupt services. After describing the interrupt process in general, it presents in detail the operating systems services offered to your programs via interrupts. The concluding chapter shows how to use Turbo C TOOLS to build your own custom interrupt service routines. Its intervention technique helps circumvent obstacles caused by non-reentrant DOS routines.

Who needs this book? You do, if you are considering serious software development for the IBM PC family, using Turbo C, or if Turbo C is a possibility and you want to find out how it supports your particular requirements. Or you may want to read it to find out how polished PC software is really constructed, what's easy and what's hard, how its systems aspects can be organized, and how to use and extend available tool kits.

Introduction

Contents

This book is an introduction to systems programming concepts and techniques for the IBM PC family. Its language is *Turbo C*, one of the most popular for PC software development, developed by Borland International Inc. The book will show you how to use Turbo C for many systems programming tasks commonly encountered in applications software development. These range from mundane but tricky string processing problems, screen handling with windows and menus, through directory searches and execution of other programs, and finally to arcane techniques for constructing keyboard and timer interrupt service routines. Heavily documented programming examples are provided throughout, and their source code is also available to you on an optional diskette. A special feature of the book is its detailed description of one of the most complete systems programming tool kits for Turbo C, the Blaise Computing Inc. product *Turbo C TOOLS*.

This introduction stresses the development and use of tool kits for systems and applications programming. It provides an overview of the contents of the book and diskette, reviews the organization of Turbo C, and gives a capsule description of the Turbo C TOOLS package. It concludes with a list of the references and documentation that you will need for programming projects of this nature.

1.1 Who needs this book?

Concepts

PC software development
Software tools
Turbo C Library
Turbo C TOOLS
Prerequisites for this book
Higher level vs. assembly language

Who needs this book? You do, if you are considering serious software development for the IBM PC family, using the Borland International Inc. Turbo C language, or if Turbo C is a possibility and you want to find out how it supports your particular requirements. Or perhaps you just want to find out how polished PC software is *really* constructed, what's easy and what's hard, how its systems aspects can be organized, and how to use and extend available tool kits.

PC software development involves a more intimate relationship with the hardware and operating system than many programmers are used to. There are two reasons for this. First, the hardware flexibility characterizing IBM's design gives independent software developers responsibility to adapt to new hardware features as they appear. Second, the standard DOS operating system doesn't fill all your needs. If you try personally to supply all required systems routines, you'll waste much time reinventing techniques in which others have already invested years of effort. You need a tool kit of known solutions to common problems, so that you can concentrate on the specific ones in which you are most interested and expert.

The Turbo C Library, a package of systems routines supplied with Turbo C, is a major step toward a comprehensive tool kit. Its approximately five hundred functions cover many of the areas considered in this book:

manipulating memory areas	file input/output
string processing	directory management
screen handling	memory management
keyboard input	executing separate programs

In addition, it includes low-level graphics, which is beyond the scope of this book. Although this product is comprehensive and professionally implemented, it will fall short of your needs in several areas.

Many commercial products can provide further support for your work. This book describes one in detail, the Blaise Computing Inc. Turbo C TOOLS package. Its routines serve basic needs, extending the Turbo C Library to deal with some of the most complex low level areas: screen and keyboard control and interrupt services, as well as some simpler tasks. Turbo C TOOLS also provides complex high-level support for text windows and menus.

The Turbo C Library and Turbo C TOOLS serve general needs. Yours may extend still farther, so that you may want to acquire or develop additional tools of this nature. For example, this book develops a broader string processing package in Chapter 3. For specific projects, you may want to consider tool kits in areas like high-level graphics, serial communications, or input editing.

What principles should govern tool kit development? First, *isolate programming problems*, and attack them independently while they occupy your entire attention. That's much more likely to produce useful tools than ad hoc solutions by a programmer really interested only in getting some particular application to work. Second, *strive for generality*. Each application will differ a little from earlier ones. A tool that is too particular will need modification again and again, and may lose a little robustness each time. Next, *test the code!* Have others use it in as many different situations as possible. Finally, *write readable, understandable, trustable code and documentation*. Programmers who can't understand how a tool works may not want to use it in products on which their job depends.

The string processing routines in Chapter 3 illustrate these principles, and can serve as a model for your work. To consider them, you must understand just the most basic aspects of the PC and Turbo C.

The Turbo C TOOLS package was also developed according to these principles. Its approximately 175 routines are organized via header files into understandable modules. Each function performs a clearly defined service, useful in many contexts. Thoroughly documented source code is provided with the package, as well as an extremely detailed manual. This product has been evolving since 1983, in various dialects of the Pascal and C languages. It has a large user base, and is very reliable.

What must you know *before* reading this book? The book assumes that you are a skilled programmer in some higher-level language and that you are familiar with Turbo C. You should also be familiar with the various hardware components of your PC and with DOS—from a user's point of view. Finally, some familiarity with machine language concepts is assumed in the last two chapters, which are concerned with interrupts. You need not have done any substantial assembly language programming.

That brings up an important point about this book. In many others, techniques like those described here are implemented in assembly language. There were once several reasons for that:

- No *popular* high-level language language was well suited to low-level programming tasks.
- High-level languages were regarded as *too slow* for these tasks.
- They were thought *unsuited* to the complex logic of low level tasks.

The first claim may have held true in the past; but one of this book's goals is to show that Turbo C is a good language for systems work as well as applications programming. The second reservation is partly true, partly misleading. Some low-level tasks, such as screen manipulation and interrupt processing, do require greater speed than possible with ordinary Turbo C techniques. A solution is to use in-line assembly code or an assembly language external routine. Many of the Turbo C Library and Turbo C TOOLS routines use that technique. On the other hand, you will find that many routines in this book do *not* require fast processing, because they are infrequently executed. However, they are often very complicated, and must be done absolutely right. Therefore, the language used should facilitate use of the clearest possible programming style in the most complex logical situations. C does that.

The techniques featured in this book avoid assembly language entirely, except in a few cases where its speed is absolutely necessary, or where direct access to the CPU registers is required. This decision was reinforced once by Philippe Kahn, who founded Borland International Inc. Commenting on problems involved in converting Borland's *Sidekick* package to assembly language—required for the reasons just given— Kahn noted that "No one over twenty-five should do assembly language programming!"

1.2 Working with tools

> **Concepts**
>
> Areas requiring systems programming tools
> Should you use a commercial tool kit or write your own?
> Other areas where tool kits can help

In the previous section you saw the need for a systems programming tool kit to fill gaps left by DOS and Turbo C. Such a package will meet needs commonly encountered in applications software development. This book shows how to build and use a basic tool kit. Here is a list of areas where you will need systems tools. Those covered in this book are indicated by (*). First is a selection of low level areas:

String processing *	Directory management *
Screen handling	Clock/calendar services *
Text *	Printer control *
Graphics	Serial communications *
Keyboard input *	Sound production
File input/output *	Graphics device interfaces

Memory management and program execution
   Executing separate programs *
   DOS memory allocation *
   Extended and expanded memory

This book has left several areas uncovered because the associated equipment is not standard. Moreover, for graphics, adequate treatment would require a second volume. A rudimentary discussion of serial communications methods is given in Section 8.8, but you are referred to other sources for information on sophisticated techniques now in common use.

Beyond these basic systems programming areas, you'll need assistance in organizing

Interrupt service routines *

Interrupts form the basis of the operating system services provided for your programs. To modify or extend these services, you must understand interrupts. An interrupt service routine can be invoked by an external event during execution of an entirely unrelated program; constructing the interface between that program and your custom Turbo C service routine requires some sophisticated techniques involving assembly language. Chapters 8 and 9 are devoted to interrupt services.

High-level techniques are being developed throughout the PC software industry to make interactive applications easier to program and use. As you learn of new methods, you will want tools for using them. Any list of areas requiring such tools is necessarily incomplete, but here is a start:

Screen windows   Input editing
    Text *   Multiprocessing and
    Graphics   multiuser systems
Menus *

As indicated, two areas are covered in this book.

With a reliable systems programming tool kit, you use techniques developed by specialists—or by yourself, when you were concentrating on a specific systems problem. Developing a sophisticated applications program is far easier if you can avoid the distractions created by complicated hardware and operating system interfaces, and if you can be certain that most programming errors will occur not in those arcane areas, but in the applications area, where you are the most expert.

This book shows how to assemble and use a tool kit sufficiently general for use in many different applications. The Turbo C Library and Turbo C TOOLS are used as examples. Their underlying techniques are covered thoroughly. When you finish this book, you should be able to construct such a package for yourself. But there's no point in doing that. Use a commercial product to give you a base of tested, understood routines. Use your own time to develop whatever more specialized tools your own application requires.

With the knowledge gained here, you'll not only be able to use and extend a basic systems programming tool kit like Turbo C TOOLS, but you will see how to organize and use custom and commercial tool kits in other areas. Among the areas that you may want to consider are

Editing	High-level graphics
Data base	Statistical analysis
Communications	Numerical analysis

Commercial tool kits are available for all these. A few are cited in Section 1.6.

1.3 This book's structure

Concepts

Overview of contents
Diskette
Header file **General.H**

Later sections of this introductory chapter review the organization of Turbo C and give an overview of the Turbo C TOOLS package. Its last section surveys documentation required for serious applications programming, and refers as well to some tool kits in areas not covered in the book.

With the very first programming discussion, in Chapter 2, you see the interplay between hardware and software. It describes the PC memory structure, and demonstrates Turbo C features that work directly with memory. The six Turbo C memory models are discussed thoroughly.

The next chapter is devoted to string processing. While this is not such an engaging topic, its techniques are required frequently, and it provides a gentle entrance into advanced Turbo C programming and the use and development of software toolkits. For that reason, perhaps string processing should have come first, but smooth exposition required prior treatment of some memory considerations.

The book continues with chapters on several basic areas covered by the Turbo C Library and Turbo C TOOLS:

- Screen handling
- Keyboard
- Directory and file manipulation

The discussion is arranged so that you can see just what Turbo C itself offers, and recognize the gaps that Turbo C TOOLS fills. For example, you'll see that the Turbo C Library fulfills practically every requirement in the directory and file manipulation areas, but fails to provide robust keyboard input routines. Turbo C TOOLS satisfies that need, and its high level windowing and menu handling features greatly extend the capabilities of Turbo C.

The most complex parts of the book, Chapters 7 through 9, are concerned with organization and execution of separate program units. Chapter 7 covers Turbo C Library techniques:

- Memory allocation among programs
- Execution of separate programs
- Chaining

The core of the book, which shows how most of the Turbo C Library and Turbo C TOOLS routines are constructed, is Chapter 8, on interrupt services. That long chapter first describes the interrupt process in general, then presents in detail the operating systems services offered to your programs via interrupts. The concluding Chapter 9 shows how to use Turbo C TOOLS to build your own custom interrupt service routines. A major question is the interface between your Turbo C service routine and the perhaps unrelated program that is interrupted. Turbo C TOOLS supplies this interface routine, some of which is necessarily written in assembly language. Interrupt service routine construction is hampered by some ill-designed DOS features (non-reentrant code). The final Section 9.4 describes a technique for circumventing those obstacles: the Turbo C TOOLS *intervention* system.

Diskette

This book contains a profusion of example routines and programs. As far as possible, the optional diskette gives you a convenient way to reconstruct and test them. You will find further information about the diskette on a page in the back of the book. Its directory is listed in Appendix A.

All source code for routines and programs written for this book is found on the diskette. Individual programming tools are in files with suffix **.C**; most demonstration program file names end in **.Dem**. Many tools have simple demonstration programs in files with similar names. Because they are routine, not all those are described in the book.

General.H

Header file **General.H** is included with compiler directive **#include** in many programs in the book. This contains some declarations used throughout the book, and prototypes for most of the generally useful functions written specifically for the book. If you find an apparently undeclared identifier in one of the programs or routines in this book, look through this file for the declaration. It's listed in Appendix B.

1.4 Turbo C

Concepts

Why use C?
Why use Turbo C?
Turbo C Library
Hardware and software used to produce this book
New DOS and Turbo C versions
C style for this book

This section's major topic is a rather argumentative discussion of the reasons for and against using the C language and Turbo C system for PC software development. It concludes with a description of the hardware and software actually used for producing this book, and a few words about the style adopted here for C programs.

Why use Turbo C?

Why should you use the C language for PC software development? In the C literature you'll find several standard responses:

- C is a high-level language, well suited to expressing algorithms of all sorts.
- C fosters writing elegant, readable programs.
- C programs are portable to many computer systems.
- Excellent compilers are available.
- Excellent software tools are available in many areas.
- C compilers produce small, fast executable code.
- C lets you access and control hardware features.
- C programming makes you consider low level details.

These propositions are considered in more detail later. At the very start, however, you should realize that the author does not feel that they are compelling reasons for using C. They do establish C as an excellent possibility. Most of these propositions are only partially true, or apply equally well to other popular languages. The first and last are even contradictory. Before continuing in this vein, however, consider a narrower question.

Why should you use the Turbo C software development system? Here, the responses are less controversial:

- Turbo C has a *wonderful* user interface.
- You can configure most features to fit your habits.
- Syntax errors are immediately flagged in the editor.
- The editor will emulate popular word processors.
- Version 2 includes a source code debugger.
- The compiler is extremely fast.
- The accompanying function Library is comprehensive, well documented, and reliable.

- Turbo C includes standard features that facilitate development of very large software systems.
- Turbo C executable code compares well with that of other C compilers.

In summary, Turbo C is delightful to work with. You should realize, however, that all these positive responses except the last apply as well to Borland's Turbo Pascal system. Thus, they are not reasons to choose Turbo C; they are reasons *not to reject* it.

The author has only three criticisms of Turbo C. The first is minor: syntax error reporting could be improved considerably. For example, the uninformative "cop out" error message

Expression syntax in function ...

occurs much too frequently. The second criticism is also minor: a few Turbo C Library functions perform or are documented incorrectly. In fact, this is hardly a criticism. You can make it a positive comment merely by inserting the word *only* before *a few*: the Library contains approximately five hundred functions. The last criticism is more substantial, and arises many times in this book: the Library is chaotically organized, and unnecessarily hard to use. This is as much a criticism of C implementation principles as of technique; it will be considered again in a later paragraph.

Now return to the question of selecting a language for a programming project. A number of standard reasons for choosing C were mentioned earlier, along with the author's reservation about their cogency. Consider them in greater detail.

First, although often termed such, C is really *not a high-level language*. As you'll see from examples in this book, *you are constantly forced to consider low level address details*. Until you become a specialist in C, you will be an inefficient C programmer, because these details are often extremely hard to get right. C is not particularly well suited to expressing most algorithms, except for those explicitly concerned with addressing. Low-level concerns often predominate, and the resulting C programs don't "look like" the algorithms. Thus, the contradiction between the first reason for choosing C and the last is resolved in favor of the last. Perhaps the only way to make C programming appear really high-level is to overexploit its preprocessor features by *defining* a comprehensive set of high-level constructs, then consistently employing them. You may succeed in using C to develop an excellent high-level language understood by exactly one programmer.

C does foster writing elegant, readable programs. The author hopes there are some in this book. But C is really neutral: it also fosters writing inelegant, unreadable programs. If anything, the scale tips negative here. The author has watched C seduce virtuous programmers away from good clean programming habits into the dark jungle of fetid definitions, nebulous declarations, and code intertwined like dangling vines. Philippe Kahn, President of Borland International Inc., once called C "an American disease."

The low nature of C is sometimes a positive quality. It does provide ready access to hardware features, and makes controlling them easy. Moreover, in forcing you to consider address details, it fosters production of small, fast code. If these are primary concerns for your programming project, C is clearly an appropriate language.

C programs are in fact portable to and from many computer systems. The author has little experience in that area, and cedes a point: if you want to move a C program from some other system to the PC environment, you should probably continue to use the C language. Be prepared, however, to make perhaps major changes in your input/output code, unless you make little use of PC screen capabilities and don't care if keyboard mistakes disrupt your program's operation. (See Chapter 5 for detailed discussion of keyboard input robustness, and Chapters 4 and 5 for techniques that fully utilize PC capabilities.) Portability in the reverse direction is not so clear a question. To provide that for a new software product, choose a language available on systems you're interested in, and avoid using techniques valid only on PCs. C may well be your choice—not necessarily by virtue of its own qualities, but simply because it's widely available.

Evaluating the Turbo C Library presents a problem. The Library is certainly comprehensive. Much of this book is devoted to describing its features:

Chapter	Feature
2	Manipulating memory areas
3	String processing
4	Screen handling
5	Keyboard input
6	File input/output and directory management
7	Memory management; executing other programs

One major Library function category is not considered in this book: graphics. Turbo C includes the same Borland Graphics Interface (BGI) routines as Turbo Pascal. Covering graphics adequately would require a book in itself.

Turbo C wouldn't be useful for PC software development without such a library. The problem is that the Turbo C Library is chaotically organized. Apparently to enhance portability, Borland incorporated into its product bad features of other libraries as well as good. Unfortunately, this strategy fosters portability of bad programs as well as good, and ensures that Library difficulties will persist. Moreover, software design problems entail documentation problems. Individual Turbo C Library functions are often reasonably documented, but there may be no indication why they were designed as they are. Often there are alternate ways to accomplish a task, but no clue to the proper function for a particular context. Some functions just transport traditional C practice into the PC world without regard to propriety in that environment. There's no reason to program that way unless you're explicitly aiming for portability—but the documentation doesn't indicate that. Without an overview, you can't see the forest for the trees—or perhaps it resembles the jungle envisioned earlier. One of the goals of this book is to provide that overview.

C apologists sometimes use function libraries to deflect language criticism. If some feature of a program is ill designed or nonportable, it's convenient to respond that there's no problem with C itself, because the feature is a library function. This argument amounts to declaring the underlying language free from criticism because it just consists of all unobjectionable features. That's nonsense: if a program requires a library function just to write **Hello, world**, that function is part of the language. If the function is to some extent nonportable, so is the language. In fact, the nonportable aspects of Turbo C are mostly in its Library. Unfortunately, they aren't segregated in a single section, so it's sometimes difficult to identify them. This book may help, although that wasn't a major goal.

A final argument for using C is that all the programs in this book were written in the language. Since the book is mostly concerned with low-level detail, this should establish C as the choice for low level programming. That argument is *invalid*: it only establishes C as a possibility. Virtually all of the programs in this book were originally written in Turbo Pascal for the author's earlier book [35]. You should realize that the Turbo C versions took as long to develop as the original ones: the advantage of previously tested designs was offset by the difficulty of low-level details.

In summary, the major reasons for opting to use Turbo C are its flexibility, its emphasis on low-level concerns and consequent executable code speed and size advantage, and its portability. The last quality is mainly due to its popularity. There are many reasons not to reject Turbo C: it *can* serve you very well for a great variety of projects. Its major disadvantages are mostly consequences of its low level: it's hard to use correctly, and C programs, no matter how well written, are often hard to understand. Opting for C may thus entail inefficient use of programmer time. In addition, the Turbo C Library suffers from immaturity of design, and current strategy probably means that order won't emerge from its chaos.

There's another reason for studying C, perhaps not so serious, but perhaps explaining some of its appeal: it's different and difficult as well as applicable. As a sophomore, the author decided to learn symbolic logic for that reason. (Russell and Whitehead's *Principia Mathematica* must certainly be understood only by a selected few.) That's a wonderful reason for learning. Great intellectual excitement and enjoyment can and did result, both with logic and with programming. But there's a somewhat negative consequence as well: if the discipline does prove practical, those few who understand it become indispensable. That's perhaps good for them, but can lead to stagnation if programming becomes overspecialized.

Producing this book

An original issue IBM PC was used to develop the software for this book. It had been equipped with a 20 MB fixed disk, and a 1.2 MB diskette drive for backup. These are really required for Turbo C work. The machine has 2.6 MB of memory, allocated as follows:

64K	extended memory for printer buffer
560K	extended memory for virtual disk
640K	conventional memory
1354K	expanded memory

The latter two areas are managed by Quarterdeck Software's DESQview multiprocessing system. Four DESQview windows are always active:

Turbo C Version 1.5, Volkswriter 3, DOS 3.3, and a database. Volkswriter 3 is the word processor used for preparing the manuscript. To ward off insanity, the author configured the Turbo C editor to work almost exactly like Volkswriter. Frequently accessed items like C headers and Volkswriter spill files are placed on virtual disk. The memory just inventoried is only barely sufficient for this setup. DESQview provides the capability to switch between windows with exactly two keystrokes, and to move text from one window to another. It's ideal for writing about programming.

New DOS and Turbo C versions

Although Turbo C Version 2 and DOS Version 4 appeared while this book was being written, these new releases are not mentioned again after this introductory chapter. Including them would have delayed completion and increased the size of the book unacceptably. This is particularly unfortunate in the case of Turbo C Version 2, because of its source code debugger, which will be a major tool in PC software development.

C style for this book

For the C programs in this book, the author adopted a somewhat unusual style. Several principles were involved. First, low-level detail is generally left exposed, not hidden by macro definitions. Among the few exceptions are the **Boolean** type and related constants **True** and **False**:

```
#define Boolean int
#define True 1
#define False 0
```

These are used because the author finds it too easy to reverse conditional statements otherwise. Prototypes of generally useful functions and frequently used declarations and definitions are included in a single header file **General.H**, listed in Appendix B. Identifiers declared or defined in this book use combination upper/lower case for readability, and to distinguish them from others declared in the Turbo C Library, Turbo C TOOLS, or Turbo C itself. Finally, indentation is used to enhance readability, but two other needs take precedence: ends of lines are used for comments when appropriate, and programs should be short, to avoid page turns and to keep the book from bloating. The author hopes this style is effective and inoffensive.

1.5 Turbo C TOOLS

Concepts
Overview Sample routine

Turbo C TOOLS is a systems programming toolkit for Turbo C, developed and marketed by Blaise Computing Inc. This book describes Version 1.5. The package contains about 175 routines under the following headings:

Mne- monic	Heading	See Chapter	Mne- monic	Heading	See Chapter
st	Strings	3	fl	Files	6
sc,vi	Screen	4	mm	Memory	7
wn	Windows	4	pr	Printer	8
gr	Graphics		is	Interrupt service	9
kb	Keyboard	5	iv	Intervention code	9
mn	Menus	5	ut	Utility	

Names of the functions under each heading begin with the mnemonics shown. Except for the Graphics functions, which lie beyond the scope of this book, nearly all these routines are discussed here, in the chapters indicated. Discussions of Utility functions are scattered. As mentioned earlier, this package's goal is to fill gaps left by Turbo C and DOS, letting you write polished applications programs without becoming preoccupied with programming details in the areas listed.

Complete source code is provided with the package. It's thoroughly documented, and a detailed *Reference manual* is included [4]. The source code for an example Turbo C TOOLS function, **utsleep**, is shown in Figure 1.5.1 to illustrate the general style and documentation. It has

```
/**
* Name         UTSLEEP — Suspend processing for some period
*
* Synopsis     rdur = utsleep(period);
*
*              unsigned rdur    The number of timer ticks the
*                               process was actually delayed.
*              unsigned period  The number of timer ticks the
*                               process is to be suspended.
*
* Description  UTSLEEP  suspends processing for at least the
*              number of ticks requested, and returns the actu-
*              al number as the functional value.  Because the
*              function checks the system clock to determine
*              whether the period has expired, it is possible
*              that the actual duration is longer than that
*              requested.
*
*              There are  1193180/65536  (about  18.2)  ticks
*              per second on  IBM  PCs.
*
*              This function temporarily enables hardware inter-
*              rupts but restores the state of the interrupt
*              flag before it returns.
*
* Version 5.00   (C)Copyright Blaise Computing Inc. 1984, 1987
**/


#include <butil.h>

unsigned utsleep(unsigned period) {
  long     initclk;              /* Initial clock count. */
  long     nowclk;               /* Moving clock count.  */
  unsigned elpticks;             /* Elapsed tick count.  */
  int      ints_were_on;         /* Whether interrupts   */
ints_were_on = utinton();        /* were on already.     */
utgetclk(&initclk);              /* Find out the current */
for (elpticks = 0;               /* clock count and wait */
     elpticks < period;          /* until period counts  */
     elpticks = (unsigned)       /* have passed.         */
        (nowclk - initclk)) {
```

Figure 1.5.1 Function **utsleep** (*continued on next page*)

```
utgetclk(&nowclk);
if (nowclk < initclk)                    /* Must have wrapped    */
    nowclk += 0x1800b0L; }               /* past midnight.       */
if (!ints_were_on) utintoff();
return(elpticks); }
```

Figure 1.5.1 *(Continued)* Function **utsleep**

been edited only slightly, to conserve space and correct one error in diction. Similar style standards are enforced in this book, and should serve as a model. Properly documented code can be understood by others—and by its programmer at a later date. Code that's understood can be trusted and used correctly. **utsleep** was chosen for display here because it's simple, but does involve some timing and other systems programming details. Further such details are hidden by the references to three other Turbo C TOOLS utility functions. You might use **utsleep** to give a user a specific amount of time to answer a question; while writing a program like that, you probably don't want bother about timing and hardware interrupt details. Turbo C TOOLS does that for you.

Function **utsleep** is considered again, along with many timing and interrupt processing details, in Chapter 8.

1.6 References and further topics

Concepts

Reference manuals and related books
Turbo C Library source code
Debuggers
Tool kits in other areas

To do serious PC software development in Turbo C you need to find answers to technical questions that arise constantly. While much of the necessary material has been gathered in this book, it certainly cannot provide *all* the answers! This section will present a number of references to help you. Some are immediately relevant—even indispensable—to the type of programming considered here. Others provide background information, and some are commercial packages that extend the tool box concept to other areas mentioned in Section 1.2. Numbers in brackets refer to the Bibliography at the end of the book.

This book assumes that you are basically familiar with Turbo C and its use in applications programming. This involves both general knowledge of C and particular knowledge of its Borland implementation. The original C reference, Kernighan & Ritchie [22], is not a good tool for learning C, but is referred to so frequently and religiously that you should have it. A number of books are available that introduce C via the Turbo C implementation and develop it to a level equivalent to or slightly beyond where this book begins. The author doesn't feel familiar enough with any of them to recommend one here. The reference work by Harbison & Steele [12] is useful, particularly concerning the proposed ANSI standard C.

The principal reference manuals that you need for the type of programming considered in this book are

Turbo C
    User's guide .... [8]
    Reference guide .... [7]
    Version 1.5 additions and enhancements .... [6]
Turbo C Library source code .... [5]
Turbo C TOOLS .... [4]
DOS reference .... [19]
Microsoft MS-DOS encyclopedia .... [28]
PC technical reference .... [20]
8086 programmer's reference .... [15]

The Turbo C manuals listed are for Version 1.5, used for this book. The *User's guide* describes Turbo C as a whole, with much material on getting started; the *Reference guide* is mostly devoted to the Turbo C Library. The organization of this documentation will change as later versions become available.

The author found the Turbo C Library source code indispensable for writing this book. Too often, the Library programmers chose software organization and implementation schemes complex or arbitrary enough to defeat Borland's competent documentation specialists. If you can't gain understanding of a routine through its documentation, you must conduct experiments or analyze its source code. The author spent too much time in both activities. In fact, investigating Library function behavior often resembled PhD level research in an experimental science. If you intend to write a major application or a software toolkit in Turbo C you should anticipate that requirement. However, a goal of this book is to minimize the time you waste that way, and in any case you won't need to analyze the *entire* Library! Although Turbo C itself is priced very reasonably, the Library source code is expensive.

The *MS-DOS Encyclopedia* [28] appeared as this book was being written. It's absolutely indispensable, beautifully constructed, and a great bargain. It covers material accessible earlier only through several Microsoft product manuals and the overpriced DOS technical reference manual [18]. The author has not yet been able to study whether the last is now completely obsolete, but suspects (and hopes) so. Two trade books, Norton's [31] and Duncan's [10], cover some of the same material in a less formal setting. Duncan is one of the authors of the encyclopedia.

Each PC model has a technical reference manual. You need access to an IBM PC, XT, or AT manual. PC clone manuals are generally inadequate; too many were written by seemingly ignorant illiterates, and are useful only in providing clues to a clone's departure from IBM's hardware implementation. The most valuable part of an IBM manual is its listing of the BIOS (the part of the operating system built into your PC's memory). Even if your BIOS is a clone, it *must* work like IBM's, and the IBM manual is its best documentation. Many PC components are Intel products or clones; you will find authoritative, if sometimes opaque, documentation in the Intel references in the Bibliography. Several trade books concentrate on PC hardware questions. Norton's [30] is fairly elementary. The author's favorite is Sargent & Shoemaker [33]. For PC/AT questions, you may want to consult the author's earlier book [34].

Software development work occasionally requires a debugger. **Debug.Com**, delivered with DOS, is sufficient for many purposes, but inadequate for some work on interrupts underlying this book. The author uses *Advanced Trace 86*, developed by Morgan Computing Co. [29]. As this book was being completed, Turbo C Version 2.0 appeared, with a full source code debugger. That will certainly become the standard way to analyze Turbo C program behavior.

Section 1.2 listed a number of areas in which you might want to acquire or build toolkits extending the reach of those described in this book. Even a survey of that subject is beyond the scope of this book. Two Blaise Computing Inc. products deserve mention, though, because their techniques are closely related to the Turbo C TOOLS package featured here:

- *ASYNCH MANAGER* [2]—a low-level toolkit for interrupt driven serial communications;
- *POWER SCREEN* [3]—a high-level package for building data entry and display screens and help files.

For further information on perhaps a hundred other packages, consult the advertisements and frequent survey articles in the trade journals.

2

Memory Organization

Contents

2.1 Segment:offset addressing
2.2 Conventional memory
2.3 Turbo C memory models
2.4 Data formats in memory
2.5 Stack and heap organization
2.6 Further topics

This chapter gathers together basic information about memory utilization by Turbo C programs. The discussion ranges from elementary to arcane, but attempts to stay practical. Since you are not relying on this as an *introduction* to your PC's memory or to Turbo C, it's organized by topic rather than degree of difficulty. You'll often find very involved aspects of one topic considered before the most elementary concepts of another.

Elementary notions covered here include segment:offset addressing and allocation of PC memory among the BIOS, ROM BASIC, DOS, and your own software; you probably have already considered these concepts while becoming familiar with your machine. The discussion continues with the overall memory organization for your programs. Turbo C provides six different organizations, or *models*, for use according to your memory needs. These are described, contrasted, and demonstrated in detail. Then your attention is turned to minutiae of data structure implementation, pointer manipulation, and stack and heap organization. Software development involves all these levels of complexity. Clearly, the overall picture helps you understand your program's role in the entire machine operation. At the other extreme, knowledge of fine details of data structures and stack format help you locate and avoid bugs, and are essential if your program incorporates code written in different languages.

Section 2.6 includes miscellaneous topics. Several Turbo C Library low-level memory manipulation functions and some higher-level sorting and searching routines are demonstrated. Special considerations for AT extended memory and Lotus/Intel/Microsoft/AST *expanded* memory are discussed briefly there as well, with references to relevant programming information. Port input/output is discussed briefly.

A few routines from the Blaise Computing Inc. Turbo C TOOLS package are considered in this chapter, but not in depth. That product does not emphasize memory management tools. It will play a featured role, however, in several later chapters.

2.1 Segment:offset addressing

Concepts

Physical addresses and the 1 MB address space
AT real mode addressing
Words and paragraphs
Segment:offset addresses
Segment registers
Pseudo-variables _CS, _DS, _SS
Near and far pointers
Memory models
Accessing segment:offset addresses from Turbo C programs
Ascertaining the PC model

Physical addresses

The Intel 8086 and 8088 CPUs in most PCs use 20-bit physical addresses. Their directly accessible memory consists of eight-bit bytes, each of which has a 20-bit binary address. Since $2^{20} = 1,048,576$, PCs can use one megabyte (1 MB) of memory directly. For legibility, addresses are normally written in hexadecimal notation.

ATs have Intel 80286 or 80386 CPUs, which can operate in two modes: *real* or *protected*. In real mode, they use the same addressing scheme, but protected mode addressing is quite different. When you start an AT, it's in real mode. Since little software is available to support protected mode operation, this book will make little reference to it. An exception is the discussion of AT extended memory in Section 2.6. Unless expressly noted, memory discussions apply both to PCs and to ATs operating in real mode.

It's customary to refer to two consecutive bytes as a *word*, and to 16 consecutive bytes as a *paragraph*, provided the address of the first byte is a multiple of 16. Since 16 = hex 10, a hexadecimal paragraph address ends in zero.

Segment:offset addresses

Because the CPU manipulates information in byte or word units (eight or 16 bits), a special arrangement is necessary to handle 20-bit physical addresses. The CPU organizes memory into *overlapping segments*, each containing $64K = 2^{16}$ bytes beginning on a paragraph boundary. Since a paragraph contains 2^4 bytes, there are $2^{16} = 2^{20}/2^4$ possible segments. Thus a byte can be located by a 16-bit number identifying the segment, and a 16-bit offset within that segment. Such a pair is called a *segment:offset* address. You can determine the corresponding physical address by multiplying the segment number by 16 = hex 10 and adding the offset. *Different segment:offset addresses can refer to the same physical address:*

segment:offset address	address calculation	physical address
hex 12b3:4f26	12b30 + 04f26	17a56
hex 1000:7a56	10000 + 07a56	17a56

The first entry of a segment:offset address is often called a *paragraph* or *segment* address; for example, segment 9000 begins at address 9000:0000. Once the segment address is understood, you can specify a byte simply by its *offset* address.

This addressing scheme facilitates modular programming and code relocation, because instruction codes, data, and the program stack can often be constrained to lie in single segments. Offset addresses can be determined in advance, relative to the beginnings of the segments, and only a few segment addresses need be supplied when the program is loaded into memory for execution.

Segment registers

To facilitate segment:offset addressing, the CPU has four 16-bit *segment registers:*

CS: Code Segment Register
ES: Extra Segment Register
DS: Data Segment Register
SS: Stack Segment Register

To access code or data in memory, the segment address is often placed in the appropriate segment register, the offset in some other register (according to certain conventions), and an instruction is selected that uses these registers to determine its operand address.

The Turbo C compiler uses three of these registers in the binary code it generates:

CS   to access code,
DS   to access global and static variables,
SS   to access local variables, parameters, and other information pertaining to function calls.

For systems programming, you will occasionally need to know the contents of these registers. Turbo C provides this via three pseudo-variables _CS, _DS, and _SS. Their use is demonstrated later in Section 2.3. (Additional registers, each with a corresponding pseudo-variable, are used for other purposes. For example, the Extra Segment Register ES, with pseudo-variable _ES, can be used more or less like the Data Segment Register. An example at the end of this section demonstrates its use.)

Memory models

If a program can use single code, data, and stack segments, the contents of registers CS, DS, and SS can remain unchanged during execution. Addressing then involves manipulating single-word offsets relative to these segments. Programs whose code or data will not fit within single 64K segments must use double-word segment:offset addresses, and consequently run more slowly. At even greater cost in efficiency, some programs must compensate for the fact that a byte's segment:offset address is not unique. In all programs, the stack is accessed so frequently that double-word stack addressing would be prohibitive. Programs virtually always limit their stacks to single segments, though sometimes different program modules use separate stacks.

Turbo C allows you to choose from six *memory models*, or addressing modes, according to your code and data addressing requirements. *Small data* models use *near* data pointers by default: single word offsets relative to constant segment addresses stored in registers DS and SS. *Large data* models, on the other hand, use *far* data pointers: double-word segment:offset addresses. Large data programs must adjust the DS register whenever a static or heap data address changes. Similar choices are available for the code segment, affecting function pointer implementation. You can override the defaults by explicitly declaring variables **near** or **far**, but you won't be able to manipulate them with Library functions that expect the default pointer type. More detail concerning memory models is given after the general organization of PC memory is described in the next section.

Accessing segment:offset addresses from Turbo C programs

Sometimes you need to access data whose segment:offset address is known, but not yet stored in a far pointer variable. One method is to use one of these Turbo C Library functions, which return the byte or word stored at the specified address:

char peekb (unsigned Segment, unsigned Offset)
int peek (unsigned Segment, unsigned Offset)

These are defined as macros in header file **DOS.H**. As an example of their use, consider program **Model.Dem** in Figure 2.1.1. It uses **peekb**

```
/****************************************************************/
/* Model.Dem        Write the  PC  model number.             */
/****************************************************************/
#include <General.H>

void main() {
printf("PC model = hex %x",
  (unsigned char) peekb(0xffff,0x000e)); }
```

Output

```
PC model = hex ff
```

Figure 2.1.1 Program **Model.Dem**

to read the PC model code, stored at address hex ffff:000e in the built-in read-only memory of IBM personal computers. Here are the current possibilities:

Code	Model	Code	Model
ff	PC	fb	PC/XT (256/640K
fe	PC/XT, Portable		motherboard)
fd	PC Jr	fa	PS/2 Model 30
fc	PC/AT, XT Model 286;	f9	PC Convertible
	PS/2 Models 50, 60	f8	PS/2 Model 80

The example output in the figure was produced on a very old IBM PC. Warning: PC cloners are under no obligation to adhere to these codes!

Program **Model.Dem** included the header file **General.H** often used with this book's programs. That file contains the line **#include <DOS.H>**, required for use of macro **peekb**. This "indirect" inclusion is commonly used for examples, to keep code as compact as possible.

Corresponding functions are available to poke a character or integer **Value** into memory at a specified segment:offset address:

void pokeb (unsigned Segment, unsigned Offset, char Value)
void poke (unsigned Segment, unsigned Offset, int Value)

The peek and poke macros are defined in terms of another **DOS.H** function, which converts a segment:offset pair into a **far** pointer:

(void far*) MK_FP(unsigned Segment, unsigned Offset)

This function has a pair of inverses, for converting a near or far pointer **P** into unsigned segment:offset address components:

(unsigned) FP_SEG(void far *P)
(unsigned) FP_OFF(void far *P)

All these are macros in **DOS.H**. Their definitions are interesting:

```
#define MK_FP(Segment,Offset) ((void far *)        \
  (((unsigned long)(Segment)<<16) | (Offset)))
#define peekb(Segment,Offset)                      \
  (*((char far*) MK_FP((a),(b))))
#define pokeb(Segment,Offset,Value)                \
  (*((char far*) MK_FP((a),(b))) = (Value))
#define FP_SEG(P) ((unsigned)((unsigned long)(P)>>16))
#define FP_OFF(P) ((unsigned)(P))
```

MK_FP casts **Segment** (assumed to be **unsigned**) to **unsigned long**, shifts it 16 bits into the high word, uses a bitwise-or operation to move **Offset** into the low word, and casts the 32-bit result to type **void far ***. Function **peekb** recasts the result as a **far** pointer to a character, and dereferences it. You can figure out the remaining macros. Those for **poke** and **peek** are similar.

If you use a peek or poke function without including the **DOS.H** header, the linker will find true functions with those names compiled in the Turbo C Library. They are implemented differently. For example, consider **peekb**:

```
char peekb(unsigned Segment, unsigned Offset) {
_ES = Segment;
return *(unsigned char _es *) Offset; }
```

This code uses the **_ES** pseudo-variable to store **Segment** in register ES, uses the modifier **_es** to cast **Offset** as an **unsigned char** pointer relative to ES instead of the default DS segment register, then dereferences it. You would not want to use this function if other parts of your code depended on the value in ES. The related functions are coded similarly.

2.2 Conventional memory

Concepts

Memory required by DOS
Transient portion of **Command.Com**
Interrupt vectors
BIOS
ROM BASIC
Display memory
Custom BIOS memory and ROM cartridges
Using reserved memory for other purposes

As noted in Section 2.1, PCs can access 1 MB of memory directly. IBM allocated this space somewhat rigidly for use by the operating system, by its built-in BASIC interpreter, and by your own software. A detailed scheme is shown in Figure 2.2.1. Several items require further explanation.

Segment address (hex)	Memory area	Size
0000	Interrupt vectors (see Chapter 8)	1K
0040	Temporary storage for the BIOS, DOS, and BASIC	5K
0060	Occupied by DOS	41K*
0a50*	Available for your programs	597.5K*
a000	Reserved for display controller memory	64K
b000	Monochrome Display Adapter memory	32K
b800	Color/Graphics Adapter memory	32K
c000	Reserved for ROM BIOS extensions	64K
d000	Reserved for ROM cartridges	152K
f600	Reserved for ROM BASIC	32K
fe00	ROM BIOS	8K
		1024K

*Approximate

Figure 2.2.1 Allocation of conventional memory

The space allocated to DOS is noted only approximately, because DOS grows with each new version. Also, any custom device drivers and optional DOS features installed during the boot process via the **Config.Sys** and **AutoExec.Bat** files are placed with DOS. The 35K figure shown is for DOS 3.3 with no custom drivers. The memory available for your software depends on these considerations as well as on the amount installed in your system. The amounts of memory installed and available are reported by the DOS **ChkDsk** utility.

A Turbo C program can ascertain the amount of conventional memory installed via Library function **int biosmemory(void)**. Its prototype is in header file **BIOS.H**. Here is a sample program, run on a fully equipped PC.

```
#include "General.H"
#include <BIOS.H>
void main() {
printf("%dK  memory is installed.",biosmemory());}
```

Output

```
640K memory is installed.
```

This figure is obtained essentially by reading a memory word that contains the tally of memory OK'd during booting. Caution: Other software can change it! On the author's machine this demonstration program yields an incorrect count when run in the *DESQview* environment.

Part of DOS, the *transient portion* of **Command.Com**, is always loaded as high as possible, but below segment a000. Since this part contains the DOS command interpreter, it is not needed while other software is executing, and programs may overwrite it. When the command interpreter is needed again, the resident portion of DOS checks to see if it is still intact; if not, it's read from an external file. On a diskette system, this can generate the annoying demand to *insert a DOS diskette*. You have some control over the location of the command interpreter file via the DOS environment variable **COMSPEC**.

The interrupt vectors are the addresses of up to 256 operating system or custom memory resident service routines. The BIOS (Basic Input/Output System) is a part of the operating system encoded in read-only memory (ROM) chips. It provides low-level control of standard peripheral equipment, and includes the Power On Self Test (POST) that tests and initializes your machine during booting. (The POST determines the amount of memory installed, and Turbo C function **biosmemory** reads this tally through a BIOS service.) Assembly language code for the IBM version of the BIOS is listed in the PC *Technical Reference* manual, Reference [20]. Although public, it was copyrighted, so PC cloners had to construct BIOS programs that function like IBM's, without actually copying the code. Those are now available from several sources. BIOS services are described in detail in Chapter 8.

On IBM machines, a rudimentary BASIC interpreter is also encoded in pre-installed ROM chips. It comes into play when you boot your machine with no operating system, and provides subroutines for the more comprehensive BASICA interpreter packaged with IBM's version of DOS.

The PC was designed to accommodate both original standard IBM display controllers together, to display graphics and text simultaneously. Each requires *display memory* to store the information appearing on the screen. IBM split segment b000 equally between them. Its first 32K is sufficient to store eight 80x25 character IBM Monochrome Display Adapter text screens. (The original IBM adapter only included memory for one screen.) The remaining 32K, starting at paragraph b800, is commonly used by display controllers compatible with the IBM Color/ Graphics Adapter (CGA). It can store text screens in the same way, or graphics information—for example, two 640x200 pixel monochrome graphics screens. This memory is normally installed on display controller boards inserted into motherboard expansion slots. For more detail, refer to Section 4.2. The newer Enhanced Graphics Adapter (EGA) normally requires even more memory. In its complete versions, it needs two entire segments: a000 and b000.

The following program demonstrates direct use of the monochrome display memory. It pokes character '*' into the even-numbered bytes, and they fill the screen. (The odd-numbered bytes control screen attributes like color, underline, and blinking.) For a CGA screen, replace segment address **b000** by **b800**.

```
#include <General.H>          /* Fill the monochrome dis- */
void main() {                 /* play segment  b000  with */
    int I;                    /* stars.  There are  25    */
for (I = 0; I <= 25*80; I++)  /* rows,  80 columns.  Use  */
    pokeb(0xb000,2*I,'*'); }  /* the even numbered bytes. */
```

If you are not using segment a000 or the first part of b000 for display memory, and your memory expansion board permits, you can install conventional memory chips with addresses in this range. For DOS to use them, your software must initialize them properly during the boot process.

Many peripheral controller boards have ROM chips containing routines supplementing the BIOS. For example, the EGA ROM contains custom BIOS code to provide video services specific to that board, and fixed disk controllers must contain routines to control particular types of disks. These codes must occupy disjoint memory areas in the c000 segment. The PC BIOS boot routine polls all possible custom BIOS starting addresses, executing any initialization routines it finds.

Finally, IBM reserved segments d000 and e000 and the first part of f000 for custom ROM units containing whole software systems. Those are not common, and many memory expansion boards permit you to install conventional memory chips with these addresses. Expansion board suppliers often provide software that implements virtual disks or printer buffers in this memory. Since DOS can address only contiguous memory segments, however, it cannot utilize directly any segments after your display memory.

2.3 Turbo C memory models

Concepts

64K data and code size limits for single source code files
Near and far pointers
Linker and loader
.Exe and **.Com** files; **Exe2Bin** utility
Intel 8086 upside down stacks
Far heap
Program for demonstrating memory usage by the six models
Tiny, small, medium, compact, large, and huge models

This section discusses Turbo C memory utilization from a broad perspective. You will see its overall strategy for allocating entire segments. Later, in Section 2.4, you will investigate some of its tactics down to the scale of individual bytes.

As mentioned in Section 2.1, Turbo C lets you choose from six memory models according to the degree to which you can confine your data and code to single 64K segments. Addressing is more efficient when constrained to a single segment, because you only need to manipulate offsets; the DOS loader can set the appropriate segment register during program initialization and your program can leave it unchanged. Since memory utilization strategy depends on the model chosen, and description of the models in the literature is often unclear, each one is described and diagrammed below in detail. A single demonstration program is compiled with each of the six models. The corresponding outputs, shown with the diagrams, illustrate the memory utilization strategies.

Before describing that program, however, it is important to note that a single Turbo C source code file cannot produce more than 64K of executable code and 64K of static (including global) data. For example, the dummy program

```
int A[15000],B[20000];
void main() {}
```

will not compile in any model: an integer requires two bytes, so arrays **A** and **B** total about 70K. You get the error message *Too much global data defined in file*. To handle more than 64K code or static data, you must use separate files. For this example, you can split the source code into files **Z1.C** and **Z2.C**, then use the huge memory model to compile them separately, and link them into an **.Exe** file under guidance of a project file **Z.Prj**:

Z1.C	Z2.C	Z.Prj
int A[15000];	int B[20000];	Z1
void main() {}		Z2
Z1.Obj (30K)	Z2.Obj (40K)	Z.Exe (71K)

Since the compiler initializes the arrays, the resulting **.Obj** and **.Exe** files reflect the array sizes.

The differences among Turbo C memory models stem mostly from how they handle code and data segments for separate source code files, and from their provisions for dynamically allocated heap storage. To permit multiple segments or unlimited heap size, some models must use double word far pointers in place of the more efficient near pointers, which are just single word offsets. The six models produce executable code that differs in pointer usage and in the linker directives encoded in the **.Obj** files. The linker arranges code and data segments as directed, and places specifications in the **.Exe** files to govern the DOS loader's action when the program is executed. (For example, the loader must set the values of the segment registers.)

The program used to demonstrate the six memory models consists of two source code files, **X.C** and **Y.C**, shown in Figure 2.3.1. The first contains function **A** and static variable **B**; the second, function **main** and global variable **D**. Each function uses an automatic variable, and **main** calls Library function **malloc** to allocate a heap variable. Files **X.C** and **Y.C** are compiled separately and linked under guidance of a project file **XY.Prj** containing the two lines

X
Y

By compiling with the six models in turn, you can see how they allocate space for the code, data, and stack segments, where they place static, automatic, and heap variables, and where they place the executable code for the functions. (As described below, some memory models use near data pointers and far function pointers, or vice versa. The %**p** format for **printf** adjusts properly for data pointers but not for function pointers. Thus the conditional compilation directives **#if**, **#else**, and **#endif** are required here.)

The ensuing text describes in detail, using the demonstration program output, the memory utilization strategy of each of the six models (tiny, small, medium, compact, large, huge):

	small code	large code
small data	*tiny* *small*	*medium*
large data	*compact*	*large* *huge*

"Small code" and "small data" mean that code and data pointers are near unless otherwise specified. "Large" means that they are far. Some of the models are described in terms of their differences from others. Dynamic memory allocation for heap variables is discussed later in Section 2.5.

File X.C

```
#include <General.H>

void A() {
  static int B;
  int C;
printf("In function  A            \n");
printf("   CS DS SS     :  %X %X %X\n",_CS,_DS,_SS);
printf("   Static    B :  %p      \n",&B);
printf("   Automatic  C :  %p      \n",&C); }
```

File Y.C

```
#include <General.H>

int D;

void main() {
    int E;
  A();
  printf("In function main            \n");
  printf("   CS DS SS     :  %X %X %X\n",_CS,_DS,_SS);
  printf("   Global    D :  %p      \n",&D);
  printf("   Automatic E :  %p      \n",&E);
  printf("   Heap address :  %p      \n",malloc(2));
#if defined(__TINY__)||defined(__SMALL__)||defined(__COMPACT__)
  printf("Function     A :  %Np      \n",A   );
  printf("Function  main :  %Np      \n",main); }
#else
  printf("Function     A :  %Fp      \n",A   );
  printf("Function  main :  %Fp      \n",main); }
#endif
```

Figure 2.3.1 Memory model demonstration program

Tiny model

The *tiny* model is designed for programs that can use a single segment for everything: for executable code, static data, stack, and heap. The linker sets up a single segment, to which the DOS loader will point the CS, DS, and SS registers when you execute the program. Within this segment the code is loaded first, then the data. The heap grows upward from the top of the data area, and the stack downward from the top of the segment. If they collide, you have run out of memory.

Because of an architectural peculiarity of the Intel 8086 CPU family, stacks always grow *downward*. Think of a spike on which you might impale bills due for payment. The bills are *stacked: last in, first out*. Now affix the spike to the ceiling: the bill in the *lowest* position, like the variable with the lowest offset in the stack segment, is at the *top* of the stack!

This memory allocation is diagrammed in Figure 2.3.2, which also includes the demonstration program output for the tiny model. This is a

Low memory

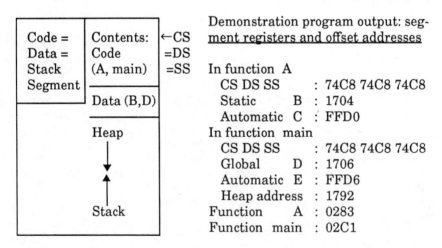

Demonstration program output: segment registers and offset addresses

```
In function  A
    CS DS SS        : 74C8 74C8 74C8
    Static      B : 1704
    Automatic  C : FFD0
In function  main
    CS DS SS        : 74C8 74C8 74C8
    Global      D : 1706
    Automatic  E : FFD6
    Heap address : 1792
Function     A : 0283
Function  main : 02C1
```

High memory

Figure 2.3.2 Tiny model memory allocation

small data, small code model, so all pointers are near: single word offsets relative to the addresses in segment registers CS, DS, and SS. You can see that these registers always contain the same value hex 74C8. Within that segment, functions **A** and **main** have the lowest offsets, followed by static and global variables **B** and **D**. The order among these is due to the fact that function A and variable **B** were defined in file **X.C**, which was mentioned first in project file XY.Prj. Next comes the heap pointer returned by Library function **malloc**. Finally, you see automatic variables **C** and **E** on the stack. **C** has the lower offset, so it's on top of the stack: function **main** was invoked first, then function **A**.

You can use the DOS **Exe2Bin** utility to convert an **.Exe** file compiled with the tiny model into a **.Com** file. Because of its simple structure, a **.Com** file is shorter, and loads faster than the original **.Exe** file.

Small model

The *small* model is the most commonly used. All program examples in other sections of this book were compiled with that model. Although it's also a small data, small code model, it differs from the tiny model in two ways:

- The code and data segments are separate.
- An additional heap, accessed with far pointers, extends from the end of the data segment to the end of conventional memory.

Since code, static data, and heap are still confined to single segments, the small model uses near pointers by default. As a consequence, you can't process far heap variables directly with Library functions. However, as long as you provide your own manipulation routines, you can store as much data there as your installed memory allows. Details of far heap usage are described in Section 2.5.

Figure 2.3.3 describes the small model memory allocation scheme, illustrated by demonstration program output. You can see that the CS register always has the same value hex 74B1, while registers DS and SS point to segment 75CC. Within those segments the functions and variables occur as they did with the tiny model.

Medium model

The *medium* model is like the small one, except that executable code resulting from separate source code files is placed in separate segments. The total amount of code is limited only by the size of the machine on which it must run. In consequence, Turbo C must use far function pointers. The medium model is thus a small data, large code model. The allocation scheme and demonstration program output are detailed in Figure 2.3.4. You can see that functions **A** and **main** occupy separate segments hex 74F9 and 74FE. (**A** comes first, because it was in file **X.C**, which was mentioned first in project file **XY.Prj**.) The CS register changes value when **A** is invoked from **main**. The variables are situated as they were in the tiny model.

Low memory

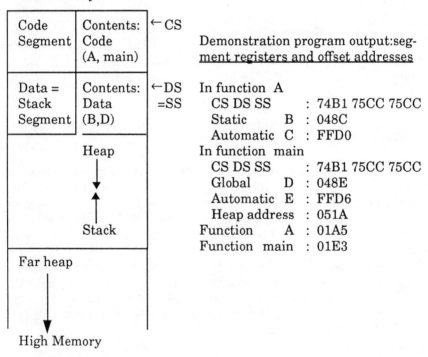

Demonstration program output:seg-
ment registers and offset addresses

In function A
   CS DS SS   : 74B1 75CC 75CC
   Static   B : 048C
   Automatic C : FFD0
In function main
   CS DS SS   : 74B1 75CC 75CC
   Global   D : 048E
   Automatic E : FFD6
   Heap address : 051A
Function   A : 01A5
Function main : 01E3

Figure 2.3.3 Small model memory allocation

Compact model

The *compact* model is the simplest in concept: code, static data, and stack all have separate single segments. The heap is implemented with far pointers like the far heap in the small and medium models. So that you can use Library functions to process heap variables, all data pointers are far. Function pointers are near since all functions lie in the same segment. The compact model is therefore a large data, small code model. Figure 2.3.5 shows the memory arrangement and demonstration program output. You can see that registers CS, DS, and SS always point to the code, data, and stack segments hex 74B1, 7629, and 767A. The static and global variables are in the data segment, and the automatic ones on the stack. The heap variable lies in a segment beyond the stack.

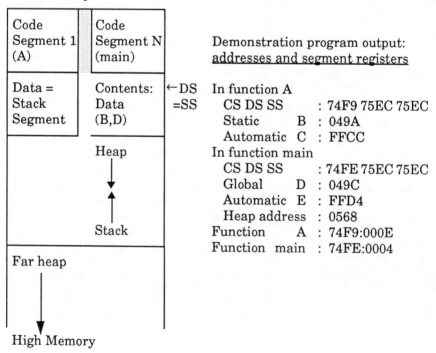

Low memory

Code Segment 1 (A)	Code Segment N (main)
Data = Stack Segment	Contents: Data (B,D) ←DS =SS
	Heap
	Stack
Far heap	

High Memory

Demonstration program output: addresses and segment registers

```
In function A
  CS DS SS      : 74F9 75EC 75EC
  Static     B  : 049A
  Automatic  C  : FFCC
In function main
  CS DS SS      : 74FE 75EC 75EC
  Global     D  : 049C
  Automatic  E  : FFD4
  Heap address  : 0568
Function     A  : 74F9:000E
Function  main  : 74FE:0004
```

Figure 2.3.4 Medium model memory allocation

Low memory

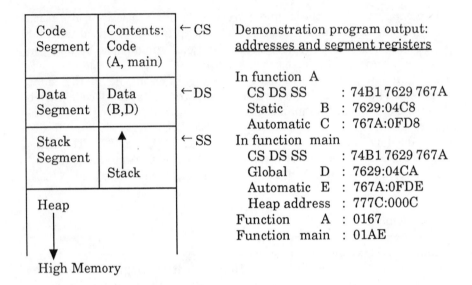

<table>
<tr><td>Code
Segment</td><td>Contents:
Code
(A, main)</td><td>←CS</td></tr>
<tr><td>Data
Segment</td><td>Data
(B,D)</td><td>←DS</td></tr>
<tr><td>Stack
Segment</td><td>Stack</td><td>←SS</td></tr>
<tr><td colspan="2">Heap</td><td></td></tr>
</table>

Demonstration program output:
addresses and segment registers

In function A
  CS DS SS   : 74B1 7629 767A
  Static   B : 7629:04C8
  Automatic C : 767A:0FD8
In function main
  CS DS SS   : 74B1 7629 767A
  Global   D : 7629:04CA
  Automatic E : 767A:0FDE
  Heap address : 777C:000C
Function   A : 0167
Function main : 01AE

High Memory

Figure 2.3.5 Compact model memory allocation

Large model

The *large* model is like the compact one, except that executable code resulting from separate source code files is placed in separate segments, as in the medium model. The total amount of code is limited only by the size of the machine on which it is to run. Thus, the large model is a large data, large code model: Turbo C must use far pointers for *both* functions and data. However, you are limited to 64K static data. Figure 2.3.6 shows the memory scheme and demonstration program output. You can see that functions **A** and **main** lie in separate code segments hex 74FD and 7502, and the CS register changes when **A** is invoked from **main**. Registers DS and SS always point to the data and stack segments 764A and 76A0.

Low memory

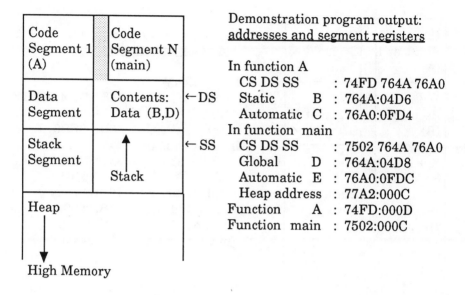

Demonstration program output:
<u>addresses and segment registers</u>

In function A
     CS DS SS   : 74FD 764A 76A0
     Static   B : 764A:04D6
     Automatic   C : 76A0:0FD4
In function main
     CS DS SS   : 7502 764A 76A0
     Global   D : 764A:04D8
     Automatic   E : 76A0:0FDC
     Heap address   : 77A2:000C
Function   A : 74FD:000D
Function main : 7502:000C

High Memory

Figure 2.3.6 Large model memory allocation

Huge model

The *huge* model—the last of the six, also a large data, large code model—removes the 64K large model static data restriction. Static data defined in separate source code files occupy separate data segments, like the two arrays in the dummy program **Z.Exe** discussed at the beginning of this section. This is revealed by the demonstration program output in Figure 2.3.7. You can see that both the CS and DS registers change value when function **A** is invoked from **main**. Of course, the functions share the same stack: otherwise, the program wouldn't be able to keep track of the chain of return addresses. Don't let the term *huge* mislead you: in this model, all pointers are by default far, not huge. Use of huge pointers is discussed later, in Section 2.5.)

Low memory

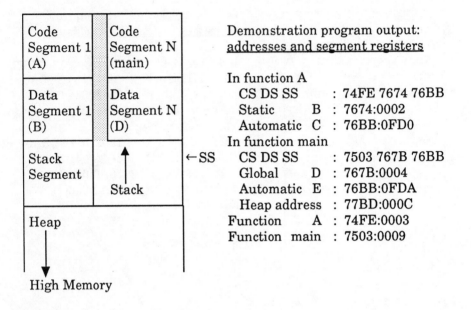

Demonstration program output:
<u>addresses and segment registers</u>

In function A
  CS DS SS   : 74FE 7674 76BB
  Static   B : 7674:0002
  Automatic C : 76BB:0FD0
In function main
  CS DS SS   : 7503 767B 76BB
  Global   D : 767B:0004
  Automatic E : 76BB:0FDA
  Heap address : 77BD:000C
Function   A : 74FE:0003
Function main : 7503:0009

High Memory

Figure 2.3.7 Huge model memory allocation

2.4 Data formats in memory

Concepts

signed and **unsigned char, int,** and **long** types
Sign extension
Twos complement interpretation of binary numbers
Manipulating high and low nybbles, bytes, and words
Values.H constants
float and **double** types; IEEE real number formats
Truncation by casting from real to integer types
Near and far pointer arithmetic; casting near to far
Normalized and huge pointers
Null pointers. Turbo C TOOLS function **utnulchk**
Arrays and C structures; bit fields

In the previous section, you considered Turbo C memory usage on the large scale: overall arrangement of the code, data, and stack segments and the heap. In this section you'll see many finer details of memory organization. Your program's static data structures are stored in the data segment in the order in which they are declared. Automatic data have the same format on stack or heap, but their order depends on that in which functions are called, and on conventions governing function call implementation. Stack and heap organization are considered in the next section; this one is concerned with the format of individual data structures.

Integer data

The simplest data structures are those stored in single eight bit bytes: **signed char** and **unsigned char** variables. (Normally, **signed char** is synonymous with **char**. However, a compiler option is available to reverse that convention.) Each of these types has $256 = 2^8$ possible values: hex 00 .. ff. Their most common use is to store codes for text characters. PC computers and Turbo C use the ASCII/IBM code to relate characters to **char** values; you'll find details in Section 3.1.

Few Turbo C features handle **char** or **unsigned char** values directly. Instead, they are often cast implicitly to the 16-bit **int** type for output or arithmetic. **char** and **unsigned char** values are cast differently, as demonstrated by program **CharCast.Dem** in Figure 2.4.1. Its first output **ff80** is an example of *sign extension:* the high order *sign bit* 1 of **char** value hex 80 is extended through the high byte of the 16-bit **int** value. This convention makes it possible to implement the standard twos complement interpretation of eight-bit arithmetic by implicitly casting **char** values to **int**, performing standard int arithmetic, then considering the low byte of the result (casting back to **char**). On the other hand, the same process makes **unsigned char** values behave as in standard eight-bit arithmetic mod 256. The correspondences between numbers and **char** and **unsigned char** values is thus given by the following table:

Stored value		Interpretation	
binary	hex	**char**	**unsigned char**
00000000	00	0	0
:	:	:	:
01111111	7f	127	127
10000000	80	-128	128
:	:	:	:
11111111	ff	-1	255

One consequence of this casting difference is that the relational operators <, <=, >, and >= work in accordance with the interpretations just described. For example,

Declaration	Turbo C	Interpretation
char A = 0x80	**(A < 0)** is true	(-128 < 0) is true
unsigned char A = 0x80	**(A < 0)** is false	(128 < 0) is false

Casting to any 16-bit type produces the same effect. This is appropriate for casting **unsigned char** to **unsigned int**, for example, but problematic in some other cases, particularly in casting **char** to a near pointer type. Casting to other types is implemented as though the **int** value were an intermediate step.

```
/****************************************************************/
/* CharCast.Dem     Demonstrate sign extension by casting char */
/*************************************** and unsigned char */
                                      /* values to int.     */
#include <General.H>                  /********************/

void main() {
  signed    char S = 0x80;
  unsigned char U = 0x80;
printf("char, unsigned char hex 80 cast to int = %04x, %04x\n",
  (int) S, (int) U); }
```

Output

```
char, unsigned char hex 80 cast to int = ff80, 0080
```

Figure 2.4.1 Program **CharCast.Dem**

There are no **char** or **unsigned char** constants. Numerical constants are regarded as **int** values if possible. Character constants like 'c' are stored as **int** values, with sign extended if necessary. Sixteen-bit **int** constants are cast to eight-bit types when necessary by using just the low bytes.

The 16-bit single word data structures include the **signed int** and **unsigned int** types. The former is synonymous with **signed** and **int**; the latter, with **unsigned**. You can include the adjective **short** in any of these designators—it has no effect. Each of these types has $2^{16} = 65536$ values: hex 0000 .. ffff. They are used for integer arithmetic, and—because most of the Intel 8086 family CPUs handle two-byte structures most efficiently—for miscellaneous storage.

Like the eight-bit types, **int** and **unsigned** values are cast differently to longer types. If you change the Figure 2.4.1 program **CharCast** to cast **int** and **unsigned** values to types **long** and **float**, you'll get the output

int, unsigned hex 8000 cast to long = ffff8000, 00008000
int, unsigned hex 8000 cast to float = -32768,   32768

The first line reveals sign extension. The second shows that **int** values are intended to be interpreted in the standard twos complement fashion, whereas **unsigned** values are interpreted simply as 16-bit binary numbers:

Stored hex value	Interpretation int	unsigned
0000	0	0
:	:	:
7fff	32767	32767
8000	-32768	32768
:	:	:
ffff	-1	65535

Arithmetic for either type is simply binary arithmetic mod 2^{16}. On the other hand, the relational operators **<**, **<=**, **>**, and **>=** work differently, in accordance with the interpretations just described. For example,

Declaration	Turbo C	Interpretation
int A = 0x8000	(A < 0) is true	(-32768 < 0) is true
unsigned A = 0x8000	(A < 0) is false	(32768 < 0) is false

Turbo C Library input/output functions do not distinguish between **int** and **unsigned** parameters. Instead, using format **%d**, the **printf** functions construct decimal numerals for values of both types using the twos complement interpretation, while formats **%u**, **%o**, **%x**, and **%X** interpret them as 16-bit binary. The **scanf** functions use the twos complement interpretation in converting numerical input only if it contains a minus sign.

Integer constants are treated unexceptionally: twos complement is used if there's a minus sign. As remarked earlier, character constants like **'c'** are really of type **int**, with the ASCII/IBM code stored in the low byte, and the signed extended if appropriate. You can also use *digraph* constants like **'ab'**, which store the two ASCII/IBM codes in the low and high bytes, respectively.

The 32-bit double word **long** and **unsigned long** integer types behave quite like **int** and **unsigned**. Turbo C will construct 32-bit constants as needed. You can force it to construct a 32-bit constant for a value that wouldn't ordinarily require that length by suffixing **L** to the numeral. For example, **printf("%08lx",-1L)** writes the string **ffffffff**. (If you omit the l, **printf** outputs the low word of the constant; if you omit the L, it will address a double word, whose low word is the **int** constant -1, and print four hex digits of garbage followed by the correct constant value **ffff**.)

Header file **Values.H** contains convenient constants for use with the three signed types:

```
#define MAXSHORT 0x7FFF
#define MAXINT 0x7FFF
#define MAXLONG 0x7FFFFFFFL
```

The Blaise Computing Inc. Turbo C TOOLS package featured in this book includes several convenient macros that help you manipulate parts of eight, 16, and 32-bit values. These extract their high and low words, bytes, and nybbles (4 bits):

uthinyb(CharValue) uthibyte(IntValue) uthiword(LongValue)
utlonyb(CharValue) utlobyte(IntValue) utloword(LongValue)

Three more will assemble eight, 16, and 32-bit values from specified high and low words, bytes, and nybbles:

utnybbyt (HiNyb,LoNyb)   utwdlong(HiWord,LoWord)
utbyword(HiByte,LoByte)

You'll find these in the Turbo C TOOLS header file **BUtil.H**.

Real data

Turbo C provides two real number types, **float** and **double**, coincident with the Intel 8087 numeric coprocessor family *short* and *long real* types, occupying four and eight bytes. Figure 2.4.2 shows their formats in memory. To determine the real number X represented, you generally calculate

$$X = \pm 1.\text{significand} * 2^{\text{biased exponent - bias}}$$

There are several exceptions: letting S = significand, E = biased exponent, and B = bias,

$E = 00 .. 0 \ \& \ S = 00 .. 0 \quad X = \pm 0$
$E = 00 .. 0 \ \& \ S \neq 00 .. 0 \quad X = \pm 0.\text{significand} * 2^{1\text{-bias}}$
$E = 11 .. 1 \ \& \ S = 00 .. 0 \quad X = \pm \infty$
$E = 11 .. 1 \ \& \ S \neq 00 .. 0 \quad X \text{ is a NaN.}$

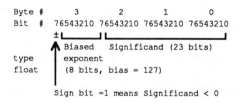

Figure 2.4.2 Memory formats for Turbo C types **float** and **double**

A *NaN* (*Not a Number*) is a value reserved for signalling an attempted invalid operation. These formats adhere to IEEE standards. Using simple algebra, you can determine that **float** and **double** values represent about six and 15 significant decimal digits. The largest and smallest absolute values of numbers representable in these formats are given by some constants conveniently declared in header file **Values.H**:

#define MAXFLOAT 3.37E+38
#define MINFLOAT 8.43E-37
#define MAXDOUBLE 1.797693E+308
#define MINDOUBLE   2.225074E-308

Constants are also provided for logarithms of these numbers. For further information on arithmetic with these types, consult the 8087 and IEEE documentation, references [16] and [14].

Real constants are ordinarily stored as **double** values. If you want one stored in the shorter **float** format, suffix an **F** to the numeral, as in **1.23E+4F**.

Casting real values to integer types is the same as *truncating* toward zero:

float values	:	65432.6	-65432.6
cast to long	:	65432	-65432
cast to unsigned	:	65432	104

Take care that this is really what you want to do. If you want to *round* a real value X, you must do it explicitly, probably by adding sign(X)/2 then truncating. (sign(X) = -1, 0, or 1 according as X is negative, zero, or positive.) Moreover, truncation by casting will fail if the real value falls outside the target type range. The first truncation on the last line of the output just shown required **printf** format %u: it's out of range for %d format. Since %u won't output negative values, in this situation you have to ascertain sign and magnitude before choosing format. The last truncation, -65432.1 to **unsigned**, is simply out of the target range, and yields garbage.

Pointers

Single word *near* pointers contain offsets relative to the Data Segment and Code Segment registers. Double word *far* and *huge* pointers contain full segment:offset addresses. Use of near and far pointers with the various Turbo C memory models was described in considerable detail in the previous section. Only a few topics remain for discussion.

Near pointer arithmetic is the same as **unsigned**. Far pointer arithmetic is **unsigned** arithmetic on the low word, which contains the offset; the segment address is unaffected. This means, for example, that the next address after offset hex ffff is offset 0000 in the *same* segment. (To address items in a data structure that "straddles" a segment boundary, you must use equivalent addresses in overlapping segments. *Huge* pointers, provided for that purpose, are discussed in the next paragraph.) According to standard C conventions, if P is a pointer to an item X of a type whose items occupy L bytes each, then you can add an integer N to P to get a pointer P + N to the Nth item of that type after X in memory (or before, if N is negative). Thus the address P + N is actually offset L*N bytes from the address P.

Casting a pointer from far to near simply removes its segment address. The opposite cast is more interesting. Turbo C obtains the segment address from the appropriate segment register. This is demonstrated by program **PtrCast.Dem** in Figure 2.4.3. First, using the address operator **&**, it outputs near pointers to a global variable in the data segment, a function in the code segment, and an automatic variable in the stack segment. Then it refers to pseudo-variables **_DS**, **_CS**, and **_SS** to print the values in the Data, Code, and Stack Segment registers. Finally, it casts the near pointers to far types and prints the corresponding segment:offset addresses. You can verify that they are constructed properly. (The data and stack segments coincide in the small model, used to compile this program.) **PtrCast.Dem** also shows how to use **typedef** statements to define the type of the far function pointer. The far pointer is then executed, as another verification that it was constructed properly.

Since their arithmetic does not affect segment addresses, you can't use far pointers directly to address items in a data structure that straddles a segment boundary. If you can't fit the entire structure into a single segment, you can use *huge* pointers. These have the same form as far pointers but their segment addresses are *normalized*: adjusted so that their offsets are less than hex 10. For example:

```
6540   : 0032
+003   ⟵──┤
6543   : 0002
```

Each memory location has a unique normalized address. The new function **Normalize** in Figure 2.4.4 normalizes any far pointer by casting it to type **long**, moving nybbles from the offset part to the

```
/***************************************************************/
/* PtrCast.Dem     Casting near to far pointers.            */
/***************************************************************/

#include <General.H>

int Data;                          /* In data segment.      */
void Code() {                      /* In code segment.      */
  printf("Hello from  Code !\n"); }
                                   /* FunctionPtr  is the   */
typedef void Function();           /* type of far pointers  */
typedef Function far *FunctionPtr; /* to functions like     */
                                   /* Code.                 */
void main() {
  int Stack;                       /* In stack segment.     */
  FunctionPtr CodePtr;             /* CodePtr  is a far     */
CodePtr = (FunctionPtr) &Code;     /* pointer to  Code.     */
CodePtr();                         /* You can execute it.   */
printf("%22s%11s%12s\n","Data","Code","Stack");
printf("Registers    : %p   %8p  %9p\n", _DS, _CS, _SS);
printf("Near pointers: %9p  %9p  %9p\n", &Data, &Code, &Stack);
printf("Cast to far  : %Fp  %Fp  %Fp\n",
  (int far *) &Data, CodePtr, (int far *) &Stack); }
```

Output

```
Hello from  Code !
                Data        Code        Stack
Registers    : 7792        767A        7792
Near pointers:        03EA        01A5        FFCE
Cast to far  : 7792:03EA  767A:01A5  7792:FFCE
```

Figure 2.4.3 Program **PtrCast.Dem**

```
/*****************************************************************/
/* Normalize.C      Function  Normalize.  Normalize far    */
/*                  pointer  *P  by removing the top three */
/* *P  offset nybbles, shifting them three nybbles leftward, */
/* and adding them to the segment address.                 */
/*****************************************************************/

void Normalize(void far **P) {
*P = (void far *)
  (((long) *P & 0xffff000f)                        /* Remove,   */
    + (((long) *P & 0x0000fff0) << 12)) ;}        /* shift, add */
```

```
/*****************************************************************/
/* HugePtr.Dem      Demonstrate huge pointer arithmetic.  Cre- */
/*                  ate a far pointer  FP.  Cast it to huge:  */
/* there's no change.  Normalize it with function  Normalize. */
/* Add  64K+1  to the non-normalized huge pointer, showing au */
/*************************************************** automatic normaliza- */
                                    /* tion and compatibil- */
#include <General.H>               /* ity with  unsigned  */
                                    /* long  arithmetic.   */
void main() {                       /* Subtract the origi- */
  char far   *FP =                  /* nal pointer.        */
    MK_FP(0x6540,0x0032);           /************************/
  char huge *HP = (char huge *) FP;
printf("Far pointer  FP :  %Fp\n",FP);
printf("Cast to huge   :  %Fp\n",HP);
Normalize((void far **) &FP);
printf("Normalize     :  %Fp\n",FP);
printf("Add  64K + 1  :  %Fp\n",HP += 0x10001);
printf("Subtract  FP  :  %ld\n",(unsigned long) (HP - FP)); }
```

Output

```
Far pointer  FP :  6540:0032
Cast to huge   :  6540:0032
Normalize      :  6543:0002
Add  64K + 1   :  7543:0003
Subtract  FP   :  65537
```

Figure 2.4.4 Program **HugePtr.Dem**

segment address part and adding, then recasting the result to a pointer type. Some feature like this function is necessary because casting a far pointer to type huge doesn't automatically normalize it, yet you may need the normalized form for comparison with other huge pointers. (You can in fact normalize a huge pointer **HP** by executing **HP += 0**. However, this seems easy to forget, tedious to document, and subject to suppression if a later maintenance programmer or optimizing compiler overzealously decides that adding zero is unnecessary. The explicit function **Normalize** is easy to remember and document.)

Normalization is carried out automatically during huge pointer arithmetic, so with these pointers you can range over all your PC's conventional memory without regard to segment boundaries. You can use either **unsigned** or **unsigned long** pointer increments, and thus directly relate addresses separated by more than 64K. Program **HugePtr.Dem** in Figure 2.4.4 demonstrates these notions as well as function **Normalize**. The program documentation describes its operation.

Far and huge pointers are commonly used in manipulating arrays and other structures on the heap, and are discussed again in that context in Section 2.5.

A final pointer topic of concern is the representation of the *null* pointer, which normally signals the end of a linked list: it's a "pointer to nothing." Its format must agree with that of other pointers, but it may not address any data that your program needs to access with pointers. Turbo C uses offset 0000 and segment:offset address 0000:0000 for its near and far null pointers. A macro **NULL** in header files **StdIO.H** and **StdLib.H** is defined to be one of these values or the other, depending on the memory model used.

The null pointer definition often collides with other design objectives, with results that hinder program development. The Turbo C null pointer format is certainly appropriate, and it's easy to check whether a pointer is null. Moreover, Turbo C sets static variables to zero when a program starts, so a pointer in which your program hasn't yet stored a valid address is null. The problem is that the near null pointer addresses the beginning of the data or code segment, which normally contains information necessary to keep your program running or to let DOS regain control after execution. Even worse, the far null pointer addresses your PC's interrupt vector table—the addresses by which the BIOS and DOS find the system routines that are constantly in use. When you mistakenly use a null pointer to store data, you destroy vital information in these areas and your program usually crashes, obliterating any clues to help you find the bug.

The Turbo C TOOLS package provides a method for checking whether you've made this error. This may let you signal the problem before you crash. To use it, invoke function **unsigned utnulchk()** before a suspected null pointer error. This records the sixteen bytes starting at the location addressed by the null pointer. On later invocations, it compares the stored values with the current contents of those bytes, and returns a nonzero value just when they have changed—presumably due to the suspected error. The prototype is in the header file **BUtil.H**.

Arrays and C structures

C is very explicit concerning array storage: arrays are one-dimensional, with their entries stored one after the other in memory. The entries themselves may be complex data structures. *Strings* are specially formatted arrays of **char** entries, discussed in great detail in Chapter 3. Arrays provide a simple way to handle enormous amounts of data, so programs involving arrays often encounter size limitations. Section 2.5 shows how to use the far heap to handle arrays whose size is limited only by your PC's memory capacity.

Like arrays, C structures are one-dimensional, their entries are stored one after the other in memory, and the entries themselves may be complicated data structures. The only interesting question involves the choice of *byte or word alignment*. Turbo C selects the former, but you may use a compiler switch to choose word alignment. With byte alignment no space is left between entries. Word alignment provides padding so that a structure and all its multibyte entries begin at even addresses. This helps PCs with 16-bit CPUs optimize memory accesses.

Bit fields within structures can be signed or unsigned. Manipulating them requires implicit casting to **int** or **unsigned**. In the former case, sign extension is used. It's not clear what rules govern bit fields that seem to overlap word boundaries; Turbo C does not signal the errors. A typical example of bit field use is given later in Figure 5.3.2: the definition of the Turbo C TOOLS structure type KEYSTATUS that indicates the current status of the shift and toggle keys.

2.5 Stack and heap organization

Concepts

Stack use in function calls
C and Pascal calling conventions
Near and far heap management
Heap fragmentation causes inaccurate memory reports
Using the far heap for arrays larger than 64K

In Section 2.3 you considered the overall arrangement of the data and stack segments and the heap for the six Turbo C memory models. Section 2.4 discussed the detailed format of individual data structures. The present section describes the arrangement of the various data structures within these memory areas. The data segment contains global variables defined outside any function and static variables defined within. They are arranged in the order in which they are declared, so need no further comment. This section is concerned with stack and heap arrangement. That information is useful in illuminating various C programming practices, and it helps solve various debugging problems. It is *essential* when you must interface your C program with code written in other languages.

Stack arrangement

The Turbo C stack is used to store variables whose lifetime coincides with a function invocation: function parameters and automatic variables declared within the function body. Its organization is best described by considering what happens when your program invokes a function: for example, one whose definition starts

```
long F(char A, int B) {
    int  C;      /* Suppose C and D are    */
    char D;      /* the only declarations.  */
```

First, your program pushes the values of the parameters in reverse order, then the address to which function **F** must return. The **int** parameter **B** requires two bytes. So does the **char** parameter **A**. (8086 family CPUs have no instruction to push a single byte.) The single or double word return address is pushed automatically by a near or far call instruction, according as a small or large code memory model is in use. At this point the stack looks like

```
        :              (previous stack contents)
        B
        A
  return address        (lowest address = top of stack).
```

The call instruction transfers control to function **F**. Turbo C functions use the Base Pointer register (BP) to keep track of stack addresses. Therefore, **F** immediately pushes the current BP value in order to restore it just before returning, then copies into BP the current value of the Stack Pointer register SP. Next, function **F** creates its automatic variables on the stack, in reverse order from their declarations. Now the stack looks like this:

```
        :              previous stack contents
        B
        A
  return address
     saved  BP          <-- BP  points here
        D
        C              lowest address = top of stack
```

Function **F** carries out its computation, locating its parameters and automatic variables easily by using positive and negative offsets relative to the BP register. When it has completed its work, function **F** places its return value in an appropriate location. **char** values are cast to **int** before return. Two-byte return values are placed in register AX, four-byte values in DX:AX, and **double** values in the numeric coprocessor's Top-of-Stack register or its equivalent in the coprocessor emulation package. A **struct** return value more than four bytes long is placed in a static variable, and a pointer to that is returned instead. Next, **F** copies BP into SP, making the saved BP value the top of the stack. **F** pops this into BP, and executes a near or far return instruction, which pops the return address and transfers control back to the calling program. At this point, register BP has been restored to the value it had before the function call, and the calling program must pop the parameters from the stack. (It may not *use* their values, since C parameters are always passed by value.)

With this invocation protocol, called the *C convention*, it's unnecessary for calling program and function to agree completely on the number of parameters. If the calling program pushes extra ones, the function will never see them, and the calling program will pop them when it regains control. On the other hand, if too few are provided, the function will probably process garbage. It's common for the first parameter to tell the function how many parameters follow.

You can use a different protocol, called the *Pascal convention*. The parameters are pushed in left-to-right order, and the function, not the calling program, pops them from the stack. This avoids inserting the parameter popping code in the calling program every time it calls the function, but requires complete agreement as to the number and lengths of the parameters. See the *User's guide* for details. (Caution: the Pascal convention is not used by Turbo Pascal! That language requires a more elaborate stack format to make automatic variables accessible from nested functions. C doesn't allow nested functions.)

Heap organization

In the small and medium memory models, the near and far heaps are handled separately. The near heap shares memory with the stack. They grow toward each other, and when they collide, you have run out of memory. The far heap can use the entire space between the top of your data segment and the end of installed conventional memory. There are two corresponding sets of Turbo C Library functions for managing the heaps:

Near heap management		Far heap management	
coreleft	realloc	farcoreleft	farrealloc
malloc	free	farmalloc	farfree
calloc		farcalloc	

Near heap functions use near pointers to address heap variables, and **unsigned** parameters to indicate their lengths and the amount of memory left. The **far..** functions use far pointers and **unsigned long** parameters.

In the tiny model there's no far heap. In the compact, large, and huge models there's only one heap, organized like the far heap just described. You can use either set of heap management functions. Because of the memory model, far pointers are used with either set, but the near heap functions will accept only **unsigned** values to indicate amounts of memory. If you want to handle pieces of memory longer than 64K, you must use the **far..** functions.

Functions **coreleft** and **farcoreleft** expect no parameters, and return the amount of memory currently available for heap variables. You can use **malloc** or **calloc** or the corresponding **far..** functions to allocate variables on the heap. Here are prototypes for the former:

void *malloc(unsigned Length)
void *calloc(unsigned Length, unsigned Number)

malloc allocates a heap variable of the specified **Length,** initializes it to zero, and returns a pointer to it. If there is insufficient memory, or if you specified **Length** ≤ 0, **malloc** returns a null pointer. Executing **calloc(Length,Number)** is the same as **malloc(Length*Number)**. Caution: you cannot use either function to allocate more than 64K! Function

void *realloc(void *P, unsigned Length)

and its **far..** counterpart adjust the **P** allocation to the specified **Length,** moving **P** if necessary to obtain the space; they return a pointer to the (possibly relocated) **P.** Space freed by the **realloc** functions is available for allocation to new variables. If you haven't sufficient memory left for a requested allocation or reallocation, these functions return a null pointer. Finally, functions

void free(void *P)
void farfree(void far *P)

free the space allocated to **P.**

Releasing heap space in arbitrary order results in a disconnected heap. Turbo C uses a linked list technique to handle this. Immediately preceding each heap variable is a header containing its length and a pointer to the header of the next variable. The header is four bytes long for small memory models, and eight for the large ones. The effects of most

of the near heap management functions are shown by program **Heap.Dem**
and its output in Figure 2.5.1. This was compiled with the small model.
First, **coreleft** reports the available memory. Next, **malloc** creates one-
and two-byte heap variables ***P** and ***Q**. The single-byte variable
actually uses two bytes; and each needs four more for the header. The
available memory decreases by six in each case. Now **realloc** is used to
enlarge ***P** to three bytes. That requires relocation, and you can see the
new address. The original space becomes available, but doesn't affect the
memory report because **coreleft** only reports the amount of available
memory after the topmost allocated heap variable. *Caution: heap frag-*

```
/****************************************************************/
/* Heap.Dem        Demonstrate heap management functions.      */
/****************************************************************/

#include <General.H>
#define Report printf("coreleft = %u\n",coreleft());

void main() {
  void *P,*Q,*R;
printf("                        ");  Report;  P =  malloc(1);
printf("P =  malloc(1)    = %p; ",P);  Report;  Q =  malloc(2);
printf("Q =  malloc(2)    = %p; ",Q);  Report;  P = realloc(P,3);
printf("P = realloc(P,3) = %p; ",P);  Report;  R =  malloc(1);
printf("R =  malloc(1)    = %p; ",R);  Report;  free(Q);
printf("          free(Q)         ");  Report;  free(P);
printf("          free(P)         ");  Report;  }
```

Output   ## Comments

```
                        coreleft = 63952
P =  malloc(1)    = 0500; coreleft = 63946   (2 for P + 4 for
                                              header.)
Q =  malloc(2)    = 0506; coreleft = 63940   (2 for Q + 4 for
                                              header.)
P = realloc(P,3) = 050C; coreleft = 63932   (Move P; release
                                              space at 0500.)
R =  malloc(1)    = 0500; coreleft = 63932   (Use space at 0500.)
        free(Q)          coreleft = 63932   (Makes a hole.)
        free(P)          coreleft = 63946   (No more hole.)
```

Figure 2.5.1 Program **Heap.Dem**

mentation causes an inaccurate memory report! A new single-byte variable ***R** is allocated in the space formerly occupied by ***P** (check the address). Now ***Q** is freed, creating a hole between ***R** and ***P**. Neither of the last two operations had any effect on **coreleft**. Finally, ***P** is freed, and **coreleft** reports the correct value, because there remains only the one allocated variable ***R** at the beginning of the heap.

Ordinarily, when you use an **..alloc** function, you need to cast its value to a pointer to the proper type: for example,

char *P;
:
P = (char *) malloc(1);

That detail was circumvented in Figure 2.5.1 to make its text simpler.

Program **FarHeap.Dem** in Figure 2.5.2 demonstrates use of the far heap to accommodate an array **A** larger than 64K bytes. In this case, **A** consists of 9000 eight byte doubles—72K. Function **farcalloc** returns a huge pointer **A** to the appropriate space. You can then use indices as usual, as shown by the two **for** loops in the program. You *must* use a huge pointer, as noted in Section 2.4.

2.6 Further topics

Concepts
Memory manipulation functions Source/target overlap problem Sorting and searching functions AT extended memory Expanded memory Port input/output

This section covers several topics related to memory that didn't seem appropriate for earlier parts of the chapter. First is the rather chaotic collection of Turbo C Library functions for manipulating memory arrays. These are described only briefly here because they are paralleled by the more commonly used string processing functions considered in great

```
/****************************************************************/
/* FarHeap.Dem     Demonstrate use of an array larger than    */
/*                 64K.  Allocate an array  A  of  N = 9000    */
/*                 doubles on the far heap.  Manipulate it by  */
/********************************** setting  A[I] = I   for     */
                            /* all  I,  adding up all          */
#include <General.H>        /* A[I],   and comparing the       */
                            /* the sum to the value of         */
void main() {               /* the equivalent formula          */
  int I, N = 9000;          /* N(N-1)/2.                       */
  double huge *A;           /****************************/
  double Sum;
A = (double huge *) farcalloc(N,sizeof(double));
for (I = 0           ;  I < N;  A[I++] = I);
for (I = 0, Sum = 0;  I < N;  Sum   += A[I++]);
printf("A[I] = I   for   I = 0 .. N-1 ;  N = %d\n",N);
printf("Sum of all   A[I] = %8.0f\n",Sum);
printf(" (N-1)N/2         = %ld  \n", (long) N*(N-1)/2);  }
```

Output

```
A[I] = I   for   I = 0..N-1 ;  N = 9000
Sum of all   A[I] = 40495500
 (N-1)N/2           = 40495500
```

Figure 2.5.2 Program **FarHeap.Dem**

detail in Chapter 3. The memory functions are loosely related to a group of slightly higher-level routines for sorting and searching. A single example program demonstrates several functions of both types. Two topics mentioned here cannot be treated in detail now because the requisite techniques are only covered later in Chapter 8: AT extended memory and Lotus-Intel-Microsoft expanded memory. Finally, port input/output is included here; it has to be included somewhere, and port addressing is (distantly) related to memory addressing.

Memory manipulation functions

The Turbo C Library contains many functions for manipulating arrays of bytes in memory. Their prototypes are in header file **Mem.H**. Generally, they assume no underlying structure: all references to the values stored are explicit, and other relationships between them are ignored. Sometimes you use these functions for manipulating data structures that are simply arrays of bytes. You can also use them to implement operations on data structures not directly supported by C: for example, assignment between arrays, and comparison of arrays or C structures.

This function set is not well designed. There is no uniformity in names, calling sequences, or values returned. There are some obvious gaps. Turbo C TOOLS fills some of the gaps, but displays the same inconsistencies. Some of the designs are inherited from earlier compilers and maintained in Turbo C to provide portability. While that quality is often desirable, it does include portability of bad code as well as good, and fosters perpetuation of bad software design. Moreover, it may ensure entrenchment of a class of programmers who find great virtue in mastering arcane distinctions that would be unnecessary had common sense, not chaos, reigned during development of C.

Four of these functions are most useful:

void *memset(void *Target, char Ch, unsigned N)
void *memmove(void *Target, void *Source, unsigned N)
void *memchr(void *Source, char Ch, unsigned N)
int memcmp(void *Source1, void *Source2, unsigned N)

These, at least, do have consistent names and calling sequences. **memset** stores copies of **Ch** in the **N** bytes starting at ***Target**; it returns the pointer **Target**. **memmove** copies **N** bytes starting at ***Source** into the **N** bytes starting at ***Target**, and returns **Target**. **memchr** returns a pointer to the first **Ch** among the first **N** bytes starting at ***Source**, or else a null pointer, if it finds no **Ch**. **memcmp** compares the **N** bytes starting at ***Source1** with those at ***Source2**, returning 0 if it finds no discrepancy, and a negative or positive value if the first discrepancy, at the Ith entry, has **Source1[I]** < or > **Source2[I]**. The first three of these functions are demonstrated later by the Figure 2.6.1 program **MiscFunc.Dem**.

Related to **memset** is function **setmem**, whose name reflects the fact that its calling sequence reverses **Source** and **Target**; it returns no value. (Assignment expressions are written **Target = Source**. Why not adhere to that order?) This function is actually more fundamental: it's written in assembly language, and **memset** just reverses the parameters and calls **setmem**. Function **memmove** is related similarly to

movmem. To maximize speed, **memchr** and **memcmp** are also written in assembly language.

Several other **memmove** relatives have trouble with *source/target overlap*. If the beginning of the target array lies within the source, like

Source[0] .. Source[N-1]
        Target[0] .. Target[N-1],

then setting **Target[0] = Source[0], ... , Target[N-1] = Source[N-1]**is incorrect. Instead, you should execute these assignments in reverse order. Function **memcpy** operates like **memmove**, but in the interest of speed, it's written in assembly language and doesn't check for overlap. Consequently it doesn't work in that case. Function **memccpy** is like **memcpy** but checks each byte transferred and stops after copying a special **char** value specified in the calling sequence.

In the small and medium models, all the functions just mentioned accept only near pointers. To copy **N** bytes from one far array to another, the Turbo C Library provides function

void movedata(int SourceSegment, int SourceOffset, int TargetSegment, int TargetOffset, unsigned N)

Like **memcpy**, this function is written in assembly language and suffers from the source/target overlap problem. Note that the order of its calling sequence is reversed and it returns no value.

Turbo C TOOLS includes a function **utmovmem** which is similar to **movedata** that avoids the overlap problem, but still has the calling sequence reversed. It also includes two macros **utpoken** and **utpeekn** that call **utmovmem** with near source and far target pointers and vice-versa.

Turbo C Library function **swab** is related to the memory manipulation functions, but its prototype

void swab(char *Source, char *Target, int N)

is in header file **StdLib.H**. It copies **N** words starting at ***Source** into **N** words at ***Target**, reversing corresponding low and high bytes. This is most useful in moving information between software or hardware systems with opposite interpretations of low and high bytes. The function is written in C and is subject to the overlap problem.

Sorting and searching

In header file **StdLib.H** you'll find prototypes for somewhat higher-level sorting and searching functions:

void qsort(void *Source, int N, int W, int (*Cf)())
void *lfind(const void *Key, const void *Source, int *N,
**   int W, int (*Cf)())**
void *lsearch(const void *Key, void *Source, int *N, int W,
**   int (*Cf)())**
void *bsearch(const void *Key, const void *Source, int *N,
**   int W, int (*Cf)())**

These operate on **Source** arrays consisting of **N** items of width **W** bytes. Each requires a pointer to a function declared like this:

int Cf(const void *P, const void *Q)

You must provide this function, which assumes that **P** and **Q** point to items of width **W** like those just mentioned. For **lfind** and **lsearch**, Cf must return 0 or a nonzero value according as items ***P** and ***Q** are equal or not. For **qsort** and **bsearch**, this nonzero value must be negative just when ***P** precedes ***Q**. (You can interpret *equal* and *precedes* as you wish.) Function **qsort** uses the Hoare-Singleton *quicksort* algorithm (reference [24, pp. 114-123]) to sort the **Source** array. The other three functions ascertain whether item ***Key** occurs in the **Source** array or not. **bsearch** requires that the array be sorted into ascending order, and performs a binary search; **lfind** and **lsearch** perform simple linear searches, not requiring a sorted array. If ***Key** occurs in the array, **bsearch** returns a pointer to such an occurrence; **lfind** and **lsearch** return pointers to the *first* one. If ***Key** does not occur there, **lfind** and **bsearch** return null pointers, but **lsearch** appends ***Key** to the end of the array, adjusts N, and returns a pointer to the new last item. (You must have allocated enough space to the array.)

Program **MiscFunc.Dem** in Figure 2.6.1 demonstrates several of the memory manipulation, sorting, and searching functions. It initializes an array with **memset**, rearranges it with **memmove**, and demonstrates what happens when **memchr** does or does not find in it a specific **char** value. The program then reinitializes the array with random values, uses **lfind** to search it linearly, sorts it with **qsort**, and searches the sorted array with **bsearch**. Macros **ShowA** and **Star** abbreviate code repeatedly used to display the array and indicate the located items. Function **DiffStar** compares two items: since they are single bytes, it just returns their difference. In function **main**, the statements invoking **lfind**, **qsort**, and **bsearch** produce *Suspicious pointer conversion* warnings from the compiler; it's not clear how to avoid those. From the output you can determine that **lfind** indeed does not assume that the array is sorted: it did not stop until it found an occurrence of the key, even though it first encountered items that succeed the key in sorted order.

On the other hand, Figure 2.6.1 output shows that **bsearch** does *not* perform as advertised: it does not return the *first* occurrence of the key. A glance at its source code shows why. It compares the key with the first item in the upper half of a subarray; if it finds the key, it declares success, or else it bisects the subarray. It neglects to search downward from a located item for the *first* occurrence.

```
/****************************************************************/
/* MiscFunc.Dem    Demonstrate several memory manipulation    */
/*                     functions.  Use  memset  to fill a  char  */
/* array  A.  Rearrange it with  memmove.  Try to find  char  */
/* values in it with  memchr.  Use  rand  to fill it with    */
/*********************** random values.  Search linearly for */
                    /* for a character with  lfind.  Sort  */
#include <General.H>   /* the array with  qsort.  Do a bina-  */
                    /* ry search with  bsearch.           */
#define N 40          /************************************/

unsigned Length = N;            /* Needed for  lfind.  */
unsigned char I, A[N], *M, Key = 5;

#define ShowA for (I = 0; I < N; printf("%u",A[I++]));
#define Star  if (M) printf("%*c*",M-A,' ');
int DiffStar(unsigned char *X,      /* Comparison function  */
        unsigned char *Y) {         /* for  lfind, qsort,  */
return (*X - *Y); }                 /* and  bsearch.        */

void main() {
printf("\nkey        : ",Key);
memset(&A[N/2],Key,N/2);            /* Create and display  */
printf("\nmemset  : ");  ShowA;     /* an array of  6s  and */
```

Figure 2.6.1 Program **MiscFunc.Dem** (*Continued on next page*)

```
M = memchr (A, Key, N);                       /* 5s.  Find and star   */
printf ("\nmemchr :  ");  Star;               /* the first  5.        */
memmove (&A[N/2], A, N/2);                     /* Cover the  5s  with  */
printf ("\nmemmove :  ");  ShowA;             /* 6s.  Display.        */
M = memchr (A, Key, N);                       /* Find the first  5    */
printf ("\nmemchr :  ");  Star;               /* (there's none).      */
for (I = 0; I < N; A[I++]=random(10);         /* Fill, display array  */
printf ("\nrand    :  ");  ShowA;             /* with random digits.  */
M = lfind (&Key, A, &Length, 1, DiffStar);    /* Linear search for a  */
printf ("\nlfind   :  ");  Star;              /* 5;  star it.         */
qsort (A, N, 1, DiffStar);                    /* Sort the array.      */
printf ("\nqsort   :  ");  ShowA;             /* Display it.          */
M = bsearch (&Key, A, N, 1, DiffStar);        /* Search sorted array  */
printf ("\nbsearch :  ");  Star; }            /* for a 5;  star it.   */
```

Output

```
key      :  5
memset   :  66666666666666666666665555555555555555555555
memchr   :                          *
memmove  :  66666666666666666666666666666666666666666666
memchr   :
rand     :  60206755864819202137910549219611534099512
lfind    :  *
qsort    :  00000111111122222334445555566667778899999
bsearch  :                               *
```

Figure 2.6.1 *(Continued)* Program **MiscFunc.Dem**

AT extended memory

Section 2.1 mentioned that an AT operates in two modes. Immediately after booting, it's in *real* mode, and addresses memory just like a PC. When you place it in *protected* mode, however, its addressing scheme is totally different. Protected mode physical memory addresses are three bytes long—24 bits—hence ATs can address $2^{24} = 2^4 x 2^{20} = 16$ MB of memory. Anything above the 1 MB PC capacity is called *extended* memory. *Caution!* The similar term *expanded* memory is used for a *different* method for increasing memory capacity, standardized by the Lotus, Intel, Microsoft, and AST Research Corporations, and described later in this section.

Extended memory can be used only in protected mode. Turbo C cannot operate in protected mode, nor can most other software packages—not even the AT BIOS. However, the BIOS does provide a service that allows assembly language programs to move data to, from, and within extended memory. The required transitions to and from protected mode are hidden. Chapter 8 discusses BIOS services in detail, and Section 8.4 describes functions that use the BIOS to determine how much extended memory is present, and to move data between conventional and extended memory.

Expanded memory

A method of addressing an amount of memory far exceeding the 640K normally accessible to DOS has been developed jointly by the Lotus Development, Intel, and Microsoft Corporations. Called *expanded* memory management (EMM), this scheme reserves some areas in the 1 MB PC main memory as *windows* for access to a much larger separately addressed memory. The windows are normally located above the conventional 640K; you can determine their addresses, avoiding areas used by custom ROM chips. To provide access to expanded memory, a memory resident management program associates required data with the windows. You must keep track of how your data is organized in the separate memory, and which data are currently available in the various windows. To refer to expanded memory locations, you request EMM services via interrupt hex 67. These services are used like the BIOS and DOS interrupt services described and demonstrated in Chapter 8. Several memory expansion boards are now available that implement EMM; this seems to have become the standard way to provide a major PC memory upgrade. For details on specific EMM techniques, consult the references in the next paragraph.

The authoritative description of the EMM standard is the original Lotus/Intel/Microsoft document, reference [25]. A description in text form is available in [10]. Shortly after EMM was developed, AST Research announced memory expansion boards implementing EMM, with several additional features that make it more versatile and convenient. The AST version, called *Extended EMS* (EEMS), is documented in reference [1]. Later still, Lotus, Intel, Microsoft, and AST produced a joint extension to both memory standards, called EMS 4.0 (reference

[26]). With EMS 4.0 memory management software, an earlier EMS board can emulate an EEMS board, but perhaps with insufficient speed.

Some EMS/EEMS memory management software will emulate AT extended memory. (This book was produced on a PC equipped with an AST EEMS board. The AST EEMS memory management program **REX.Sys** emulates extended memory, enabling use of AST virtual disk and print buffer software written for ATs.) Conversely, AT software is available that will—at least partially—make extended memory behave like EMS memory.

Port input/output

Each input/output port of an 8086 family CPU has a 16-bit *port address*. Although 64K different ports are possible, a PC usually has fewer than a hundred. Usually, a port inputs or outputs a single byte, but occasionally a 16-bit port is implemented. Different CPU instructions are required for input and output with eight-bit and 16-bit ports. Four Turbo C Library functions implement these processes:

int inport(int Port)   **void outport(int Port, int Word)**
int inportb(int Port)   **void outportb(int Port, char Byte)**

Each is a three- or four-line assembly language program, with prototype in header file **DOS.H**.

String Processing

Contents

Most programming tasks require some character string processing. Even when the data are mainly numerical or graphical, strings usually play some role in the user interface or in interfaces between software systems. Thus it's important to consider string processing early in a book on systems and application programming. This chapter covers Turbo C string handling features in detail, augmented by a few from Turbo C TOOLS and some routines especially constructed for this book.

The chapter begins with a section on handling individual characters, then discusses data structures for organizing them into strings. Manipulating the simplest such structures—character arrays—has already been discussed in Section 2.6. The standard C language string structure, however, is slightly more specialized: a character array, called a *Z-string,* ending with a terminal zero. Very general techniques for analyzing, constructing, and manipulating Z-strings are described in Sections 3.2..3.5, followed by more particular methods for text strings and numerals in the next two sections. The chapter concludes with some very specialized techniques for currency and time strings, file names, command line parameters, and the string values of program environment variables. Since the latter two items can be viewed as program inputs, the last section includes a discussion of the value returned by a program—i.e., by function **main**.

On the accompanying diskette, source codes for the special string processing routines constructed in this chapter are gathered into file **Strings.C**, with related definitions and prototypes in header file **General.H**. The diskette also contains many simple demonstration programs; their names generally reflect those of the functions demonstrated, with extension **.Dem**.

3.1 Characters

Concepts

char data
signed char vs. **unsigned char**
ASCII/IBM code, control characters
char constants, escape sequences
getchar and **putchar** input/output
To **fflush** the input buffer
Order of characters; comparing and classifying
CType macros
Upper/lower case conversion
Side effect and non-reentrancy problems caused by macros

Character data and constants

This chapter is about string processing, and strings are sequences of characters. Thus it's appropriate to begin by considering character data.

In Turbo C, they have type **char** and require one byte, 8 bits, to store. The correspondence between text and control characters and the $256 = 2^8$ **char** values is known as the *ASCII/IBM code.*

Before discussing the code, it's necessary to consider how numerals represent **char** values—a delicate matter. Most PC software assumes that a single-byte data type represents the integers in the range 0..255, but C ordinarily uses the range -128..127. The question is whether the **char** type is by default **signed** or **unsigned**:

	char values	
signed	hex	unsigned
0	00	0
:	:	:
127	7f	127
-128	80	128
:	:	:
-1	ff	255

Turbo C defaults to **signed char**, although you can change that via the **Options/Compiler/Code Generation** menu. This text will use the ordinary C default, but will describe the ASCII/IBM code in terms of the **unsigned char** values 0..255, in accordance with common PC practice.

Because Turbo C rarely manipulates single bytes, **char** values are cast to type **int** before almost all operations. As described in Section 2.4, this process involves sign extension: replicating the high bit of the **char** value through the high byte of the corresponding word.

Codes 0..127 were standardized once by ASCII (American Standards Committee for Information Interchange) to represent the digits, upper and lower case letters, some punctuation marks and special symbols, and some commands commonly used for teletype control. This standard is still respected, although some control codes became obsolete and are now used differently. Use of codes 128..255 varies widely among different input/output equipment. All codes represent distinctive characters on PC displays according to a *de facto* standard established by the IBM Monochrome Display Adapter. See Appendix C for a complete listing. Codes 0, 32, and 255 all correspond to the blank screen character; these are the only such duplications.

Turbo C provides several ways to designate **char** constants. The most common is to enclose the character itself in single quotes: for example, **'A', '2', ')'**. Sometimes this is impossible, particularly when the hardware or software used to prepare the program is insensitive to or misconstrues the character involved. In that case you can use the signed decimal constant corresponding to the ASCII/IBM code number. You can also use an unsigned decimal, hex, or octal constant or a hex or octal *escape sequence* beginning with a backslash. Program **ChrConst.Dem** in Figure 3.1.1 demonstrates all seven ways to designate ASCII 130 character **'é'**. (Like most PC software, the Turbo C editor allows you to enter characters like **'é'** by holding down the <Alt> key and typing the ASCII/IBM code on the numeric keypad.) As discussed in Section 2.4, all these are really **int** constants obtained by sign extension from the corresponding bytes. Thus the value of **'é'** and **-126** is the twos complement of **130** = hex 82. Under %c format, **printf** simply ignores the high byte of the value to be output.

ASCII codes 0..31, commonly called *control* codes, have familiar names like *Control-A*, and are often entered via keystrokes like <Ctrl-A>. They are sometimes displayed like **^A** (different from the corresponding IBM screen character, which for ASCII 1 = **^A** is an outlined happy face). You could use hex or octal escape sequences to enter these characters. For several of them C also provides mnemonic escape sequences. These are listed in Figure 3.1.2, with some remarks about their effect on normal screen output (DOS output requested by **printf**) and on printers. A few additional escape sequences are provided to permit unambiguous syntax in other contexts.

```
/********************************************************************/
/* ChrConst.Dem     Demonstrate char constants and values.      */
/********************************************************************/

#include <General.H>
                                        /*  'é' = ASCII 130 */
void main() {                           /* = -126 (mod 256) */
printf("%c %c %c %c %c %c %c\n",'é',    /* = hex 82         */
   130,-126,'\x82',0x82,'\202',0202); } /* = octal 202.     */
```

Output

é é é é é é

Figure 3.1.1 Program **ChrConst.Dem**

C code	ASCII code name	Effect
\a	7 <BEL>	DOS beeps (alarm)
\b	8 <BS>	DOS backspaces.[1]
\t	9 <TAB>	DOS tabs.[1]
\n	10 <LF>	**printf** expands this to <CR> <LF> , causing DOS to start the next line.[1]
\v	11 <VT>	DOS writes a male symbol.[2]
\f	12 <FF>	DOS writes a female symbol.[2]
\r	13 <CR>	DOS restarts the current line.
\?	63 Question mark	These permit unambigu-
\\	92 Backslash	ous syntax in various
\'	39 Single quote	situations.
\"	34 Double quote	

[1] DOS's exact behavior depends on the cursor location.
[2] Printers may interpret <VT> as vertical tab and <FF> as form feed.

Figure 3.1.2 Escape sequences

There should be a mnemonic constant for the blank character ASCII 32 that's more visible than ' '. Therefore, the macro

#define Blank ' '

is included in the header file **General.H** for this book. Various others are included as well, and used without comment when the meaning is clear.

Character input/output

Because of the complexity, the high-level **printf** function was used for character output in Figure 3.1.1. For single-character input/output, the

Turbo C Library provides macros **getchar** and **putchar**. Use them as though they were functions with these prototypes:

int getchar(void) **int putchar(char)**

The macro definitions, in header file **StdIO.H**, are complicated enough to defy understanding at this point, mainly because they invoke a succession of deeper and deeper functions that ultimately request DOS standard (redirectible) input/output. They are discussed in more detail in Sections 5.1 and 4.1. (There you will find recommendations for using other functions when fine keyboard and screen control are required. Except in the next demonstration program, that's not the case in this chapter. Since **getchar** and **putchar** are the most standard C character input/output functions, they are used here.)

The header file **General.H**, for use with all programs in this book, contains a simple macro

#define NewLine putchar('\n')

that places the cursor at the beginning of the next line (scrolling the screen if necessary).

Program **CharIO.Dem** in Figure 3.1.3 demonstrates **getchar** and **putchar**. A typical example of the demonstration programs for functions described in this book, it's an endless loop that you must terminate with <Ctrl-Break>. During each iteration, it inputs data, demonstrates a computation involving the input, then outputs the results. Writing such routines is fairly simple; few will be shown explicitly in the text.

CharIO.Dem uses high-level function **printf** for complex output, but inputs and outputs the single character **Ch** via **getchar** and **putchar**. Standard C input/output is buffered. The first invocation of **getchar** reads into the input buffer as many characters as you type. Your <CR> triggers it to move one character from the buffer into **Ch**. Function **fflush** empties the buffer before the next **getchar**, lest the loop continue reading from the buffer. (This is necessary even if you know you'll enter only a single character. DOS adds an <LF> after your <CR>. The <CR> is discarded, but the <LF> remains, and unless you flush, **getchar** will read it on the next iteration.)

To produce the second sample **CharIO.Dem** output, ASCII 21 was entered via the numeric keypad. Still responding to the **getchar** request, DOS produced the top line *echo* ^U (Control-U). Then it responded to **putchar** by outputting the *single* character § on the second line. You'll find that other control characters produce different, sometimes bizarre, effects. The worst is the DOS end-of-file character **^Z**: **getchar** reports that it has read the C end-of-file signal, but doesn't remove **^Z** from the buffer. These examples should convince you that programming robust keyboard input requires more sophisticated methods, like those discussed in Chapter 5.

```
/*****************************************************************/
/* CharIO.Dem      Demonstrate character input/output.        */
/*****************************************************************/

#include <General.H>

void main() {
  char Ch;
  for (;;) {                             /* You must terminate */
    printf("\nEnter a character:  ");    /* this endless loop  */
    fflush(stdin);                       /* with  <Ctrl-Break>. */
    Ch = getchar();
    putchar(Ch);
    printf(" in  %%d  format:  %d\n", Ch);
    printf("It's  ASCII %d .\n", (unsigned char) Ch); }}
```

Sample executions

```
Enter a character:  A
A  in  %d  format:  65
It's  ASCII 65 .

Enter a character:  ^U
§ in  %d  format:  21
It's  ASCII 21 .

Enter a character:  é
é  in  %d  format:  -126
It's  ASCII 130 .
```

Figure 3.1.3 Program **CharIO.Dem**

Classifying characters

The ASCII code was designed so that the usual order of letters and digits coincides with the numerical order of the corresponding **char** values. The blank precedes all digits, which precede all upper case letters, which precede the lower case. (All these fall within codes 0..127.) Moreover, the difference between corresponding upper and lower case codes is the same for all letters: for example, **'a'** - **'A'** = **'z'** - **'Z'**. Thus it's easy to determine the alphabetic order of two **char** values once you know they're in the same case, and it's easy to change from upper to lower case or vice versa by adding or subtracting **'a'** - **'A'**.

The Turbo C Library provides facilities for this kind of character classification and conversion. The functions in Figure 3.1.4, each with a single parameter **int c**, return **int** values. Nonzero values signify membership in the character sets noted. For example, **isascii(c)** has value 1 if $0 \le c < 128$, and 0 otherwise. These functions are all implemented as macros in header file **CType.H**: for example,

#define isascii(c) ((unsigned)((c) + 1) < 0x81)

Functions **isgraph** and **isprint** mention argument **c** twice, so are subject to side effect errors. (That problem is considered in the last paragraph of this section.) Macros **islower** to **ispunct** all refer to an

Function	Set			Value
isascii	ASCII	=	{0..127}	1
isgraph	graph	=	{33..126}	1
isprint	print	=	{32} + graph	1
isupper	upper	=	{'A'..'Z'}	4
islower	lower	=	{'a'..'z'}	8
isalpha	alpha	=	upper + lower	4+8
isdigit	digit	=	{'0'..'9'}	2
isalnum	alnum	=	alpha + digit	2+4+8
iscntrl	cntrl	=	{0..31} + {127}	32
isspace	space	=	{9..13} + {32}	1
ispunct	punct	=	cntrl + space	64
isxdigit	xdigit	=	digit + {'A'..'F'} + {'a'..'f'}	2+16

Figure 3.1.4 Character classification functions

external array _ctype preset in Library source file **CType.C** with classification values for the 128 characters: for example,

#define IS_UPP 4
#define isupper(c) (_ctype[(c) + 1] & IS_UPP)

Since $'A' = 65$ and _ctype[66] = 20 = 16 + 4, **isupper('A')= 4**.

Each Library function in the next list maps arguments from one character set to corresponding values in another. Other arguments are unchanged.

int toupper(int c)   lower case --> upper case
int tolower(int c)   upper case --> lower case

The prototypes are in **CType.H**. The same header file contains macro versions of these functions, namely

#define _toupper(c) ((c) + 'A' - 'a')
#define _tolower(c) ((c) + 'a' - 'A')

These clearly don't work unless **c** is in the case opposite that of the intended value. Therefore, each service is provided by a bonafide function, which checks the case first, then invokes the corresponding macro.

Macro design

The problem with these macros presents an opportunity to discuss some questions about macro design. If you try to improve **_toupper(c)** by having it check first whether **c** is lower case, you will probably evaluate **c** twice. This causes a problem when **c** is the value of a function with a side effect, as shown by macro **ToUpper1** in Figure 3.1.5: **c** is the value of a function that writes a message. Evaluating **c** twice writes the message twice. *A general purpose macro should evaluate its argument only once!*

You can avoid repeated evaluation of **c** by storing it first in a scratchpad variable, as in this macro **ToUpper2(c)**:

char V;
#define ToUpper2(c) (islower(V = (c)) ? _toupper(V) : V)

```
/*********************************************************************/
/* ToUpper.Dem    Macro _toupper(c)  fails when  c  isn't   */
/*                lower case.  ToUpper1(c)  checks  c first, */
/* hence evaluates it twice, causing a side effect problem.   */
/*************************************** Function  toupper(c) */
                                      /* works properly.      */
#include <General.H>                  /***********************/
#include <CType.H>

#define ToUpper1(c) (islower(c) ? _toupper(c) : (c))

int F(int c) {                        /* Function  F  has a   */
printf("Hello from  F !  ");          /* side effect.         */
return c; }

void main () {
printf("_toupper(F('A')) = %c\n", _toupper(F('A')));
printf("ToUpper1(F('A')) = %c\n", ToUpper1(F('A')));
printf(" toupper(F('A')) = %c\n",  toupper(F('A'))); }
```

Output

```
Hello from  F !  _toupper(F('A')) = !
Hello from  F !  Hello from  F !  ToUpper1(F('A')) = A
Hello from  F !   toupper(F('A')) = A
```

Figure 3.1.5 Program **ToUpper.Dem**

Since the macro expansion must be a syntactically valid *expression*, you can't declare scratchpad variable **V** within the macro; it must be *global*. (Clearly, you should use a variable name more distinctive than **V**, that no containing program is likely to use.) There will be trouble if other software should interrupt **ToUpper2** between references to **V**, then itself use **ToUpper2**. The first value of **V** would be overwritten by the second, hence unavailable for use after the interruption. Such a situation may seem unlikely in this context. However, it occurs in DOS itself and is the root of the famous "non-reentry problem" that makes it so difficult to write memory resident DOS software. *A general purpose macro should not use a global variable.*

The global variable problem was caused by an attempt to avoid repeated evaluation of a macro argument that could be the value of a function with a side effect; the macro expansion had to be a valid expression. In some situations, you may want to use a scratchpad variable, but may require only that the macro yield a valid *statement*. (All expressions are statements, but not vice-versa.) In that case you can declare a *local* variable, as in this last version **ToUpper3(c)**:

```
#define ToUpper3(c) { char V = c;        \
                    if (islower(V))   \
                        c = _toupper(V); }
```

This macro creates a copy **V** of **c** on the stack, converts **V** if necessary, copies the result back into **c**, then pops **V** from the stack. Since **ToUpper3(c)** creates a *new* stack variable each time it's used, its code is reentrant. But it expands to a *statement* and *changes* the value of **c**; both of these qualities prevent its use as a function like the previous versions.

3.2 Strings

Concepts

Data structures for strings
Z-strings
Allocation
Constants
Indexing
String length function **strlen**
gets and **puts** input/output
String processing tools: chapter preview

There are several ways to design a data structure for character strings. In some languages, strings have limited length, the length is included in the structure just before the data, and the data are stored in consecutive memory locations. In Turbo Pascal, for example, a single byte encodes the length, so strings must be shorter than 256 characters. Easy access to the length enhances efficiency of many string operations that depend on or affect it, but consecutive data storage makes rearranging strings awkward and time-consuming. A fixed maximum string length simplifies memory allocation for strings. But a short maximum hampers use of the structure for major text processing applications, and a long one leads to inefficient storage if many strings are much shorter. An alternative structure, a linked list, provides ease of manipulation and essentially unlimited length, at the expense of space for the link pointers and time for allocating links and for stepping from one to the next.

C uses a compromise structure called a *Z-string:* an array of character data followed by a special *terminator*. You allocate memory for a string just as you would for any other array: N characters require N bytes plus 1 for the terminator. This structure permits essentially unlimited string length. However, ascertaining a string's length requires searching it from the beginning for the terminator. Efficiency requires avoiding that operation when possible. Another problem with Z-strings is that you can't use the terminator, ASCII 0 (Z stands for *Zero*), as a character in the string. That control character is not often used for other purposes, but it does occur whenever ASCII characters are used to encode numerical information—for example, in some printer control sequences.

You can declare and allocate memory for a string S of limited length—for example, length ≤ 100 —in two ways:

char S[101];   **char *S;**
                                       S = (char *) malloc(101);

The first creates an array in the data or stack segment, and a pointer S to it. The second creates a pointer S to an array allocated on the heap. You should enter a terminating **S[I] = 0** for some **I** ≤ 100 in either case; don't rely on automatic initialization.

The last paragraph referred to S as a string *pointer*. For precise writing it's appropriate to distinguish between the pointer and the string *S itself. However, this becomes tiresome and leads to overly complex prose. This text will employ ambiguity where it can simplify the discussion without jeopardizing clarity: the term *string* will denote both the pointer and the sequence of characters in memory.

String constants look like **"this"**. Turbo C allocates space for them as needed. An assignment statement **S = "this"** makes a previously declared **char *** pointer S point to the constant string. No prior space allocation for S is necessary because just the pointer value is changed. (In fact any previously allocated space should be freed, lest it become unusable.)

The constant "" stands for the empty string: a **char** array with one entry, the terminal 0. Since this symbol is easily misconstrued, a more visible macro is included in this book's header file **General.H**, as well as a macro for ascertaining whether a string **S** is empty:

#define EmptyStr   ""
#define StrEmpty(S) (*(S) == 0)

The latter returns 1 or 0 depending on whether **S** is empty or not.

You can access the entries of a string **S** of length **N** by indexing: **S[0]..S[N-1]** and **S[N]** are its constituent characters and terminal 0. The indices may have any type compatible with **unsigned int**. Since any **unsigned int** value could be a valid index, a general string processing routine can't use indices 0, -1, etc., to signal special situations. If **I** is an **unsigned** index, then **S + I** is a pointer to **S[I]** (as long as **I ≤ N**). Conversely, given a **char** * pointer **P** to an **S** entry, **I = P – S** is the corresponding index: **P** points to **S[I]**.

Library function **strlen** takes a string argument of type **char** * and returns its length, of type **unsigned**. Its prototype

size_t strlen(const char *s);

is in header file **String.H**. The function, coded in assembly language, simply searches for the terminator and returns its index. (Actually, the **strlen** value has type **size_t**, which is defined in **String.H** to be the same as **unsigned**. Apparently Turbo C uses this method to comply with a C convention that various data have the type **size_t** of the value of the **sizeof** operator. Since Turbo C documentation doesn't emphasize that distinction, this book won't either.)

Program **StrIndex.Dem** in Figure 3.2.1 displays some of these concepts, as well as the standard Library string input/output functions **gets** and **puts**. It uses these to input and echo a string **S**. **gets** is more appropriate here than the high level input function **scanf**, which doesn't allow you to enter an empty string. The prototypes

char *gets(char *S)   int puts(const char *S)

are in header file **StdIO.H**. **gets** returns **S**; **puts** returns the last character written. **StrIndex.Dem** outputs the length of **S**, uses pointer arithmetic to locate its last entry, and displays an entry specified by an

```
/*****************************************************************/
/* StrIndex.Dem    Demonstrate string allocation, input/out-  */
/*                 put, length and indexing.                  */
/*****************************************************************/

#include <General.H>

void main() {
  char S[101];
  unsigned I,L;
for (;;) {                                  /* Endless loop!     */
  printf("Enter a string  S :  ");
  fflush(stdin);
  gets(S);
  printf("Your string is  ");
  puts(S);
  printf("strlen(S)         =  %d\n",L = strlen(S));
  printf("Its last entry is  %c\n",*(S+L-1));
  printf("Enter an index  I :  ");
  scanf ("%u",&I);
  printf("S[I]              =  %c\n\n",S[I]); }}
```

Sample execution

```
Enter a string  S :  untied!
Your string is  untied!
strlen(S)         =  7
Its last entry is   !
Enter an index  I :  9
S[I]              =  ?
```

Figure 3.2.1 Program **StrIndex.Dem**

index **I** that you enter. There's no protection against references to **S[I]** with **I ≥ strlen(S)**; the sample output shows that garbage results. In Chapters 4 and 5 you'll find arguments against general usage of **gets** and **puts** and the higher level functions **scanf** and **printf**. These objections apply mostly when you need really precise keyboard and display control. That's not the case in the present chapter, and since these are the most standard C string input/output functions, they are used here.

You can check that your <CR> that signalled DOS to terminate your input is not stored with **S**. In fact, DOS read the <CR> into the standard input buffer, and added an <LF>. When **gets** moved your input into **S**, it removed the <CR> from the buffer but not the <LF>. Therefore, it was necessary to use **fflush(stdin)** to clear the buffer for the next input. You can also verify from the sample **StrIndex.Dem** output that **puts** appends <CR><LF> to its output. If you need to suppress that, you'll have to use screen handling techniques described later in Chapter 4.

The rest of this chapter considers string processing in depth, by detailing the extensive Turbo C Library facilities and describing the development of a string processing toolkit to supplement them. Each section covers a single topic. The first three are general:

3.3 Analysis   gaining information about the entries of a string,
3.4 Synthesis   building strings,
3.5 Manipulation   changing them.

The remaining sections apply the general techniques to specific areas in systems and applications programming.

3.6 Text   text string considerations;
3.7 Numerals   converting between internal representations of numbers and numerical strings;
3.8 Money   describing monetary amounts according to national currency conventions;
3.9 Time   constructing time and date strings according to national conventions;
3.10 Further topics interpreting and assembling full file names; interpreting a Turbo C program's DOS command line and environment.

Most of the functions discussed later in this chapter belong to the Turbo C Library. A few are provided by the Blaise Computing Inc. Turbo C TOOLS package featured throughout the book. Finally, many new ones are specified to fill in gaps. Some are constructed here, but others are just described and left to you as exercises. By working out the details, you'll gain familiarity with many C techniques used in the rest of this book.

3.3 String analysis

```
Concepts

String length
Empty string
Ascertaining where strings differ
Searching a string for a character
Searching a string for a character in or not in a given set
Searching a string for a substring
```

This section describes routines that return information about strings, but do not alter them: they report string length, compare two strings, or locate a character or substring within a given string. The Turbo C Library provides many functions of this sort that you'll need for everyday work. Their names begin with **str** and prototypes are in header file **String.H**. The Library leaves a few gaps, some of which are filled by functions presented in this section. These you will find in source code file **Strings.C** on the accompanying diskette, with prototypes and associated definitions in this book's header file **General.H**. The header file is listed in Appendix B. Demonstration programs for various functions are contained in similarly named **.Dem** files. Others you can code yourself as exercises, following guidelines suggested here.

The first string analysis routine is **strlen**, already mentioned in Section 3.2. To determine the length of a string **S** it must search memory forward from the address **S** for the first terminal 0. For speed, it's implemented in assembly language.

You can easily determine whether a string is empty, by asking whether its first entry is the terminating 0. Header file **General.H** defines a macro for that, as well as a mnemonic for the empty string:

#define StrEmpty(S) (*(S) == 0)
#define EmptyStr   ""

A fundamental operation with any data structure is ascertaining whether two instances are the same. A comparison function should return the value 1 to indicate equality, and 0 for inequality. When a comparison function reports inequality, more information is often required. Just where do two structures differ? After comparing two strings, you often take some action, depending on their equality or on the first entries where they differ. For example, strings **S** and **T** are equal if they have exactly the same entries; otherwise, **S** precedes **T** in lexicographic order if $S[I] < T[I]$, where **I** is the first index for which $S[I] \neq T[I]$. (This includes the case where **S** is a proper initial substring of **T**: then $S[I]$ is the terminating 0 of **S**.) While the Turbo C Library provides several high-level functions (described in Section 3.6) that consider the ASCII/IBM lexicographic ordering of two strings, none identifies first differing entries so that you could ascertain precedence with respect to some other ordering, or take some other action. You would need such a feature, for example, if you wanted to alphabetize Spanish words containing letter ñ. Function **StrEqualsF** in Figure 3.3.1 performs this task: when $S \neq T$, it returns 0 as well as pointers to the first differing entries. (Turbo C warns against including the assignment within the **while** statement in this function. That practice is usually objectionable, because the code is hard to understand. Here it seems justified, particularly since the remedy suggested in the *Reference Guide,* Appendix B, leads to even more obscure code.)

Occasionally, you may need to process strings in the backward direction, starting from their ends. You could reverse them with Library function

```
/*****************************************************************/
/* StrEqualsF       Compare strings S,T  in the forward direc- */
/*                  tion.   If equal, return  1  and point  PS  */
/* and  PT  to the terminators.  Otherwise, return   0  and     */
/* point to the first differing entries.  If one string is a    */
/* proper initial substring of the other,  PS  or  PT  will     */
/****************************************** point to the sub-    */
                                         /* string terminator.   */
int StrEqualsF (char *S,                 /*********************/
                char *T,
                char **PS,               /* PS,PT  are pointers */
                char **PT) {             /* to pointers.        */
   int Equals;
  *PS = S;
  *PT = T;
  while ((Equals = (**PS == **PT)) && (**PS != 0)) {
    ++*PS; ++*PT; }
  return Equals; }
```

Figure 3.3.1 Function **StrEqualsF**

strrev (described in Section 3.5) then use forward-directed routines. However, unless you don't mind destroying the original strings when you reverse them, you must allocate space for the backward copies. In any case, reversing them takes time. It may be better to adapt the analysis routines. Figure 3.3.2 contains function **StrEqualsB**, a backward version of **StrEqualsF**. Writing these functions brings up a design question: is it better to return *pointers* or *indices* to first differing entries? Pointers seem easiest for the forward direction, and indices for the backward. So **StrEqualsB** is written in a slightly different style, with indices. For your own string processing tool kit you should probably pick one style, and rewrite the other routine, to avoid confusion in applications.

StrEqualsF is a little more general than it appears. You don't need to start at the strings' beginnings, but may point **S** and **T** to any entries for starting the comparison. Providing analogous functionality with **StrEqualsB** would have required an extra pair of parameters. Alternatively, for **StrEqualsB** you could use ***PM** and ***PN** as inputs, indicating the first entries to be compared.

```
/*************************************************************/
/* StrEqualsB      Compare strings  S,T  in the backward di- */
/*                 rection.  If equal, return  1  and set *PM */
/* = 0 = *PN.  Otherwise, return  0  and let  *PM  and  *PN  */
/* indicate the first differing characters, counting back    */
/* from the ends. If one string is a proper final substring  */
/* of the other,  *PM  or  *PN  will be  0 and the other will */
/* indicate the substring's start.                           */
/*************************************************************/

int StrEqualsB(        char *S,
                       char *T,
                unsigned *PM,              /* PM,PN  are pointers  */
                unsigned *PN) {            /* to indices.          */
*PM = strlen(S);
*PN = strlen(T);
while ((*PM > 0) && (*PN > 0) && (S[*PM] == T[*PN])) {
  --*PM; --*PN; }
return (*PM == 0) && (*PN == 0) && (S[*PM] == T[*PN]); }
```

Figure 3.3.2 Function **StrEqualsB**

You can use **StrEqualsF** and **StrEqualsB** to ascertain whether one string is a proper initial or final substring of another:

- **S** is a proper initial substring of **T** just when **StrEqualsF** returns 0 and **PS** points to the terminator, i.e. *****PS** = 0;

- **S** is a proper final substring of **T** just when **StrEqualsB** returns 0 and **M** = 0.

A demonstration program **StrEqual.Dem** for these two routines is included on the accompanying diskette.

Another common string analysis task is searching a string **S** forward or backward from a given position for a specified character **Ch**. For example, if **S** is a common English name like "James Thomas Smith", you could separate the Christian name by searching for the first blank, or the surname by searching for the last. These tasks are performed by two Library functions:

char *strchr(char *S,   Search forward from the
      char Ch)   beginning.

char *strrchr(char *S,   Search backward from the
      char Ch)   end.

Each returns a pointer to the first occurrence, or a null pointer, if there is none. Both routines are implemented entirely in C. If you already know the length **N** of **S**, you can use the slightly faster function

void *memchr(void *S, int Ch, unsigned N)

already discussed in Section 2.6; it's implemented in assembly language.

Searching forward or backward from a given entry is a fairly common task. For example, you may want to locate each newline character '**\n**' in succession to determine the lengths of lines for arranging output of a text string. While **strchr** can start anywhere, **strrchr** is limited to starting from the end. In Figure 3.3.3 is a new backward search routine **StrChrB**. In this chapter, names of forward and backward directed routines end in **F** or **B**; if you decide to use **StrChrB** in your tool kit, you may want to rename **strchr** consistently using

```
/**************************************************************/
/* StrChrB          Search string  S  backward from pointer  P */
/*                  for character  C,  returning a pointer to  */
/************************************** the first one found,  */
                                 /* or the null pointer,  */
char *StrChrB(char *S,           /* if there's none.      */
             char *P,            /**********************/
             char  C) {
   unsigned I = P-S;                 /* Convert pointer  P  */
   while (S[I] != C && I != 0) --I;  /* to index  I,        */
   return (S[I] == C ? S + I : NULL); } /* then back again.   */
```

Figure 3.3.3 Function **StrChrB**

#define StrChrF strchr

You will find on the accompanying diskette a demonstration program **StrChr.Dem** for functions **StrChrF** and **StrChrB**.

Four variants of the **StrChr** functions are useful in applications: search a string **S** forward or backward for the first occurrence of a character in a given string **Seek** or *not* in a given string **Ignore**. For example, **S** might be a forward or reverse Polish algebraic expression:

Parenthesized	Polish	Reverse Polish
(a+b/c)*(d-e)	*+a/bc-de	abc/+de-*

Interpreting **S** you might want to search forward or backward for the first character not occurring in the operator string **Ignore = "+-/*"**. To ascertain whether **S** involves certain variables, you might search forward for the first entry that also occurs in **Seek** = "abc". Here are prototypes for the four functions:

char *StrPBrkF(char *S,
               char *Seek)

Search forward for the first **S** entry occurring in **Seek**.

char *StrPBrkB(char *S,
               char *T,
               char *Seek)

Search backward from **T** for the first **S** entry occurring in **Seek**.

char *StrCPBrkF(char *S,   Search forward for the
              char *Ignore)   first **S** entry not in
                                       Ignore.

char *StrCPBrkB(char *S,   Search backward from **T**
              char *T,   for the first **S** entry
              char *Ignore)   not in **Ignore.**

(The **C** in the last two names stands for *complement.*) The first function is already available as **strpbrk** in the C Library, so all that's required is to include

#define StrPBrkF strpbrk

in header file **General.H**. (Turbo C literature uses the **pbrk** pseudo-mnemonic without comment. Members of the C insiders club allegedly use knowledge of its origin as a secret recognition device.)

    Function **StrCPBrkF** is easy to implement using C Library function **strspn**:

char *StrCPBrkF(char *S,
                    char *Ignore) {
unsigned N = strspn(S,Ignore);
return (N != strlen(S) ? S + N : NULL); }

strspn(S,T) returns the length of the longest initial segment of **S** consisting of characters in **T**. The related Library function **strcspn(S,T)** returns the length of the longest initial segment consisting of characters *not* in T. Here are their prototypes:

unsigned strcspn(const char *S1, const char *S2);
unsigned strspn (const char *S1, const char *S2);

These two functions and **strpbrk** are implemented entirely in C.
    The other two routines, in the backward direction, are most safely implemented with the forward versions, using the string reversing function **strrev** described later in Section 3.5. They are left as exercises. String reversal requires allocating a temporary variable as large as the string; if your application requires **StrPBrkB** or **StrCPBrkB** to process

```
/****************************************************************/
/* StrStrB        Search string  S backward from its end for */
/*                substring  T.  Return a pointer to the       */
/*                start of the first occurrence found, or      */
/****************************************** the null pointer if */
                                      /* there's none.         */
char *StrStrB(char *S,                /************************/
             char *T) {
  unsigned K,L,M,N;
if (StrEmpty(S)) return NULL;         /* Special case.         */
M = strlen(S);                        /* Know  M > 0.          */
if (StrEmpty(T)) return S+M-1;        /* Special case.         */
N = strlen(T) - 1;                    /* T[N]  is last entry.*/
while (M > N) {                       /* N Ú 0,  so  M > 0.    */
  K = M - 1;                          /* Imitate code for      */
  L = N;                              /* StrEqualsB.           */
  while ((L > 0) && (S[K] == T[L]))   /* Step left in  S,T     */
      { --K; --L; }                   /* while they agree.     */
  if ((L == 0) && (S[K] == T[0]))     /* Check  T[0]           */
      return S + K;                   /* separately.           */
    else                             /* Mismatch;  M > 0,     */
      --M; }                          /* so step left in  S.   */
  return NULL; }                      /* Match is impossible.*/
```

Figure 3.3.4 Function **StrStrB**

very long strings or to run as fast as possible, you might want to write them from scratch, avoiding the reversal.

The final string analysis functions considered in this section search a string **S** for the first occurrence of a given substring. You could use one of these with common names like **S** = "James Thomas Smith" to identify individuals with middle or last name " Smith". Library function **strstr(S,T)**, written in assembly language for speed, searches string **S** forward for an occurrence of string **T**, returning a pointer to its first occurrence, or the a pointer if there's none. Here is its prototype:

char *strstr(const char *S1, const char *S2);

This routine gives a perhaps inappropriate result when **T** is empty. In that case, **strstr(S,T)** points to the terminator of **S**, whereas it should point to the first entry, or have the null value if **S** is empty. (**T** is a substring of **S** starting at **S[I]** if for all **J** < **strlen(T)**, **S[I+J]** = **T[J]**. If **T** is empty, this is true for all **I** < **strlen(S)**, so **strstr(S,T)** should point to the first such **I**, if there is one.) The following function **StrStrF** fixes this problem, calling **strstr** for the hard work.

```
char *StrStrF(char *S,
              char *T) {
return (StrEmpty(S) ? NULL :
       StrEmpty(T) ? S      : strstr(S,T)); }
```

Its backward directed counterpart **StrStrB** in Figure 3.3.4 is written from scratch in C, hence will operate more slowly. While **StrStrF** can start the search with any entry of **S**, **StrStrB** must start at the end. You might want to modify it to start at an entry specified by **T**. On the accompanying diskette you'll find a demonstration program **StrStr.Dem** for these two functions.

3.4 String synthesis

> **Concepts**
>
> Allocating memory space
> String filling
> Duplicating strings
> Inserting characters and substrings
> Concatenation
> String copying
> Justification

In earlier sections, you have used and developed some sophisticated routines to analyze strings, but have tested them with example strings constructed only from constants and input. This section considers methods for building strings: replicating characters, inserting characters and strings, concatenation, copying, and justification. Many of these functions are provided by the Turbo C Library; a few others are constructed here from scratch. The last example, which justifies a string in a longer one filled with a "background" character, is a feature of the Blaise Computing Inc. Turbo C TOOLS package.

The first step in building a string **S** of length $\le$ **N** is to allocate space: either

- declare it an array **char S[N+1]**, or
- execute **S = (char *) malloc(N+1)** to allocate heap space.

The job's not done yet, because **S** may contain garbage. You need to clear that away and set the terminator. Function **StrAlloc** in Figure 3.4.1 allocates heap space for **S**, fills it with **N** copies of character **Ch**, sets the terminator, and returns a pointer to **S**. If there's insufficient memory available, or if you specify **N** < 0, it returns the null pointer instead. It's implemented using Library function **memset**, described in Section 2.6. Since **StrAlloc** hides the allocation procedure from the calling function, you must be particularly careful to free the space allocated to strings when they are no longer needed, lest you waste memory resources. A demonstration program, **StrAlloc.Dem**, is included on the accompanying diskette.

Related to **StrAlloc** are two Library routines:

char *strset (char *S, char Ch)
char *strnset(char *S, char Ch, unsigned N)

Function **strset** fills an existing string **S** with copies of **Ch**, and returns a pointer to **S**; **strnset** is similar, except it fills at most **N** characters. These functions neither allocate space nor set the terminator.

```
/******************************************************************/
/* StrAlloc          Allocate and return a pointer to a string  */
/**************************************** of   N   copies of      */
                                        /* character  Ch.  If    */
char *StrAlloc(     char Ch,            /* memory isn't suffi-   */
               unsigned N) {            /* cient, or  N < 0,     */
  char *S = (char *) malloc(N+1);       /* return the null       */
if (S != NULL) {                        /* pointer.              */
  memset(S,Ch,N);                       /************************/
  S[N] = 0; }
return S; }
```

Figure 3.4.1 Function **StrAlloc**

The only Library **str..** function that actually allocates space for a new string is

char *strdup(char *S)

It makes a copy of **S** (allocating space), and returns a pointer to the copy, or the null pointer if there's not enough memory. **strdup** is implemented in C, calling Library function **memcpy** (described in Section 2.6) to make the copy. Other Library **str..** functions concatenate or copy source strings into target strings that you have already constructed.

Before turning to concatenation and copying, consider two custom string *insertion* routines.

char *StrInsChr(char *T, char *P, char Ch)
char *StrInsStr(char *T, char *P, char *S)

These allocate memory for a new string U, formed by inserting **Ch** or **S** at the location specified by **P** in **T**. They return a pointer to **U**, or the null pointer if there isn't sufficient memory. Figure 3.4.2 contains source code for the more complex function **StrInsStr**; you'll find **StrInsChr** in file **Strings.C** on the accompanying diskette. They call Library function **memcpy** (described in Section 2.6) for the actual copying. A demonstration program is on the diskette.

Special cases of string insertion include concatenation—i.e., prefixing and suffixing (inserting at beginning or end)—and copying (inserting into an empty string) as special cases. You could use the insertion routines for all these operations, or you could construct individual functions imitating or calling them. The latter strategy is probably unwise, since more functions would allocate string space, making it harder to keep track of. Alternatively, you can allocate strings yourself using **StrAlloc**, and rely on several Library functions for concatenation and copying.

There are two concatenation functions:

strcat (char *T, char *S)
strncat(char *T, char *S, unsigned N).

Function **strcat** appends a copy of **S** to the end of **T**, and returns a pointer to **T**. You must have allocated enough space to **T** to permit that operation. **strncat** is similar, except that it appends at most **N** characters. Both

```
/*********************************************************************/
/* StrInsStr       Return a pointer to a string formed by in- */
/*                 serting string  S  at pointer  P  in string*/
/* T.  Assume that  P  points within  T  or to its terminator */
/* —in  which case append. S.  Allocate memory to the new     */
/***************************************** string, or return   */
                                     /* the null pointer if */
char *StrInsStr(char *T,             /* there isn't enough. */
                char *P,             /* Leave  T  unchanged.*/
                char *S) {           /*********************/
   unsigned L,M,N;
   char *U;
   L = strlen(T);
   N = strlen(S);
   U = (char *) malloc(L+N+1);       /* Space for the new   */
   if (U == NULL)                    /* string.             */
      return NULL;                   /* Not enough memory.  */
   M = P-T;                          /* Index of new entry. */
   memcpy(U,T,M);                    /* Copy the first part.*/
   memcpy(U+M,S,N);                  /* Insert  S.          */
   memcpy(U+M+N,T+M,L-M+1);          /* Copy the rest.      */
   return U;  }
```

Figure 3.4.2 Function **StrInsStr**

functions are implemented in C, calling Library function **movemem** (described in Section 2.6) to move the data.

The Turbo C Library provides three copying functions:

strcpy (char *T, char *S)
strncpy(char *T, char *S, unsigned N)
stpcpy (char *T, char *S)

Function **strcpy** copies **S** to **T**, and returns a pointer to **T**. You must have allocated sufficient space to **T**. Function **strncpy** copies **N** characters from **S** to **T**. For each one beyond the end of **S**, a zero byte is copied into **T**. (This is the only way a terminal zero is copied into **T**.) For example, consider the output of the program in Figure 3.4.3. Function **stpcpy** is like **strcpy**, except it returns a pointer to the *terminator* of the copy. You can use it to build up a string by repeated concatenation, as in Figure 3.4.4. Functions **strcpy** and **strncpy** are implemented entirely in

```
void main() {
  char *S = "abcd";
  char *T = "123456789";
  char *U = "123456789";
printf("%s\n",strncpy(T,S,3));
printf("%s\n",strncpy(U,S,7)); }
```

Output

```
abc456789
abcd
```

Figure 3.4.3 **strncpy** demonstration

assembly language; but **stpcpy** calls function **memcpy** (described in Section 2.6).

The last string synthesis operation discussed here is *justification*. Especially in preparing screen output, you'll want to left justify, center, or right justify a string of varying length within a longer one that's padded with background fill characters like blanks or underscores. The first Turbo C TOOLS string processing routine under consideration performs that task:

stpjust(char *T, char *S, char Ch, int N, int Code).

```
void main() {
  int I;
  char *P;
  char T[33];
T[0] = 0;                      /* Make  T  empty.        */
P = T;                         /* Start at beginning.    */
for (I = 1; I <= 8; ++I)       /* Repeatedly append      */
  P = stpcpy(P,"Choo");        /* Choo,  move to end.    */
printf("%s",T); }              /* Print from start.      */
```

Output

```
ChooChooChooChooChooChooChooChoo
```

Figure 3.4.4 **stpcpy** demonstration

```
void main() {
  char *S = "Purse";
  char Ch = '$';                         /* Fill with $.        */
  char *T = "01234567890123456789";      /* Truncate T to      */
  int  N = 10;                           /* length 10.         */
  int  Code;                             /* -1,0,1 = left,     */
for (Code = -1; Code <= 1; ++Code)       /* center, right.     */
  printf("%s\n", stpjust(T,S,Ch,N,Code)); }
```

Output

```
Purse$$$$
$$Purse$$$
$$$$$Purse
```

Figure 3.4.5 stpjust demonstration

This function truncates **T** to **N** characters, within which **S** is justified and padded with copies of **Ch**; it returns a pointer to **T**. Use **Code = -1,0,1** for left, center, or right justification. You must have allocated **T** at least **N** + 1 bytes. (Parameter **N** seems redundant, since you'll probably use **N** = **strlen(T)**.) Function **stpjust** is implemented entirely in C. Figure 3.4.5 shows a brief demonstration program and its output.

3.5 String manipulation

Concepts

Reversing a string
Character substitution
String substitution (a recursive function)
String deletion
Tokenization

In Sections 3.3 and 3.4 you have been considering routines for gaining basic information about strings and for building new ones. This section treats some further aspects of string manipulation which don't fit clearly in either category:

- reversing the order of a string;
- substituting one string for all occurrences of another;
- extracting and deleting substrings; and
- dividing a string into pieces, or *tokens*, delineated by characters in a specified set of *separators*.

Except for the first operation, these probably fall together in this section because the corresponding routines are more complex than earlier ones.

Reversing a string is quite simple, though. The Turbo C Library function

char *strrev(char *S)

simply reverses string **S** in place, without creating a new copy. One use of this routine was mentioned earlier in Section 3.3: constructing a backward-directed analog of a familiar routine. There you were invited to design a function

char *StrPBrkB(char *S, char *T, char *Seek)

to search backward from ***T** for the first **S** entry occurring in **Seek**. Figure 3.5.1 shows a possible solution. Function **strdup** makes a copy of **S**, **strrev** reverses it, **strpbrk** searches forward in the reversed copy,

```
/******************************************************************/
/* StrPBrkB        Search string  S  backward from  *T  for a */
/*                 character occurring in string  Seek.  Re-  */
/* turn a pointer to the first character found.  If there's   */
/* none, return the null pointer.                             */
/******************************************************************/

char *StrPBrkB(char *S,
               char *T,
               char *Seek) {
  char *R = strrev(strdup(S));       /* This allocates  *R.  */
  char *Q = strpbrk(R, (char *)Seek); /* Search reversed copy */
  free(R);                           /* then release it.     */
  return (Q == NULL ? NULL           /* Vector result to  T  */
                    : T - (Q - R)); } /* =  vector RQ.        */
```

Figure 3.5.1 Possible code for function **StrPBrk**

and the **return** statement in effect reverses the result. The memory that **strdup** allocated for the reversed copy is released by function **free** when it's no longer needed. This design has a major flaw: it will crash if **strdup** cannot allocate enough memory. In that case, **strdup** returns a null pointer, either offset 0000 in the data segment or segment:offset address 0000:0000. **strrev** reverses —scrambles—whatever string starts there, which is usually some information vital to DOS. You can check for the **strdup** error condition easily, but you would have to redesign the **StrPBrkB** specification to return an error code. You can find in file **StrPBrk.Dem** on the accompanying diskette the source code from this figure, analogous code for the routine **StrCPBrkB** also mentioned in Section 3.3, and a demonstration program.

Working with text editors, you've had experience with *string substitution*. The simplest case is character for character substitution, a facility provided by Turbo C TOOLS function

char *stpxlate(char *Source, char *Table, char *Trans)

For every occurrence in **Source** of a character in **Table**, **stpxlate** substitutes the corresponding character in **Trans**. The left-hand example in Figure 3.5.2 is a typical application. Only the first occurrence of a character in **Table** is considered. If **Trans** is shorter than **Table**, it's padded with blanks to agree in length. These two exceptional cases are demonstrated in the right-hand example of the figure. Function **stpxlate** is implemented entirely in C.

The general string for string substitution operation is much more complicated. How would you construct the string **T** resulting from string **S** when you substitute string **B** for all occurrences of substring **A** in **S**? First, you need to make the definition more precise, to take care of overlapping occurrences of **A**: substituting "**&**" for "**aa**" in "**aaa**" yields "**&a**" if you proceed from left to right, and "**a&**" if you proceed from right to left. Let's agree on left to right.

```
Table   : abc           Table   : abac
Trans   : 123           Trans   : 123
Source  : aaacbbb        Source  : aaacbbb
Result  : 1113222        Result  : 111 222
```

Figure 3.5.2 Applying function **stpxlate**

Implementing string substitution in C, you encounter two problems:

- allocating space for the result and temporary storage,
- building the result without unnecessarily shuffling string entries.

You could step through S from left to right, building initial substrings of the result T as in Figure 3.5.3. However, you can't allocate space for all of T until you know how many times A occurs in S. You would have to construct each initial T substring by allocating space for the previous one plus a copy of B, then moving all those characters. Can you avoid this shuffling? Once you ascertain the number N of occurrences of A in S, you know that

$$strlen(T) = strlen(S) + N * (strlen(B) - strlen(A)),$$

so you can allocate space for all of T. Now you could carry out the substitution as shown for the earlier example. However, you'd have to find all occurrences of A *again*. That's inefficient; you should record the location of each occurrence as you count it. In a temporary array of pointers? No—you'd have to know N in order to allocate space for the array.

At this point, a solution should come to mind. An essentially unlimited temporary storage structure is *always* available: the program stack. Moreover, substitution is an essentially recursive operation, as shown in the example earlier: you substitute for one occurrence of A, then carry out the same process for the shorter final substring of S. Recursive functions automatically use the stack for temporary storage. There's still a problem: if you stack the locations of A in S proceeding from left to right, you'll retrieve them in the opposite order. You don't want to search for A from right to left, because of the overlap problem mentioned earlier.

		Initial T substring	Final S substring
S	= "xaaxyaaaxyz"		"xaaxyaaaxyz"
A	= "aa"	"x&"	"xyaaaxyz"
B	= "&"	"x&xy&"	"axyz"
		"x&xy&axyz"	

Figure 3.5.3 First algorithm for finding the result T of substituting B for A in S

	Analyze	**xaaxyaaaxyz**	Push pointers
		↑↑	1,2 onto the
	Find **A** :	1 2	stack.

S = "xaaxyaaaxyz"   Analyze   **xyaaaxyz**   Push pointers
A = "aa"   ↑ ↑   3,4 onto the
B = "&"   Find **A** : 3 4   stack.

Analyze **axyz**

No **A**	Result **T** :
Copy the end of **S**	**axyz**
Use pointers 3,4	**xy&axyz**
Use pointers 1,2	**x&xy&axyz**

Figure 3.5.4 Recursive substitution algorithm

Thus you need to build the result **T** from right to left. Figure 3.5.4 is a diagram of this process, using the same example.

This recursive substitution algorithm is implemented by function **StrSubst(S,A,B)** in Figure 3.5.5. This routine sets up some static variables, then calls the recursive function **Subst** that corresponds to the algorithm. Since **Subst** counts the number of occurrences of **A** in **S**, one occurrence per invocation, the count must be tallied in a global variable, declared **static** so that it will be inaccessible outside the file containing this code. **Subst** itself is declared **static** for the same reason. Each invocation of **Subst** requires some static information about **S,A,B** as well. The program follows the algorithm as described in Figure 3.5.4, except for one detail. If the innermost invocation cannot allocate enough memory for the result, the null pointer error signal must be propagated out through all invocations, and back to **StrSubst**. You will find a demonstration program for **StrSubst** on the accompanying diskette.

Substring *deletion* is a special case of substitution. Just substitute the empty string for the one to be removed. Here is example output from the **StrSubst(S,A,B)** demonstration program:

Enter S : Repeal Coopers beeper
Enter A : pe
Enter B :
Result is   Real Coors beer

```
/***************************************************************/
/* StrSubst        Return a pointer to a new string construct-*/
/*                 ed by substituting  B  for all occurrences */
/* of  A  in  S.   Return the null pointer if  A  is empty or */
/* there is insufficient memory for the result.            */
/***************************************************************/

char *StrSubst(char *S,
               char *A,
               char *B) {
if (StrEmpty(A)) return NULL;
LengthS = strlen(S);                    /* Set up for recursive */
LengthA = strlen(A);                    /* function  Subst  by  */
LengthB = strlen(B);                    /* storing fixed data   */
PA = A;                                 /* in static variables. */
PB = B;                                 /* The  A  count's used */
NumberOfAs = 0;                         /* to allocate memory   */
return Subst(S); }                      /* for the result.      */


/***************************************************************/
/* Subst          Recursively construct the result  T  of    */
/*                substituting  B  for  A  in  S.   Static    */
/* PA,PB,PS  point to  A,B  and the yet unanalyzed part of    */
/* S.  Subst  finds the first  A,  prepares to substitute     */
/* B,  and calls itself to analyze the rest of  S.   When no  */
/* more  As  remain, it allocates memory for  T,  copies the  */
/* end of  S,  then returns through earlier invocations, sub- */
/* substituting  Bs.  Subst  returns a pointer to the final   */
/******************************************** segment of  T  just */
                                        /* constructed, or it   */
static unsigned LengthS,LengthA,        /* returns the null     */
             LengthB,NumberOfAs;        /* pointer if there's   */
static char *PA,*PB;                    /* not enough memory.   */
                                        /************************/
static char *Subst(char *PS) {
  char *P,*T;
  unsigned L,M;
if ((P = strstr(PS,PA)) == NULL) {      /* If no  A  occurs in  */
  L = LengthS + NumberOfAs *            /* the rest of  S, set  */
    (LengthB -LengthA);                 /* L = length of  T,    */
  T = (char *) malloc(L+1);             /* allocate space for   */
  if (T == NULL) return NULL;           /* it (returning  NULL  */
```

Figure 3.5.5 Function **StrSubst** (*Continued on next page*)

```
M = strlen(PS);                           /* if impossible), and */
T += L - M;                               /* copy the rest of  S */
memmove(T,PS,M+1);                        /* to the end of  T.   */
return T; }

                                          /* Found another  A.   */
++NumberOfAs;                             /* Call  Subst  recur- */
if ((T = Subst(P+LengthA)) == NULL)       /* sively to analyze   */
  return NULL;                            /* the part of  S  af- */
                                          /* ter the first  A.   */
                                          /* Pass on an out-of-  */
T -= LengthB;                             /* memory signal.      */
memmove(T,PB,LengthB);
M  = P - PS;                              /* Copy  B  to the     */
T -= M;                                   /* front of  T,  then  */
memmove(T,PS,M);                          /* the part of  S  be- */
return T; }                               /* fore the first  A.  */
```

Figure 3.5.5 (*Continued*) Function **StrSubst**

Other forms of string deletion can be regarded as special cases of *copying*, which was discussed in Section 3.4. Deleting the initial substring preceding a pointer is the same as copying the final substring starting at the pointer, which you can do with **strcpy**. Deleting the final substring starting at index **N** is the same as copying the initial substring of length **N**, a **strncpy** operation. With **strcpy(S,S+N)** you can delete the first **N** entries of **S** *in place*. With the other two methods, you have to make a new string with the required entries. (**strncpy** won't move the terminator.) In file **Strings.C** on the accompanying diskette is a new function

char *StrNDel(char *T, char *S, char *P, unsigned N)

that will remove **N** characters from string **S**, starting at pointer **P** (but stopping at the end of **S**) and place the result in string **T**. You must have allocated sufficient space for **T**; it could be the same as **S**. The code for this routine involves no new ideas, so it's not shown here.

The last general string manipulation routine considered in this chapter is the Turbo C Library *tokenization* function **strtok**, which is particularly useful in interpreting algebraic or natural language input. You specify a string of *separators*: characters like blanks or other punctuation that you use to separate strings into pieces, or *tokens*. Then you call **strtok** repeatedly to separate one token after another from the beginning of a string **S**. The first call takes the form

strtok(S,Separators)

and returns a pointer to the leftmost token. Subsequent calls like

strtok(NULL,Separators)

return pointers to successive tokens from the left end of **S** until a null pointer signifies that none remains. Program **StrTok.Dem** in Figure 3.5.6 demonstrates this technique. While processing **S**, **strtok** replaces

```
/*****************************************************************/
/* StrTok.Dem      Demonstrate function  strtok.              */
/*****************************************************************/

#include <General.H>

void main() {
  char *S = "Do-wop, daba do-wop, do-wop bam boom!";
  char *Separators = ", !";
  char P[10];
  int  I;
printf("%s\n",strtok(S,Separators));
while ((P = strtok(NULL,Separators)) != NULL)
  printf("%s\n",P);
for (I = 0; I <= 10; ++I)
  printf("%d ",(unsigned) S[I]); }
```

Output

```
Do-wop
daba
do-wop
do-wop
bam
boom
68 111 45 119 111 112 0 32 100 97 98
```

Figure 3.5.6 Demonstrating function **strtok**

the first separator after each token by a terminal 0. You can see this on the last output line: the codes 44,32 for the comma and blank separators after the first **S** token **Do-wop** show now as 0,32 (underlined). Function **strtok** is implemented entirely in C, and uses a static variable to keep its place in string **S**.

3.6 Text strings

Concepts
Ascertaining lexicographic order of strings Eliminating white space and control characters Converting between upper and lower case Turbo C Tools string functions Converting consecutive blanks to tabs and vice versa

Earlier sections of this chapter have considered strings in a general context, with little attention to particular applications. This section describes several Turbo C and Turbo C TOOLS features clearly intended for handling text strings. Later sections will emphasize even more specific applications.

In Section 3.3 on string analysis, you worked with functions that compare two strings. These ascertained only whether two strings were identical, or where they differed. With text strings, *order* is important. The Turbo C Library provides four functions that report whether one string precedes another:

int strcmp(char *S, char *T)
int stricmp(char *S, char *T)
int strncmp(char *S, char *T, unsigned N)
int strnicmp(char *S, char *T, unsigned N)

Function **strcmp** is the simplest: it returns a negative, zero, or positive value according as **S** precedes, equals, or follows **T** in lexicographic order with respect to the ASCII/IBM code. The value is actually $S[I] - T[I]$, where **I** is the first index for which $S[I] \neq T[I]$. The empty string precedes all others. Trailing blanks are significant: for example, **"ab"** precedes "ab ". Characters are compared as if they were unsigned: characters 128..255 follow 0..127. Function **stricmp** is similar, except that it treats all letters as upper case. (This can cause a minor problem with ASCII 91...96, some punctuation marks that fall between the upper and lower cases. For example, according to **strcmp**, the character '^' = ASCII 94 precedes 'a', but with **stricmp**, it follows 'a'.) Functions **strncmp** and **strnicmp** are like the first two, except that they consider at most the first **N** characters. They are also closely related to Library functions **memcmp** and **memicmp**, described in Section 2.6, that compare *exactly* **N** characters. All these functions (except **memicmp**) are implemented in assembly language for speed.

In many applications the text string order is different from ASCII/IBM lexicographic: consider alphabetic order in languages with character sets different from English, or even the order of names in your telephone book. To compare strings **S** and **T** based on a different character ordering, use the Section 3.3 function **StrEqualsF** to find the first **I**, if any, for which **S[I]** ≠ **T[I]**, then compare those two characters. Applications like the telephone book are more complicated; it is used as an example later in this section.

Turbo C TOOLS function

char *stpcvt(char *S, int Code)

converts string **S** in several ways according to the **Code** values in Figure 3.6.1. To perform more than one conversion, add the codes. (The

Code	Effect
1	Delete all white space.[1]
2	Delete leading white space.[1]
4	Delete trailing white space.[1]
8	Reduce contiguous white space[1] to a single blank.
16	Don't convert substrings within single or double quotes.
32	Convert lower case to upper.
64	Convert upper case to lower.
128	Delete control characters.[2]

[1] defined by **CType** macro **isspace**.
[2] defined by **CType** macro **iscntrl**.

Figure 3.6.1 stpcvt string conversion codes

inconsistent sum 32+64 is interpreted like 32.) Turbo C TOOLS macros provide convenient mnemonic code value constants: for example, **RWHITE** and **TOUP** stand for 1 and 32. Turbo C Library functions

char *strlwr(char *S)
char *strupr(char *S)

provide less general functions, changing all letters in **S** to lower or upper case, respectively.

The problem of determining the order of names in the telephone book leads to an interesting application of **stpcvt** and several functions considered earlier. If you study the first pages of A listings and several with names that include blanks or punctuation marks, you may infer the following algorithm to determine whether one name precedes another.

1. Considering first and last names separately, construct temporary names for use in comparison, as follows.
2. Spell out all numerals in English. (These are not all done consistently.)
3. Remove other non-alphabetical characters.
4. Ignore upper/lower case distinctions.
5. A last name may be designated "initials"; if so, insert a blank after its first letter.
6. The telephone-book order is the ASCII lexicographic order of the comparison versions of the last names, or if they are equal, of the first names.

Figure 3.6.2 lists some examples, in telephone book order. In each case the order would be different if you skipped one of the steps of the algorithm.

Here is a program fragment that will construct the comparison version **CName** of a first or last **Name** that contains no numerals.

```
char *T = strdup(Name);
stpxlate(T,"-'&",EmptyStr);
stpcvt(T,RWHITE+TOUP);
if (Initials) {
    CName = StrInsChr(T,T+1,Blank); free(T); }
  else
    CName = T;
```

Last name	First name	Initials?	Last name: Comparison Version
A	-Acme	Yes	A
A-A	Bakery	Yes	A A
Aa	Audio Visual Center	No	AA
Davies	Symphony Hall	No	DAVIES
Da Vinci	Pizzeria	No	DAVINCI
One	Hundred Per Cent	No	ONE
1	Potato 2	No	ONE
O'Neill's	Tree Service	No	ONEILLS
Smith	X	No	SMITH
Smith Kline	Clinical Lab	No	SMITHKLINE

Figure 3.6.2 Names from the telephone book

To avoid destroying **Name**, the code uses **strdup** to make a temporary copy **T**. To delete non-alphabetic characters, it changes them all to blanks with **stpxlate** (described in Section 3.5—the empty string is automatically padded with blanks to equal the length of the string "-'&" of punctuation marks). Then **stpcvt** deletes all blanks (**RWHITE**) and converts to upper case (**TOUP**). If the variable **Initials** has been set ≠ 0 to indicate that the last name is initials, Section 3.4 function **StrInsChr** inserts a blank after the first character. Since **StrInsChr** must allocate space for a new copy of **T**, the old one is released. **EmptyStr** and **Blank** are constants defined in this book's header file **General.H**.

Once you have constructed comparison versions of the names, it's easy to use **strcmp** to ascertain their order. The program fragment just given does not address the problem of converting numerals to English equivalents. That is discussed in the next section.

Two Turbo C TOOLS functions support use of tabs:

```
char *stptabfy(char *S, int I)
char *stpexpan(char *T, char *S, int I, int TSize).
```

stptabfy replaces groups of blanks in **S** as if tab stops were set at characters $I, 2I, 3I,..., - I = 8$ is commonly chosen—and returns **S**. **S** never gets longer, so you can use the same string for the result. The inverse function **stpexpan** expands tabs in source string **S** to blanks, as if tab stops were set the same way. Since **S** will normally grow longer in this case, you must allocate a target string **T** long enough for the result, and pass its maximum length as parameter **TSize**. The function will process as much of **S** as it can, given the size of the target string, then return the null pointer if it's finished, or else a pointer to the first character not processed.

Program **StpTabfy.Dem** in Figure 3.6.3 demonstrates both of these functions. Their prototypes are included via Turbo C Tools header file **BStrings.H**. The program "tabifies" a typical columnar text string—a

```
/************************************************************/
/* StpTabfy.Dem    Demonstrate  Turbo C Tools  functions   */
/*                 stptabfy and  stpexpan.  Use  stptabfy   */
/****************************** to replace groups of consecu- */
/*                  /* tive blanks in a typical text */
#include <General.H>        /* string, with tabs set at      */
#include <BStrings.H>       /* at characters  8,16,24,....   */
                            /* Then use  stpexpan  to expand */
#define TabInterval 8       /* the tabs back to blanks.      */
                            /************************************/
void main() {
  char *S = "         1 Potato 2           No      ONE";
  unsigned I,N = strlen(S);
  char *T,*U;
printf("\nLength  String     ");
for (I = 1; I <= N; ++I) putchar('.');
printf("\n %u    Original  %s",N          ,S);
stptabfy(S,TabInterval);
printf("\n %u    Tabified  %s",strlen(S),S);
T = (char *) malloc(N+1);
U = stpexpan(T,S,TabInterval,N+1);
printf("\n %u    Expanded  %s",strlen(T),T);
printf("\nstpexpan  returned  %s",U);  }
```

Output

```
Length  String    ......................................................
  52    Original           1 Potato 2              No      ONE
  28    Tabified  °    1 Potato 2°° N°° ONE
  52    Expanded           1 Potato 2              No      ONE
stpexpan  returned  (null)
```

Figure 3.6.3 Program **StpTabfy.Dem**

line from Figure 3.6.3 —then expands the result, thus regaining the original string. In the output, ASCII 9 symbol o represents a tab. You can see that tabification can greatly reduce the length of such strings, hence the length of text files. For that reason, Blaise Computing Inc. source code files are tabified. This presents a problem to software that does not recognize tabs (for example, the word processor with which this text was written). Thus, it's often useful to expand them back to blanks.

3.7 Numerals

Concepts

Integer conversion with **sscanf** and **sprintf**
Real conversion with **sscanf** and **sprintf**
Organization of the Library conversion functions
atol and related functions
Low-level integer conversion: **strtol**, **ltoa**, and related functions
Low-level real conversion: **strtod**, **ecvt**, and related functions
A recursive function to produce English-language numerals

Conversion between internal and external number representations is sometimes a perplexing programming problem. Internal representations are usually versions of binary integer or binary floating point notation. Externally, some text format is used, commonly with binary, decimal, or hexadecimal digits, perhaps in floating point significand/exponent form. All these representations are types of *numerals*—that is, *names* of abstract entities called numbers. The problem is to convert between different systems of numerals. Internal representations are generally closely related to hardware designs. Software developers usually choose a particular external representation for a combination of reasons:

- An application may require a certain degree of accuracy.
- It may use numbers varying widely in magnitude.
- An input or output medium may restrict the numerals' length or style.
- Certain conversions may be easier to program.

The Turbo C Library provides extensive, robust conversion facilities. This section gives them an overview, concentrating on the less common ones, since you have probably used the standard ones since you began C programming. No matter how comprehensive the facilities at hand, however, sometime you'll need a different variation. A few new tools are provided here to show how you can extend the Library functions. These will produce additional digital forms, as well as English-language numerals.

Integer conversion with sscanf and sprintf

Since you began C programming, you've probably used high-level Library functions **scanf** and **printf** for numerical input/output. Each converts between internal and external representations using two logical steps: **scanf** reads a string of numerical characters, then converts it to the internal representation; **printf** reverses these steps. This chapter is not concerned with input/output, so will concentrate on the conversion routines. The Turbo C Library gives direct access to them through functions **sscanf** and **sprintf**. Their calling sequences are identical to those of **scanf** and **printf**, except that each has a new **char *** parameter, first in the list—the numerical string to be converted or constructed. **sscanf** and **sprintf** return the number of fields converted and the length of the string constructed. Since these functions are used like the input/output routines, only their high points and some trouble spots are discussed here. Check the *Turbo C reference guide* for further details.

Program **IntCvt1.Dem** in Figure 3.7.1 demonstrates integer conversion with **sscanf** and **sprintf**, using common hexadecimal formats and an unusual left justified decimal format. It's necessary to perform some **printf** output to display the results. To keep **printf** and **sprintf** effects separate, output is postponed until the end of the program, and uses only common %d and %s formats.

As shown in program **IntCvt1.Dem**, functions **sscanf** and **sprintf** use formats %x and %X differently:

	sscanf	**sprintf**
%x	Convert from hex to **int** or **unsigned int**.	Construct a lower case hex numeral.
%X	Convert from hex to **long** or **unsigned long**.	Construct an upper case hex numeral.

The hex example also points out a failing of the Turbo C Library integer conversion facilities: although you can *interpret* negative numerals using any radix in the range 2..36, you can *construct* them only in decimal. You'll find a solution to that problem later in this section.

```
/******************************************************************/
/* IntCvt1.Dem      sscanf  and  sprintf  integer conversion.  */
/*********************************** Convert numeral  S =*/
                                   /* hex -8a = -138  to   */
#include <General.H>              /* internal form  N.    */
                                   /* Convert  -N,N  back  */
void main() {                      /* to a fancy decimal   */
  int Fields,N,Length;            /* and a different  hex*/
  char *S = "-8a";                /* format.  Show that  */
  char T[18],HexN[5],HexMinusN[5]; /* X  format converts a*/
Fields = sscanf(S,"%X",&N);        /* negative integer as  */
Length = sprintf(T,"%+-17d",-N);   /* if it were unsigned.*/
sprintf(HexN     ,"%X", N);        /* Display the results */
sprintf(HexMinusN,"%X",-N);        /* using  printf  %d,%s*/
                                   /* formats.            */
printf("Converting  S = %s ,  "    /************************/
  "sscanf  returned  %d  field  "
    "N = %d .\n",S,Fields,N);
printf("Left justify  -N  with  +  in a blank filled string\n"
  "%sof length  %d .\n",T,Length);
printf("In  %%X  format,  N = %s  and  -N = %s .",
  HexN,HexMinusN); }
```

Output

```
Converting  S = -8a,  sscanf  returned  1  field  N = -138 .
Left justify  -N  with  +  in a blank filled string
+138             of length  17 .
In  %X  format,  N = FF76  and  -N = 8A .
```

Figure 3.7.1 Program **IntCvt1.Dem**

Real conversion with sscanf and sprintf

The similar program **RealCvt.Dem** in Figure 3.7.2 demonstrates conversion between external and internal forms for fixed and floating point numerals. It uses **sprintf** to convert a **double** variable **X** to numerical strings **E** and **F** in different formats, converts those back to internal format, and prints the results.

To perform numerical conversions correctly, you'll almost always have to experiment. There are so many possibilities and fine distinctions that documentation may be obscure or unreliable. For example, it's not easy to predict the behavior of **sprintf** formats %e,%f,%g. Here are the results of a simple experiment with %g:

N	1.23e±N	in format %9.2g
0	1.23	1.23
1	12.3	0.123
2	123	0.0123
3	1.23e+003	0.00123
4	1.23e+004	0.000123
5	1.23e+005	1.23e-005

As the *Turbo C reference guide* indicates, %g uses fixed point %f format when the %e exponent would fall in the range -4..p, where p is the precision specifier (.2 in format %9.2g). Moreover, it trims trailing zeroes and decimal point. Another experiment verifies that %e and %f formats don't trim:

In formats	%.3e	%.2f	%.2g	%.3g	%.4g
12.499 =	1.250e+001	12.50	12.5	12.5	12.499

These %g results are mystifying until you use the # flag to retain trailing zeroes:

In formats	%#.2g	%#.3g	%#.4g
12.499 =	12.5	12.50	12.499

In fact, when the %e exponent n falls in the range -4..p, %g uses %f format with precision p-n (= 1,2,3 in these cases) then trims trailing zeroes.

```
/**********************************************************/
/* RealCvt.Dem    sscanf  and  sprintf  real conversion.      */
/************************************* Convert a real value*/
                                     /* X  to numerals  E,F */
#include <General.H>                 /* with  %e,%f  formats*/
                                     /* and convert back to */
void main() {                        /* internal forms  XE, */
  char E[25],F[25];                  /* XF  with  %E.  Use  */
  double XE,XF;                      /* printf  with  %s,%E */
  double X = 1234.5678;              /* formats to display  */
sprintf(E,"%12.7e",X);               /* the results.        */
sprintf(F, "%8.2f",X);               /************************/
sscanf(E,"%E",&XE);
sscanf(F,"%E",&XF);

printf("%9.4f  in  %%12.7e,  %%8.2f  formats:  %s,%s.\n"
  "%%E  reconversion yields  %.7E, %.7E.",X,E,F,XE,XF); }
```

Output

```
1234.5678 in  %12.7e, %8.2f  formats:  1.2345678e+003, 1234.57.
%E  reconversion yields  1.2345678E+003, 1.2345700E+003.
```

Figure 3.7.2 Program **RealCvt.Dem**

Functions **sscanf** and **sprintf** use formats %e,%f,%g,%E,%G
differently:

	sscanf	**sprintf**
%e	Convert fixed or floating point to **float**.	Construct floating point numeral with 'e'.
%E	Convert fixed or floating point to **double**.	Construct floating point numeral with 'E'.
%f	Same as %e.	Construct a fixed point numeral.
%g	Same as %e.	Same as %f, if appropriate, else %e.
%G	Same as %E.	Same as %f, if appropriate, else %E.

sscanf formats **%E** and **%G** are equivalent to **%le** and **%lg**. (Flag l signals a *long* parameter.) There is *no* corresponding **%F** format: **F** specifies a *far* parameter, and ordinarily produces garbage.

Organization of the Library conversion functions

Often you don't need the full high-level **sscanf** and **sprintf** conversion machinery, so the Turbo C Library provides functions that give shortcuts to the low level routines on which **sscanf** and **sprintf** are based. Figures 3.7.3 and 3.7.4 show the relationships among the various functions. Those written in C are identified by subscript C; all others are written in assembly language. Prototypes for the Library functions are found in several header files:

String.H	**StdIO.H**	**StdLib.H**			**Math.H**
strtol	sscanf	atof	itoa	ecvt	atof
strtoul	sprintf	atoi	ltoa	fcvt	
strtod		atol	ultoa	gcvt	

The other functions, whose names begin with underscores, are intended only for internal use by the Library functions. Although you won't be

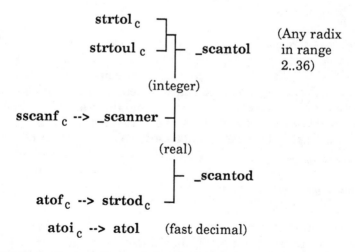

Figure 3.7.3 Turbo C external to internal numerical conversion functions

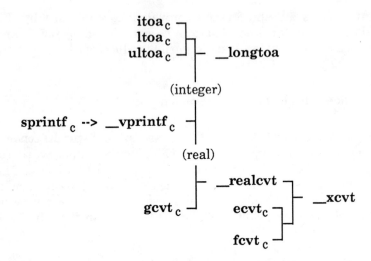

Figure 3.7.4 Turbo C internal to external numerical conversion functions

using the internal functions directly, they're shown here so that you can understand the Library organization.

To convert decimal numerals to **long** integer values, you can use the Library function

long atol(char *S).

This returns zero if **S** is not a valid input, hence is dangerous unless the routine that constructed **S** is totally reliable. If you are certain that **S** will always be valid, it's reasonable to use **atol** because it avoids some of the overhead of the more general internal function **_scantol**. Similar routines **atoi** and **atof** provide conversion to **int** and **double** values. **StdLib.H** defines **atoi** as a macro: **atol** followed by a cast to type **long**. There is no point in using **atof**, because it simply calls **strtod**, which is a little safer.

Low level integer conversion

Library function **strtol** lets you analyze a string from start to end in a manner like **strtok**, interpreting numerals as you find them. Here is its calling sequence:

long strtol(char *S, char **T, int Radix)

strtol scans **S** for the longest initial substring that is a numeral under the specified radix, and returns the corresponding value and a pointer **T** to the next character in **S** (the one that terminated the scan). You can use any radix in the range 2..36: the digits are the appropriate initial subset of 0..9a..z or the corresponding upper case. A **strtol** demonstration program is described later, in connection with Figure 3.7.7. If **S** is invalid—i.e., no initial substring is a valid numeral—or **Radix** is out of range, then **T** will point to the beginning of **S**, and **strtol** will return the value zero. If **S** is a valid numeral but yields a value outside the range of the specified type, **strtol** sets global variable **errno** = **ERANGE** = 34 and returns the appropriate overflow value,

LONG_MAX = 231 - 1 = hex efff ffff
LONG_MIN = -232   = hex 8000 0000.

These mnemonic identifiers are defined as macros in header files **Limits.H** and **Math.H**. Although **strtol** uses the same low-level routines as **sscanf**, the latter doesn't necessarily respond exactly the same way to overflow situations, because the low-level responses are moderated by function **_scanner**. The only way to be sure what happens is to analyze the Library source code. Error handling is discussed in general in Chapter 8.

The Library includes another function, **strtoul**, for conversion to an unsigned long value. It's used exactly like **strtol**, except that the overflow value is **ULONG_MAX** = 2^{32} - 1 = hex ffff ffff.

The inverse of **strtol** is Library function

char *ltoa(long N, char *S, int Radix)

for converting **long** integer values **N** to numeric strings **S**. Analogous routines **itoa** and **ultoa** convert **int** and **unsigned long** values. (The **a** in these names, as well as in **atoi**, etc., stands for ASCII.) You must allocate sufficient memory for **S** before calling these functions. Figure 3.7.5 gives its maximum length for hexadecimal, decimal, and binary numerals. When **Radix** > 10, these routines use lower case letters for digits after 9. You may use Library function **strupr**, described in Section 3.6, to convert them to upper case.

Maximum	Decimal Numeral	No. of digits	Hex Numeral	No. of digits	No. of binary digits
int	±32767	6	efff	4	16
unsigned	65538	5	ffff	4	16
long	±2147483647	11	efffffff	8	32
unsigned long	4294967295	10	ffffffff	8	32

Figure 3.7.5 Maximum lengths of integer numerals

Like **sprintf**, function **ltoa** constructs negative numerals only when **Radix** = 10; otherwise **ltoa** treats **N** as if it were unsigned. The new function **StrLtoA** in Figure 3.7.6 converts a positive or negative **long** integer value **N** to a positive or negative numeral for any radix. It calls **ltoa** to convert | **N** |, then appends a minus sign if **N** < 0. Figure 3.7.7 program **IntCvt2.Dem** demonstrates **StrLtoA** as well as the Library functions **ltoa** and **strtol** discussed earlier. The program uses **strtol** to interpret a binary numeral, shows how **ltoa** represents a negative integer as unsigned, then calls **StrLtoA** to construct a negative hex numeral.

```
/*************************************************************/
/* StrLtoA     Return a pointer to a signed numeral S       */
/********************************** corresponding to N   */
                                   /* under the specified */
char *StrLtoA(long N,              /* Radix. You must      */
              char *S,             /* allocate sufficient */
              int Radix) {         /* memory for S be-     */
  char *T;                         /* fore calling this    */
T = S;                             /* function.            */
if (N < 0) *T++ = '-';             /***********************/
ltoa(abs(-N),T,Radix);
return S; }
```

Figure 3.7.6 Function **StrLtoA**

```
/************************************************************/
/* IntCvt2.Dem   Demonstrate strtol, ltoa and StrLtoA      */
/*               integer conversion. Convert a binary nu-   */
/*               meral to an integer N Ú 0. Convert N,      */
/**************************************** -N to hex numerals, */
                                    /* showing that ltoa    */
#include <General.H>                /* treats -N as if it   */
                                    /* were unsigned. Call  */
void main() {                       /* strupr to get upper  */
  long N;                           /* case, and StrLtoA    */
  char *S = "11111111b";            /* to build a negative  */
  char *T,U[10];                    /* hex numeral.         */
N = strtol(S,&T,2);                 /************************/
printf(" N = binary %s = %d .\n",S,N);
printf(" strtol   returned a pointer to  %c .\n",*T);
printf(" N = hex %s .\n",ltoa(N,U,16));
printf("-N = hex %s .\n",strupr(ltoa(-N,U,16)));
printf("-N = hex %s .\n",StrLtoA(-N,U,16)); }
```

Output

```
 N = binary 11111111b = 255.
 strtol   returned a pointer to  b.
 N = hex ff.
-N = hex FFFFFF01.
-N = hex -ff.
```

Figure 3.7.7 Program **IntCvt2.Dem**

Low-level real conversion

Analogous to routine **strtol** described earlier, Library function **strtod** lets you analyze a fixed or floating point numeral that begins a string **S**, and returns the corresponding **double** value and a pointer to the next entry in **S**. Use it like **strtol**, but of course with no radix parameter. Its overflow value is **HUGE_VAL** = 1.797693e+308.

Three Turbo C Library functions convert real values to numerals:

char *ecvt(double X, int N, int *Point, int *Sign)
char *fcvt(double X, int N, int *Point, int *Sign)
char *gcvt(double X, int N, char *S)

These correspond roughly to **sscanf** formats %e,%f,%g. Rather than discuss a long demonstration program, consider what each of these functions does with a particular example:

```
double X  = -1234500;        T = ecvt(X,N,&Point,&Sign)
int N = 4;                   T = 1234            length  4
int Point,Sign;              Point = 7           Sign = 1
char *T;
                             T = fcvt(X,N,&Point,&Sign)
gcvt(X,N,T)                  T = 12345000000     length 11
T = -1.2345e+006             Point = 7           Sign = 1
```

Functions **ecvt** and **fcvt** return a non-zero **Sign** value to indicate that **X** < 0. The former returns the significand for the floating point representation of **X**, rounded after **N** = 4 digits. (The discarded digit 5 rounds downward because its predecessor is even.) The returned value **Point** = 7 indicates that the point should be located after the 7th digit. Function **fcvt** returns the digits of a fixed point representation, rounded **N** digits after the point, which is to be located similarly. Finally, **gcvt** attempts to produce a %f format numeral for **X** with **N** significant digits (or fewer, if trailing zeroes can be trimmed); failing that, it produces a numeral in %.4e format (**N** = 4). Functions **ecvt** and **fcvt** return pointers to strings in a static data area that is reused every time they are called; you must copy the numerals into your own work area as soon as they are constructed. Function **gcvt** works in a more usual way: before invoking it, simply allocate memory sufficient for the numeral **T**.

Unfortunately, no numeric conversion facility ever seems to offer every format that you might want. In numerical analysis, for example, you often want error estimates with only a single significant digit. The numerals should be as short as possible, to fit unobtrusively into a crowded output table. The Turbo C Library functions do provide single significant digit floating point format. But you can't suppress the point nor the plus sign and leading zeroes of the exponent. The new function

char *StrShrtE(double X, char *S)

in Figure 3.7.8 does just that. It calls **ecvt** to construct a two digit significand for **X**, rounds that to one digit, then constructs a numeral from the remaining information supplied by **ecvt**. A simple demonstration

```
/**************************************************************/
/* StrShrtE       Return a pointer to the shortest possible  */
/*                %e format numeral S for X. You must        */
/************************************* allocate sufficient */
                                     /* memory for  S be-   */
char *StrShrtE(double X,             /* fore invoking this  */
char *S) {                           /* function.           */
char *T,*U;                          /***********************/
int Point,Sign;
T = ecvt(X,2,&Point,&Sign);          /* Get a two digit sig-*/
if (T[1] >= '5')                     /* nificand and round  */
if (T[0] == '9') {                   /* it to one, moving   */
T[0] = '1';                          /* the point to the    */
++Point; }                           /* right if you round  */
else                                 /* 9  up to  10.       */
++T[0];
U = S;                               /* Start with  -  if   */
if (Sign) *U++ = '-';                /* X < 0  (Sign ≠ 0).  */
*U++ = T[0];                         /* Copy significand and*/
*U++ = 'e';                          /* e.  Point-1  is the */
itoa(Point-1,U,10);                  /* exponent.  Copy its */
return S; }                          /* decimal numeral.    */
```

Figure 3.7.8 Function **StrShrtE**

program is included on the accompanying diskette. Here is some sample output:

X	0	-.00095	12345
StrShrtE	0e0	-1e3	1e4

The result isn't always properly rounded, because the significand is rounded twice in succession, and the odd-even distinction for rounding 5 is ignored. However, it's good enough for the intended purpose. You may want to add more elaborate rounding.

English-language numerals

The last topic considered in this section was mentioned in the previous one while discussing the telephone book ordering of names. To ascertain that order, you must first spell out any numerals in English. For example, *1000 Post* is alphabetized as though it were spelled *One thousand Post*. This numeric conversion occurs in other contexts too: for example, in writing checks. Thus you may find use for a function

char *StrULtoE(unsigned long N)

that returns a pointer to the English-language numeral for **N**.

A recursive algorithm for this conversion is shown in Figure 3.7.9, which displays the tree corresponding to a typical computation. Essentially, you find the largest *break point* B = 1,000,000, 1000, 100 or 20 not exceeding **N**, compute Q = N / B and M = N mod B, find the numerals for Q and M recursively, and place between them the word or particle for B.

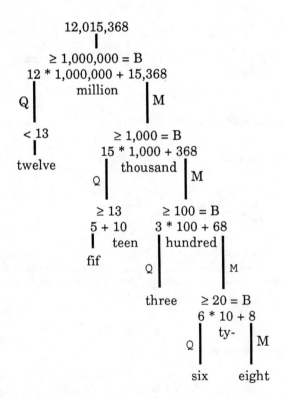

Figure 3.7.9 Recursive algorithm for English numerals

When B = 20, divide by 10 instead, and use the decade particle (**twen, thir,** etc.) as numeral for Q. When $13 \leq N < 20$, the numeral is the decade particle followed by **teen.** (**fourteen** is an exception.) When $N < 13$, look up the numeral in a table. Each inequality shown in the figure corresponds to a recursive invocation of the algorithm.

Figure 3.7.10 displays source code for **StrULtoE,** implementing this algorithm. It uses some static storage for the English words corresponding to the break points, and for the decade particles and numerals for 0..12. There are only a few complications in coding the algorithm itself. First, you have to allocate space for the numerals as you progress; and after you assemble some parts into a larger piece, you must release their space. Finally, there are some minor problems with the blanks and hyphens between words, and with the numeral **zero.** You can follow the details in the source code documentation. Note the "cascaded" calls to Library function **stpcpy.** A simple demonstration program is included on the accompanying diskette. It outputs the numeral

twelve million fifteen thousand three hundred sixty eight

corresponding to the example integer 12,015,368 in Figure 3.7.9.

```
/******************************************************************/
/* StrULtoE        Return a pointer to the English name for  */
/*                 number  N.  This allocates a new string.  */
/******************************************************************/
static unsigned long Break[]  = {1000000,1000,100,20};
static char *Middle[]      =
  {" million "," thousand "," hundred ","ty-"};
static char *Digit[]       =
  {"zero","one","two","three","four","five","six",
   "seven","eight","nine","ten","eleven","twelve"};
static char *Decade[]      =
  {"twen","thir","for","fif","six","seven","eigh","nine"};

char *StrULtoE(unsigned long N) {
  char *S,*T,*U,*V;
  unsigned D,L;
  unsigned long M;                          /* Compare  N  with    */
```

Figure 3.7.10 Function **StrULtoE** (*Continued on next page*)

```
for (D = 0; D <= 3; ++D)              /* break values   1M,1K,*/
  if (N >= Break[D]) {                /* 100,20.  Unless  N   */
    if (D < 3) {                      /* < 20,   translate    */
        T = StrULtoE(N/Break[D]);     /* left, right parts    */
        M = N % Break[D]; }           /* T,U  separately.     */
      else {                          /* Treat  Break[3] = 20*/
        T = Decade[N/10 - 2];         /* specially.  Use      */
        M = N % 10; }                 /* "zero" only on the   */
    U = (M == 0 ? EmptyStr            /* left, when  N = 0.   */
               : StrULtoE(M));
    L = strlen(T) + strlen(Middle[D]) /* Allocate space for   */
      + strlen(U);                    /* the result   S = left*/
    S = (char *) malloc(L+1);         /* + middle + right.    */
    V = stpcpy(stpcpy(S,T),Middle[D]);/* Copy the left, mid-  */
    if (D < 3) free(T);               /* dle, and right parts*/
    if (!StrEmpty(U)) {               /* to  S.  If the       */
        stpcpy(V,U);                  /* right part is empty, */
        free(U); }                    /* delete the middle's  */
      else                            /* final blank or  -.   */
        *(V-1) = 0;                   /* Free  T,U  when you   */
    return S; }                       /* no longer need them. */
  if (N >= 13) {
    T = (N == 14 ? "four"             /* If  13 <= N < 20,    */
               : Decade[N-12]);       /* construct the result*/
    L = strlen(T) + 4;                /* from the decade and */
    S = (char *) malloc(L+1);         /* the particle "teen".*/
    stpcpy(stpcpy(S,T),"teen"); }     /* "Fourteen" is an ex-*/
  else {                              /* ception.            */
    L = strlen(Digit[N]);             /* If  0 <= N < 13,    */
    S = (char *) malloc(L+1);         /* just look up the    */
    stpcpy(S,Digit[N]); }             /* result.             */
  return S; }
```

Figure 3.7.10 (*Continued*) Function **StrULtoE**

You may want to check your understanding of this algorithm by considering the following modifications.

- Include *billions*. (This is useful only in the United States. In this country, the largest unsigned long integer **ULONG_MAX** = 2^{32} - 1 is counted in the billions, but for Europeans and **StrULtoE** it's between four and five thousand million.)

- Include a provision for the word *and,* as in *one hundred and one.*
- Consider the problem of French numerals, in which 99 is *quatre-vingt-dix-neuf,* like *fourscore and nineteen* in English.
- Consider German numerals, in which 99 is *neunundneunzig,* like *nine and ninety* in English.

3.8 Money and time

Concepts

Country-dependent DOS string formats
country function
Outputting monetary amounts
Turbo C Library time and date formatting functions
More flexible time and date formatting functions
Handling dates before 1980

Country dependent formats

Often you may want to output strings denoting amounts of currency. Their format varies from country to country. For example, in the United States you could spend $1234.56, whereas in France it might be 1234,56 F. Several other common notations depend on the country, particularly those for the time and date. Since DOS is marketed internationally, it makes a polite effort to use the time and date format of the country selected by the user. It provides this information, as well as some other formatting details, to your programs, so that they too can respond appropriately. Otherwise, users would always have to consider whether 4/12/88 means April 12 or December 4, and whether 08:00 might be an evening hour or not. Since some currency, time, and date formatting details are handled similarly, they are considered together in this section.

   DOS provisions for country dependent formatting are connected with its *code page* mechanism for assigning ASCII/IBM codes above 127 to the non-English characters used by various languages. This book does not cover code pages at all. All its programs assume that the standard United States code page 437 is in use.

With a **Config.Sys** command, you can tell DOS during booting which country's formats you want to use. DOS expects to find all its formats in a file that you can specify via the **Config.Sys** command **COUNTRY**. If you don't, it defaults to file **\Country.Sys** on the boot drive (supplied with DOS). The **COUNTRY** command lets you select the country by its telephone code. Unfortunately, rather few choices are available:

United States	1	Italy	39	Norway	47
Netherlands	31	Switzerland	41	Germany (BRD)	49
Belgium	32	United Kingdom	44	Australia	61
France	33	Denmark	45	Finland	358
Spain	34	Sweden	46	Israel	972

If you don't supply full information, DOS defaults to the United States formats. Normally, DOS reads the appropriate information just during booting, to determine the formats for the *current* country. If you want access to other formats later, you must execute the memory resident DOS utility **NLSFunc** to make them available. After that, DOS will respond to your program's requests for format information. (This description is specific to DOS 3.30. Corresponding features of earlier versions were less complicated.)

Turbo C programs can ascertain the formats for the current and other countries through Library function

struct country *country(int Code, struct country *C)

Given a pointer to structure **C**, this routine requests a DOS service to fill **C** with the format data for the country with the specified code, or for the current country, if **Code** is zero. It returns the same pointer. Unfortunately, in Version 1.5, **country** doesn't work properly when **Code** > 255. Fixing the bug is a good example of programming with DOS interrupt services; so an improved version of the function is described later, in Chapter 8. The prototype for function **country** is in header file **DOS.H**, along with the following declaration:

```
struct country {
    int co_date;        /* Date style  (0..2)        */
    char co_curr[5];    /* Currency symbol           */
    char co_thsep[2];   /* Thousand separator        */
    char co_desep[2];   /* Decimal separator         */
```

```
char co_dtsep[2];    /* Date separator                    */
char co_tmsep[2];    /* Time separator                    */
char co_currstyle;   /* Currency style  (0..3)            */
char co_digits;      /* Significant digits in currency    */
char co_time;        /* 0: 12 hr clock; 1: 24 hr          */
long co_case;        /* Obsolete                          */
char co_dasep[2];    /* Data separator                    */
char co_fill[10]; }; /* Unused                            */
```

All these character arrays are in ASCII Z-string format: their last characters are terminating zeroes. Here are the contents of this structure for the United States and France.

Country	Separators		Formats		Currency	
0 :	Data	, Time :	Currency	0	Symbol	$
United	Thousand	, Date -	Time	0	Digits	2
States	Decimal	.	Date	0		
33 :	Data	; Time :	Currency	3	Symbol	F
France	Thousand	Date /	Time	1	Digits	2
	Decimal	,	Date	1		

The **country** structure lacks an entry for the country code itself: you cannot use function **country** to ascertain what country is current!

Most of the table entries will be described later in this section in connection with money matters and time. Three, however, have more general use: the data, thousand, and decimal separators. It's not clear what the first one is for: the author hasn't noticed any French tendency to separate list items with semicolons where commas would be used in this country. The United States and French thousand separators (comma and blank) are distinctive and common: 1,000,000 and 1 000 000. As a numerical string processing exercise, you might want to write a function that inserts the proper separator in an integer numeral. The decimal separators are also distinctive: 1234.56 and 1234,56. Although DOS *informs* you in this way which character is conventional, DOS doesn't *use* it. Even though Turbo C **printf** output is channeled through DOS, your real number output will have the standard decimal point even when the current country is France. If you want to use the alternative decimal separator, you'll have to substitute it for the point using one of the routines **StrSubst** or **stpxlate** described in Section 3.5.

Money

Outputting currency amounts is harder than you might think. The currency style entry **co_currstyle** in the structure filled by function **country** tells where to put the currency symbol:

Style	0	1	2	3
Left or Right	Left	Left	Right	Right
Separated from numeral by blank?	No	Yes	No	Yes

The symbol itself is entry **co_curr**, a string of length ≤ 4. Entry **co_digits** gives the number of digits after the decimal separator. (For most countries it's 2, but for Italy it's 0.) Function

char *StrToMoney(double X, int Code)

in Figure 3.8.1 constructs a numerical string for the amount **X** in the currency units of the country with the specified **Code**. Perhaps such tedium shouldn't be displayed in public, but it does provide a typical numerical string processing example. Basically, it calls function **country** to get the format information, then **fcvt** (discussed in the previous section) to construct a numerical string ready for insertion of the decimal separator. A new string, of the proper length, is allocated. (You have to move **fcvt** output from its static string buffer.) Standard string-handling techniques are used to generate a minus sign if necessary, copy the digits, and the decimal separator if necessary. Given **X** = 1234.56 and **Code** = 1 and 33 (United States and France), this function constructs strings **$1234.56** and **1234,56 F**. You might want to write an alternative version with parameters for currency style, symbol, and number of digits, avoiding reference to the **country** function. That version would not be limited to the countries that DOS supports.

To reverse this process—i.e., convert to a **double** value a string specifying a monetary amount—you could use techniques from earlier sections to delete leading or trailing non-digits and change the only possible embedded non-digit—the decimal separator—to a point, then use Library function **strtod** to read the resulting numeral.

```
/************************************************************/
/* StrToMoney      Convert a real value  X  to a numeral in  */
/*************************************** the money format of */
                                       /* the country with the*/
char *StrToMoney(double X,             /* specified  Code.    */
                int Code) {            /* Space is allocated  */
  struct country C;                    /* for the numeral.    */
  char *T,*S,*M;                       /***********************/
  int Point,Sign,L;
country(Code,&C);                      /* Get country format.  Tem-*/
T = fcvt(X,C.co_digits,                /* porary numeral  T  with  */
  &Point,&Sign);                       /* rect number of decimal   */
L = strlen(T) + 12;                    /* places.  Space for numer-*/
S = M = (char *) malloc(L);            /* al  M.  S  steps through */
if (C.co_currstyle & 1 == 0)           /* M.  Style  0,2:  cur-    */
  S = stpcpy(M,C.co_curr);             /* rency at left.  Style 2: */
if (C.co_currstyle == 2)               /* with a blank.            */
  *S++ = Blank;
if (Sign) *S++ = '-';                       /* Minus if negative.  */
strncpy(S,T,Point);                         /* Copy digits up to   */
S += Point;                                 /* the decimal point.  */
T += Point;
if (C.co_digits != 0)                       /* Decimal point if    */
  *S++ = C.co_desep[0];                     /* required.           */
strncpy(S,T,C.co_digits);                   /* Copy rest of digits.*/
S += C.co_digits;
if (C.co_currstyle == 3)                    /* Styles  1,3:  cur-  */
  *S++ = Blank;                             /* rency at right.     */
if (C.co_currstyle & 1 != 0)                /* Style 3:  with a    */
  S = stpcpy(S,C.co_curr);                  /* blank.              */
*S = 0;                                     /* Terminator.         */
return M; }
```

Figure 3.8.1 Function **StrToMoney**

Time

PC clock/calendar hardware provides both large- and small-scale time services. The latter, involved mainly with real-time aspects of various applications, are discussed latter in Chapter 8. This section is concerned with the former, which give the current time and date and related

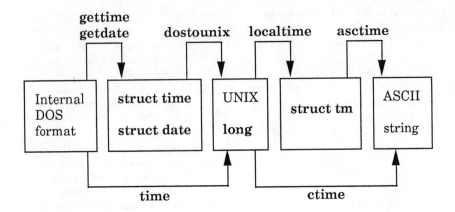

Figure 3.8.2 Turbo C time and date functions

information. You will see how the Turbo C Library functions obtain time and date information from DOS and make it available to your programs. There are some obvious gaps in these services, and new software tools are presented to fill some of them.

During booting, DOS obtains the time and date from a non-volatile battery driven clock in your PC, or from keyboard input. During operation, it uses periodic signals from the PC's timer chip to keep its time current. (With DOS 3.3 on a PC/AT, you reset the non-volatile clock by changing the DOS time or date. With earlier DOS or PC versions, the clock and the DOS time and date are independent: during operation, you can reset either without affecting the other.)

The Turbo C Library includes several functions for obtaining the DOS time and converting it to a form appropriate for your programs and their users. Four formats are used; Figure 3.8.2 shows which functions convert from one to another.

Library functions

void getdate(struct date *D)
void gettime(struct time *T)

convert the internal DOS information to corresponding C data structures of types **struct time** and **struct date** defined in header file **DOS.H** as follows:

```
struct time {
   unsigned char ti_min;      /* Minutes          */
   unsigned char ti_hour;     /* Hours  (0..23)   */
   unsigned char ti_hund;     /* 0.01  seconds    */
   unsigned char ti_sec; }    /* Seconds          */

struct date {
   int  da_year;              /* Year  (1980..)     */
   char da_day;               /* Day of the month   */
   char da_mon; }             /* Month  (1..12)     */
```

The time unit 0.01 second is misleading. The smallest time unit that DOS can handle is one *tick* = 1/18.2 ≈ 0.055 sec, a unit defined by PC hardware.)

Turbo C Library function

long dostounix(struct date *d, struct time *t)

converts a time and date from structures of the specified types to UNIX format: a single **long** value giving the number of seconds since 1 January 1970. (But DOS won't report any date before 1980.) The inverse of this function,

void unixtodos(long UnixTime, struct date *d, struct time *t),

is available for converting from UNIX format back to the **struct time** and **struct date** formats. The shortcut function

long time(long *UnixTime)

gets the time from DOS, returns the UNIX equivalent, and stores it in the specified variable **UnixTime**. It merely calls **gettime, getdate,** and **dostounix**.

Library function

struct tm *localtime(const long *UnixTime)

converts UNIX time to a C data structure of the type **struct tm** defined in header file **Time.H** as follows:

```
struct tm {
    int tm_sec;          /* Seconds                    */
    int tm_min;          /* Minutes                    */
    int tm_hour;         /* Hours  (0..23)             */
    int tm_mday;         /* Day of the month  (1..31)  */
    int tm_mon;          /* Month  (0..11)             */
    int tm_year;         /* Year - 1900                */
    int tm_wday;         /* Day of the week (Sun = 0)  */
    int tm_yday;         /* Day of the year  (0..365)  */
    int tm_isdst; }      /* ?                          */
```

Careful: the month and year formats differ from their **struct date** counterparts! The last field is supposed to indicate whether daylight savings time is in effect. Although there is a way to inform the C runtime system about this (but not DOS), it's not clear how it works. Equally unclear is another function **gmtime** that gives the Greenwich Mean Time. You'll need the Library source code and perhaps a debugger to figure these out.

To convert **struct tm** time information to an ASCII string, use function

char *asctime(const struct tm *T).

It returns a pointer to a string of the form

Sat Apr 23 23:13:44 1988

in a static data area. You should move it to your own storage immediately, because each call to this function overwrites the same static area. **asctime** uses function **sprintf** to construct the string. Finally, the shortcut function

char *ctime(const long *UnixTime)

combines **localtime** and **asctime**, producing an ASCII string from a UNIX time.

The time and date function prototypes are found in two header files, as follows:

<u>**DOS.H**</u>   <u>**Time.H**</u>

gettime	dostounix	time	asctime
getdate	unixtodos	localtime	ctime

All these functions are written in C. A program showing the use of some of them is given later, in Figure 3.8.4.

Although the Turbo C Library supports several time and date formats, there are a number of gaps in its list of features. A principal one is the lack of any connection with the international notation conventions reported by the **country** function. The time conventions include 12- or 24-hour clock specification, and the choice of character to separate hours, minutes, and seconds. Figure 3.8.3 contains a new function **StrTime** that converts the **struct tm** time to an ASCII string of the form 21:38:57, allowing you to specify these notation conventions. Program **StrTime** in the figure shows how to use it, as well as the Library conversion functions **time** and **localtime**.

The Turbo C Library functions' lack of access to date notation conventions is more severe. While using the **struct country** format and separator conventions, you may want to refer as well to full month and day names, or to different abbreviations, perhaps in other languages. The header file **General.H** for this book includes two global variables

char *DayName[7]   char *MonthName[12]

containing the full English month and day names. The new function **StrDay** in Figure 3.8.4 converts **struct tm** information to an ASCII string **DateStr** in any of the following formats:

Format	DateStr
0	88-04-20
1	04-20-88
2	20-04-88
3	April 20, 1988
≥ 4	20 April 1988

(Formats 0..2 agree with the **struct country** conventions.) You can specify the separator (-). A simple demonstration program is on the accompanying diskette. If you need abbreviations or names in other languages, you can use **StrDay** as a guide or simply translate the name arrays.

```
/********************************************************/
/* StrTime        Construct time string  TimeStr  in format  */
/*                  21:38:57.  You must have allocated it  9  */
/* bytes, and have built a  struct tm  variable  *T  with the */
/* time data.  You may select a  24  or  12  hour clock, and  */
/* specify the separator  (:  in the example).  StrTime  re-  */
/* turns a pointer to  TimeStr.                               */
/********************************************************/

char *StrTime(         char *TimeStr,
              const struct tm *T,
                  Boolean  TwentyFourHours,
                    char  Separator) {
sprintf(TimeStr,"%02d%c%02d%c%02d\0",
  (TwentyFourHours ? T->tm_hour : T->tm_hour % 12),Separator,
    T->tm_min,Separator,T->tm_sec);
return TimeStr; }


/********************************************************/
/* StrTime.Dem      Demonstrate functions  time, localtime,  */
/*                  and  StrTime.  Use the first two to get   */
/* the time from  DOS  in  Unix  format and build that into a */
/************************************** struct tm  variable */
                                    /* *T.  Call   StrTime   */
#include <General.H>                /* to convert  *T  to    */
                                    /* strings in  12  and   */
void main() {                       /* 24  hour formats.     */
  long      UnixTime;               /**********************/
  struct tm *T;
  int       XXIV;                   /* 1,0  for  12,24  hr.*/
  char      TimeStr[9];
time(&UnixTime);                    /* DOS  to  Unix.*/
T = localtime(&UnixTime);           /* Unix  to  tm. */
for (XXIV = 0; XXIV <= 1; ++XXIV)
  printf("%s\n",
    StrTime(TimeStr,T,XXIV,':')); }          /* tm  to string.*/
```

Figure 3.8.3 Demonstrating time functions and the new function **StrTime**

The final topic in this section concerns anyone who works with historical data: determining the day of the week for a given date, and determining the number of days between two dates. Turbo C Library

```
/**************************************************************/
/* StrDay          Day and date strings.  Construct a date    */
/*                 string DateStr  in the specified format.    */
/*                                Formats   0,1,2   agree with*/
/* Format..DateStr..........L      the specification of  struct*/
/*       0  88-04-20         9     country  in DOS.H.  You     */
/*       1  04-20-88         9     must first allocate  DateStr*/
/*       2  20-04-88         9     at least  L  bytes as shown,*/
/*       3  April 20, 1988  19     supply a pointer to a       */
/*      ≥ 4  20 April 1988  18     struct tm  variable  T  that*/
/*                                contains the date informa-   */
/* tion, and specify the date separator    (-  in the exam-    */
/* ples.)  The function returns a pointer to the name of the   */
/* weekday in a string stored in a global variable.            */
/**************************************************************/

char *DayName[7] = {"Sunday","Monday","Tuesday","Wednesday",
  "Thursday","Friday","Saturday"};
char *MonthName[12] = {"January","February","March","April",
  "May","June","July","August","September","October","November",
    "December"};

static int F[3][3] = {2,1,0,    /* These are the permutations */
                      1,0,2,    /* of the  struct tm  entries */
                      0,1,2};   /* for formats  0..2.         */

char *StrDay(          char *DateStr,
             const struct tm *T,
                       int Format,
                       char Separator) {
  int U[3];
if (Format < 3) {                /* For short formats, change  */
  U[0] = T->tm_mday;             /* month from  0..11  to      */
  U[1] = T->tm_mon + 1;          /* 1..12  and rearrange date  */
  U[2] = T->tm_year;             /* components as necessary.    */
  sprintf(DateStr,
    "%02d%c%02d%c%02d\0",U[F[Format][0]],Separator,
      U[F[Format][1]],Separator,U[F[Format][2]]);  }
  else if (Format == 3)
  sprintf(DateStr,"%s %d, %d\0",MonthName[T->tm_mon],
    T->tm_mday, (T->tm_year)+1900);
  else
```

Figure 3.8.4 Function **StrDay** (*Continued on next page*)

```
sprintf(DateStr,"%d %s %d\0",T->tm_mday,
   MonthName[T->tm_mon], (T->tm_year)+1900);
return DayName[T->tm_wday]; }
```

Figure 3.8.4 *(Continued)* Function **StrDay**

functions provide these services, but only for dates since 1 January 1980. For earlier ones new functions are required. These are not really string processing features, but are included here because they are more closely related to this section than any other. The main problem is accounting for leap years. Our current Gregorian calendar conventions were established by Pope Gregory XIII in 1582. The older Julian calendar accounted for leap years incorrectly, and had become more than 10 days out of phase with the seasons. Unfortunately, it remained in use in Europe alongside the Gregorian until about 1750, causing much confusion in interpreting historical records.

Figures 3.8.5 to 3.8.8 contain a suite of functions for obtaining Gregorian calendar information. The calculations are valid for dates since Day 1 —Saturday, January 1, 1583. However, they clearly do not apply to dates reckoned before or after that in the obsolete Julian calendar. Here is a list of the routines:

Function	Figure	Description
Leap	3.8.5	Report whether a specified year is a leap year.
DayOfYear	3.8.6	Return the number of the given day in the year, having indicated if it's a leap year.
Gregorian	3.8.7	Return the number of days since Day 1.
Weekday	3.8.8	Return the day of the week for a given date.

The number of days between two dates is the difference of the corresponding values of function **Gregorian**. **Leap** and **WeekDay** are implemented as macros in the header file **General.H** for this book. These functions duplicate some Library features, but are valid for a much wider range of dates. The algorithms are described briefly in the program documentation in the figures. A simple demonstration program is provided on the accompanying diskette.

```
/******************************************************************/
/* Leap          Return  1  or  0  indicating whether a    */
/*               specified year  (≥ 1583)  is a leap year.  */
/* Since then, years divisible by  4  are leap years, except */
/* centennial years, unless they are divisible by  400.      */
/******************************************************************/

#define Leap(Year) ( (Year) % 4   == 0 && \
                     ( (Year) % 100 != 0 || \
                     (Year) % 400 == 0  ))
```

Figure 3.8.5 Function **LeapYear** (a macro)

```
/******************************************************************/
/* DayOfYear     Return the number of the given day in the  */
/*               year.  Specify leap year or not.           */
/******************************************************************/

static int DaysBefore1stOf[]          /* Days in a non-leap  */
  = {  0, 31,59, 90,120,151,          /* year before  1st  of*/
     181,212,243,273,304,334};        /* the indicated month.*/

int DayOfYear(    int Day,            /* Day, Month in ranges*/
                  int Month,          /* 1..31, 0..11.       */
              Boolean LeapYear) {
  int N = DaysBefore1stOf[Month] + Day;
if (LeapYear && Month > 1) ++N;       /* Feb  is month  1.   */
return N; }
```

Figure 3.8.6 Function **DayOfYear**

```
/******************************************************************/
/* Gregorian     Return the number of days since day  1  = */
/*               1 January 1583.                            */
/******************************************************************/

long Gregorian(int Day,              /* Day, Month in ranges    */
               int Month,            /* 1..31, 0..11.           */
               int Year) {           /* Year  Ú 1583.           */
```

Figure 3.8.7 Function **Gregorian** (*Continued on next page*)

```
long N = DayOfYear(Day,Month,     /* Days this year, plus 365 */
   Leap(Year));                   /* for each previous year,  */
N += (long) (Year-1583)*365;      /* plus 1 for those di-     */
N += (long) (Year-1581)/4;        /* visible by 4, except     */
N -= (long) (Year-1501)/100;      /* centennial years, unless */
N += (long) (Year-1201)/400;      /* they're divisible by     */
return N; }                       /* 400.                     */
```

Figure 3.8.7 *(Continued)* Function **Gregorian**

```
/*****************************************************************/
/* WeekDay          Return the day of the week (Sunday = 0)    */
/*                  for any day since  Saturday, 1 Jan 1583.   */
/*****************************************************************/
```

```
#define WeekDay(Day,Month,Year)  (Gregorian(Day,Month,Year)+5)%7
```

Figure 3.8.8 Function **WeekDay** (a macro)

3.9 Further topics

```
Concepts

File names
Function main parameters
Ascertaining the program file name
Command line parameters
Environment variables
Function main value and DOS ErrorLevel variable
```

This section is concerned with some very specialized string processing topics: constructing and parsing DOS file names, ascertaining the complete file name of the program itself (hence its location in a drive's directory tree), reading its command line parameter strings, and reading the values of the environment variables it inherits from its parent program (usually **Command.Com**). The last three techniques involve the parameters for function **main**. The section concludes with a related topic, the value returned by function **main**.

File names

Handling file names often involves string processing. For example, you may want a user to enter a drive name or a file name extension, so that you can construct a full path name. The Turbo C Library provides two functions for file name synthesis and analysis:

void fnmerge(char *PathName,
                char *Drive, char *Dir, char *Name, char *Ext)

int fnsplit(char *PathName,
              char *Drive, char *Dir, char *Name, char *Ext)

Their prototypes are in header file **Dir.H**; they are written in C, and use the C string handling functions. **fnmerge** constructs a full path name from its constituent parts; some of those may be empty. **fnsplit** reverses the process, returning as well a word of flags indicating which parts were present and signalling the occurrence of any wild card character (**?** or *****).

A program **FN.Dem** demonstrating these functions is included on the accompanying diskette; it is too long and repetitive to reproduce here. However, two sample outputs are shown in Figure 3.9.1. **FN.Dem** inputs and echoes strings **Drive, Dir, Name**, and **Ext**; then it calls **fnmerge** to construct the full **PathName**, which it outputs. It passes **PathName** to **fnsplit** for analysis, writes the resulting constituent parts, and displays the flags returned by **fnsplit**. It outputs these by a sequence of statements of the form

if (Flags & DRIVE) printf("Drive ");

Header file **Dir.H** contains appropriate definitions of **DRIVE** and other constants corresponding to the flags.

You can see from Figure 3.9.1 that the **fnsplit** analysis agrees with the original input when the latter is valid. *Caution: neither function guards against invalid input!*

Evidently, **fnmerge** accepts characters that may not appear in valid file names, and a misplaced period can lead to misinterpretation. Robust file handling involves elaborate validation of names before you attempt to use them to identify actual files. That in itself is a good exercise in string analysis, and requires some detective work to discover the official DOS file name syntax.

Valid fnmerge input

Drive	= a
Directory	= bcd\efg.hij
Name	= klm
Extension	= .n*
Full name	= a:bcd\efg.hij\klm.n*

fnsplit analysis:

Drive	= a:
Directory	= bcd\efg.hij\
Name	= klm
Extension	= .n*
Flags	= Drive Dir Name Ext Wild

Invalid fnmerge input

Drive	= ax
Directory	= bcd>!
Name	= ef.g
Extension	= hi
Full name	=a:bcd>!\ef.ghi

fnsplit analysis:

Drive	= a:
Directory	= bcd>!\
Name	= ef
Extension	= .ghi
Flags	= Drive Dir Name Ext

Figure 3.9.1 Demonstrating functions **fnmerge** and **fnsplit**

Command line

Turbo C always parses the DOS command line that executes a program, and provides access to its constituents via the function **main** parameters. In all previous examples in this book, function **main** had a void parameter list. However, you may also define it with one, two, or three parameters like this:

void main(int N, char *ComLine[], char *Environ[])

(You can use any names you want to identify the **main** parameters.) Consider the first two now; the last will be discussed later. (**main** can also return a useful value, described at the end of this section.)

Parameter **N** is always positive. It specifies the length of the **ComLine** array: one greater than the number of parameters in the DOS command line that executed the file containing **main**. Array entry **ComLine[0]** is the *full* path name of that file—not just the abbreviation used on the command line. The remaining entries are the command line parameters. This is demonstrated by program **ComLine.Dem** in Figure 3.9.2. The first line of the sample execution is the author's DOS prompt, which identifies the current directory. The first item on the next line is the command to execute the file **ComLine.Exe**.

You can use the program file name feature to install a multifile software system. If you insist on placing multiple files all in the same directory as the main program file, it can find them by using **fnsplit** to parse **ComLine[0]**. That convention is unnecessarily inconvenient for users who wish to place some files on a virtual disk, or who must use

```
/****************************************************************/
/* ComLine.Dem      Show how to ascertain the program file name*/
/*                  and read command line parameters.          */
/****************************************************************/

#include <StdIO.H>

void main(int N, char *ComLine[]) {
  int I;
printf("Program file: %s\n",ComLine[0]);
printf("%d  command line parameters:\n",N-1);
for (I = 1; I < N; printf("%s\n",ComLine[I++])); }
```

Sample execution

```
DESQview 21:32 Sun  5-22-1988 C:\TURBOC\WORK
ComLine First Second
Program file:  C:\TURBOC\WORK\COMLINE.EXE
2  command line parameters:
First
Second
```

Figure 3.9.2 Program **ComLine.Dem**

diskettes too small for all the required files. A much more flexible convention would be to require a short installation file in the same directory as the main program. It would simply contain the full path names of all the auxiliary files for the system.

Environment

Besides the command line, you can also use the DOS *environment* feature to communicate small amounts of information to your program. The environment consists of ASCII Z-strings of the form **VARIABLE=Value**. Substring **Value** is regarded as the value of the environment variable **VARIABLE**. Each program inherits an environment from its parent program—usually the DOS command line interpreter **Command.Com**. (The **Command.Com** environment is initialized by several DOS features, including command **Set**. Chapter 7 discusses techniques a parent C program can use to create proper environments for child programs it may spawn.)

The third parameter for

void main(int N, char *ComLine[], char *Environ[])

is a pointer to an array **Environ** of strings copied from the DOS environment by the Turbo C code that executes function **main**. (**Environ** is not the environment itself; for reasons discussed in Chapter 7, it's best for your program to work with a copy.) Unfortunately, no **main** parameter gives the length of the **Environ** array. That's not hard to find, however: the last **Environ** entry is always an empty string, consisting solely of the terminating 0.

Program **Environ.Dem** in Figure 3.9.3 demonstrates use of the **Environ** array, as well as the Turbo C Library function

char *getenv(char *V)

This function will return a pointer to the value of environment variable **V** if it's present; otherwise, **getenv** returns a null pointer. Its prototype is in header file **StdLib.H**, and it's written in assembly language. Program **Environ.Dem** outputs **Environ** entries while they're not empty, then enters an endless loop, prompting the user to inquire about environment variables, and responding appropriately. The first line of

```
/*****************************************************************/
/* Environ.Dem    Show how to display the program environment*/
/*               strings, and how to ascertain their values.*/
/*****************************************************************/

#include <General.H>

void main(int N, char *ComLine[], char *Environ[]) {
  int  I;
  char Variable[80];
  char *Value;
printf("Program environment:\n");         /* Print  Environ    */
for (I = 0; !StrEmpty(Environ[I]);        /* strings while they */
  printf("%s\n",Environ[I++]));            /* aren't empty.      */
for (;;) {                                 /* Endless loop!      */
  printf("\nVariable:  ");
  fflush(stdin);                           /* On demand, display */
  gets(Variable);                          /* the value of an en-*/
  Value = getenv(Variable);                /* vironment variable.*/
  if (Value == NULL)
      printf("Not the name of an environment variable.");
    else
      printf("Value = %s",Value); }}
```

Sample execution

```
DESQview 22:00 Sun  5-22-1988 C:\TURBOC\WORK
Environ
Program environment:
COMSPEC=C:\COMMAND.COM
PATH=D:\;C:\DISPATCH;C:\;C:\DV
PROMPT=DESQview $t$h$h$h$h$h$h $d $p$_
Variable:  comspec
Not the name of an environment variable.
Variable:  COMSPEC
Value = C:\COMMAND.COM
```

Figure 3.9.3 Program **Environ.Dem**

the sample execution is the author's DOS prompt line. The first item on the next line executes the file **Environ.Exe**. The sample execution displays the three variables normally present in the environment of every program: **COMSPEC** locates the command processor, **PATH** specifies the directories DOS searches for executable files, and **PROMPT** specifies the DOS prompt format. The output shows, incidentally, that environment variable names are always upper case.

ErrorLevel

You can define function **main** to return a value. Although the Turbo C literature is not explicit about this matter, inspection of the Turbo C Library source code file **C0.Asm** shows that the low byte of the value returned in register AX is transmitted to DOS for use as the value of its **ErrorLevel** variable. (See Section 2.5 for the use of AX.) The DOS **if ErrorLevel** command gives you access to use that value after execution is completed. For example, consider program **Main.Dem**:

```
char main() {
return 17; }
```

Compile it to an executable file **Main.Exe**, and execute the following batch program **ErrorLvl.Bat**:

```
@Echo Off
Main
for %%1 in (16,17,18) do if ErrorLevel %%1 Echo %%1
```

The DOS **ErrorLevel** function returns a true value when the value of its parameter %%1 does not exceed that of the **ErrorLevel** variable. Here is a sample execution:

```
ErrorLevel
16
17
```

You can use a variant of the last little C program to input a keystroke via a batch program. Program **GetKey.Dem** in Figure 3.9.4 merely inputs a character from the keyboard and returns it as the **ErrorLevel** value. The Figure includes a batch program that invokes it, and sample output. You can make a more elegant version of **GetKey.Dem**, with a shorter executable file (**GetKey.Exe** is 4350 bytes long) by using one of the **ConIO** keyboard input functions described in Chapter 5.

```
Batch program  GetKDem.Bat
@Echo Off
Echo Enter a letter of the alphabet.
GetKey
if ErrorLevel 91 GoTo Lower
  Echo Upper case!
  GoTo End
rem (Z  is  ASCII 90)
:Lower
  Echo Lower case!
:End
```

```
Program  GetKey.Dem
#include <StdIO.H>
char main() {
  return getchar(); }
```

Sample execution
```
GetKDem
Enter a letter of the alphabet.
Z
Upper case!
```

Figure 3.9.4 Using **ErrorLevel** to input to a batch program

Chapter 7 gives more detail on the use of **ErrorLevel** in spawning child programs.

4

Text Mode Screen Handling

Contents

4.1 Turbo C screen handling
4.2 Display buffer and attributes
4.3 Screen handling with Turbo C TOOLS
4.4 Turbo C TOOLS screen windows

This chapter will show you how to achieve *nearly complete* control over screen output—sufficient control to use the screen effectively in an interactive user interface. Text mode screen handling usually involves two types of output at once. Your program is outputting text information, and simultaneously sending codes to control the display unit. These techniques are stressed equally.

A major problem with this kind of programming is the variety of display equipment. Turbo C supports only the two original IBM display controllers—the Monochrome and Color/Graphics Adapters. It falls far short of an effective methodology for even these. Sections 4.3 and 4.4 are devoted to the much more comprehensive Turbo C TOOLS screen and window handling features. That package fills in most of the gaps for the adapters just mentioned, providing straightforward techniques for controlling them and some features of the newer IBM Extended Graphics Adapter. Now, however, the IBM VGA Adapter is becoming a standard, and others specially designed for advanced word processing are common. No commercial package can cover the whole field. However, if you master the methodology described in this book, you should be able to extend the Turbo C and Turbo C TOOLS features to new and more powerful display devices as they continue to appear.

There are several general methods for displaying text information with Turbo C. Here are three sets of corresponding Library functions, with the header files that contain their prototypes:

Output	StdIO.H		ConIO.H
Character	fputc	putc	putchar	putch
String	fputs		puts	cputs
Formatted	fprintf		printf	cprintf

The **StdIO** functions in the left-hand column are designed mainly for file output. They require a parameter to identify the file, and use DOS file output services. Since DOS has a standard file name for the screen, they can be used for screen output, but that's unusual. The functions in the middle column are intended mainly for screen display via the DOS *standard output* service, hence their output can be redirected at run time to a file. Since these two output methods must make sense in the general file handling context, they can't take advantage of many special properties of the screen, and can't be used very effectively for interactive screen input/output. They are considered in some detail in Chapter 6 with other file processing techniques. The **ConIO** functions in the right-hand column, on the other hand, are designed specifically for screen handling; their output cannot be redirected to a file. They are described in detail in this chapter.

The **ConIO** screen functions may utilize output services provided by the PC's or display controller's BIOS (the program stored in ROM that directly controls the hardware). For some applications, these services are too slow, so Turbo C normally controls the hardware itself: instead of asking the BIOS to store data in the display controller memory at addresses appropriate to specified screen positions, Turbo C stores the data there itself. The screen output strategy is governed by the value of a Turbo C Library global variable, which you can reference by including this declaration in your program:

extern int directvideo

Normally, **directvideo** = 1, and the **ConIO** functions control the hardware directly. However, if you set **directvideo** = 0, Turbo C will use the BIOS services. You will gain some portability at the cost of speed, as discussed later.

Producing effective screen output requires more control over your display unit than the functions just mentioned provide. Turbo C fills part of this gap with routines for the following tasks:

- confining output to a given screen window,
- clearing part or all of the screen,
- inserting and deleting screen rows,
- controlling and ascertaining cursor location,
- setting the text mode of a color/graphics adapter,
- setting text attributes (color, underline, blink),
- ascertaining information about the current window,
- moving text among windows and memory.

These features are described in detail in Sections 4.1 and 4.2. The latter also demonstrates absolute memory addressing techniques for direct display buffer access.

Although the Turbo C screen handling functions give you great power over the display, they are still insufficient for effective interactive input/output. For example,

- You cannot associate attributes with screen areas independent of their content.
- Window handling is primitive.
- You cannot handle more than one screen page, even if your display controller permits it.

Turbo C TOOLS provides solutions for these problems, as well as several other features. They are described in Sections 4.3 and 4.4. The latter is devoted to window handling. Like the **ConIO** functions, the Turbo C TOOLS routines use BIOS screen output services, or even directly access display controller memory, instead of using the higher level DOS output facilities.

When you use the **ConIO** functions or Turbo C TOOLS to bypass DOS output, you gain control and speed, but lose compatibility with some software and hardware. Your programs become *ill-behaved* in the sense that DOS cannot control their output and process it for further use by other routines. In particular, text information cannot be redirected to other files or devices. Even if you set **directvideo** =0 so that **ConIO** functions output via BIOS services, your programs will run only on machines with completely compatible BIOS video services. When **ConIO** functions bypass the BIOS, they will run only on machines whose hardware is completely IBM compatible. You lose portability to machines with non-standard hardware that must be driven by customized DOS or BIOS versions. You must choose: speed and control, or portability.

One problem with **ConIO** output affected the production of this book: incorporating screen output in a manuscript or report. The standard <Shift-PrtSc> method produces hardcopy of a single screen, but it can't be redirected to a file for further editing. The most direct method for producing hardcopy of multiple output screens is the <Ctrl-PrtSc> facility. However, this is a DOS feature, and does not capture **ConIO** output, so you must use mainly the **StdIO** functions. Moreover, it does not work in the Turbo C integrated software development environment: you have to compile, exit to DOS, toggle <Ctrl-PrtSc>, then run the **.Exe** file. It's just as easy in that case to redirect the **.Exe** output to a file for further editing. (You can correct blunders that way.) Chapter 9 describes in detail a memory resident <Shift-PrtSc> program that can copy *any* text screen image to a file. The outputs shown in this book, however, were for the most part captured by the mark/transfer facility of the *DESQview* operating environment.

Occasionally, you may need to request DOS or BIOS screen output services yourself, like the Turbo C Library and Turbo C TOOLS routines operate. General techniques for obtaining DOS and BIOS services are described in Chapter 8; the material there is sufficient to show you how most of the Library and TOOLS functions were constructed. Sometimes you may even want to go below that level and use input/output ports directly. For example, you may want to turn off the display. That kind of programming is discussed as appropriate in this book, but without many examples, because they usually require detailed knowledge of the technical manuals for the equipment involved.

4.1 Turbo C screen handling

Concepts

TTY output conventions
ConIO output functions
Screen coordinates
Turbo C screen windows
Cursor control
Display controllers and text modes
Setting CGA and Monochrome text modes
Ascertaining mode and window information
Ascertaining which display controller is installed
Hercules Monochrome and IBM Extended Graphics Adapters
Using **TCInst.Exe** to select display type

This section describes Turbo C techniques that will give you almost complete position control of your screen output. Turbo C functions **putch, cputs,** and **cprintf** output a character stream that produces a TTY style display, with standard cursor placement conventions. You will find prototypes of these functions in header file **ConIO.H**. (Corresponding functions in **StdIO.H** produce similar output when directed to the screen, but ignore some important screen control features, described later.) Several other **ConIO** routines provide additional cursor control and rudimentary window handling. With care, you can place your output text almost anywhere you want. Example programs are given here to illustrate these methods.

Turbo C also provides means for setting screen text attributes (color, underline, blink). Since these features require detailed knowledge of display buffer format, and since they are greatly expanded by the Turbo C TOOLS package, attribute manipulation is described separately in Section 4.2.

TTY output conventions

Since all text output will ultimately be displayed by some device, it usually includes some *control characters,* which are transmitted like text, but used to control devices. Thus there is a small overlap between text and display control output. Only five such control characters are relevant for Turbo C **ConIO** screen output:

ASCII	Name	Effect when output by ConIO functions
0	NUL	No effect.
7	BEL	Beep.
8	BS	Move cursor left one column, if possible (back-space).
10	LF	Move the cursor to column 1 (carriage return). Then move it down one row, if possible; otherwise, scroll the screen contents up one row, leaving the bottom line blank (line feed).
13	CR	Carriage return.

After displaying any other character, the cursor is moved right one column, if possible. Otherwise, it acts as if the character were followed by an LF. The text display conventions just described are called *TTY* output. (TTY is an abbreviation for *teletype,* a primitive output device.)

Some TTY fine points need consideration. First, you must distinguish the ASCII 0 NUL character, which has no effect, from the two blank characters ASCII 32 and 255, which move the cursor (and *are* visible if you use a background color or underline). Second, DOS screen output—hence **StdIO** output when directed to the screen—interprets the ASCII 9 TAB character as though tab stops were installed every eighth column, and inserts blanks accordingly. The **ConIO** output functions just display a little circle. The Turbo C *Reference guide* is incorrect concerning the effect of ASCII 10.

These output effects are all demonstrated by program **TTYCtrl.Dem** in Figure 4.1.1.

ConIO screen output

Turbo C functions **putch, cputs,** and **cprintf** produce TTY output. Their prototypes, as well as those of the remaining functions described in this section, are in header file **ConIO.H**:

```
int putch(int Ch)
int cputs(const char *S)
int cprintf(const char *Format, ...)
```

```
/***********************************************************/
/* TTYCtrl.Dem    Demonstrate effect of  ASCII  control char-*/
/*                acters  0,7,8,9,10,13  and blanks  32,255  */
/************************************** on  putch  output.  */
                                    /* Output some stars    */
#include <General.H>               /* and dots to show     */
#define N 10                       /* cursor placement.    */
                                   /***********************/
unsigned Ch[N]
  = {'*',0,7,8,9,10,13,32,255,'*'};
void main() {
  int I;
for (I = 0; I < N; ++I) {
  printf("ASCII %3u = ",Ch[I]);  putch(Ch[I]);  printf(".\n"); }}
```

Output

```
ASCII  42 = *.         (For alignment)
ASCII   0 = .          (No effect)
ASCII   7 = .          (Hear a beep)
ASCII   8 =.           (Backspace)
ASCII   9 =        .   (Tab character displayed)
ASCII  10 =            (Carriage return, line feed)
.
.SCII  13 =            (Carriage return)
ASCII  32 =  .         (Blank)
ASCII 255 =  .         (Blank)
ASCII  42 = *.         (For alignment)
```

Figure 4.1.1 Program **TTYCtrl.Dem**

The last is a variable length parameter sequence, like that of **printf**.
Functions **putch** and **cputs** return **Ch** and the last character output;
cprintf returns the number of characters output. Note that the no-effect
convention concerning ASCII 0 doesn't really occur with **cputs** and
cprintf: these output *strings*, and interpret ASCII 0 as a terminator!
  To produce neat displays, you must be able to control precisely the
position of all your screen output. You can do that with functions **putch**,
cputs, and **cprintf** as long as

- you know where the cursor is at the start,
- all output stays in top to bottom sequence, and
- you avoid writing in the rightmost column.

Under these conditions, the only control signals affecting the position of your output are those produced *directly* by your program and data. (Remember that writing in the rightmost column produces an automatic carriage return and line feed, and when the cursor is on the bottom line, a line feed produces automatic scrolling.

One provision is missing from this method of output positioning. Unless you can control which row you start on, you can never tell which row you are writing on. One way to do that is to use Turbo C function

void clrscr(void)

which wipes the screen clean and moves the cursor to the top left corner. That corner has minimum screen column, row coordinates X,Y = 1,1. The maximum X,Y coordinates depend on the current display mode, which is considered later.

Often you may want to confine your output to a rectangular *window* on the screen, which you would like to treat as if it were the entire screen. Turbo C provides a simple method for this. Turbo C TOOLS includes more powerful window handling features, described in Section 4.3. To use the Turbo C facility, specify the *current* screen window by executing function

void window(int X1, int Y1, int X2, int Y2)

where **X1,Y1** and **X2,Y2** are the screen coordinates of the upper left and lower right window corners. (The default current window is the entire screen.) **window** moves the cursor to the top left corner—position 1,1— of the current window—and all subsequent **ConIO** functions locate cursor and output relatively. The corresponding **StdIO** functions ignore the window entirely.

Program **Window.Dem** in Figure 4.1.2 illustrates function **window**. It produces rapid scrolling in a small window in the middle of the screen.

Turbo C provides several cursor control routines:

void gotoxy(int X, int Y)
int wherex(void)
int wherey(void)

These all use the screen coordinate system described earlier, relative to the current window. The first moves the cursor to location **X,Y**. It has

```
/************************************************************/
/* Window.Dem      Demonstrate function  clrscr  and  ConIO  */
/*********************************** output in a window. */
                                /***********************/
#include <General.H>

void main() {
  int X,Y;
  clrscr();                          /* Clear the screen,    */
  for (X = 1; X <= 80; ++X)          /* then fill it with    */
    for (Y = 1; Y <= 25; ++Y)        /* dots.                */
      putch('.');
  window(30,8,50,17);                /* Clear a window in    */
  clrscr();                          /* the screen center,   */
  for (X = 1; X <= 100; ++X)         /* then fill it with    */
    for (Y = 1; Y <= 22; ++Y)        /* lots of output,      */
      cprintf("%d",X%10); }          /* scrolling rapidly.   */
```

Figure 4.1.2 Program **Window.Dem**

no effect if **X** or **Y** is out of bounds. The latter two functions return the current cursor coordinates; you can use them to find the cursor when some other routine has moved it to an unknown location.

There is an ambiguity in the notion "relative to the current window." When you change the current window dimensions with function **window**, do the values of **wherex** and **wherey** change, or does the cursor physically move to the analogous location relative to the new window? The latter occurs: **window** does not change the value of **wherex** or **wherey**; it may move the cursor physically on the screen.

Three more **ConIO** functions use the cursor location to help you arrange the display in a screen window:

void clreol(void)
void delline(void)
void insline(void)

The first clears the current row rightward from the cursor. Function **delline** deletes the current row and moves the text in all lower rows up one, creating a blank row. **insline** moves the text in the current row and all lower ones down one (losing the bottom row of text), then clears the current row. None of these affects the current cursor location.

Program **Cursor.Dem** in Figure 4.1.3 illustrates the use of several of these routines. It writes a rippling pattern in a screen window until you press a key, then clears the current column and row. Rippling is produced by using **gotoxy** to resume writing at top left when the cursor reaches bottom right; otherwise the cursor would remain on the bottom row. Pressing a key again resumes the pattern; press <Ctrl-Break> to exit.

Program **Window.Dem** in Figure 4.1.2 showed that you can scroll a window upward by causing a line feed on its bottom row. Similarly, you can scroll downward by using functions **gotoxy** and **insline** to insert a new top row, then writing text there. A more convenient and versatile Turbo C TOOLS scrolling routine is described in Section 4.3.

```
/***************************************************************/
/* Cursor.Dem      Demonstrate  ConIO  output, cursor control.*/
/***************************************************************/

#include <General.H>
#define  M 25                              /* Number of rows.    */

void main() {
  int  N,X,Y;
clrscr();
window(1,1,M,M);
for (;;) {                                 /* Endless loop!      */
  for (N = 0; !kbhit(); ++N) {             /* Loop 'til keystroke.*/
    if (wherex() == M & wherey() == M)     /* When you reach lower*/
      gotoxy(1,1);                         /* right, start over.  */
    cprintf("%d",N%5); }
getch();                                   /* Discard keystroke.  */
X = wherex();                              /* Save current  X.    */
gotoxy(1,wherey());                        /* Clear current row.  */
clreol();
for (Y = 1; Y <= M; ++Y) {                 /* Clear current       */
  gotoxy(X,Y);                             /* column.             */
  putch(Blank); }}}
```

Figure 4.1.3 Program **Cursor.Dem**

Program **Window.Dem** used the construct

```
for (N = 0; !kbhit(); ++N)
  /* Insert action here */
getch();
```

to repeat an action until any key is pressed. Functions **kbhit** and **getch** are discussed in greater detail later in Chapter 5. The former returns 0 just when the keyboard buffer is empty. Your keystrokes place input codes in that buffer. Function **getch** removes one; that's required for the program to work.

Display controllers and text modes

Several standard PC display controllers are available, some of which can drive displays of several types, and in several modes of operation. Beginning execution, a Turbo C program must determine what equipment is present and set it to produce the effect you want. This information is available to your program, so that it can operate differently with different equipment. To develop really graceful software, you need to be able to ascertain as well the detailed state of the display equipment, because that is often used for communication. Sometimes this is obvious—other software records information on the screen, and your program must read it. Sometimes it's more subtle. For example, suppose another program is using cursor shape and position to convey status information, and your software intervenes. If you change the cursor, you must restore it to its original state before you return to the interrupted program, or else you'll destroy needed information.

With the graphics unit in Version 1.5, Turbo C provides fairly comprehensive information about installed equipment. Because of the constantly expanding repertoire of available display equipment, however, no software system can even approach completeness. On the other hand, Turbo C provides only rudimentary information about the current state of the installed equipment. Turbo C TOOLS routines discussed in Section 4.3 provide somewhat more information, but cannot achieve completeness because some controllers fail to provide readable records of all status information.

Two display controllers were provided for the original IBM PC: the Color/Graphics and Monochrome Display Adapters (CGA and MDA).

Both controllers can be present at once, connected to different displays. The intent was to provide simultaneous graphics and text displays. Since this chapter considers only text display, graphics features are ignored. Together, these adapters have five text modes:

Mode	Turbo C constant	Adapter	Display	Columns x Rows
0	BW40	CGA	Composite Monochrome	40 x 25
1	C40	CGA	Color	40 x 25
2	BW80	CGA	Composite Monochrome	80 x 25
3	C80	CGA	Color	80 x 25
7	MONO	MDA	IBM Monochrome	80 x 25

The constants in the second column are conveniently defined as macros in header file **ConIO.H**. Color features are described in later sections. The values in the right-hand columns are the maximum X,Y screen coordinates. Depending on the active mode, the PC BIOS outputs text to different adapter memory locations and control codes to different output ports. A screen display reflects the most recent output to the adapter to which it's connected. Switching modes is not uncommon. For example, you might want to switch to the more visible 40-column mode CGA for emphasis, or switch between CGA graphics and Monochrome text if you're using two displays. Turbo C provides a simple technique to switch to a text mode: Use function

void textmode(int Mode)

where **Mode** = 0,1,2,3,7. You can use a **ConIO** constant for the mode: **textmode(C40)** will switch to 40-column CGA color text. You can also use the parameter value **Mode = LASTMODE** = -1 to return to the previous text mode. This procedure always clears the screen, selects the full screen as default window, and moves the cursor to the top left corner. If the appropriate equipment isn't present, it apparently has no effect.

Sometimes you may need to ascertain what mode is currently active, as well as other display information. Partial information is supplied by the **ConIO** function

void gettextinfo(struct text_info *T)

You must allocate sufficient memory for the **text_info** structure *T, defined in **ConIO.H** as follows:

```
struct text_info {
    unsigned char winleft;       /* Current window boundaries. */
    unsigned char wintop;
    unsigned char winright;
    unsigned char winbottom;
    unsigned char attribute;        /* Current and normal text */
    unsigned char normattr;                  /* attributes. */
    unsigned char currmode;            /* Current mode. */
    unsigned char screenheight;       /* Number of rows. */
    unsigned char screenwidth;      /* Number of columns. */
    unsigned char curx;         /* Current cursor position rel- */
    unsigned char cury; };     /* ative to the current window. */
```

(Items **attribute** and **normattr** are the attribute codes corresponding to foreground and background colors, intensity, underline, and blink, described in Section 4.2.)

Turbo C provides two functions for identifying installed display controllers. The first is primitive: function

int biosequip(void)

declared in header file **BIOS.H**, returns a word, bits 4,5 of which designate the video mode activated during booting:

Value in bits 4,5	Mode	Turbo C constant
1	0	**BW40**
2	2	**BW80**
3	7	**MONO**

You can inspect the value stored in these bits by executing

(biosequip() & 0x30)) >> 4

It's generally safe to use the corresponding mode. (**biosequip** obtains this value via a BIOS service; the BIOS obtained it by reading some motherboard switches, and stored it somewhere for later reference. That reference value can in fact be changed by misbehaving software.)

The second method for identifying a display controller actually specifies the equipment. Header file **Graphics.H** includes the prototype

void far detectgraph(int far *Controller, int far *Mode)

This function stores an integer in **Controller** as follows:

Controller value	Graphics.H Constant	Interpretation
-2		MDA (no graphics controller)
1	**CGA**	
2	**MCGA**	
3	**EGA**	EGA driving color display
4	**EGA64**	EGA with only 64K
5	**EGAMONO**	EGA driving monochrome display
6	**IBM8514**	
7	**HERCMONO**	Hercules Monochrome Graphics Card
8	**ATT400**	
9	**VGA**	
10	**PC3270**	

This function will not detect a Monochrome Adapter (MDA) installed *in addition* to a graphics controller. Turbo C TOOLS function **scequip**, described in Section 4.3, is sensitive to that, however. The list of controllers detected by **detectgraph** includes several boards developed more recently than the original MDA and CGA equipment. Two of these are described briefly later.

Caution: Unlike most Turbo C Library functions, **detectgraph** requires far pointer parameters. If you're using a small-data model, either construct far pointers explicitly or include **Graphics.H** so that the prototype forces implicit casting of near to far pointers. Otherwise your program will crash. This function returns no information about which text mode might be active. (Parameter **Mode** is used for another purpose.) To ascertain the current mode, use **gettextinfo**.

Hercules Monochrome and IBM Extended Graphics Adapters

Two display controllers have emerged as standards parallel to the CGA and Monochrome Adapter: the IBM Extended Graphics Adapter (EGA) and the Hercules Monochrome Graphics Card. Both are now imitated by several suppliers of compatible controllers. Neither Turbo C nor Turbo C TOOLS supports these controllers completely. As long as you are interested only in text output, it's not difficult to adapt a program to use all special text display features provided by the Hercules controller. Moreover, programs written for the CGA or Monochrome Adapter usually produce the same output with an EGA. Some additional EGA text display features are supported by Turbo C TOOLS, as described in Section 4.3, but others require some lower-level programming.

The Hercules Monochrome Card is the simpler one. Its main distinguishing feature is its ability to produce medium resolution graphics on display units compatible with the IBM Monochrome Display. Its graphics operation mode is totally incompatible with the CGA. However, in *text mode*, it is almost indistinguishable from the IBM Monochrome Adapter. All Monochrome Adapter features described above are identical in the Hercules Card, except for the number of text pages (displayable screen images). The IBM controller has only one, but the Hercules provides two. Virtually no commercial software makes use of the extra Hercules page, because it was originally very difficult for software to tell when a Hercules is installed. (Hercules Computer Technology has more recently publicized a suitable technique.)

The EGA is an extremely complicated device. Its properties vary with the amount of display buffer memory included; fortunately, only the original IBM models are commonly found with less than the full 256K. Fully equipped clones are now readily obtainable at a fraction of the original IBM price. The main EGA attraction is its ability to produce monochrome or multicolor medium resolution graphics on display units compatible with the IBM Monochrome, Color, and Enhanced Color Displays. Various EGA operating modes imitate all functions of the IBM Monochrome and CGA Adapters, extending them somewhat. You should note the following EGA extensions of features described earlier:

- 80x43 text screen mode.
- You may add 256 custom characters to the ASCII/IBM set.
- You may split the text screen into independent upper and lower screens.
- Multiple text pages are available.

Some additional enhancements are noted in later sections.

As mentioned earlier, neither Turbo C nor Turbo C TOOLS completely supports the EGA. Several programming techniques required to take advantage of new EGA text features are described in Chapter 8. Note, however, that the PC BIOS screen output service routines described there are automatically replaced by new ones when an EGA is installed.

Thus, to do any programming for the EGA, you will almost certainly have to consult the EGA reference material contained in the *IBM PC Technical Reference: Options and Adapters* manual, Reference [21], and in the *IBM Personal Computer Seminar Proceedings,* Reference [13]. Since these manuals are often unclear, some experimentation will be necessary, too. References [23] and [32] may also be helpful.

Using TCInst.Exe to select display type

When you use Turbo C program **TCInst.Exe** to install your Turbo C compiler, it lets you choose the default display mode, one of the CGA modes, or the Monochrome mode. If you choose the default mode, the compiler and its compiled programs will always adjust themselves to whatever controller is present. Otherwise, both compiler and compiled programs will assume that a specific adapter is present, and they will not run on the other. Thus, if your software must run on systems with either type of display controller, you should select the default screen mode. Use **textmode** or the more elaborate Turbo C TOOLS routines only when you must switch modes, or do something infeasible with the standard controllers.

Caution: A composite monochrome display's response to a color mode depends on the model. Sometimes characters lose readability. Determining whether color software you're developing will also work with a composite monochrome monitor requires experimentation.

4.2 Display buffer and attributes

Concepts

Changing text color and background
Display buffer
Text attributes
Direct display buffer access
Copying screen rectangles
Snow
Display pages

Section 4.1 concentrated on techniques for *positioning* text displays. This section introduces the problems of controlling their color and other *attributes,* and considers as well some situations in which position and attribute interact. Several Turbo C attribute control functions are described. Some experience with color text display poses the following question: Should attributes like color be associated with the text itself, or with the screen locations where it will be displayed? Both alternatives are common. Text editors commonly associate attributes with specific text items, no matter where they appear on the screen. Data entry routines, however, often use color to distinguish the roles of different screen areas, independent of the text to be placed there. Turbo C takes the former approach.

To consider display attributes, you must be familiar with the display buffer format. It's described in detail here, and an example program shows how to output information directly to it. For some video controllers, direct buffer access can degrade display quality; a solution to that problem is mentioned in this section but treated in detail later. Turbo C provides only rudimentary control over screen attributes. Sophisticated attribute manipulation is made feasible by Turbo C TOOLS routines discussed in Section 4.3.

Turbo C text attributes

Turbo C provides six functions for setting output text attributes:

void lowvideo()	void textcolor(int C)
void highvideo()	void textbackground(int B)
void normvideo()	void textattr(int A)

Each applies an attribute to all subsequent screen output.

Functions **lowvideo** and **highvideo** assign low- or high-intensity foreground attributes to subsequent **ConIO** screen output. (Output from **StdIO** functions is unaffected.) **normvideo** reestablishes the attribute active when the program started. The Turbo C startup routine ascertains that information when it switches to the screen mode specified by the **TCInst** program. This causes the BIOS to clear the screen, and Turbo C observes what attribute was used. To produce reverse video, blinking, and underlining—the other attributes available with the Monochrome Adapter—you must use the other routines, as follows:

Reverse video
textbackground(LIGHTGRAY)
Incompatible with underlining, except with EGA

Blinking
Low intensity—
   textcolor(LIGHTGRAY+BLINK)
High intensity—
   textcolor(WHITE+BLINK)

Underlining
Low intensity—
   textcolor(BLUE)
High intensity—
   textcolor(LIGHTBLUE)
With blinking—add
   BLINK to the color
Incompatible with re-
verse video, except
with EGA

The color name constants and **BLINK**, defined as macros in header file
ConIO.H, are described later. Program **MonoAttr.Dem** in Figure 4.2.1
illustrates several of these features. You should modify it to check the
other attributes.

Some features of this program seem reasonable, but **LIGHTBLUE?**
This curiosity stems from the Color/Graphics Adapter (CGA) screen
attribute codes. The Monochrome Adapter codes were designed for CGA
compatibility. To understand what's going on, it's best to consider the
organization of the display buffers in these adapters.

```
/*******************************************************************/
/* MonoAttr.Dem    Demonstrate monochrome display attributes. */
/*******************************************************************/

#include <ConIO.H>

void main() {
  lowvideo();              cputs("ABC");      /* Low intensity. */
  highvideo();             cputs("DEF");      /* High intensity.*/
  textcolor(BLUE);         cputs("GHI");      /* Underline.     */
  textcolor(LIGHTBLUE);    cputs("JKL"); }    /* High intensity */
                                              /* with underline.*/
```

Output

ABCDEFGHIJKL

Figure 4.2.1 Program **MonoAttr.Dem**

Display buffer

A *display buffer* is part of the PC main memory, physically located in the display controller, which contains an exact encoded image of the display. The image reflects not only the displayed text, but its attributes as well. In fact, the buffer contains an attribute code for every character position on the screen. Thus, the attribute concept from the video controller standpoint is different from that associated with the Turbo C functions described earlier. An attribute is assigned to a screen position, independent of the text displayed there. The Turbo C functions, on the other hand, assign an attribute to text as it is output, independent of its ultimate position on the screen.

For text display, each screen position requires two bytes in the display buffer: one for the ASCII/IBM code of the displayed character, and one for the code of the attribute assigned that position. The Monochrome and CGA adapters support screens with either 80 or 40 text columns, and 25 rows. Consider the larger one; the smaller is handled similarly. This screen displays 80 x 25 = 2000 characters, so the buffer requires 2 x 2000 ≈ 4K bytes to store a screen image. (PC memory is installed in banks with multiples of 1K = 1024>1000 bytes; hence, there is some space left over. You can use it as you wish.) The screen codes are stored in the display buffer consecutively, row by row, from top left to bottom right. The first byte of a screen code, always stored at an even offset, is the character code; the attribute code follows. The 256 ASCII/IBM character codes and their screen images are tabulated in Appendix C. The next paragraphs give a detailed description of the attribute codes.

Text attribute codes

The text attribute code format, shown in Figure 4.2.2, was designed for the CGA and modified slightly for the Monochrome Adapter. For the CGA, interpreting this code is fairly simple. The character at the corresponding screen location blinks if the (high order) *blink bit* is set. Its background is one of eight colors that can be specified by the RGB *background bits*, and the color of the character itself is determined by the four *foreground bits*.

The 16 colors determined by the intensity, red, green, and blue bits IRGB can be described roughly in accordance with your intuition for color mixing:

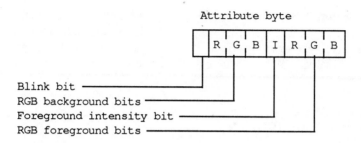

Figure 4.2.2 Text attribute format

IRGB	Hex	Dec	Color	
0000	0	0	**BLACK**	
0001	1	1	**BLUE**	
0010	2	2	**GREEN**	
0011	3	3	**CYAN**	Dark Colors
0100	4	4	**RED**	Foreground/
0101	5	5	**MAGENTA**	Background
0110	6	6	**BROWN**	
0111	7	7	**LIGHTGRAY**	
1000	8	8	**DARKGRAY**	
1001	9	9	**LIGHTBLUE**	
1010	a	10	**LIGHTGREEN**	
1011	b	11	**LIGHTCYAN**	Light Colors
1100	c	12	**LIGHTRED**	Foreground only
1101	d	13	**LIGHTMAGENTA**	
1110	e	14	**YELLOW**	
1111	f	15	**WHITE**	

These color names are defined in header file **ConIO.H** as constants (macros) with the appropriate values. Moreover, **BLINK** is a predeclared constant with value **128**.

With this information Turbo C functions **textbackground** and **textcolor** can be precisely described. The former requires a parameter B in the range 0..7 = **BLACK..LIGHTGRAY**. Executing **textbackground(B)** sets according to B the background RGB bits of the attribute bytes of all characters subsequently output to the screen. Function **textcolor** is slightly more complicated. It requires a parameter

C in the range 0..31, which determines five bits. Executing **textcolor(C)** sets according to **C** the blink, foreground intensity, and foreground RGB bits for all characters subsequently output to the screen. For example, to produce blinking blue characters on a brown background, use these statements:

textcolor(BLINK + BLUE)
textbackground(BROWN)

If you wish to assemble attribute byte **A** yourself from its background and foreground nybbles, you can set the attribute with a single function call **textattr(A)**.

The colors actually produced by a color display connected to a CGA depend on the technology. Some inferior models don't distinguish between the dark and corresponding light colors. The response of a monochrome display attached to the CGA composite video output is somewhat unpredictable, too. Making color software produce attractive output on various displays requires experimentation.

This discussion of screen attribute codes has so far been confined to the CGA Adapter. The codes are interpreted slightly differently by the Monochrome Adapter. The blink bit is handled similarly. The various attributes are produced as follows:

	Background		Foreground	
	Color	RGB	IRGB	Color
Invisible	BLACK	000	0000	BLACK
Underline	BLACK	000	0001	BLUE
Normal (**lowvideo**)	BLACK	000	0111	LIGHTGRAY
High Intensity Underline	BLACK	000	1001	LIGHTBLUE
High Intensity (**highvideo**)	BLACK	000	1111	WHITE
Reverse Video	LIGHTGRAY	111	0000	BLACK

As you see, the major difference in interpretation is that foreground color **BLUE** means *underline* to the Monochrome Adapter. This underlies the choice of color codes in program **MonoAttr**. The remaining background and foreground codes are interpreted more or less reasonably by the Monochrome Adapter, although there are some "unexpected features." The exact interpretation of each attribute code is detailed in Appendix C of the IBM PC *Technical Reference* manual, Reference [20]. You may need to consult that table to build software that produces attractive output on both the CGA and Monochrome Adapter.

With the CGA, it's possible to trade the blink feature for the availability of light background colors by sending the appropriate code to CPU port hex 3d8, which is connected to the CGA Control Register. This is an unexpectedly delicate operation because you must send a whole byte, whose other bits reset other CGA parameters. The problem is that you can't *read* the previous settings, so you can't restore them when your software is done. Refer to your adapter's technical reference manual for details. On the EGA, this operation is simpler, and is implemented by Turbo C TOOLS function **scblink**, described in Section 4.3.

The EGA also allows you to select which 16 of its 256 possible colors are produced on the screen. The CGA color list given earlier is merely the *standard EGA palette*, or color map. Turbo C TOOLS functions described in Section 4.3 allow you to change that at will. (Of course, you will no longer use the intuitive IRGB interpretation of the bits of the color code.)

Direct display buffer access

Sometimes you want to move data to and from the display buffer directly, without DOS or BIOS intervention. For example, you may need to preserve a copy of some portion of the screen in order to restore it later. You can do this with Turbo C absolute addressing techniques, described earlier in Section 2.1, provided you know these display buffer segment addresses:

Display buffer segment address
Monochrome Adapter   hex b000
Color/Graphics Adapter   hex b800

IBM chose different addresses to permit simultaneous installation of both adapters, thus supporting simultaneous text and graphics displays. Program **CharSet.Dem** in Figure 4.2.3 illustrates this technique. First, it fills the entire screen with blanks in reverse video. Then, it displays all 256 ASCII/IBM character codes in normal video starting at top left. Even the four control characters ASCII 7,8,10,13 (BEL,BS,LF,CR) that function **putch** will not display are visible. This version of the program is for a Monochrome Adapter. Change the constant **Buffer** to **0xb800** to run it with a CGA.

```
/****************************************************************/
/* CharSet.Dem    Demonstrate direct output to the monochrome*/
/*               display buffer.  Display all  256  ASCII/  */
/* IBM  characters.  First fill the screen with reverse video */
/*************************************** blanks, then display*/
                                        /* the characters in   */
#include <General.H>                    /* normal video, start-*/
                                        /* ing at top left.    */
#define Columns   80                    /************************/
#define Rows      25
#define Size      Columns*Rows          /* Buffer dimensions.  */
#define Segment   0xb000                /* Buffer segment.     */
#define Reverse   0x70                  /* Text attribute      */
#define Normal    0x07                  /* codes.              */

void main() {                          /* Make a far pointer   */
  int far *Buffer = MK_FP(Segment,0);  /* to the buffer.       */
  int I;
for (I = 0; I <= Size; Buffer[I++] = Reverse<<8 | Blank);
for (I = 0; I <= 0xff; Buffer[I++] = Normal <<8 | I    ); }
```

Figure 4.2.3 Program **CharSet.Dem**

Turbo C provides three functions that let you avoid some of the detail required for direct display buffer access:

int gettext(int SourceTop,   int SourceLeft,
             int SourceBottom,   int SourceRight,
             void *Target)

int puttext(int TargetTop,   int TargetLeft,
             int TargetBottom,   int TargetRight,
             void *Source)

int movetext(int SourceTop,   int SourceLeft,
             int SourceBottom,   int SourceRight,
             int TargetTop,   int TargetLeft)

Function **gettext** copies data from a screen rectangle to a memory array. The rectangle is specified by the coordinates of its top left and bottom right corners. Both character and attribute codes are copied, so you must have allocated to the memory array twice as many bytes as the number of characters in the rectangle. The screen data are stored in the target array row by row, and within a row, each character code is followed by the corresponding attribute. Function **puttext** performs the reverse copying operation, and **movetext** copies from one screen rectangle to another. These functions are supposed to return 1 to report success; if any rectangle coordinate parameter is invalid, they are supposed to abort and return 0. (In Version 1.5, however, **puttext** always attempts the copy and returns 1. If you specify a rectangle that extends beyond the screen, **puttext** will overwrite memory adjacent to the display buffer.) Program **PutText.Dem** in Figure 4.2.4 demonstrates all three routines, constructing a circular design from a small screen rectangle. Its output depends on what that rectangle contains when the program is executed; in the case pictured it consisted of part of the DOS prompt and the command line (outlined). (Incidentally, the constant **M_PI** used in this program has the value π; it's defined as a macro in header file **Math.H**.)

Snow

If you modify the display buffer segment address and run program **CharSet.Dem** with a CGA adapter, you may notice screen "snow." This is caused by a poor IBM design. In short, when the CPU is moving data to the display buffer, various bits are briefly altered and restored in the memory update cycle. Unfortunately, while scanning the buffer to update the display, the adapter finds these bits in the altered state, and reproduces that on the screen. The fault has been corrected in many display controllers compatible with the CGA. Nevertheless, to avoid this ugly effect on thousands of machines, you may want to use a more sophisticated method. That involves waiting to access the buffer only when the display is turned off during retrace periods while the electron beam moves from the right end of one scan line to the left end of the next, or from the bottom line back to the top. Implementing this method requires inputting from a CPU port attached to a CGA register to detect when the display turns off, then moving data to or from display memory as fast as possible (normally using assembly language) during the retrace period.

If you selected the appropriate option while installing Turbo C with the **TCInst.Exe**, your compiled programs will always wait for retrace

```
/*****************************************************************/
/* PutText.Dem     Demonstrate functions  gettext, puttext,   */
/**************************************** and   movetext.      */
                                        /* Copy a small screen */
#include <Math.H>                       /* box into a memory   */
                                        /* array with gettext  */
#define DX  7     /* Box dimen-  */     /* then reproduce it  N*/
#define DY  1     /* sions, -1.  */     /* times with  puttext */
#define XC 40     /* Center of   */     /* in a circular pat-  */
#define YC  8     /* circle.     */     /* tern. Use  movetext*/
#define N  10                           /* to copy the last one*/
                                        /* into the center.    */
void main() {                           /*********************/
  int Box[(DX+1)*(DY+1)];
  int   I,X,Y;
  float T;
gettext(1,2,1+DX,2+DY,Box);             /* Screen to array.    */
for (I = 0; I < N; ++I) {               /* Step around circle. */
  T = 2*M_PI*I/N;                       /* Angle.              */
  X = XC*(1+0.5*cos(T));                /* X  and  Y  coordi-  */
  Y = YC*(1+0.5*sin(T));                /* nates of new box.   */
  puttext(X,Y,X+DX,Y+DY,Box); }         /* Array to screen.    */
movetext(X,Y,X+DX,Y+DY,XC,YC);          /* Copy last to center.*/
getch(); }                              /* Pause for snapshot. */
```

Output

```
┌────────┐
│DESQview│12:33 Sat   6-04-1988 D:\
│puttext │
└────────┘
                         DESQview    DESQview
              DESQview   puttext     puttext    DESQview
              puttext                           puttext
              DESQview
              puttext                DESQview              DESQview
                                     puttext               puttext
              DESQview                                 DESQview
              puttext    DESQview    DESQview  puttext
                         puttext     puttext
```

Figure 4.2.3 Program **PutText.Dem**

periods when accessing the display buffer directly with **ConIO** functions. A Turbo C TOOLS routine described in Section 4.3 also implements this strategy. On the other hand, if you use your own routines for direct access, you may have snow unless you wait explicitly for retrace periods. You can use the Turbo C Library or Turbo C TOOLS source code as a guide.

Scrolling the screen display requires extensive data shuffling in the display buffer. To avoid the resulting snow produced by a CGA, the BIOS scrolling routine determines whether it's using one, and if so, turns it off during scrolling. That produces the characteristic scrolling blink. To IBM, this was the lesser evil. The blink persists even with a compatible video controller properly designed to avoid the snow, unless it uses a technique described in Chapter 9 to replace the BIOS screen output service routine.

The Hercules Monochrome Graphics Card also produces snow, especially when it displays large reverse video areas. While the snow removal methods just described work for the Hercules card, neither Turbo C nor Turbo C TOOLS implements them in that case.

Display pages

Most video controllers have more display buffer memory than the 4K required for an 80x25 text screen. This provides room for multiple text *pages:* screen images that can be displayed alternatively. For example, the CGA has 16K (the minimum necessary for a 640x200 monochrome graphics display), providing four 80x25 or eight 40x25 text pages. You can instruct these controllers which page to display at any time. Turbo C does not directly provide techniques for that, but they are included in Turbo C TOOLS, as described in Section 4.3. The Hercules Monochrome Graphics Card provides two pages, but neither Turbo C nor Turbo C TOOLS supports that feature.

4.3 Screen handling with Turbo C TOOLS

> **Concepts**
>
> Turbo C TOOLS screen output features; coordinate system
> Identifying display equipment and its mode
> Switching between color and monochrome displays and modes
> EGA 43 row modes
> Controlling multiple screen pages
> Adjusting border color
> Vertical and horizontal scrolling
> Cursor location and appearance
> EGA palette and blinking
> Setting attributes and characters independently
> Drawing screen boxes
> TTY output in a rectangle with word wrap
> Screen output speed comparisons
> Reading from the screen

The Turbo C screen handling features described earlier in this chapter fall far short of what you need for really polished programs. Particularly lacking are facilities for

- ascertaining display controller status details,
- controlling certain display features,
- using multiple display pages,
- associating display attributes with screen locations independent of the displayed text,
- reading text from the screen,
- keeping track of multiple screen windows.

You need the first three of these to utilize the full capability of your equipment. The last three are particularly important for using the display effectively in interactive programs.

Turbo C TOOLS meets most of these requirements. It has a general screen handling unit, and one devoted to window manipulation. In the present section you will find a detailed survey of the general techniques; windowing is considered in Section 4.4. In all cases the relationship of the Turbo C TOOLS routines to features already present in Turbo C is discussed, and several example programs are provided.

Figure 4.3.1 lists most of the Turbo C and Turbo C TOOLS general screen handling routines according to their function. Related routines are grouped together, or in analogous locations. No window handling routines are listed, because they are discussed in the next section. In fact, this reveals a major difference between the Turbo C and Turbo C TOOLS routines shown here: Turbo C routines observe current window boundaries set by the **window** function; these particular Turbo C TOOLS routines ignore windows. Another pervasive difference is that Turbo C does not support multiple display pages. All relevant Turbo C TOOLS routines do; this is explained later. The figure shows an unfortunate feature of this part of Turbo C TOOLS: chaotic, forgettable function names.

Another, rather unfortunate, difference between the Turbo C and Turbo C TOOLS routines is their coordinate systems. Turbo C uses the

Type	Turbo C Screen Functions			Turbo C TOOLS Screen Functions		
Equipment, mode	biosequip textmode gettextinfo detectgraph			scequip scchgdev	scnewdev	scmode scrows
Page control				scpages b_curpage [1]	scpage scapage	
Entire screen	clrscr	insline delline		scpclr scborder	viscroll vihoriz	
Cursor control	wherex wherey	gotoxy		sccurst viptr	sccurset	scpgcur
Attributes	textcolor textbackground textattr	lowvideo highvideo normvideo		scpall scpalett	viatrect	scblink
Text output	putch cputs cprintf	clreol	puttext movetext	scttywrt scttywin scwrap vidspmsg	scclrmsg scattrib scwrite	scbox viwrrect
Screen input	gettext			scread		virdrect

[1] Global variable

Figure 4.3.1 Turbo C and Turbo C TOOLS general screen handling routines

Borland X,Y coordinate system: X is the column coordinate, Y is the row coordinate, and the top left corner has coordinates 1,1. Turbo C TOOLS uses a reverse system: Row,Column coordinates are listed in that order, and the top left corner has coordinates 0,0. (Turbo C TOOLS is in fact the older product—it's descended from a package originally designed for use with Microsoft Pascal. It maintains the Row, Column 0,0 convention because of the large number of users it inherited from earlier versions. The Row,Column order agrees with the Microsoft BASIC language, and the 0,0 location with the BIOS specifications. Borland's choice of the X,Y order clearly makes more sense, while its 1,1 convention is debatable.) The difference between coordinate systems is particularly troublesome if you need to use functions from both sets in the same program. Since the Turbo C TOOLS package includes its source code, you could easily modify its screen functions, however, to make the coordinate system agree with Borland's.

Some of the Turbo C TOOLS routines in Figure 3.4.1 begin with **sc..**; others, with **vi...** Their prototypes and related definitions are included in header files **BScreens.H** and **BVideo.H**. The former call on BIOS services for screen input/output; the latter access the display buffer directly. As you have seen with the Turbo C functions, direct access is much faster, but somewhat less portable. Later in this section, the speeds of the various output routines are compared.

Display equipment and mode

Five Turbo C TOOLS routines help you discover what display equipment is present, ascertain and set its mode, and change between color and monochrome displays:

scequip   **scnewdev**   **scmode**
           scchgdev   **scrows**

Although they are logically similar to Turbo C functions described in the previous section, you may find them a useful addition because they support a somewhat different selection of equipment and features. The functions are described in detail next; an example program is considered later, after the discussion of display pages.

Function **scequip** is logically straightforward but complex in detail. It answers five questions:

- Is a Monochrome Adapter present?
- Is a CGA present?
- Is an EGA present? Is it in a color or monochrome mode? How much memory is installed? How are its switches set?
- Is a Professional Graphics Controller (PGC) present? Is it in a CGA mode?
- What machine ID code is stored in your BIOS?

Here is the prototype:

char scequip(void)

The machine ID code is returned via the function value. See Section 2.1 for a list of the codes. To answer the remaining questions, **scequip** sets various global variables described in the Turbo C TOOLS manual, Reference [4].

Function **scequip** tests for a Monochrome Adapter by reading from the CPU input/output port used to ascertain and set the cursor location, then writing an invalid parameter there. It reads from the port immediately, then restores the original value. If **scequip** reads a value different from the one it wrote, the port must not be connected, and the Adapter is absent. Otherwise, it's present; because the test parameter is invalid, the cursor doesn't move. The CGA and PGA tests are similar. The EGA is detected and its mode ascertained via a BIOS service peculiar to that controller. (ROM on the EGA contains an extension of the BIOS. When you boot a machine with an EGA, the RAM copy of the BIOS video service routine address is changed from the one on your system board to the custom EGA routine. The interrupt mechanism for obtaining BIOS services is described in Chapter 8.) Finally, **scequip** obtains the machine ID from address f000:fffe as described in Section 2.1.

Various clones answer these questions like the real IBM products. When you use Turbo C TOOLS, you are trusting such a clone to respond like the IBM controller in *all* relevant ways!

The difficulty of ascertaining information about installed display controllers illustrates an IBM design flaw. The original PC design should have included a "display controller information" port. The original IBM display controllers should have responded to certain signals from the CPU by placing in this port codes that identify themselves and indicate the current mode of operation. The EGA design approaches this, but earlier controllers, from independent suppliers or IBM itself, are notoriously difficult for software to recognize.

Once you are sure what equipment is installed (or at least have enough information to proceed), you can use function

int scnewdev(int Mode, int Rows)

to select a display mode. Although two devices may be installed simultaneously, their mode repertoires may not overlap; thus this operation activates a unique device. The **Mode** parameter can specify an IBM text or graphics mode. The possible text modes are the same as those in the previous section:

Turbo C Mode	ConIO Constant	Description	
0	**BW40**	40x25	composite monochrome
1	**C40**	40x25	16 color[1]
2	**BW80**	80x25	composite monochrome
3	**C80**	80x25	16 color[1,2]
7	**MONO**	80x25	monochrome[2]

[1] With an EGA you can select a palette of 16 from 256 colors.
[2] With an EGA you can select 25 or 43 rows.

For the complete list of graphics modes supported by Turbo C TOOLS, see its reference manual [4]. Parameter **Rows** lets you specify 25 or 43 screen rows for EGA mode 3 or 7. (The 43-row option involves selecting the font and adjusting BIOS parameters that specify the number of rows for operations like scrolling, clearing the screen, and screen hardcopy. Ill-behaved software that doesn't obtain these parameters from the BIOS will continue operating on the top part of the screen only, as though it had just 25 lines.) Function **scnewdev** uses its return value as an error status code.

When **scnewdev** selects a new device, it sets various Turbo C TOOLS global variables. It identifies the device as color or monochrome if modes 0..3 or mode 7 is supported. At most one of each can be installed. After a device has been identified, you can use the simpler function

int scchgdev(int Device)

to change to it from another device. **Device** = 0 or 1 specifies a switch to the monochrome or the color device. The function value returns a status code.

Sometimes you may need to ascertain not only what display controller is active, but what state it's in. Turbo C TOOLS provides two functions for that purpose:

int scmode(int *Mode, int *Columns, int *VisiblePage)
int scrows (void)

Function **scmode** sets variables ***Mode, *Columns**, and ***VisiblePage** accordingly, and returns 0 or 1 to indicate that the controller is monochrome or color; **scrows** returns the number of rows.

There is no Turbo C nor Turbo C TOOLS routine to tell which mode of an inactive device was last active. You may be able to do that by reading input ports, if you can precisely identify the equipment and learn enough about it from its manuals.

You can turn a display on or off by outputting certain codes to a port. This operation is delicate: You must activate a mode when you turn the device on, so you must determine what mode to select. (It's possible to break some monitors by turning them on in the wrong mode.) There is no way to tell whether a display has been turned on or off: The information is not recorded in readable form. By inputting from a port you can tell whether it's off at least temporarily during a retrace period. Since this question is concerned with high-speed operation, it's normally relevant only in assembly language programming. Retrace period detection underlies the CGA snow prevention methods described in the previous section.

Display pages

Most video controllers have more memory than the minimum required for one *page*, or screenful, of text. For example, the CGA has 16K, which can store four pages of 80x25 text or eight pages of 40x25 text. In certain configurations, the EGA also stores multiple pages. Such controllers generally have some mechanism for regarding one page as active, or visible. To let you display one page while constructing another, software packages may provide a way to regard one page as *current*—i.e., the one you're now writing. The PC and EGA BIOS implement these concepts, and Turbo C TOOLS carries them over into C software. One function,

int scpages(void)

returns the number of pages available in the current display mode. (For the EGA, this depends not only on the mode, but on the amount of memory installed and the current number of screen rows.) Function **scmode**, described earlier, sets a parameter to identify the visible page. The Turbo C TOOLS global variable

extern int b_curpage

identifies which page is current, or writeable. You cannot easily ascertain the page that previously executing software was writing on: this variable is always initialized to page 0.

Turbo C TOOLS does not support the additional display pages available on the Hercules Monochrome Graphics card. With the techniques covered in this book, however, you should be able to extend page control to the Hercules device easily. See the Hercules manual for details.

Two additional functions,

int scapage(int VisiblePage)
int scpage(int WriteablePage)

allow you to change the visible and writeable pages. The first forces parameter **VisiblePage** to lie in the valid range, and returns the number of the page actually displayed. The second is implemented as a macro that simply assigns a value to the global variable **b_curpage**.

To compute the display buffer address of the character on the current (writeable) display page with specified coordinates, you can use this function:

char far *viptr(int Row, int Column)

It returns a null pointer to indicate any error.

Caution: While most Turbo C TOOLS functions operate on whatever page is currently writeable, there are some exceptions. Moreover, the

Turbo C screen output functions always write only on page 0. Choose your output functions carefully.

Figure 4.3.2 contains a program fragment illustrating the use of many of the Turbo C TOOLS screen handling routines just discussed. Suppose your system has Monochrome and EGA adapters connected to IBM Monochrome and Enhanced Color Displays. The figure shows the function calls for a program that starts on either display, switches to 40x25 color text, to 320x200 color graphics, to monochrome text, back to graphics, then back to the original display. It restores the original mode, number of lines, and visible page.

```
/******************************************************************/
/* Displays.Frg    Program fragment demonstrating use of two    */
/*                 displays.                                     */
/******************************************************************/

#include <BScreens.H>    /* Turbo C TOOLS header file        */
#define C40   1          /* 40x25   color text mode          */
#define Lo4   4          /* 320x200  4 color graphics        */
#define Mono  7          /* Standard  80x25  monochrome text */

int OldDevice,OldMode,OldColumns,OldVisiblePage,OldRows;
    :
OldDevice = scmode(&OldMode,              /* Record mode, visible*/
   &OldColumns,&OldVisiblePage);          /* page, and number of */
OldRows = scrows();                       /* rows.               */
if (scnewdev(C40,25)  == C40 ) {          /* Include code to pro-*/
    .... }                                /* duce a big title.   */
else puts("Can't do mode  1 !");
if (scnewdev(Lo4,25)  == Lo4 ) {          /* Code for  320x400  4*/
    .... }                                /* color graphics.     */
   else puts("Can't do mode  4 !");
if (scnewdev(Mono,25) == Mono) {          /* Code for standard   */
    .... }                                /* monochrome text.    */
   else puts("Can't do mode  7 !");
scchgdev(COLOR);                          /* Change to  COLOR    */
    :                                     /* device for graphics.*/
scchgdev(MONO );                          /* Change to MONO de-  */
    :                                     /* vice for more text. */
scnewdev(OldMode,OldRows);                /* Restore old device  */
scapage(OldVisiblePage);                  /* in proper state.    */
```

Figure 4.3.3 Turbo C TOOLS display switching technique

Routines that affect the entire screen

Several standard Turbo C routines affect the entire screen. The clear screen function **clrscr** is an obvious example, and the insert and delete routines **insline** and **delline** can also be mentioned because of the way they may rearrange the screen. (The text output functions **putch**, **cputs**, and **cprintf**, described in Section 4.1, could also be included by virtue of their scrolling effect, but they will be discussed later.)

Turbo C TOOLS expands this repertoire considerably, with routines

scborder   **scpclr**   **viscroll**
                                      vihoriz

The first function,

int scborder(unsigned Color)

lets you set the screen border in certain CGA and EGA modes. The **Color** parameter should be one of the **ConIO** color constants described in Section 4.2. On the EGA, the border color depends also on the palette selection, discussed later. The function value is an error status code. Although you can set the border color, there is no way to ascertain its current color — the controllers do not record that information in readable form.

The remaining entire-screen functions operate on whatever display page is current, but ignore any windows in effect. Function

void scpclr(void)

clears the current (writeable) page, filling the corresponding part of the display buffer with blanks, and normal white-on-black attribute codes. (If you want to retain the attributes already present or set a new one for the entire screen, you can use functions **scwrite** or **viscroll**, described later.)

Turbo C TOOLS includes both vertical and horizontal scrolling functions:

int viscroll(int Rows, int Attribute,
**   int Top, int Left, int Bottom, int Right,**
**   int Direction)**

int vihoriz (int Columns, int Attribute,
int Top, int Left, int Bottom, int Right,
int Direction)

You specify the number of rows or columns to scroll, the attribute to be assigned the new blank rows or columns, the boundary coordinates of the scrolling rectangle, and the scrolling direction. (Remember, Turbo C TOOLS screen coordinates differ from Borland's.) For your convenience, these direction constants are predefined as macros:

SCR_UP   = SCR_RIGHT = 0
SCR_DOWN = SCR_LEFT   = 1

If you specify 0 rows or columns to scroll, the functions clear the entire rectangle to blanks with the specified attribute. They adjust the boundary coordinates if necessary to fit within the screen. Each accesses the display buffer directly, bypassing the BIOS, and waits for retrace periods, if necessary, to avoid CGA snow. A pair of closely related window scrolling routines is demonstrated in Section 4.4.

Cursor control

The only standard Turbo C cursor control routines are **wherex** and **wherey**, which report its column and row coordinates, and **gotoxy**, which moves the cursor. Coordinates are specified relative to any Turbo C window in effect. These routines operate only on display page 0, even with a multipage display controller.

Turbo C TOOLS extends this positional control slightly: its corresponding routines **sccurst** and **sccurset** ignore any window, but operate on whatever display page is current. Remember, they use a coordinate system different from Borland's. Function

int sccurset(int Row, int Column)

is similar to **gotoxy(Column,Row)** except for two features. First, it operates on the current (writeable) page; you won't see the screen cursor move unless the writeable page is also visible. Second, it adjusts **Row** and **Column**, if necessary, to fit within the screen boundaries; its return value contains the new coordinates in the high and low bytes.

The effect of **wherex** and **wherey** is similarly relativized by function

int sccurst(int *Row, int *Column, int *Top, int *Bottom)

This reports in ***Row** and ***Column** the cursor position on the writeable page. The function also returns 0 or 1 to indicate whether the cursor on the visible page is on or off. Further, it reports the dimensions of the visible cursor (described later) in ***Top** and ***Bottom**. The third cursor control function,

int scpgcur(int Off, int Top, int Bottom, int Adjust)

sets the visible cursor dimensions, adjusting them, if desired, for certain CGA and EGA text modes, and turns it on or off. This function has no effect (not even on the visible page) unless the current page is visible.

The cursor *dimensions* are its top and bottom scan lines. This refers to the screen box, or dot matrix, in which a character is written. For the Monochrome Adapter, the box is 9 dots wide by 14 deep; its horizontal scan lines are numbered 0..13 from top to bottom. To use **scpgcur**, specify the top and bottom cursor scan lines. For example, the cursor fills the entire box if **Top,Bottom** = 0,13, and is a simple underscore for 13,13. For the CGA, the box is 8x8 and the scan lines are numbered 0..7. You obtain a simple underscore cursor with the CGA by specifying **Top,Bottom** = 7,7. This is simple enough unless you are writing software whose output should appear roughly the same with either Adapter. A CGA underscore cursor will appear in the middle of the character box if you switch to a Monochrome Adapter, and a cursor with top or bottom below line 7 may not look right with the CGA. (You have probably observed that with commercial software!) If you select the **Adjust** = 1 option, **scpgcur** will help solve this problem by proportionally adjusting scan line values if the current display device is using a 7 line box. Turbo C TOOLS recommends that you use one of the following dimension settings:

Appearance	Top	Bottom
Top line	0	1
Top half box	0	4
Full box	0	13
Bottom half box	8	13
Bottom line	12	13

These tools permit you to control the cursor appearance completely in your own software. Moreover, if you execute **sccurst** on entrance to your program and save the reported cursor information, then you can restore the cursor position and appearance with **scpgcur** when you leave.

Displaying text

In Sections 4.1 and 4.2 you have seen that the standard Turbo C text display routines specify characters and display attributes separately. Functions **textcolor, textbackground, textattr, lowvideo, highvideo**, and **normvideo** set foreground and/or background attributes that will apply to all ensuing text, which is displayed in TTY fashion by **putch, cputs**, or **cprintf**. Thus, attributes are associated with the text as it is produced. These routines observe window boundaries, but operate only on display page 0, even with a multipage display controller.

Turbo C TOOLS provides much greater flexibility. Its routines operate on whatever display page is current, but ignore any window. (Corresponding functions for use with windows are described in Section 4.4.) Display attributes may be associated with the corresponding characters as in **ConIO** output, or you may associate them with screen location, independent of the displayed text.

In concept, the simplest function is

int viatrect(int Top, int Left, int Bottom, int Right,
int Foreground, int Background)

It sets the attribute code as indicated for all positions in the specified rectangle of the current (writeable) page, adjusting the specified boundary coordinates, if necessary, to fit within the screen. **viatrect** returns the area, or number of character positions in the resulting rectangle.

Three other functions are concerned solely with attributes, but only for the EGA display controller. You can use functions **scpal1** and **scpalett** to change a single palette entry or the entire palette for its 16-color modes. Thus, you can choose for simultaneous display any 16 of its 256 possible colors. For the color codes and calling sequences of these functions, consult the EGA technical reference manual in Reference [21] and the Turbo C TOOLS manual, Reference [4]. The third routine,

int scblink(int Blink)

controls the function of bit 7 of the attribute byte in EGA color text modes. Specifying **Blink** = 1 restores the default setting: When this bit in an attribute byte is set, the corresponding character blinks. **Blink** = 0 makes that bit govern the background intensity: when bit 7 is set, the background of the corresponding character is intensified. With **Blink** = 0, you can select the background color from all 16 colors, not just the eight dark ones. The function value is used as a status code. Although you can set the current palette and blinking features, there is no way to ascertain their current status—the controllers do not record that information in readable form. (The 6845 chip in the CGA display controller also allows the trade-off between blinking and background intensity; however, function **scblink** works only with the EGA.)

The simplest Turbo C TOOLS functions that write characters are

int scattrib(int Foreground, int Background,
char Ch, unsigned N)
int scwrite (char Ch, unsigned N)

The first displays **N** copies of character **Ch** with the specified attribute, starting at the cursor position on the current (writeable) page. The second just writes **Ch**, preserving the attributes already assigned. There is no scrolling, and neither function checks against overwriting the end of the display buffer. They don't move the cursor.

Function **viwrrect** is a much more elaborate version of the Turbo C Library function **puttext**. It copies characters from a ***Source** array in memory to a rectangle on the current (writeable) display page, with several options. Here is its prototype:

int viwrrect(int Top, int Left, int Bottom, int Right,
char *Source,
int Foreground, int Background,
int Option)

The function adjusts the rectangle boundary coordinates, if necessary, to fit within the screen. The options are selected via the last three parameters:

Option 0   The ***Source** array contains only characters—no attribute bytes. Its length must match the rectangle dimensions. If **Foreground = Background = -1**, attributes within the rectangle will be left undisturbed. Otherwise, they are all filled with the specified foreground and background nybbles.

Option 1   ***Source** contains character/attribute pairs. Its length must match the rectangle dimensions, and the **Foreground** and **Background** parameters are ignored.

A related function is intended for displaying messages on single rows:

int vidspmsg(int Row, int Column,
                 int Foreground, int Background,
                 char *Message)

Actually, this is implemented as a macro: These two function calls are identical:

vidspmsg(Row,Column,Foreground,Background,Message)

viwrrect(Row,Column,Row,Column+strlen(Message)-1,
                 Foreground,Background,Message,0)

From this you can see two reasons for caution when using **vidspmsg**. First, it's clearly not useful for displaying strings that may extend over more than one screen row. Second, since the **vidspmsg** macro makes multiple references to its parameters, it is subject to side effect errors. (See Section 3.1.)

Program **ViSc.Dem** in Figure 4.3.4 demonstrates several of the Turbo C TOOLS routines just discussed: **viatrect**, **vidspmsg**, **sccurset**, and **scattrib**. The rhythm of this method of text display is evident: set the attributes of a screen rectangle, construct a string, display it using the attributes already present, and move the cursor independently. If you don't need the cursor for **scattrib** or **scwrite**, you can leave it in a more meaningful or less obtrusive place, or turn it off. You should experiment with alternatives to this output technique. If you use Turbo C **ConIO** output functions like **cprintf** in place of **vidspmsg**, you have to reset the attributes every time. **StdIO** functions like **printf** use the existing

```
/*****************************************************************/
/* ViSc.Dem        Demonstrate  Turbo C TOOLS  screen handling*/
/*                 functions.  First,  viatrect  changes the  */
/* bottom half of the screen to reverse video.  Next,         */
/* vidspmsg displays copies of each row number near the mar- */
/* gins as guides, using attributes already in place.  Final- */
/* ly,  scattrib displays ten copies of the character corres-*/
/* ponding to the row number, in high intensity, overlapping  */
/* the right margin.  Note that  ASCII  0,7..10,13  are not   */
/* interpreted as control characters, but displayed instead,  */
/****************************************** and the last five   */
                                         /* characters are lost */
#include <StdIO.H>                       /* off the end of the  */
#include <BScreens.H>                    /* screen.  There is no*/
#include <BVideo.H>                      /* scrolling.          */
                                         /***********************/
void main() {
  char Row,S[80];                        /* NORMAL = white.     */
  int  N;                                /* Black on white = re-*/
viatrect(13,0,24,79,BLACK,NORMAL);       /* verse video.        */
for (Row = 0; Row < 25; ++Row) {         /* Construct message,  */
  sprintf(S,"%2d%66d",Row,Row);          /* and display it.  -1 */
  N = vidspmsg(Row,6,-1,-1,S);           /* = save attributes.  */
  sccurset(Row,N+7);                     /* Move cursor.  10 cc.*/
  scattrib(NORMAL+INTENSITY,BLACK,       /* of character  Row,  */
  Row,10); }}                            /* very white on black.*/
```

Figure 4.3.4 Program **ViSc.Dem**

attributes, but are so slow that you can see the cursor move from character to character. Another alternative, Turbo C TOOLS function **scwrap**, is discussed later.

A sort of opposite to **vidspmsg** is function

int scclrmsg(int Row, int Column, int N)

This displays **N** blanks starting at the given position on the current (writeable) display page, retaining existing attributes. In effect, it clears a message written there previously, often in preparation for another. It does not move the cursor, and does not check whether the region to be cleared extends (in error) beyond the end of the display buffer.

A handy function, which Turbo C TOOLS, in fact, uses to construct window borders (see Section 4.4) is

int scbox(int Top, int Left, int Bottom, int Right,
**   int Type, char Ch, int Attribute)**

This draws a box around the specified rectangle on the current (writeable) page. The function simply returns an error code if the dimensions are invalid. The border is actually *within* the rectangle, so that the interior space usable for text is smaller by two rows and two columns. The specified attribute is applied to the border, not the interior. If **Type** < 0, the border is constructed from copies of character **Ch**. Otherwise, **Ch** is ignored and one of 16 box styles selected, using the ASCII/IBM box drawing characters. See the Turbo C TOOLS manual, Reference [4], for details.

Three final Turbo C TOOLS routines provide TTY output. The first,

int scttywrt(char Ch, int Foreground)

simply writes character **Ch** at the cursor location. It works only when the current (writeable) display page is also visible. The **Foreground** attribute is used only in graphics modes. In text modes, the attribute already assigned the character position applies. When scrolling occurs, the attribute of the new blank line is taken from that at the cursor location when the line feed occurred (the left-hand column if scrolling is caused by overflowing the bottom line). The remaining functions provide TTY output relative to a screen rectangle:

void scttywin(int Top, int Left, int Bottom, int Right,
**   char Ch, int Foreground, int Background,**
**   int ScrollForeground, int ScrollBackground)**

void scwrap (int Top, int Left, int Bottom, int Right,
**   int N, char *S,**
**   int Foreground, int Background,**
**   int Option)**

The first displays a single character, and you can specify attributes for both the character and any new blank line created by scrolling. Function **scwrap** displays a character string; words—substrings delineated by white space and the string ends—aren't split unless their length exceeds that of the rectangle. The **Option** parameter works like the one for function **viwrrect**, indicating that ***S** consists of characters or of character/attribute pairs. In the former case, **N** = 0 signifies that **S** is an ASCII Z-string; otherwise **scwrap** regards it as a character array. For both functions, a foreground or background parameter value -1 means to use the attribute nybble already present.

Screen output efficiency

A comparison of execution speeds for the various screen output methods is quite revealing. Figure 4.3.5 shows the time (seconds) required to fill the screen with copies of a single character. The same program—discussed later—was run on two machines: an original IBM PC with an original Hercules Monochrome Graphics Card, and a 10-MHz AT clone with an Everex EGA. The ranking of the methods was the same for both configurations: **StdIO** DOS output is slowest, and direct display buffer output of preformatted text rectangles is far faster. The speed-up factors between the two machines differ among the output methods, in a complicated way that's not easy to analyze. Evidently, the greatest improvement is witnessed by the slow DOS functions, which involve the most CPU processing. The fastest functions, however, experience the least improvement. They do the least formatting, so their speed is largely limited by that of the display controller memory, which didn't differ significantly between the two configurations.

These data imply that care in selecting fast screen output can bring great benefits—as much as a thousand-fold speed-up. However, some aspects of display performance are heavily dependent on the choice of display controller.

Here is a fragment of the program used to produce Figure 4.3.5:

```
for (K = 0; K < 80; S[K++] = '@'+I); S[80] = 0;
M = 50;
T = biostime(0,0);
for (K = 0; K < M; ++K)
  for (Row = 0; Row < 25; ++Row)
    vidspmsg(Row,0,7,0,S);
DT[I] = (biostime(0,0) - T)/(18.2*M) - DT[0];
```

It first constructs a string **S** for the Ith test—in this example, for timing function **vidspmsg**. Then it selects the number **M** of screenfuls of **S** to display, and reads the time **T**. The function displays **S** on each row, repeating the test **M** times. Finally, it reads the clock again, computes the elapsed time since time **T**, divides by **18.2** to convert to seconds, divides by **M** to get the average time, then subtracts a previously computed value **DT[0]** representing the loop overhead—the average time for the loop **for (K = 0; K < M; ++K)**. The result **DT[I]** is the average time reported in the figure. Function **biostime**, described in detail in Section 8.7, reports the time in *ticks*; there are approximately 18.2 ticks per second. (You will find the program on the accompanying diskette.)

Reading from the screen

Although the screen is not normally thought of as an *input* device, one routine may use it to store data to be processed by another, especially if

| | | Seconds | | |
| | | 4.77 MHz | 10 MHz | Speed-up |
Output function		PC Time	AT Time	Factor
printf		20.0	1.6	10
puts		20.0	1.6	10
scwrap	(pairs)	13.0	3.5	4
scwrap	(chars)	12.0	3.4	4
scttywin		12.0	3.2	4
scttywrt		5.3	1.0	5
puttext	(BIOS)	2.8	1.1	3
cprintf	(BIOS)	2.8	1.1	3
cputs	(BIOS)	2.7	1.1	2
cprintf	(direct)	0.87	0.14	6
cputs	(direct)	0.77	0.12	6
vidspmsg		0.15	0.048	3
scattrib		0.13	0.033	4
scwrite		0.13	0.027	5
viwrrect	(chars)	0.033	0.013	3
viwrrect	(pairs)	0.024	0.011	2
puttext	(direct)	0.022	0.011	2

Figure 4.3.5 Average execution times for screen output functions

the data just arrived through the user interface. For such situations, convenient and efficient screen *reading* routines are useful. The Turbo C Library includes one such function, **gettext**. It's limited to page 0, and reads the attributes as well as the text. Turbo C TOOLS provides two somewhat more flexible functions:

char scread(int *Foreground, int *Background)
int virdrect(int Top, int Left, int Bottom, int Right,
char *S, int Option)

The first simply returns the character at the cursor location on the current (writeable) page, and records the foreground and background attribute nybbles as well. It uses a BIOS service. The second routine accesses the display buffer directly, moving characters—or character/ attribute pairs, according to the **Option** selected—from the specified rectangle on the current (writeable) page into array **S**. You must have allocated **S** enough space for this. It returns the number of characters read.

4.4 Turbo C TOOLS screen windows

Concepts

Desk tops and screen windows
Turbo C TOOLS window concepts
Window descriptors
Descriptor list maintenance is transparent
Creating and displaying windows
Window output and scrolling
Ascertaining and changing window status
Removing and destroying windows
Demonstration program **WhirlWin.Dem**
Incompatibility with Turbo C Library window features

An effective design technique for an interactive user interface is emulation of a busy *desk top*. Screen areas correspond to documents on the desk. Those corresponding to documents in full view—not covered by others—function like *windows* through which you can see data "inside" your computer. A screen window is a little more flexible than the corresponding document, because text visible through the window can be changed more easily and rapidly than a document. Some software packages make more use of this flexibility than others. The design chosen for Turbo C TOOLS adheres rather closely to the desk top paradigm. You can understand it easily by thinking of a window as a document on your desk. The following descriptive paragraph is phrased in that way.

Before you can manipulate any document, you must instruct Turbo C TOOLS to make a *descriptor* for it. The descriptor format is not important yet; it will be discussed later. A document comes into existence only when its descriptor is created. You put a document on your desk by *displaying* it at a specified location. It may wholly or partially cover others already displayed. At any time, one document is regarded as *current:* it's the one you can work on. When you display a document, it becomes current, but you may change the current document to any other one. You may *remove* a document, *uncovering* any material that it alone obscured. If you remove the current document, you must designate another as current. Removing a document does not destroy it; you can redisplay it later, if you wish. Finally, you may *destroy* a document—this destroys its descriptor. You must remove it before destroying it, because removal requires the descriptor.

To become yet more familiar with the concepts underlying Turbo C TOOLS window techniques, read the previous paragraph again with the word *document* replaced by *window.* You should be comfortable with the notion of the current window, and what it means to *display, remove,* and *destroy* a window.

Turbo C TOOLS has elaborated the window paradigm, introducing some concepts that aren't mirrored on real desktops. First, it uses the page control technique described in the previous section to support windows on two devices with multiple screen pages (just like multiple desks). Second, each window has its own current cursor style and position, which you can change at will. These two concepts interact in the notion of *active* window: the only window on a given page that may display its cursor. Cursor display is not mandatory: the current style may be invisible. Moreover, the cursor is not displayed if any part of the active window is obscured by another one. A visible cursor is principally used to cue user input, so the active window concept really pertains to Turbo C TOOLS keyboard input features, discussed in the next chapter.

As a final elaboration, Turbo C TOOLS lets you output to obscured windows. On a real desktop, you have to uncover a document before writing on it. With some window management systems, a window must be *totally* visible before you can output to it. With Turbo C TOOLS, you can output to any window, any time. If your output window is even partially covered, however, you'll see no effect on the screen until all obscuring windows are removed. Moreover, you can designate any window as *delayed*, to postpone screen changes until you officially *update* it. (Even then, changes won't take effect until the window is totally uncovered.) This feature is particularly useful when window output results from a long computation, and immediate—hence partial—screen updating would appear disorderly. Delayed screen updating requires maintaining memory images of all screen windows, with machinery to keep track of their status compared to the screen.

Implementing all these features requires a tremendous amount of attention to detail. The Turbo C TOOLS window management unit is thus a major accomplishment. Its source code, exclusive of the general screen handling routines described in the previous section, is about 120 pages long! Using it, you benefit from years of experience, refined through several product generations.

Caution: The Turbo C TOOLS window management unit is unrelated to the rudimentary window handling features in Turbo C itself. Don't try to mix these methods!

Information pertaining to a screen window can be divided into three categories:

Static window
properties
Window dimensions
Border description
Cursor style
Default text attributes
Screen update delayed?

Properties affected by
window display, removal
Window location
Contents of obscured area
Pointers to previous and
  next windows
Is window wholly visible?

Dynamic window information
Cursor location
Is cursor off?
Current text, attributes

The first type is *static*: usually determined when you *make* a window—i.e., when you instruct Turbo C TOOLS to create a descriptor—and you don't ordinarily change it. Second, some information is determined only when you display a window, or display or remove one that obscures it. Finally, *dynamic* information changes *often* during window output. These categories correspond roughly, but not exactly, to the organization of the Turbo C TOOLS routines.

The window descriptor, a structure declared as type **BWINDOW** in the Turbo C TOOLS header file **BWindow.H**, records all this information except the last item noted. The current text and screen attributes are stored in the window's memory image. They are also present in the display buffer, unless covered by a more recently displayed window. Since the obscured information cannot be shown again until that window is removed, it's associated with the covering window. That is, every window descriptor contains a pointer to a memory buffer that stores the text, with attributes, that it covered when it was first displayed.

The window location is specified by the Turbo C TOOLS screen coordinates of its upper left corner. Its border can be omitted, constructed from any single character, or any reasonable combination of the single and double line IBM graphics character set. It may have top and/or bottom titles, centered or left or right justified. The border and titles can have any foreground/background attributes. The cursor style, as usual, is specified by its top and bottom scan lines.

For each display page, the descriptors of windows currently displayed are organized as a doubly linked list. The list order reflects that in which the windows were displayed. A window may obscure only windows displayed earlier. Windows may be removed in any order. When one is displayed or removed, earlier windows must be inspected to ascertain if their visibility status is changing. (Windows that are not wholly visible cannot be updated on screen, so a visibility flag is maintained as an entry of the window descriptor.) When you remove a window, Turbo C TOOLS can restore the obscured screen area in one step; but any later windows must then be redisplayed one by one from their memory images, to maintain screen consistency.

Figure 4.4.1 gives an overview of the Turbo C TOOLS window handling functions. Operations are listed in temporal sequence: from a window's creation and display, through manipulation of its contents, to its removal and destruction. The scopes of the operations progress in step from your program's data area, where window descriptors are created, to individual screen windows, to particular sites of window data manipu-

Operation	Scope				
	Program	Window	Rectangle	Row, col	Starting at cursor
Create	wncreate				
Status	wnerror wnsetbuf	wngetopt wnsetopt			
Display	wnredraw	wndsplay wnupdate			
Activate		wncursor wnselect			
Cursor				wncurmov [c]	wncurpos [c]
Attributes		wnattr [c]	wnatrblk	wnatrstr	
Text output				wnwrap [c] wnwrbuf [c]	wnprintf [c] wnwrstr [c] wnwrstrn wnwrtty [c]
Screen input				wnrdbuf [c]	
Scroll		wnhoriz [c] wnscroll [c]	wnscrblk		
Remove		wnremove			
Destroy	wndstroy				•

[c] Operates on the current window.

Figure 4.4.1 Turbo C TOOLS window functions

lation, and back to broader areas as a window disappears from the scene. Functions with superscript **c** in the figure operate on the current window, designated by **wnselect**. The routines are sensibly named, and their calling sequences consistently designed, except that four routines **wnatrblk**, **wnscrblk**, **wnatrstr**, and **wnwrstrn** require a parameter to specify which window is affected, instead of referring to the current one. Perhaps this reflects a change in programming staff rather than functionality.

About half of these routines, as well as some features of the window and border descriptor data structures, are used in the demonstration program **WhirlWin.Dem** in Figure 4.4.3. Thus, it's efficient to describe

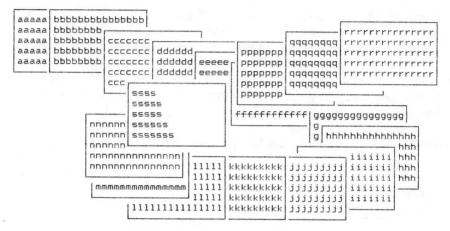

Figure 4.4.2 WhirlWin.Dem output

them in terms of that program. You'll find its source code and **.Exe** file
on the accompanying diskette. It was not possible to include the required
Turbo C TOOLS source code there, so you won't be able to alter the
program.

Before considering the individual routines, look at the output in Figure
4.4.2. **WhirlWin** creates and displays the windows in alphabetical order.
As soon as a window is displayed, it's filled with text in an eye-catching
way. After the last window is displayed and filled, only one other—
window **o** —is wholly visible. The program selects it as the current
window, and scrolls there an echelon **s** pattern, awaiting a keystroke.
The figure is a screen snapshot taken during that time. Next, every third
window **a,d,...,p** is removed. You can see in each case that obscured
earlier windows are restored instantly, but later ones are redrawn in
order. Finally, the remaining windows are cleared, removed, and destroyed in the order opposite that in which they were displayed: **r,q,...,a**.
The text is wiped away by smooth horizontal scrolling.

Program **WhirlWin.Dem** includes Turbo C TOOLS header file
BWindow.H, which in turn includes many other headers from that
package and the Turbo C Library. In particular, it includes prototypes
and definitions for the following routines that it uses:

clrscr delay getch kbhit max scpgcur

Some have been described or mentioned earlier. Functions **delay** and **max** have the obvious effect, and **kbhit** returns 0 unless a key has been pressed but not yet read by an input routine.

WhirlWin creates and manipulates **NW** = 18 windows. Window descriptors are structures of type **BWINDOW**, defined in **BWindow.H**. In the program, **W** is an array of pointers to **NW** of these descriptors. As you can see, to use function

BWINDOW *wncreate(int Height, int Width, int Attribute)

to build a window descriptor, you need only specify the dimensions and default foreground/background attribute byte. In this case, that is selected by the predefined macro **NORMAL**: normal monochrome video. The function allocates memory for the descriptor, and returns a pointer to it. Although border specification might seem to be appropriate, too, at this stage, Turbo C TOOLS allows alternate display of the same window with different borders, so you describe the border later.

```
/*******************************************************************/
/* WhirlWin.Dem   Demonstrate  Turbo C TOOLS  window hand-  */
/*                   ling.  Display and write in a series of  */
/* overlapping windows.  Change the current window, then re-  */
/* move windows in a scrambled order.  Demonstrate vertical  */
/* and horizontal scrolling.                                 */
/*******************************************************************/

#include <BWindow.H>            /* Includes other headers.  */
#define  NW       18            /* Number of windows.       */
#define  Height    5            /* Window height.           */
#define  ALittle  50            /* Delay length  (msec).    */

void main() {
    int    I,J;                       /* Loop indices.       */
    int    X,Y;                       /* Curve coordinates.  */
```

Figure 4.4.3 Program **WhirlWin.Dem** (*Continued on next page*)

```
float    T         = -0.25;              /* Curve parameter.    */
WHERE    Location = {MONO,0};              /* Device, page.   */
char     *S        = "aaaaaaaaaaaaaaa";    /* String to show.*/
int      Width     = strlen(S);            /* Window width.   */
BORDER   Border    = {1,NORMAL};          /* Type 1, norm. video.*/
BWINDOW *W[NW];                            /* Window pointers.    */
int      WhereIs;                          /* wngetopt response. */
clrscr();                                  /* Clear screen, loop  */
for (I = 0; I < NW; ++I) {                 /* through the windows.*/
  X = 52*T*(T-1)*(T-2) + 40;                 /* Curve equations*/
  Y = 18 - 10*(T-1)*(T-1);                   /* determine the  */
  Location.corner.col = max(X-Width /2,1);   /* window center. */
  Location.corner.row = max(Y-Height/2,1);   /* Create window, */
  W[I] = wncreate(Height,Width,NORMAL);      /* normal video.  */
  wnsetopt(W[I],WN_CUR_OFF,1);               /* Cursor off.    */
  wndsplay(W[I],&Location,&Border);          /* Border defined */
  for (J = 0; J < Height; ++J) {             /* earlier. Out- */
    wnwrbuf(J,0,0,S,-1,-1,CHARS_ONLY);       /* put a line, de-*/
    delay(ALittle); }                        /* lay to see it. */
  for (J = 0; J < Width; ++S[J++]);        /* Next string, parame-*/
  T += ( (T < 0) || (T > 2)                /* ter. Uneven steps  */
    ? 0.06 : 0.20 ); }                     /* for best appearance.*/
wnselect(W['o'-'a']);                        /* 'o' window.    */
for (I = 0; !kbhit(); I = (I+1)%Width) {     /* Loop until you */
  wnscroll(1,-1,-1,SCR_UP);                  /* hit a key:     */
  wncurmov(Height-1,0);                    /* Scroll up, keeping attri-*/
  wnwrstr(S+Width-I,-1,-1);                /* butes, and write a vary- */
  delay(ALittle); }                        /* ing amount of string S. */
getch();                                   /* Clear keyboard buffer.   */
for (I = 0; I < NW; I += 3) {              /* Remove every third window*/
  wnremove(W[I]);                          /* from bottom up. Wait for*/
  getch(); }                               /* a keystroke each time.   */
for (I = NW-1; I > 0; --I) {                /* Visit each window,  */
  wngetopt(W[I],WN_DEVICE,&WhereIs);         /* from top down. If   */
  if (WhereIs != ABSENT) {                   /* it's present, scroll*/
    wnselect(W[I]);                          /* it leftward.        */
    for (J = 0; J < Width; ++J) {            /* In any case, remove */
      wnhoriz(1,-1,-1,SCR_LEFT);             /* and destroy it. (No*/
      delay(ALittle); }}                     /* matter if it's not  */
    wnremove(W[I]);                          /* actually present.)  */
    wndstroy(W[I]); }                      /* Restore the cursor to   */
scpgcur(0,12,13,0); }                      /* normal for  MONO.       */
```

Figure 4.4.3 *(Continued)* Program **WhirlWin.Dem**

The **wncreate** routine does select a default cursor style (normal shape, cursor on). To change it, you need to change an item in the window descriptor structure. Function

BWINDOW *wnsetopt(BWINDOW *W, int Item, int Value)

serves this purpose. In **WhirlWin**, the appropriate item is designated by a constant **WN_CUR_OFF** defined as a macro in **BWindow.H**, and given the value **1** (true). This avoids distracting "cursor chaff." For further details about the **BWINDOW** structure, consult the Turbo C TOOLS manual, Reference [4].

To display a window with function

BWINDOW *wndsplay(BWINDOW *W, WHERE *Location,
                        BORDER *Border)

you must specify pointers not only to the window descriptor, but also to structures indicating the window's location and border type. The former is defined in two stages in **BWindow.H**:

```
typedef struct {
    int row,col; }        /* Turbo C TOOLS  screen coordinates. */
    LOC;
typedef struct {
    int dev;              /* Device = COLOR, MONO,  or  ABSENT. */
    int page;                          /* Display page number. */
    LOC corner; }        /* Top left corner, not including border. */
WHERE;
```

COLOR, MONO, and **ABSENT** are predefined Turbo C TOOLS macro constants. The last is used to indicate that the window is not displayed on any page of any device. In **WhirlWin** a single structure of type **WHERE** is declared, and its first two items initialized to **MONO** and page 0. The corner coordinates for each window are determined by evaluating parametric equations for points on a cubic curve. (Some experimentation led to the graceful appearance and convenient window locations in Figure 4.4.2.) The border descriptor structure, defined as type **BORDER** in **BWindow.H**, lists border design details, including box characters, title location and text, and box and title attributes. There are too many possibilities to catalog here; see the Turbo C TOOLS manual. A single **BORDER** structure is declared in this demonstration program, and its first two items initialized to specify border type 1, with the normal monochrome video attribute. No title is specified.

Turbo C TOOLS function

int wnwrbuf(int Row, int Column, int N, char *S,
        int Foreground, int Background, int Option)

writes characters from array **S** to the current window at the specified location with the specified attributes. (For some reason, the designer decided not to refer to the cursor for the location.) Valid **Option** values include the constant **CHARS_ONLY** used in this program, which indicates that **S** consists of just characters, no attributes. In that case, **N** = 0 tells the function that **S** is an ASCII Z-string. The foreground/ background parameter value -1 is used here to preserve the attribute bytes already present in the window. There are several further options concerning the structure of **S** and placement of the cursor after the operation. See the Turbo C TOOLS manual for details. This function does *not* support TTY output. Control characters are merely displayed. The output string wraps from the end of one row to the beginning of the next. Output is terminated at the end of the window; there is no scrolling. (Some TTY window output functions are described at the end of this section.)

Short delays are inserted in **WhirlWin** after all screen output operations. Otherwise, you might not catch the action! After each window is displayed, each character in string **S** is incremented to obtain the next letter, and the curve parameter is incremented as well. The latter adjustment was determined experimentally for best visual effect.

The next phase of WhirlWin uses the simple function

BWINDOW *wnselect(BWINDOW *W)

to select the 'o' window as current, then repeatedly scrolls up one row, clearing the bottom line, and writes a tail end of the string **S**, achieving a rolling echelon effect. It uses functions

BWINDOW *wnscroll(int N, int Foreground, int Background,
        int Direction)
BWINDOW *wncurmov(int Row, int Column)
BWINDOW *wnwrstr(char *S, int Foreground,
        int Background)

The first scrolls **N** rows; the direction may be given by one of the predefined constants **SCR_UP, SCR_DOWN**. The foreground/background attributes apply to the new blank line. The second function moves the cursor. *Caution:* This function, or perhaps other Turbo C TOOLS window management functions, seems to interfere with Turbo C **ConIO** cursor handling. Don't try to mix the techniques! Function **wnwrstr** writes string **S** at the cursor location with the specified attributes. For each function, an attribute parameter value -1 indicates that attributes already present should be preserved.

To demonstrate removal of windows that may be partially obscured, **WhirlWin** removes windows **a,d,g,...,p,** using function

BWINDOW *wnremove(BWINDOW *W)

After each operation, the program awaits a keystroke, so that you can observe the commotion on screen: in each case, obscured earlier windows are restored instantly, but later ones are redrawn in succession. In the final phase, **WhirlWin** visits each window in turn, starting from the end. First, it ascertains whether the window is present by calling function

BWINDOW *wngetopt(BWINDOW *W, int Item, int *Value)

This is the reverse of **wnsetopt**. The **BWINDOW** item in question is **WN_DEVICE**; its value is stored in variable **WhereIs**. In most cases, the window is scrolled horizontally, using function **wnhoriz**, analogous to **wnscroll**; but if **WhereIs = ABSENT**, this step is skipped to save time. In any case, the window is removed. (Note that removing an absent window has no ill effect.) At last, the window descriptor is destroyed— its memory released—by function

int wndstroy(BWINDOW *W)

As a finishing touch, **WhirlWin** must restore the cursor, because it was turned off during execution. A more sophisticated program would have called function **sccurst** at the beginning to ascertain the current cursor status. This one, however, takes that information for granted, and directly executes **scpgcur(0,12,13,0)** These parameters specify cursor *on,* top and bottom scan lines **12,13** (monochrome underscore), and no adjustment for color display.

In the previous discussion, return values of several functions were incompletely specified. Usually they return status information. If a window handling function detects an error or other abnormal situation during execution, it sets a Turbo C TOOLS global error code variable, proceeds if the situation is harmless, or else aborts. If its type permits, it may return the error code as well. More often, however, it must simply signal the calling program to inspect the error code variable. Most frequently, the function normally returns a pointer, and uses a null pointer to indicate an error. You can inspect and reset the error code variable by executing function

int wnerror(int NewCode)

This returns the code for the error reported most recently, and sets the error code value equal to **NewCode**. For a complete error code list, see the Turbo C TOOLS manual.

Turbo C TOOLS includes a considerable repertoire of window handling functions beyond those already discussed. This paragraph gives a brief overview of most of those intended for common use. For details, consult the Turbo C TOOLS manual. First, there are three TTY text output functions: **wnwrtty** outputs a single character, **wnprintf** mimics **printf** output, and **wnwrap** outputs a string with word wrapping. Three functions are concerned solely with display attributes: **wnattr** will change the default foreground/background attribute for a window; **wnatrstr** outputs a string of attribute bytes (analogous to **wnwrbuf**); and **wnatrblk** lets you reset the attributes of a rectangle within a window. This last function is related to **wnscrblk**, which scrolls such a region. You can use **wncursor** to activate the cursor in a window (excluding other windows on the same page), and **wncurpos** to ascertain the cursor position for the current window. Cursor manipulation often is involved with screen input. You can read from a window into a buffer in memory using function **wnrdbuf**—an inverse of the function **wnwrbuf** used in **WhirlWin**. If screen input, delayed updating, or intervention of other software makes your screen inconsistent with window images in memory, you can use function **wnupdate** to update a particular window (provided it's wholly visible), or **wnredraw** to redraw an entire page. (Many lower-level functions are involved in the implementation of these functions. While unmentioned in the manual, those are thoroughly documented in the source code, and could prove very useful.)

5

Keyboard Input

Contents

Beginning programmers, especially those who start on timesharing systems, usually visualize keyboard input as the process in which they type values for certain variables, verify their work on the screen, use the backspace key as necessary to permit error correction, then touch the enter key to send presumably valid input to their program. In fact, this is a composition of three processes: keyboard handling, screen display, and simple editing. To acquire real facility in keyboard input programming, you should separate these notions.

Screen manipulation techniques have been discussed already in the previous chapter. Keyboard input editing is generally simple, and some of the keyboard handling routines described in this chapter take care of it automatically. The first three sections of this chapter are devoted mostly to low-level keyboard handling. The only real complications are due to the lack of uniformity and robustness of the Turbo C Library functions that support keyboard input. They are generally unsuitable for programming interactive user interfaces. Several more convenient and reliable Turbo C TOOLS input routines are described in Section 5.3. Techniques for invoking memory resident software through *hot keys* are postponed until Chapter 9.

In Section 5.4, screen display and keyboard input are brought together again in a discussion of high-level keyboard input: the powerful and comprehensive Turbo C TOOLS *menu handling* features. With these and the lower-level Turbo C TOOLS keyboard routines, you will be able to handle almost any interactive input situation with grace and efficiency.

5.1 Turbo C keyboard input

Concepts

Underlying DOS services
Choosing input functions
ConIO keyboard input functions
Pushback functions
Extended ASCII keystroke codes
Input echoing
Detecting whether keyboard input is ready
StdIO keyboard input functions
DOS keyboard input editing features
cscanf and **scanf** garbage in input buffers
Flushing the input buffer
<Ctrl-Z> disrupts input control

This section describes the Turbo C Library keyboard input functions, concentrating on their inadequacy. In fact, they are hardly useful for interactive input/output. Complete keyboard control requires features of a product like Turbo C TOOLS, covered in later sections.

There are three sets of Turbo C Library keyboard input functions, listed below with the header files that contain their prototypes:

Input	StdIO.H		ConIO.H	
Push back	ungetc		ungetch	
Character	fgetc	fgetchar	getch	getche
	getc	getchar		
Ready?			kbhit	
String	fgets	gets	cgets	getpass
Formatted	fscanf	scanf	cscanf	

The **StdIO** functions in the left-hand column are designed mainly for file input. They require a parameter to identify the file, and use DOS file input services. Since DOS has a standard file name for the keyboard, they can be used for keyboard input, but that's unusual. Those functions are described later, in Chapter 6. The functions in the middle column are intended mainly for keyboard input via the DOS *standard input* file, using the same services. The **ConIO** functions in the right-hand column also employ DOS —not its file input services, but features specifically designed for keyboard input. Thus, Turbo C keyboard input features are *entirely* DOS-based. They're inadequate because DOS is. Effective interactive keyboard input programming must use lower-level BIOS keyboard services. In this section, however, you'll see what you can and cannot do with the Turbo C Library functions.

Selecting a keyboard input method, you must ask several questions, as follows.

1. Can the technique really ascertain enough about keyboard events to discover your user's intent?
2. Does it support keyboard editing (backspace, etc.)?
3. Can your program detect and handle <Ctrl-Break> properly? *Should* it? How about other special keystrokes?
4. Is your keyboard input echoed on screen? If so, where? With what attributes? Does the cursor move? How are control and non-ASCII keystrokes echoed?
5. Can your keyboard input be redirected to come from a file?
6. Will invalid input disrupt your display or crash your program?

You will see that for Turbo C input the answers to (1) and (6) are often *no* and *yes*, respectively. Moreover, complete answers to some of the other questions are difficult to obtain, because DOS is inadequately documented. The Turbo C Library source code shows when DOS services are used, but you can't tell exactly how those services work, without exhaustive experimentation. One major DOS keyboard input feature is the possibility of redirection to a file. This involves detailed consideration of some file processing concepts, and is discussed later in Chapter 6.

Consider the **ConIO** input functions. The very first, logically, is the *pushback* function

int ungetch(int Ch)

This processes character **Ch** so that the next invocation of **getch** or **getche** in the current program will behave as if you had just input that character. The implementation is simple: **ungetch** just stores **Ch** in a variable it shares with the other functions. A zero in that variable indicates that it's empty; a nonzero value is a character awaiting input. The function returns the integer -1 if a character was already present; otherwise it returns **Ch**. The intent of **ungetch** is to let a routine inspect an input, process it if appropriate, or push it back for later processing by another routine in the same program. For example, the low-level input formatting routine _scanner called by **cscanf** for interpreting input characters uses **ungetch** in this way. For several reasons, **ungetch** fails to meet most other requirements for pushback routines. First is its limitation to a single character. Second, it only handles the ASCII/IBM character set—it can't process the cursor keystrokes, for example. Finally, it can't push back a character for processing by another *program*. Those techniques, available through Turbo C TOOLS, are considered in Section 5.3.

The next most basic **ConIO** input function is more common:

char getch(void)

If **ungetch** has remembered a character, **getch** returns that; otherwise, **getch** reads a character from the keyboard, waiting if necessary. It won't distinguish between different ways of entering the same character—for example, <Ctrl-A> and <Alt-(keypad)1>, or the white and grey + keys. It will report non-ASCII/IBM keystrokes, in a strange way: first it returns zero, then the next invocation of **getch** will return the same keystroke's *extended ASCII* code. For example, if you press the up arrow key, **getch** returns 0, and its next invocation returns extended ASCII code 72. Extended ASCII code, and keyboard events in general, are discussed in much more detail in the next section. This awkward behavior stems from one of the less well-designed DOS input services. (See Section 8.5.)

If you need to input extended ASCII keystrokes, you'll probably want a more graceful function. Figure 5.1.1 shows a new software tool, function **ASCIIIBM**, that returns equivalent information in a single call, by executing **getch**, twice if necessary. A demonstration program and commented output are included. From the output, you can see another property of **getch**: it treats <Ctrl-Break> as just another way of

```
/**************************************************************/
/* ASCIIIBM.Dem    Demonstrate function ASCIIIBM:  read a   */
/*                 keystroke, using getch. If it's ASCII/    */
/*********************************** IBM, put the corre-      */
                                  /* sponding character in   */
#include <ConIO.H>               /* *Ch and return it. Oth-*/
                                  /* erwise, put the extended */
int ASCIIIBM(char *Ch) {         /* ASCII code in *Ch and */
  char X = *Ch = getch();        /* return zero.           */
if (X == 0) *Ch = getch();       /***************************/
return X; }

void main() {                    /* Demonstration program.  */
  int I;
  char Ch;
for (I = 0; I < 10; ++I) {       /* Loop through ten tests. */
  cprintf("Keystroke:  ");
  if (ASCIIIBM(&Ch))
    cprintf("ASCII/IBM       %3u %c\n",(unsigned) Ch,Ch);
  else
    cprintf("Extended ASCII  %3u   \n",(unsigned) Ch   ); }}
```

Output   Keystroke:

Keystroke:	ASCII/IBM	122	z	<Z>
Keystroke:	ASCII/IBM	90	Z	<Shift-Z>
Keystroke:	Extended ASCII	44		<Alt-Z>
Keystroke:	ASCII/IBM	26	→	<Ctrl-Z>
Keystroke:	Extended ASCII	77		<→>
Keystroke:	ASCII/IBM	3	♥	<Ctrl-Break>

(<CapsLock> was toggled off during execution.)

Figure 5.1.1 Program **ASCIIIBM.Dem**

entering ASCII 3. The ensuing **cprintf** prints the corresponding ASCII/IBM heart symbol. Of course, your program can interpret ASCII 3 as a signal to abort; the keystroke just won't trigger the usual DOS user break response. (For most programs, it's *desirable* to replace the DOS <Ctrl-Break> handler with a custom routine, so that you can clean up files and restore the display status before terminating.)

The related function

char getche(void)

operates like **getch**, but echoes its input at the current cursor location. In fact, it's implemented as **getch** followed by the single-character TTY output function **putch**, so the echo respects the current **ConIO** output window and text attribute. (See Section 4.2.)

Often you want to know whether keyboard input is ready, so that you can proceed with other business if it's not. You can't use **getch** or the other **ConIO** input routines, because they will stop and *wait* for input. Function

int kbhit(void)

fills this need. Implemented as a call for a DOS service, it returns a nonzero or zero value to indicate whether a keystroke is ready or not, and does not process the input at all. The program

```
void main() {
while (!kbhit());
printf("Input ready!"); }
```

loops until you press a key, then prints a message. (Actually, it detects only the keystrokes and keystroke combinations that the BIOS recognizes, listed in Appendix D.) You can check that **kbhit** interprets <Ctrl-Break> as a user break signal: after that keystroke, the program will abort without printing the message. Once it signals input ready, **kbhit** will continue to do so until some routine or program has emptied the BIOS keyboard buffer (described in the next section). Thus the program

```
void main() {
for (;;)
  if (kbhit()) printf("Input ready!\n"); }
```

will wait for a keystroke, then print messages endlessly.

Function **cgets** is designed for inputting strings of limited length, with echo, and permits use of the backspace key for minor editing. Its prototype

char *cgets(char *S)

doesn't betray its complexity. To input a string up to N characters long, allocate N + 3 bytes to character array **S**. Set **S[0]** = N + 1, then call **cgets**. The function will input up to N characters, with echo. The number of characters actually input, including the terminating <CR>, is reported as **S[1]**, and they are stored in **S[2]**, **S[3]**,.... The <CR> becomes the terminating 0 for the string. **cgets** returns a pointer to **S[2]**. Although bizarre in design—it reflects too closely a low-level DOS service—this function is fairly useful. It can read any ASCII string, including the empty one. Input is echoed TTY fashion at the current cursor location, and uses current screen attributes, but ignores the current Turbo C window. It does not move the cursor. The function ignores extended ASCII keystrokes, but <Ctrl-Break> (i.e., ASCII 3) does terminate the program.

Whereas **cgets** inputs a string of specified maximum length *with* echo, function

char *getpass(char *Prompt)

inputs a string of up to eight characters *without* echo. First, it displays the **Prompt** string at the cursor, TTY fashion, with the current attributes, but ignoring the current window. It returns a pointer to the input string, a static variable that is overwritten by each call to **getpass**. The intent of this function is to provide reasonably secure password entry. You should erase a recorded copy of a password as soon as you validate it.

The high-level **ConIO** input function is **cscanf**, which you invoke exactly like **scanf**. In fact, the two functions use the same low-level routine to interpret formatted input. (This text has assumed that you are familiar with the elaborate **scanf** formatting conventions, and has used them earlier without much comment.) The functions differ in the way they obtain their input and produce the screen echo: **cscanf** uses **getche**, while **scanf** uses the **StdIO** file input function **fgetc**. That is, **cscanf** uses DOS services designed specifically for keyboard input, while **scanf** uses general file services with the standard input file. Where **cscanf** uses **ungetch** to postpone processing a character, **scanf** uses **ungetc**.

These functions are nearly useless for robust input programming. Because it ultimately calls **putch**, the **cscanf** echo does occur, TTY fashion, at the current cursor location and respects the current **ConIO** window and attributes. However, no reliable editing is provided. Like **getch**, **cscanf** ignores the user-break function of the <Ctrl-Break> keystroke, reporting it merely as ASCII 3. It will not permit you to enter an empty string, either. Even worse, there is no provision for handling extended ASCII keystrokes; your program behaves unpredictably if they occur in **cscanf** input. On the other hand, the **scanf** echo ignores the **ConIO** window, preserves screen attributes already present, and interprets <Ctrl-Break> as a user break signal. Both functions replace the cursor where it was before input; but they both suffer the empty string and extended ASCII problems. The program and output in Figure 5.1.2 (discussed in the next paragraph) betray another difference between these functions: **cscanf** does not echo the terminating <CR> keystroke, but **scanf** does.

You have seen another fault of the **cscanf** and **scanf** functions in demonstration programs earlier in this text. Neither function entirely empties the input buffer: each leaves a single garbage character there. Unless you flush the buffer somehow, your next input function of the same type will read that garbage (an ASCII 13 carriage return) and probably cause your program to fail. Program **LeftOver.Dem** in Figure 5.1.2 illustrates this design error. Each function is used in turn to read an input string **S**. The program prints **strlen(S)** so you can verify how many characters it read. A succeeding invocation of **getch** or **fgetchar** (the analogous **StdIO** function) will not await your next input. Instead, it will input the leftover garbage character. That's the only leftover, because the *next* input function *will* wait. **LeftOver.Dem** traces exactly what **cscanf** did wrong by executing **ungetch** just before the first **getch**: this function fails, indicating that **cscanf** had pushed back the garbage character (an ASCII 10 line feed) and neglected to remove it. Presumably, the **scanf** fault is similar, but the corresponding pushback function **ungetc** is not sensitive enough to verify that.

The remedy for the fault demonstrated by **LeftOver.Dem** is to flush the input buffer after keyboard input. For **cscanf**, execute **getch()** and ignore its return value. For **scanf**, execute **fgetchar()** or **fflush(stdin)**. The latter flushes the buffer associated with the DOS standard input

```
/********************************************************************/
/* LeftOver.Dem    Show how  cscanf  and  scanf  each leave a */
/*                 garbage character in an input buffer.  Read*/
/* a string with  cscanf.  Try to push back a character;      */
/* ungetch  returns  -1 to show that it's already remembering*/
/* one.  getch  returns that character, a  <CR>.  A following */
/* call to  getch  waits for input, indicating that only the  */
/* <CR>  was left over.  A similar experiment with  scanf     */
/*************************************** shows that it leaves*/
                                    /* an  <LF>  in a buf- */
#include <ConIO.H>                  /* fer.  You can't use */
#include <StdIO.H>                  /* ungetc,  however,   */
                                    /* to tell if it was   */
void main() {                       /* pushed back.        */
  char S[81];                       /***********************/
printf("\nEnter a string:    ");
cscanf("%s",&S);
printf("\ncscanf  read        %s",S            );
printf("\nstring length       %d",strlen(S)    );
printf("\nungetch('A') =       %d",ungetch('A'));
printf("\ngetch() =     ASCII %u",getch()      );
getch();                                              /* Await in- */
cputs("\n");                                          /* put, skip */
printf("\nEnter a string:    ");                      /* a line.   */
scanf ("%s",&S);
printf("\nscanf  read         %s",S            );
printf("\nstring length       %d",strlen(S)    );
printf("\nfgetchar() = ASCII %u",fgetchar()    );  /* Await in- */
fgetchar(); }                                      /* put, quit.*/
```

Output

```
Enter a string:     abcde
cscanf  read        abcde
string length       5
ungetch('A') =      -1
getch() =     ASCII 13

Enter a string:     abcde
scanf  read         abcde
string length       5
fgetchar() = ASCII 10
```

Figure 5.1.2 Program LeftOver.Dem

file; that is discussed in more detail in Chapter 6. Earlier chapters used **fflush** because its name reflects what's happening.

Like **scanf**, the other **StdIO** keyboard input functions **gets, getchar,** and **fgetchar** are based on function **fgetc**, hence ultimately on the DOS general file services, applied to the standard input file. When this file is connected to the keyboard device, it operates in a line buffered mode. You can use the following standard editing keystrokes just as for editing DOS commands:

<←> <→> <BS> <Del> <Esc> <F1> <F3> <Ins>

<CR> terminates editing and triggers actual input to your program. The functions produce echoes and treat <Ctrl-Break> just like **scanf**, but *don't* suffer the **LeftOver.Dem** garbage problem.

The **StdIO** function

char *gets(char *S)

simply inputs characters into string **S**; you must have allocated sufficient space for them. There's no way to limit the number of characters input. Thus, **gets** input can easily overwrite the end of **S**, and its echo can easily interfere with other parts of your display.

The two single-character input functions

int getchar(void)   int fgetchar(void)

seem identical, except that the former is really a macro defined in file **StdIO.H**. You might want to use the latter, as in program **LeftOver.Dem**, to avoid including that header file. On the other hand, line buffering is inappropriate for most single-character input, so these two functions are nearly useless.

All the **StdIO** keyboard input functions suffer a final, fatal problem: they will *never* remove ASCII 26 = ^Z from the input buffer, because C uses that as an end-of-file signal. Once your user enters <Ctrl-Z>, these functions will never *wait* for an input. They just report the presence of that character by returning the value **EOF = 65535**, and your program sails away, out of control. Program **^ZSticks.Dem** in Figure 5.1.3 demonstrates this failure by receiving ^Z as input, reporting that, then trying to wait for new input. Then it flushes the buffer, tries again, and fails.

As the examples in this section show, if you use Turbo C Library keyboard input functions, you often can't detect non-ASCII keystrokes, and your program and display are vulnerable to disruption by unintended input. You cannot use those functions if you need complete information about keyboard events, or if your program must survive invalid inputs. The Turbo C TOOLS package provides techniques for surmounting these problems. These are based on the PC BIOS keyboard control features, so it's necessary to consider those in some detail in the next section, before surveying the Turbo C TOOLS functions in Section 5.3.

```
/******************************************************************/
/* ^ZSticks.Dem    Show that once   ^Z  enters the  stdin  buf-*/
/*                 fer, you can't get rid of it, and   StdIO   */
/* keyboard input functions won't wait for input.             */
/******************************************************************/

#include <StdIO.H>
#define  InputReport                                         \
  printf("getchar() = ASCII %u\n", (unsigned) getchar())

void main() {
printf("Enter  Ctrl-Z :  ");
InputReport;                   /* Echoes  ^Z,  returns  EOF. */
InputReport;                   /* Doesn't wait, returns  EOF. */
fflush(stdin);
printf("Flushed  stdin\n");
InputReport; }                 /* Doesn't wait, returns  EOF. */
```

Output

```
Enter  Ctrl-Z :   ^Z
fgetchar() = ASCII 65535
fgetchar() = ASCII 65535
Flushed  stdin
fgetchar() = ASCII 65535
```

Figure 5.1.3 Program ^ZSticks.Dem

5.2 BIOS keyboard buffer

Concepts

BIOS keystroke processing
Keystroke codes
Keystrokes that trigger special BIOS responses
An example DOS keyboard input service
<Ctrl-Break> and <Ctrl-C>
Other services

The Turbo C keyboard handling techniques discussed in Section 5.1 don't give you complete control over your keyboard, nor the ability to interpret completely arbitrary keyboard input. The extended ASCII keystroke code was considered there only briefly. Other keystroke questions arise, as well. For example, how can you distinguish different keystrokes that produce the same character? How can you ascertain and set the numerical keyboard status? How can you detect weird combinations like P and Q depressed simultaneously? Your experience tells you that keystrokes are stored in a queue before they are processed, because you frequently type faster than software can process your input. Therefore, the key your user touches *now* in response to a screen prompt might not be the next in line for processing. How do you insure that it *is?* Most of these problems can be solved easily using the Turbo C TOOLS package, but others require its sophisticated use. *All* of them require further knowledge of the PC keyboard controller and BIOS operation. This section will cover that area, as much as possible without becoming involved in general details of interrupt processing. That aspect is covered later in Chapters 8 and 9.

BIOS keystroke processing

PC keyboards contain varying numbers of keys, between 80 and 127, numbered consecutively from 1 upward. (Their exact number and order is irrelevant; for details, consult Appendix D.) Keyboard events—touching or releasing keys—are monitored independently of your computer's CPU by an Intel 8048 microprocessor, which describes them by means of *scan codes.* The scan code corresponding to touching a key is simply the key number. To obtain the code for releasing it, just add 128 = hex 80. Each keyboard event causes the 8048 to place the corresponding scan code in a register connected to CPU port hex 60, and to send a signal to the Intel 8259A Interrupt Controller Chip requesting that the CPU service that port. The 8259A prioritizes simultaneous service requests from the keyboard and other peripherals that compete for CPU attention. The keyboard signal comes to it on Interrupt Request Line IRQ1, a high priority line.

As soon as the 8259A can give priority to the keyboard service request, it sends signals to the CPU that cause immediate execution of an interrupt 9 instruction. In short, this interrupts whatever the CPU was doing, but stores just enough information that it can find its place again. Then the CPU transfers control to a routine whose address is stored in entry 9 of the interrupt vector table described in Section 2.2. Unless you have installed some memory resident custom keyboard handling software, interrupt vector 9 remains as it was initialized by the PC's boot routines, pointing to the BIOS keyboard handler in ROM. On a machine with an IBM ROM BIOS chip, this procedure is called **KB_INT**. Other suppliers' BIOS chips operate according to the same general specifications, but must vary in detail.

KB_INT first decides whether you released or touched a key. Releases are ignored, except releases of the **Shift, Ctrl,** and **Alt** keys. **KB_INT** maintains a record of the status of these keys and the toggle keys **CapsLock, NumLock,** and **Ins.** When you *touch* a key, however, **KB_INT** must make a complicated analysis of the key number and the status of the shift and toggle keys to ascertain your intent. The assembly language for this analysis is published in the PC *Technical Reference* manual (Reference [20]). It is entertaining reading! Based on this analysis, **KB_INT** may

- ignore the event;
- update its record of shift and toggle key status, if you pressed one of those;
- generate a two-byte *keystroke code,* and place it in a 15-place queue called the *keyboard buffer;*
- beep at you and ignore the keystroke, if it attempts the previous alternative and finds the buffer full;
- or take a special action like printing the screen.

The keyboard buffer is a BIOS feature, and has nothing to do with the DOS standard input file buffer mentioned in the previous section.

Before considering keystroke codes in detail, note that **KB_INT** must also inform the 8048 keyboard processor that service is at hand, and take certain precautions to insure that it is not itself interrupted—and thus disrupted—during vital phases of its analysis. Note that some detail involving interpretation of <Alt-(keypad)> keystrokes has been skipped.

If you touched a key corresponding to a character with an ASCII/IBM code, the keystroke code consists of this code followed by the scan code of the event. Thus, for example, the keystroke code distinguishes which + key you may have touched. ASCII keystrokes entered via the numeric keypad have scan code 0. Certain other keystrokes have *extended ASCII* keystroke codes consisting of a zero byte followed by a code tabulated in Chapter 3 of the PC *Technical Reference* manual and in Appendix D of this book. For example, <Alt-F10> has keystroke code hex 00,71.

KB_INT takes special action on several keystrokes, as follows:

<Shift-PrtSc>	Execute interrupt 5, which normally triggers a screen hardcopy.
<Ctrl-Alt-Del>	Execute interrupt hex 19, which normally causes a warm boot.
<Ctrl-NumLock>	Set a *hold-state* flag and enter a loop that does nothing until the flag is turned off. While processing ordinary keystrokes, **KB_INT** turns the flag off, so the effect of **Ctrl-NumLock** is to suspend execution, waiting for an ordinary keystroke.
<Ctrl-Break>	Execute interrupt hex 1b and place keystroke code 00,00 in the keyboard buffer. This process is discussed in more detail under a later heading.

When **KB_INT** has finished processing a keystroke, it informs the 8259A (so that chip can keep its priorities straight) and transfers control back to the interrupted program, restoring its previous state of execution.

Custom keyboard handlers carry out a process similar to **KB_INT**. They simply vary in detail, particularly concerning the keystrokes singled out for special treatment. To install a custom keyboard routine, you must load it into memory and arrange for interrupt vector 9 to point to it.

An example DOS keyboard input service

So far, you have seen how keystrokes are recorded and queued in the keyboard buffer by the PC BIOS procedure **KB_INT**. It remains to see how your program obtains keyboard input information from the keyboard buffer and some other information sources. One typical way is for the machine language version of your program to execute an interrupt hex 21 instruction after setting CPU register AH = 7. This is the main instruction in the Turbo C Library function **getch**. Executing interrupt 21 preserves the vital aspects of your machine's status, and transfers control to a routine whose address is stored in interrupt vector hex 21: the DOS function call dispatcher. Based on the value in AH, the dispatcher invokes a procedure called *Direct Console Input without Echo*. This DOS routine operates as follows, using CPU register AL to transmit input to your program.

0. Wait, if necessary, until the buffer contains at least one keystroke code.
1. Remove a keystroke code from the buffer.
2. If it's the <Ctrl-Break> 00,00 code, change it to <Ctrl-C> 03,00.
3. If it's an extended ASCII code, set AL = 0 and arrange that the next invocation of this procedure start with step 5 below;
4. else put the ASCII/IBM character code in AL and return to your program.
5. Put the extended ASCII code from the previous invocation in AL.
6. Arrange that the next invocation of this procedure starts with step 0 above; return to the calling program.

This is a somewhat complex routine, but it provides very simple information. Note that Step 2 explains why **getch** treats <Ctrl-Break> and <Ctrl-C> similarly.

<Ctrl-Break> and <Ctrl-C>

You must have noticed the varying treatment of the <Ctrl-Break> keystroke among different input functions. Also, you may have observed that the <Ctrl-C> keystroke often, but not always, has the same effect as <Ctrl-Break>. Moreover, you certainly have used <Ctrl-Break> to abort some programs that don't even input from the keyboard. With this knowledge of the BIOS keyboard handler, it's just possible to begin considering how these features are implemented and why they vary. As noted earlier, when the BIOS keyboard handler detects a <Ctrl-Break> keystroke, it executes interrupt 1b and puts ASCII 0 in the keyboard buffer; when it detects <Ctrl-C>, it just places ASCII 3 there. DOS keyboard input services, like the preceding example, change the ASCII 0 to ASCII 3. Most of them, but not the one just considered, then transfer control to a DOS routine that aborts the program currently running.

What if your program never asks DOS for keyboard input? When DOS boots, it points interrupt vector 1b to a little routine that sets an internal flag, to signal that the BIOS has detected a <Ctrl-Break>. Periodically, DOS checks the keyboard buffer, to see if a <Ctrl-C> keystroke has occurred, and the internal flag, to see if it signals <Ctrl-Break>, and it aborts your program accordingly. Just *when* DOS performs this test is determined in part by its **BREAK** switch, which is controlled by the DOS command **Break** and a corresponding program service. When **BREAK is on**, all DOS services perform the test. Normally, however, **BREAK is off**, and only a subset of the services do.

Thus you can terminate your program with <Ctrl-C> or <Ctrl-Break> if it requests DOS services, and DOS checks the buffer and the flag during those services. <Ctrl-C> and <Ctrl-Break> are handled differently. For example, <Ctrl-C> must be at the *head* of the keyboard buffer to be detected when a DOS service checks the buffer. <Ctrl-C> has no effect while another character is waiting to be processed or if it's removed from the buffer before DOS can check it. To ascertain whether a break check occurs during your program, you must inspect the source code to determine which DOS services are used, and consult the *MS-DOS Encyclopedia* (Reference [28]) to see whether they include the test. You must also keep track of the status of the **BREAK** switch. The situation is even further complicated by the fact that some DOS services—for example, the one described earlier, on which function **getch** is based— regard <Ctrl-C> and <Ctrl-Break> merely as ASCII 3 input and actually *turn off* the <Ctrl-Break> flag. Later, in Chapters 8 and 9, you will see how to control the events that occur when DOS does decide to process a user break signal.

Other services

Further keyboard services are offered both by DOS and directly by the BIOS. In particular, DOS can flush the buffer so that your program can interpret its next input as a response to a screen prompt, and the BIOS can report the status of most shift and toggle keys. Moreover, by paying very close attention to the details of the BIOS code, you can provide services left unfilled by both the BIOS and DOS. For example, you can place codes in the keyboard buffer so that your program or some other will interpret them as though they were keystroke data. Turbo C provides a way to invoke the appropriate interrupts, and with absolute memory addressing you can access the buffer. However, it is difficult and tedious to keep track of the necessary address details and to set and interpret the CPU registers. A complicated example of this kind of programming for a custom keyboard service routine is described in Section 9.3. For ordinary work, the Turbo C TOOLS keyboard handling routines are sufficient to handle this kind of detail for you. They are described in the next section.

5.3 Turbo C TOOLS keyboard handling

> **Concepts**
>
> Inspecting, flushing and reading from the keyboard buffer
> Monitoring and setting shift and toggle keys
> String input routines
> Stuffing the keyboard buffer
> Looking up scan codes

Earlier in this chapter, you saw that Turbo C key handling methods cause problems and leave some serious gaps. The BIOS provides most of the assembly language techniques necessary to correct these deficiencies, and Turbo C TOOLS packages them in C. Thus they become convenient and intuitive to use, free from much of the detail required for low level coding.

Turbo C TOOLS provides four groups of keyboard routines, as follows:

kbready	**kbstatus**	**kbquery**	**kbqueue**
kbflush	**kbset**	**wnquery**	**kbplace**
kbgetkey			**kbstuff**
			kbscanof

The first two groups consist of low-level routines for interacting with the keyboard buffer and with the BIOS flags that reflect the status of the shift and toggle keys. The third set of functions is slightly higher level, inputting and echoing strings. The last group is concerned with buffer *stuffing*: placing keystroke codes in the keyboard buffer, so that other software will execute as if a user had actually pressed the corresponding keys.

The first Turbo C TOOLS keyboard routine, function

int kbready(char *Ch, int *Key)

is an elaboration of the Turbo C Library function **kbhit**. It returns 0 or 1 to indicate whether the keyboard buffer is empty or not; if a keystroke is present, it stores the two-byte keystroke code in *Ch and *Key. For an ASCII/IBM keystroke, *Ch is the corresponding character and *Key is the scan code; otherwise, *Ch is zero and *Key is the extended ASCII code. This function does not change the buffer in any way.

To flush the keyboard buffer, use function

int kbflush(void)

It returns the number of keystroke codes removed. The most common use of this routine is to ensure that the next keystroke to be processed is a response to a prompt of some sort. Remember, the keyboard buffer is different from the DOS standard input file buffer, so **kbflush** has no effect on that buffer, and the Turbo C Library routines **fflush** and **flushall** have none on the keyboard buffer.

The third function,

int kbgetkey(int *Key)

reads and removes a keystroke code from the buffer, waiting for input if necessary. It returns the ASCII/IBM code or 0, and stores the scan or extended ASCII code, respectively, in ***Key**. Thus, **kbgetkey** is a considerable improvement on the Turbo C Library single-character keyboard input functions.

Function **kbgetkey** is implemented in C, whereas **kbready** is written in assembly language, apparently just because it requires more delicate manipulations. **kbflush** invokes the other two: it simply reads keystrokes until the buffer is empty. These routines use BIOS services only; they do not call DOS, so input can *not* be redirected to come from a file. Functions **kbready** and **kbflush** are demonstrated by program **KBReady.Dem** in Figure 5.3.1. The sample output shows how you can distinguish between different keystrokes that yield the same ASCII code, and how you can read extended ASCII keystrokes with a single invocation of **kbready** (or **kbgetkey**). Moreover, you can see that <Ctrl-Break> places keystroke code 0,0 in the buffer, which **getch** reports as ASCII 3.

The useful function

int kbstatus(KEYSTATUS *Status)

tells you the status of various shift and toggle keys. The BIOS constantly monitors the *shift keys* <Alt>, <Ctrl>, <LeftShift>, and <RightShift>. It sets bits at address 0040:0017, called **KB_FLAG** in the IBM BIOS listing, to reflect whether the keys are depressed or not. The BIOS bootstrap routine, moreover, sets other bits at the same address to indicate that the *toggle keys* <CapsLock>, <Ins>, <NumLock>, and <ScrollLock> are in the inactive status; afterward, the BIOS monitors them and maintains these bits accordingly. The next byte in memory, offset hex 0018, provides similar, but less commonly needed, information. **KEYSTATUS** is a type of C structure predeclared in Turbo C TOOLS header file **BKeybrd.H,** as in Figure 5.3.2. This entire structure is packed into a single word; **kbstatus** returns the information as an integer value, and fills the specified structure variable with it as well. The function is implemented as a macro in the same header file.

Two of these special keys, <LeftShift> and <NumLock>, are monitored with **kbstatus** in the Figure 5.3.3 demonstration program **Shft&Num.Dem**. It uses just two entries **left_shift** and **num_state** of the **KEYSTATUS** records. The current status Up/Down of the shift key and Numeric/Cursor of <NumLock> is updated on screen every time you

```
/**************************************************************/
/* KBReady.Dem    Demonstrate  Turbo C TOOLS  functions    */
/*                kbready and  kbflush.  Use the former to  */
/**************************************** detect keystrokes  */
                                  /* and report the full */
#include <General.H>              /* codes.  Report the  */
#include <BKeybrd.H>              /* codes returned by   */
                                  /* getch,  then flush  */
void main() {                     /* the buffer.         */
  char Ch = 0;                    /**********************/
  int  Key;
cprintf("Touch keys!\n");         /* Press  <CR>  to exit*/
for (;Ch != CR;)                  /* from this loop.     */
  if (kbready(&Ch,&Key)) {
    cprintf  ("Ch,Key  = %3u,%2d\n",Ch,Key);
    cprintf  ("getch() = %3u\n",Ch = getch());
    if (Ch == 0)                              /* Extended */
      cprintf("getch() = %3u\n",getch());     /* ASCII.   */
    kbflush(); }}
```

Output			Comment	Output			Comment
Ch,Key	=	8,14	<BS>	Ch,Key	=	72,35	<Shift-H>
getch()	=	8		getch()	=	72	
Ch,Key	=	8, 0	<Alt-(keypad) 8>	Ch,Key	=	0,35	<Alt-H>
getch()	=	8		getch()	=	0	Extended
				getch()	=	35	ASCII
Ch,Key	=	8,35	<Ctrl-H>	Ch,Key	=	0, 0	<Ctrl-Break>
getch()	=	8		getch()	=	3	
Ch,Key	=	104,35	<H> with	Ch,Key	=	3,46	<Ctrl-C>
getch()	=	104	<CapsLock> off	getch()	=	3	

Figure 5.3.1 Program **KBReady.Dem**

do anything to those keys. Note that the right shift key has no effect on this. Touching any ordinary key terminates the program.

After twiddling the <NumLock> key, you're likely to exit from the program with it in **Numeric** state. This is disconcerting, because then the cursor keys don't work. Courtesy demands that such a program

```
typedef struct kstatus
    unsigned right_shift    : 1;    /* <RightShift>    depressed */
    unsigned left_shift     : 1;    /* <LeftShift>     depressed */
    unsigned ctrl_shift     : 1;    /* <Ctrl>          depressed */
    unsigned alt_shift      : 1;    /* <Alt>           depressed */
    unsigned scroll_state   : 1;    /* <ScrollLock>    toggled   */
    unsigned num_state      : 1;    /* <NumLock>       toggled   */
    unsigned caps_state     : 1;    /* <CapsLock>      toggled   */
    unsigned ins_state      : 1;    /* <Ins>           toggled   */
    unsigned filler         : 3;    /* Filler for word alignment */
    unsigned hold_state     : 1;    /* <Ctrl-NumLock>  toggled   */
    unsigned scroll_shift   : 1;    /* <ScrollLoc      depressed */
    unsigned num_shift      : 1;    /* <NumLock>       depressed */
    unsigned caps_shift     : 1;    /* <CapsLock>      depressed */
    unsigned ins_shift      : 1;    /* <Ins>           depressed */
} KEYSTATUS;
```

Figure 5.3.2 Turbo C TOOLS **KEYSTATUS** structure

restore the default **Cursor** state. In fact, you often need to switch the keypad from one type of input to another. To do this, you can use function

void kbset(KEYSTATUS *Status)

Just set the appropriate entry of the structure ***Status**. The function will copy the structure into the BIOS data area, and the BIOS will then interpret keyboard input according to the new settings. This technique is also demonstrated in program **Shft&Num.Dem**. The program uses several Turbo C TOOLS routines already described in Chapter 4 to produce graceful screen output.

To set keyboard status flags, you generally read them first with **kbstatus**, change the appropriate entries in the **KEYSTATUS** structure, then set the flags with **kbset**. To guard against inconsistent flag settings, it might be prudent to disable the BIOS keyboard service routine during this brief period by turning off maskable interrupts. That process is discussed in Chapters 8 and 9.

The two functions

char wnquery(char *Response, int N, int *Code)
char kbquery (char *Response, int N, int *Code,
                int *Scrolled)

```
/****************************************************************/
/* Shft&Num.Dem    Demonstrate  Turbo  C TOOLS  keyboard status*/
/*                 functions, by continuously reporting the    */
/* <LeftShift>  and  <NumLock>  status.  An ordinary keystroke*/
/********************************************* ends the test and */
                                        /* sets  <NumLock> to */
#include    <ConIO.H>                   /* cursor key status.  */
#include  <BKeybrd.H>                   /***********************/
#include   <BVideo.H>

char *Shift  [2] = {"Up      ","Down    "};
char *NumLock[2] = {"Cursor ","Numeric"};

void main() {
  int X,Y,High,Low;                     /* Cursor pos., style. */
  KEYSTATUS Old,New;
clrscr();                               /* Clear screen.      */
cputs("\nLeft shift key      ");        /* Write caption.     */
cputs("\n  NumLock key     ");
sccurst(&Y,&X,&High,&Low);              /* Where to report.   */
scpgcur(1,High,Low,0);                  /* Turn off cursor.   */
kbstatus(&Old);                         /* Get current status. */
while (kbhit() == 0) {                   /* Loop until  kbhit.  */
  kbstatus(&New);                       /* Change in status?   */
  if (New.left_shift != Old.left_shift ||
     New.num_state  != Old.num_state) {
    Old = New;                          /* Record and report.  */
    vidspmsg(Y-1,X,-1,-1,Shift  [New.left_shift]);
    vidspmsg(Y ,X,-1,-1,NumLock[New.num_state ]); }}
New.num_state = 0;                      /* Set  <NumLock>     */
kbset(&New);                            /* status off.        */
scpgcur(0,High,Low,0); }                /* Turn cursor back on.*/
```

Figure 5.3.3 Program **Shft&Num.Dem**

provide higher-level keyboard input: you can enter a string of length <
N, which is stored in ***Response**. Input is echoed TTY fashion: **kbquery**
tallies the number of consequent new lines in ***Scrolled, wnquery**
echoes are positioned relative to the current Turbo C TOOLS window
(see Chapter 4), and **wnquery** input stops when the window is full.
Input also stops if you reach length **N - 1**. You may terminate the input
string with ASCII 10 or 13 (CR or LF) or any extended ASCII keystroke.

In the former cases, the functions return 10 or 13 and place the terminal keystroke's scan code in ***Code**; if the terminal keystroke is extended ASCII, they return zero and place the extended ASCII code in ***Code**. If the current window isn't entirely visible, **wnquery** sets an error code and has no further effect—see the Turbo C TOOLS manual, Reference [4]. Both functions are written entirely in C and use BIOS services but not DOS.

The last group of Turbo C TOOLS keyboard handling functions is concerned with *buffer stuffing:* placing keystroke codes in the keyboard buffer, so that other software will execute as if a user had actually provided keyboard input. This is useful mainly for memory resident software—especially keyboard enhancement utilities—and will be mentioned again in that context in Chapter 9. Memory resident concurrent execution is required, for example, to simulate an input string longer than the buffer. However, you can sometimes use the technique in normal operation: for example, to provide the first few keystrokes for the *next* program to be executed by a **.Bat** routine (provided that software doesn't flush the buffer before input). Moreover, buffer stuffing techniques can be demonstrated easily in ordinary operation, as in the Figure 5.3.4 program **KbStuff.Dem**.

To operate **KbStuff.Dem**, think of three strings **S[0],S[1],S[2]** of lengths **L,M,N** where **L + M + N < 15**: for example,

S[0], S[1], S[2] = "aaa", "bbbb", "ccccc"

KbStuff.Dem gives you five seconds to enter **S[0]** —just the characters, without a <CR> or other terminal keystroke, then it gives you five more for **S[1]** and then for **S[2]**. Constructing S[0] and S[1], it empties the keyboard buffer. But it never actually constructs S[2]: that's just left in

```
/******************************************************************/
/* KbStuff.Dem    Demonstrate  Turbo C TOOLS  queue stuffing.*/
/*                Read two strings.  Have the user type a      */
/*                third, then stuff the second ahead of it     */
/*****************************************  and the first be-   */
                                         /* hind, with a  <CR>. */
#include <General.H>                     /* Read the buffer with*/
#include <BKeybrd.H>                     /* gets.               */
                                         /***********************/
```

Figure 5.3.4 Program **KbStuff.Dem** (*Continued on next page*)

```
void main() {
  char *Index = "LMN";
  int  I,SpaceLeft,BufferSize,KeysTyped,K,Key;
  char S[2][16],T[16];
printf("Think of integers %c,%c,%c Ú 0  with sum  < 15 .",
  Index[0],Index[1],Index[2]);
for (I = 0; I <= 2; ++I) {              /* Have user enter  3  */
  printf("\nYou have  5  seconds "      /* strings.          */
    "to type  %c  characters: \a",      /* \a  beeps.        */
       Index[I]);
  delay(5000);                          /* 5000  millisec.   */
  if (I == 2) break;                    /* Just read 1st 2.  */
  SpaceLeft = kbqueue(&BufferSize);     /* Compute input length*/
  KeysTyped = BufferSize - SpaceLeft;   /* from buffer status. */
  for (K = 0; K < KeysTyped; ++K)       /* Read string S[I],  */
    S[I][K] = kbgetkey(&Key);           /* terminate it.      */
  S[I][K]  = 0;
  printf("\n  %c = %d .  ",Index[I],KeysTyped);
  if (Index[I] > 0) cprintf("You typed %s .",S[I]); }
printf("\n Your last  %c  keystrokes are still in the buffer. "
     "\n  I'm stuffing your middle  %c  inputs ahead of them,"
      "\n  and your first  %c  after, followed by  <CR> .   ",
  Index[2],Index[1],Index[0]);
kbstuff(KB_HEAD,S[1]);                  /* Middle string S[1]. */
kbstuff(KB_TAIL,S[0]);                  /* First string  S[0]. */
kbplace(KB_TAIL,CR,0);                  /* CR triggers gets.  */
printf("\nNow  gets  is reading and echoing them:\n  ");
gets(T); }
```

Output

```
Think of integers  L,M,N ≥ 0  with sum  < 15 .
You have  5  seconds to type  L  characters:
  L = 3 . You typed  aaa .
You have  5  seconds to type  M  characters:
  M = 4 . You typed  bbbb .
You have  5  seconds to type  N  characters:
  Your last  N  keystrokes are still in the buffer.
I'm stuffing your middle  M  inputs ahead of them,
  and your first  L  after, followed by  <CR> .
Now  gets  is reading and echoing them:
  bbbbccccaaa
```

Figure 5.3.4 *(Continued)* Program **KbStuff.Dem**

the buffer. Now the program stuffs S[1] into the buffer at the head, S[0] at the tail, and finally inputs and echoes the concatenated string

T = S[1] S[2] S[0] = "bbbbaaacccc"

This demonstration requires computing the lengths of S[0] and S[1], which would be tedious to do directly. **KbStuff.Dem** achieves that by calling function

int kbqueue(int *BufferSize)

This function returns the number of free buffer positions and, for your convenience, stores the total buffer capacity in ***BufferSize**. Thus the number of keystrokes in the buffer at any time is given by

KeysTyped = BufferSize - SpaceLeft

Once the constituents of target string **T** are in memory and in the buffer, **KbStuff.Dem** calls function

char *kbstuff(int AtHead, char *S)

twice, to stuff strings **S** into the buffer, indicating the head or tail as destination by setting parameter **AtHead** = 1 or 0. Function **kbstuff** stuffs only as many characters as will fit, and returns a pointer to the first character of **S** that wasn't stuffed (or zero if all were).

Finally, program **KbStuff** uses function

int kbplace(int AtHead, char Code0, char Code1)

to stuff a <CR> code into the buffer at the tail. Parameters **Code0,Code1** are the two bytes of the keystroke code. In this demonstration, the buffer will be read by Turbo C Library function **gets**, which requires **CR** = ASCII 13 to terminate its input. That function doesn't care how you enter the **CR**, so **KbStuff** simulates keystroke <Alt-(keypad)13> by setting **Code0,Code1** = 13,0. Function **kbplace** returns 0 or 1 to indicate success or failure.

Functions **kbqueue**, **kbstuff**, and **kbplace** may not work in the presence of memory resident keyboard enhancement software. Keyboard enhancers may use a different buffering technique by substituting their own keyboard service routines for those of the BIOS. Turbo C TOOLS compensates for that as much as it can, but nevertheless may remain incompatible. For example, program **KbStuff.Dem** won't work in the author's DESQview environment. These questions are considered again in Chapters 8 and 9.

For your convenience in coding buffer stuffing applications, Turbo C TOOLS provides a function **kbscanof** that returns the most common scan code corresponding to a given ASCII character in the range 0..127. You can use its return value as parameter **Code1** in functions **kbstuff** and **kbplace**. See the manual for details.

5.4 Turbo C TOOLS menu features

Concepts

Menu concepts
Turbo C TOOLS menu handling functions
Lotus-type menu items
Integrating menu selection with spreadsheet data entry

Programming effective user interfaces for interactive software requires complementary screen handling and keyboard input methods. One of the most pleasing techniques is the use of menus. Text suddenly appears on screen, giving you information about alternative actions. You can enter a keystroke identifying one of the choices, or perhaps use the cursor keys to move a pointer to the right one. Once your selection is noted, the menu disappears, restoring the previous screen appearance, and new information or alternatives may be presented. This is extremely high-level input of very simple information. The keyboard techniques introduced in earlier sections are clearly sufficient for the input itself, but portraying the choices so vividly puts a great demand on screen output techniques. What is required is facility with window displays, like that provided by the Turbo C TOOLS routines described in Section 4.4, a convenient and general set of data structures for describing menus, and routines that put the two together. If the data structures are general enough, you will be able to use the routines for menu input in a great variety of situations.

Turbo C TOOLS includes data structure definitions and routines that make it easy to program menu selections. They are illustrated here in two stages. The simple menu in Figure 5.4.1, produced by program **Menu1.Dem** in Figure 5.4.2, illustrates the basic menu concepts. The more complex program **Menu2.Dem** in Figure 5.4.3 shows the elaborate organization necessary to coordinate menu selection and data entry.

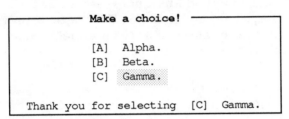

Figure 5.4.1 Program **Menu1.Dem** output

Menu1.Dem displays in mid-screen a menu like Figure 5.4.1. You can move the highlight bar from one item to another with the cursor and tab keys. You select an item by pressing the corresponding letter key, or by touching <CR> when the item is highlighted. Following a selection, the program writes the appropriate bottom line. Pressing <Esc> causes the program to remove the menu and terminate. Other keystrokes merely cause beeps.

A menu is a Turbo C TOOLS window, on which is imposed further structure. Therefore, it shares many properties with ordinary windows. First, it has

- horizontal and vertical dimensions, and
- default foreground and background attributes.

You can create and destroy a menu like other windows. The properties just mentioned are recorded in a *menu descriptor* when you create a menu. You can also display it and remove it from the screen. The following properties are assigned when it's displayed:

- its location on any page of any device, as specified by the Turbo C TOOLS screen coordinates of its top left corner;
- its border design, which follows the Turbo C TOOLS conventions and may include top and/or bottom titles.

The two major features that distinguish a menu from a more general sort of window are its *item* and *keystroke* lists, which describe and help you select from the available alternatives. Turbo C TOOLS items are identified by their coordinates relative to the menu window. The menu in Figure 5.4.1 includes three, with coordinates Row,11 for Row = 1,2,3. With various keystrokes, described later, users may highlight an item or select the corresponding alternative. In addition to location, items have other properties:

- text string (short description),
- foreground and background attributes,
- protected or unprotected status.

Users are not allowed to highlight a protected item. This distinction is useful if you want the menu always to have the same overall appearance, but some items aren't always appropriate. For example, menu alternatives might include data entry and manipulation, but the latter choice may not be valid until a user has actually entered data.

Turbo C TOOLS menu items feature an optional *long description* text string, with its own location and attributes. This allows you to provide emphasis and avoid screen clutter by displaying the long description only when the item is highlighted. The long text may describe the effect of various keystrokes associated with the item. The Turbo C TOOLS manual calls this kind of menu item *Lotus-style*.

Constructing a menu requires attention to seven sets of foreground/background attributes. The default attributes apply to the short description text strings of unprotected items, as well as other text written in the window by Turbo C TOOLS routines. Attributes for protected items, long description strings, and the highlight bar are specified separately when you create the menu. Finally, the border and top and bottom title attributes are determined when the window is displayed.

The keystrokes associated with a menu may result in any combination of the following effects:

1. move the highlight bar,
2. beep,
3. return to the calling program, transmitting item coordinates, keystroke code, and status code.

Keystrokes are described for the entire menu—they must produce the same combination of these effects, no matter what item is highlighted. (This is a minor defect in the Turbo C TOOLS design, considered again at the end of this section.) The cursor keys always move the highlight bar to the next item left or right, above or below, in the same row or column. Rows and columns wrap around in cyclic fashion. The <Tab> and <Shift-Tab> keys also move the highlight from item to item, but in the order of their installation, considered below. The <Home> and <End> keys move it to the first and last items installed. The <CR> and <Esc> keys both produce effect 3), returning status codes indicating success or failure.

The Figure 5.4.1 menu was produced by program **Menu1.Dem**, shown in Figure 5.4.2. Its first task is to construct the menu descriptor, using function

BMENU *mncreate(int Height, int Width,
int DefaultAttribute,
int HighlightAttribute,
int ProtectedItemAttribute,
int LongTextAttribute)

```
/**************************************************************/
/* Menu1.Dem      Demonstrate  Turbo C TOOLS  menu handling. */
/*                Display a simple menu offering three alter-*/
/* natives, then write a message in the same window reflecting*/
/**************************************** the user's choice.  */
                             /***********************/
#include <BMenu.H>

char *ThankYou   = "Thank you for selecting  ";
char *Caption[3] = {"[A]  Alpha.","[B]  Beta. ","[C]  Gamma."};
char *Keys[3]    = {"Aa","Bb","Cc"};

void main() {
  int    Width,I,Row,Col,Ch,Key;
  BMENU  *Menu;                    /* Pointer to menu.        */
  WHERE  Where = {MONO,0,{6,10}};  /* Page 0,  corner  6,10.  */
  BORDER Border;                   /* Window border descriptor.*/

Width = strlen(ThankYou)               /* Menu width.  Create */
  + strlen(Caption[0]) + 2;            /* menu with appropri- */
```

Figure 5.4.2 Program **Menu1.Dem** (*Continued on next page*)

```
Menu = mncreate(6,Width,                /* ate dimensions and   */
   NORMAL,REVERSE,NORMAL,NORMAL);       /* usual attributes.    */

Col = 11;                               /* Install items  A,B,C*/
for (I = 0; I < 3; ++I)                 /* at column   11,      */
   mnitmkey(Menu,I+1,Col,MN_NOPROTECT,  /* with keys to select  */
      Caption[I],Keys[I],MN_TRANSMIT);  /* them.                */

Border.type    = BBRD_SSSS | BBRD_TCT;  /* Single line  (SSSS) */
Border.attr    = NORMAL;                /* border with top cen-*/
Border.ch      = 0;                     /* ter title   (TCT)  in*/
Border.pttitle = " Make a choice! ";    /* boldface.           */
Border.ttattr  = NORMAL | INTENSITY;

mndsplay(Menu,&Where,&Border);          /* Display the menu.   */

Row = 1;                                /* Start highlight at  */
while (mnread(Menu,Row, Col,            /* item  A.  Loop un-  */
                 &Row,&Col,             /* til  <Esc>  returns */
                 &Ch,&Key,              /* an error code.  Set */
                 MN_UNKNOWN_BEEP)       /* Row,Col,Ch,Key   to */
       == WN_NO_ERROR) {                /* reflect selection.  */
  wncurmov(5,1);                        /* Write message on row*/
  wnprintf("%s%s",ThankYou,             /* 5  depending on the */
    Caption[Row-1]); }                  /* item selected.      */

mndstroy(Menu);                         /* Remove menu, restore*/
scpgcur(0,12,13,0); }                   /* monochrome cursor.  */
```

Figure 5.4.2 *(Continued)* Program **Menu1.Dem**

The function returns a pointer to the descriptor, a structure of type **BMENU** defined in header file **BMenu.H**. It's unnecessary to describe that structure in detail. It includes entries for the menu dimensions and attributes, for a pointer to a Turbo C TOOLS window descriptor, and for pointers to lists of items and keys. **Menu1.Dem** computes the menu **Width** to neatly encompass the text on the bottom line of Figure 5.4.1.

The next task for **Menu1.Dem** is to construct the item and key lists by making three calls to function

BMENU *mnitmkey (BMENU *Menu,
                 int Row, int Col,
                 int Option, char *Text,
                 char *Keys, int Effect)

Like other menu functions, it has a parameter pointing to the menu, and it returns the same value or a null pointer, indicating success or failure. The item is identified by its coordinates relative to the menu window. The available options correspond to constants defined in **BMenu.H**: **MN_NOPROTECT** or **MN_PROTECT**. The entries of string **Keys** represent ASCII keystrokes that will select this item, transmitting the coordinates and keystroke code to the calling program. In **Menu1.Dem** items are selected by the corresponding upper and lower case keystrokes. The **Effect** parameter is the sum of a code specifying the intended highlight motion and flags representing beep, return, success, and failure. **BMenu.H** defines constants for all the possibilities. The one used in this example is **MN_TRANSMIT**, which means return item and keystroke information with status code **WN_NO_ERROR** indicating success. (The <CR> key has the same effect.)

In Turbo C TOOLS there's no provision for preventing the text of one item from overlapping that of another; you have to lay out a menu in detail. You can't use function **mnitmkey** to change an item or keystroke, but you can do that with either of the functions **mnitem** or **mnkey**. These can add, change, or remove an item or keystroke. In fact, **mnitmkey** just calls these functions in succession. Function

BMENU *mnkey(BMENU *Menu,
             int Row, int Col,
             int Ch, int Key,
             int Effect, int Option)

gives you much more complete control over keystrokes. The pair **Ch,Key** constitutes the full two-byte keystroke code, so you can specify non-ASCII keystrokes, as well as distinguish different keystrokes that produce the same ASCII characters. (**Menu1.Dem** doesn't accept <Alt-(keypad)65> for '**A**', for example.) Using an appropriate **Effect** code, you can also make a keystroke select the item with the specified coordinates; otherwise, parameters **Row** and **Col** are ignored. Neither **mnitem** nor **mnitmkey** support Lotus-type long description text strings. However, the analogous functions **mnlitem** and **mnlitkey**, used in the same way, have additional parameters for the extra string and its coordinates. The order in which **mnitem** and **mnlitem** install menu items determines the way in which the <Tab>, <Shift-Tab>, <Home> and <End> keys move the highlight bar. Functions **mnkey** and **mnlitkey** are demonstrated later in program **Menu2.Dem**.

Once all the items and keystrokes have been installed in a menu, and you have defined window location and border descriptors of types **WHERE** and **BORDER** as in Section 4.4, you can display the menu using function

> BMENU *mndsplay(BMENU *Menu,
> WHERE *Where,
> BORDER *Border)

Figure 5.4.2 gives a typical example. This function simply validates its parameters then calls the window display function **wndsplay**. (Function **mnitmkey** actually wrote the items' text strings in the window's memory image.) To avoid "cursor chaff" in the menu, **mndsplay** turns the cursor off; thus you'll have to restore it to its original state before terminating your program.

Menu1.Dem now enters a **while** loop which repeatedly asks the user to select an item—either through a letter key or by moving the highlight bar and pressing <CR>. After selection, it writes a message reflecting the choice. In fact, the message is determined by the row coordinate of the selected item. The loop terminates when the user presses <Esc>: **while** detects the resulting error code. The user's choice is obtained through function

> int mnread(BMENU *Menu, int StartRow, int StartCol,
> int *Row, int *Col,
> int *Ch, int *Key,
> int Option)

Parameters **StartRow** and **StartCol** tell it where to start the highlight bar. The function responds to user keystrokes, moving the highlight and beeping as directed by the menu's keystroke list and the **Option** parameter, until it detects a keystroke designated to cause a return. Then it places the highlighted item's coordinates and the keystroke code in *Row, *Col, and *Ch, *Key, and returns a status code. The latter can be the success code **WN_NO_ERROR** or an error code. In either case, when **mnread** returns, **Menu1.Dem** uses the value *Row to select a message to print. It invokes Turbo C TOOLS window handling functions to move the cursor to the appropriate spot and emulate **printf**.

The **Option** parameter for **mnread** is the sum of some flags by which you can control

- response to keystrokes not in the menu's list;
- when keystrokes cause beeps;
- whether you remove the highlight bar or the whole menu after the function returns; and
- in the last case, whether you destroy the menu's data structures, or save them for repeated use.

When **while** detects the error code and exits from the loop, **Menu1.Dem** executes function **mndstroy** to remove the menu and destroy its associated data structures. Finally, the program turns the cursor on— **mndsplay** had turned it off to provide a clean display.

Program **Menu1.Dem** showed only the most basic menu handling techniques. At the risk of overwhelming you with detail (or underwhelming you with tedium), a second menu is presented in Figure 5.4.3. It was generated by the longer, more realistic program **Menu2.Dem** in Figure 5.4.4. This represents a typical scientific programming task: using a menu structure to select which of several variables to change, performing the input as smoothly as possible, then outputting some values dependent on the input. In short, **Menu2.Dem** is a simple spreadsheet program. Its data are related by three equations:

$$X_0/A + Y_0/B = 1$$

$$Y_1 = X_1{}^2$$

$$D^2 = (X_0 - X_1)^2 + (Y_0 - Y_1)^2$$

```
┌──────── Distance  D :   (X0,Y0)   to    (X1,Y1) ─────────┐
│  A  =        12.34    X0 =     1234.56    X1 =      -789.01 │
│  B  =       -56.78    Y0 =     5623.80    Y1 =    622536.81 │
│                                                            │
│  Enter  X1 =                              D  =    616916.31 │
└────────────────────────────────────────────────────────────┘
```

Figure 5.4.3 **Menu2.Dem** output

```
/********************************************************************/
/* Menu2.Dem      Demonstrate sophisticated  Turbo C TOOLS    */
/*                Lotus-type menu handling, integrating item */
/*                selection and data entry.                   */
/********************************************************************/

#include    <Math.H>
#include <BKeybrd.H>
#include    <BMenu.H>

float A = 1, B = 1;     /* For  X/A+Y/B = 1:  shouldn't = 0.  */
float X0,Y0,X1,Y1,D;    /* Two points and their distance.     */

#define K 7                     /* Length of  "Enter  ".         */
#define L 9                     /* Length of a  float  numeral.  */
#define M 3                     /* Spaces between grid columns.  */
#define N 7                     /* Number of cells.              */

#define  Col(J)  J*(K+L+M) + 1      /* Locates Jth Col of cells.*/
#define VCol(J) Col(J)     + K      /* Locates column for value.*/

typedef                            /* Structure corresponding*/
  struct {                         /* to a menu item.        */
        int    Row;                /* Cell row.              */
        int    Col;                /* Cell caption column.   */
        int    VCol;               /* Cell value column.     */
        char   Caption[K+L+1];     /* +1  for the terminator.*/
        char   Keys[3];            /* Keys that select cell. */
        float  *VPtr; }            /* Pointer to cell value. */
    CellType;

CellType Cell[N] =
  {{0,Col(0),VCol(0),"A  =        ","Aa",&A },       /* [0]*/
   {1,Col(0),VCol(0),"B  =        ","Bb",&B },       /* [1]*/
   {0,Col(1),VCol(1),"X0 =        ","Xx",&X0},       /* [2]*/
   {0,Col(2),VCol(2),"X1 =        ","Xx",&X1},       /* [3]*/
   {1,Col(1),VCol(1),"Y0 =        ","Yy",&Y0},       /* [4]*/
   {1,Col(2),VCol(2),"Y1 =        ","Yy",&Y1},       /* [5]*/
   {3,Col(2),VCol(2),"D  =        ",""  ,&D }};       /* [6]*/

int CellIndex(int Row, int Col) {     /* Find  Cell[I]  with */
  int I;                              /* specified  Row  and */
```

Figure 5.4.4 Program **Menu2.Dem** (*Continued on next page*)

```
for (I = 0; I < N; ++I)            /* Col.  Return  I  or */
  if (Cell[I].Row == Row &&        /* -1  in case of suc- */
      Cell[I].Col == Col)          /* cess or failure.    */
    return I;
return -1; }

void Display(CellType C) {         /* Display the cell  C */
  char S[80];                      /* value, using stars  */
sprintf(S,"%*.2f",L,*C.VPtr);      /* if it doesn't fit.  */
if (strlen(S) > L) strnset(S,'*',L);
wnwrbuf(C.Row,C.VCol,L,S,-1,-1,CHARS_ONLY); }


BMENU   *Menu;
WHERE   Where = {MONO,0,{5,5}};    /* Page 0,  corner  5,5.   */
BORDER Border;                     /* Set up in  main.        */

char *DigitsEtc                    /* These keystrokes trigger*/
  = "0123456789+-.";               /* entry of a new value.   */
#define CR  13                     /* Carriage return.        */
#define Esc 27                     /* Escape.                 */

void main() {
  int   I,Ch,Key,Row,Col;
  char S[L];
Menu = mncreate(4,Col(3)-M+1,      /* Create a menu with ap-  */
  NORMAL,REVERSE,NORMAL,NORMAL);   /* propriate dimensions,   */
wnselect(Menu->pwin);              /* etc.  Menu = current win-*/
wnwrbuf(3,Col(0),0,"Enter   ",     /* dow.  Write data entry  */
  -1,-1,CHARS_ONLY);               /* cue.                    */

for (I = 0; (Ch = DigitsEtc[I]) != 0; ++I)   /* Set up numeric */
  mnkey(Menu,0,0,Ch,kbscanof(Ch),            /* keys to start  */
    MN_TRANSMIT,MN_ADD);                     /* data entry.    */

for (I = 0; I < N; ++I)            /* Install all menu items.  */
  mnlitkey(Menu,
      Cell[I].Row,Cell[I].Col,     /* Caption location.       */
      (I < 4 ? MN_NOPROTECT        /* First  4  items active,  */
      : MN_PROTECT),               /* the rest protected.     */
      Cell[I].Caption,             /* Caption text.           */
      3,VCol(0),                   /* Location, text of Lotus  */
      Cell[I].Caption,             /* style description.      */
```

Figure 5.4.4 (*Continued*) Program **Menu2.Dem** (*Continued on next page*)

```
       Cell[I].Keys,MN_SELECT);        /* Keys to select the item. */

Border.type    = BBRD_SSSS | BBRD_TCT;      /* Menu border      */
Border.attr    = NORMAL;                     /* specification.  */
Border.ch      = 0;
Border.pttitle = " Distance  D :  (X0,Y0)  to  (X1,Y1) ";
Border.ttattr  = NORMAL;

mndsplay(Menu,&Where,&Border);              /* Display menu.   */
for (I = 0; I < 2; Display(Cell[I++]));     /* Display A,B.    */

Row = 0; Col = Col(0);                      /* Start highlight at   */
for (;;) {                                  /* item A.  Loop un-    */
   mnlread(Menu,Row,Col,&Row,&Col,          /* til <CR> or          */
       &Ch,&Key,MN_UNKNOWN_BEEP      |      /* <Esc> keeping the    */
              MN_KEEP_HIGHLIGHT  |          /* display neat. You    */
              MN_KEEP_DESCRIPTION);         /* can use only a nu-   */
   if (Ch == CR || Ch == Esc) break;        /* meric key to select  */
   kbplace(KB_HEAD,Ch,Key);        /* an item.  Push it back into  */
   wncurmov(3,VCol(0)+K);          /* the buffer, then go to the da-*/
   wnquery(S,L,&Ch);               /* ta entry site and read a num- */
   I = CellIndex(Row,Col);         /* ber.  Determine which cell was*/
   *Cell[I].VPtr = atof(S);        /* chosen, and update its value. */
   if (I <= 2)                     /* Changing Cells  0,1,2  (A,B,  */
      Y0 = B * (1 - X0/A);         /* X0)  requires changing Y0.    */
   if (I == 3) Y1 = X1*X1;         /* Y1  depends on  X0  (Cell 3). */
   D = hypot(X0-X1,Y0-Y1);            /* Compute distance.     */
   for (I = 0; I < N; ++I)            /* Display all cell      */
      Display(Cell[I]); }            /* values.               */
mndstroy(Menu);                      /* Remove menu, restore  */
scpgcur(0,12,13,0); }                /* monochrome cursor.    */
```

Figure 5.4.4 (*Continued*) Program **Menu2.Dem**

You may change the values of A, B, X_0, and X_1, but the others are computed from those. In the Figure 5.4.3 menu, items Y0, Y1, and D are protected; you can't move the highlight to any of them. The cue line that appears here as **Enter X1** is handled as a Lotus-type long description text string. Actually, the text **Enter** is just output to the window; **X1** is a Lotus-type description that reflects the highlight bar position. Aside from the usual keystrokes, <A> and <B> select the corresponding items, while <X> selects either X0 or X1, depending on which comes next in the installation list.

Besides the Lotus-type items, a second nicety is featured in this program: integration of the item selection and data entry processes. Any numerical keystroke—a digit, minus, plus, or decimal point—selects the highlighted item, and is also the first input character. Moreover, users can backspace to revise the input, then accept it with <CR>. Input is echoed in the space near the lower left corner, and transferred to the menu upon acceptance. Then the spreadsheet is updated, and users may make other selections.

Updating the spreadsheet raises a problem that Turbo C TOOLS doesn't address. In this type of application, the mathematical variables are usually manipulated by routines independent of the user interface. They are often components of larger structures like vectors and matrices, and the mathematical routines are included in packages of scientific software tools. You need a convenient way to associate the screen locations, or item coordinates, with the corresponding mathematical variables. Turbo C TOOLS doesn't provide a direct method for doing that—a possible modification is suggested at the end of this section. Program **Menu2.Dem** uses an array **Cell** of structures of type **CellType** that correspond to the menu items. Each structure contains the item's coordinates, the column in which its numeric value starts, its text, and a pointer to the corresponding mathematical variable. Several of these components are used with function **mnlitkey** to install the menu items. The text string doubles as the ordinary and Lotus-type descriptions. The Lotus-type description is used here not to provide additional detail, but for redundancy to help prevent data entry errors. The string includes a number of trailing blanks so that the highlight bar will underlie the entire numeric value in the menu and the Lotus-type descriptor will overwrite, hence erase, the old value in the data entry area.

The **Cell** array insulates the user interface from the mathematics. Since each **Cell** structure contains a pointer to the mathematical variable, you can display a **Cell** value on screen without even knowing the variable name. This is implemented in **Menu2.Dem** by function

void Display(CellType C)

The function avoids collisions with cell or window boundaries—a tedious precaution. It uses Turbo C TOOLS window output function **wnwrbuf**, described in Section 4.4.

If you know the **Cell** index, it's easy to find the corresponding item coordinates. On the other hand, the menu selection function **mnread** and the analogous Lotus-type function **mnlread** report the coordinates of a selected item, and to find the corresponding **Cell** index you must search through all the **Cell** structures for a match. Function

int CellIndex(int Row, int Col)

performs this service, returning the index (or -1 if it fails to find a match). To process numerical input, **Menu2.Dem** uses the Turbo C TOOLS high-level keyboard input function **wnquery** and Turbo C Library function **atof** to read and echo a numeric string and convert it to a **float** value. Then it calls **CellIndex** to find the appropriate **Cell** structure, and stores the **float** value in the mathematical variable designated by the structure's data pointer entry. Once a new value has been stored, the program updates the dependent variables, then calls function **Display** to update the spreadsheet on screen.

How are the numeric keystrokes (digits, plus, minus, decimal point) used *both* to select the highlighted item *and* as numerical input? First, each of the corresponding ASCII codes is stored in turn in variable **Ch**, then **mnkey** is called to augment (option **MN_ADD**) the menu's keystroke list:

mnkey(Menu,0,0,Ch,kbscanof(Ch),MN_TRANSMIT,MN_ADD)

Turbo C TOOLS function **kbscanof** returns the most common scan code associated with the stored ASCII code. Thus, only the numeric keys on the typewriter part of the keyboard will work. (Enabling numeric keypad entry would require another set of **mnkey** calls.) This makes the numeric keys select the highlighted item for input. The Lotus-type menu selection function places the keystroke code in **Ch** and **Key**:

mnlread(Menu,Row,Col,&Row,&Col,&Ch,&Key,
MN_UNKNOWN_BEEP
MN_KEEP_HIGHLIGHT
MN_KEEP_DESCRIPTION)

Thus, this function reads the first numeric input character. You can use a conventional keyboard input function to read the rest. However, really smooth data input requires enabling the backspace key <BS> to revise input before accepting it. Even if you use such a sophisticated routine, you can't backspace over that first character—you're stuck with it. The solution is to push it back to the head of the keyboard buffer, using the Turbo C TOOLS function **kbstuff** described in the previous section. Then the high-level input function **wnquery** will read and echo a string, with <BS> editing, at the data entry site near the lower left corner.

As you've seen, the menu handling features of Turbo C TOOLS are very comprehensive. The programs in Figures 5.4.2 and 5.4.4 demonstrate that once you understand the basic rhythm of menu creation, display, and item selection, it's possible to program sophisticated interactive input/output fairly easily. However, the second example shows that if you mix menu selection and data display, as in spreadsheet work, you will have to use some complex and tedious data structures to relate the user interface to the mathematics.

Some limitations have come to light. You can't easily vary the attributes within the text of a single item, as Turbo C does in its integrated development environment. This could be remedied by changing the text from strings of characters to arrays of character/attribute pairs, which is probably not a severe programming task. Second, you can't vary the meaning of a keystroke according to the item highlighted, so you can't generally use the Lotus-type long text descriptions as subsidiary menus. Changing that might require major redesign of the menu handling functions.

Another perhaps simple change to the menu functions would simplify their use in data entry contexts like **Menu2.Dem**. If the menu reading functions **mnread** and **mnlread** returned a pointer to the selected item rather than its coordinates, and the item descriptor structure were expanded to include a **void** * pointer **P**, users could make **P** address the corresponding data. That would make the **Menu2.Dem** function **CellIndex** unnecessary.

File Handling

Contents

The Turbo C Library provides a rich selection of file handling services for your programs. Your problem will probably lie not in finding a function for the task at hand, but rather in deciding which one to use. The Library functions are organized by dividing their prototypes and related definitions among seven header files:

IO.H	**Dir.H**	**DOS.H**	**FCntl.H**
StdIO.H		**ErrNo.H**	**Stat.H**

The three on the left are the most important. The scattering of file handling features among the others really reflects disorganization.

The **IO** and **StdIO** headers include five nearly parallel suites of functions, typified by these output routines:

Level	IO functions	StdIO functions
Low	_write write	fwrite
High		fprintf printf

The low-level functions themselves form a hierarchy. For example, _write merely provides DOS file output, while write incorporates some Turbo C protection features. fwrite, the standard C Library stream output function, includes yet more security features as well as a general input/output buffering system. The two versions of the familiar high-level output function printf are more easily distinguished: fprintf outputs to a specified stream, while printf uses the *standard* output stream. The latter is associated with the DOS standard output file handle. This normally uses the console screen device for output, but can be redirected at run time to any output file or device.

Clearly, a program should use a single suite of file input/output functions if possible, lest the associated data structures for protection and buffering become inconsistent with the actual state of the file. Criteria for choosing functions are not clear. For compatibility with C programs written for other operating systems, the StdIO stream functions are the choice. But they are implemented on top of the DOS file input/output system, and duplication of features like buffering will decrease efficiency and increase confusion. For the greatest control over input/output, use the low-level functions in IO.H.

This chapter first gives an overview of the file input/output systems. Then it considers the IO and StdIO functions in detail in Sections 6.2 and 6.3. Parallel demonstration programs in these sections let you compare the two types of service. Finally, Section 6.4 covers functions that manipulate DOS file system units, like directories and volumes, that are more comprehensive than single files. Most of those functions are organized in the Dir.H header file.

Turbo C TOOLS is not mentioned much in this chapter because Turbo C left only a few gaps for it to fill. (In fact, this version of the Blaise Computing Inc. product includes far fewer file handling routines than earlier ones that support other C compilers.)

6.1 Directory/file system overview

Concepts

The file concept
File access levels
DOS file handling
IO and **StdIO** file handling functions
Volume and directory manipulation
Input/output devices regarded as files

Files organize data intended for storage on or communication via some electronic medium. A language's file handling system forms the interface between applications programs and that hardware. Higher-order languages normally treat files as sequences of records. The records may be as simple as individual bytes, or arbitrarily complex, but they must all be of the same type. Usually, the records are created and appended to the file in sequence. However, you may read or update them either sequentially or in random order. The latter requires that the entire file be accessible at once, but that's not necessary for sequential access. For a higher-level language, file handling features must be as independent as possible from details of the data storage or communications medium. Moreover, if the language is to be general purpose, its facilities must not depend on the definitions of the records, which vary with individual applications.

DOS and Turbo C file handling

To maintain balance between these requirements, both Turbo C and DOS handle files as sequences of bytes: The constituent records are as simple as possible. Both above and below this level of abstraction, more structure is apparent. Below, you need structure to describe how the data are arranged on the medium. Above, record structure may be imposed by a particular application. You can give structure to a byte sequence to make it fit the design of a storage or communication device, and remove structure from a more complex record to transform it into a simple sequence.

For various purposes, programs must access files at several levels, as depicted in Figure 6.1.1. The highest and much of the lowest level in the figure are beyond the scope of this book. The highest level is considered in works on data processing. Programs at the lowest level are almost totally hardware dependent, usually optimized for speed, and written in assembly language. The **IO.H** and **StdIO**.H functions are described in Sections 6.2 and 6.3. Four Turbo C functions represent the lowest level of abstraction: **ioctrl**, **biosdisk**, **absread**, and **abswrite**. Some **ioctrl** features are discussed later. The other three functions are not considered further here, because most programming tasks at this level require the interrupt mechanism, discussed in Chapter 8, to access BIOS services. Two other Turbo C functions, **randbrd** and **randbwr**, are comparable to some of the **IO** functions, but are based on the obsolete DOS file control block (FCB) mechanism. Microsoft recommends against using this technique, so the functions are not described here.

Level of abstraction	File access methods
Highest: sequences of highly structured records.	High-level language facilities specialized for data processing.
High: byte sequences with sophisticated buffering and security features.	C programs using the **StdIO** stream processing functions.
Low: sequences of bytes with minimal additional structures for buffering and access protection.	DOS file handle services. Turbo C programs access these via the **IO** functions.
Lowest: bytes grouped for direct storage on or transmission via particular hardware.	BIOS services and low-level device dependent DOS services.

Figure 6.1.1 Selected file handling methods

Volumes and directories

You're familiar with DOS's organization of files into directories, and with its method of regarding directories as subdirectories of others, until you get to a single root directory on a volume. DOS uses directory entries to store volume name and time; directory name, time, and type; file name, time, type and size; and information that will lead DOS to the actual data stored on the medium. You use many DOS commands for manipulating this directory structure. Turbo C programs can perform the same operations; functions paralleling the DOS commands, as well as for performing wildcard directory searches and a few other directory operations, are discussed in Section 6.4.

File attributes, time stamp, and file size

Three items mentioned in the last paragraph can be regarded as belonging either to the directories in which they're entered, or to the files which they describe: the file time, type, and size. Since the functions for manipulating them are grouped among the file handling functions, they should be considered here, before the detailed descriptions of those functions in the next two sections.

The directory entry for a DOS file includes an *attribute byte,* whose bits are defined in Figure 6.1.2. Most of these attributes are familiar to a DOS

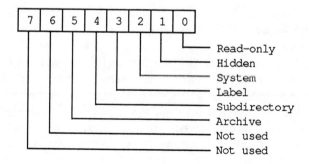

Figure 6.1.2 File attribute byte

user; note that some are mutually incompatible. DOS will not alter or erase a *read-only* file. Its directory operations won't find *hidden* or *system* files. (Under current DOS usage, these attributes are synonymous.) The label bit identifies an entry in a root directory used for its volume label. Subdirectories are just ordinary files with a special format, identified by the subdirectory bit. The DOS **Backup** utility turns off the archive bit; DOS turns it on whenever it alters the file. **Backup** inspects this bit to enable you to select for backup just those files that have changed since the previous backup. Combinations of attributes are permitted, as long as they make sense. For example, DOS files **IBMBIO.Com** and **IBMDOS.Com** are read-only hidden system files.

Another directory field called the *time stamp,* four bytes long, reports the date and time when the file was last altered. This information is reported by DOS command **Dir**.

The directory entry for a file also includes a four-byte field for the file size. This is the number reported by DOS command **Dir**. Unfortunately, the notion of file size is not always clear, because there are several ways to compute it, which rarely agree with each other. The reported file size is the actual number of bytes written in the file. However, DOS allocates space on a recording medium in *cluster* units. A cluster is a multiple of 512 bytes, determined to make the most efficient use of the medium. Normally, the file does not wholly occupy its last cluster, so that storing a new file decreases the space available by more than the file size. Finally, many text file processors, and some Turbo C Library functions, recognize <Ctrl-Z> as an end of file (EOF) mark, and may reckon file size as the number of bytes before EOF. That number is unlikely to agree with the DOS file size.

Input/output devices regarded as files

Files form a very general class of data structures. They can be finite, with all entries present at once for random access. Or they can be used for sequential access only, in which case all you need is the current record (or byte) and a way to get the next one. Files need not be permanently recorded; they can be ephemeral streams of data received or transmitted by your computer. It's common to handle keyboard and serial port input, and screen, serial, and printer output as files. Of course, some aspects of these input/output devices don't fit readily into the file concept, and there are some other differences between these applications of the file concept and the more familiar data storage files. As you saw in Chapter 4 you can't regard display output simply as a character stream: too much control information is required. Similarly, some aspects of serial communication depend on timing as well as the characters. And you do send a few control codes to a keyboard and receive a few status codes *from* a printer. Also, when a file is recorded on a permanent medium, it's ordinarily available for random access and has a beginning and an end. But an input/output character stream ordinarily permits access only in strict sequence; its beginning is inaccessible after the start of processing, and it often has no obvious end.

You will see the complications caused by DOS provisions for handling input/output devices like files. These are perhaps unavoidable because DOS is attempting to treat unlike ideas similarly, and the devices and file handling mechanisms were designed independently. Moreover, DOS grew in stages, and some of its earlier features are nearly incompatible with aspects of its design that were developed later.

IO vs. StdIO functions

The Turbo C features in Sections 6.2 and 6.3 are all based on DOS, so share its problems. The low-level **IO** functions are virtually exact counterparts of the DOS services. The **StdIO** functions are only slightly more powerful. In fact, they serve mainly to make a Turbo C program more compatible with C programs written for other machines. This actually increases complexity—the **StdIO** functions use software techniques not universally available for PCs. They are built on top of the DOS file handle system, and at times it's not easy to predict exactly how the two work together. For example, sometimes the **StdIO** functions will not increase file input/output speed, as the Turbo C *Reference guide,* Reference [7], suggests, but will decrease it by installing a superfluous level of buffering. Although source code for the Turbo C functions is available for analysis, that for DOS is not. Unfortunately, in some respects DOS is inadequately documented.

6.2 File handle input/output

Concepts

File handles, standard handles
DOS input/output buffer
File access byte
File sharing
File handle attributes, binary and text mode files
Reporting errors
File creation
Opening a file
Ascertaining and setting file and handle attributes
Reading, writing, and closing files

This section begins with an overview of the DOS file handle features. These underlie the input/output functions declared in header file **IO.H**, the family of low-level Turbo C file input/output functions. The method used by the functions to report failures is described, then there is an overview of the entire family. The most fundamental functions are considered in detail, with a demonstration program.

Officially, file handles are just integers that DOS uses to identify open files. They lie in the range 0..N, where N is specified by the **FILES** command in the **Config.Sys** file. (The default is N = 8, which is too small. Although DOS permits the maximum value N = 255, Turbo C will consider only file handles in the range 0..20. You should set N = 20 for complete compatibility with Turbo C.)

Opening a file means assigning it a handle and initializing various associated data structures in preparation for file input/output. You *close* a file by saving with it any necessary information stored in those structures, emptying them, and freeing the handle for assignment to another file. What's important about handles is the list of file features that you can access via references to them, and the set of operations that you can perform on files through such references. Here is a list of accessible features:

The file itself—a sequence of bytes.
The file pointer (current location for reading or writing).
Is the pointer at the end of the file?

Directory information:
  Time stamp,
  Attribute byte,
  File length.
The drive where the file is located.

Further, you can ascertain whether a file handle represents a data storage file or an input/output device, distinguish among various types of devices, and determine whether a device is in raw or cooked mode (see the description of the DOS hex 44 IOCTL function in Section 8.5). This list also contains some properties that affect access in a file sharing environment. Some of these are mentioned; others are beyond the scope of this book.

One obvious file feature is *not* accessible via file handles: the file name. A program cannot determine the name of a file to which a handle refers, unless it opened the file itself.

When it executes a program, DOS automatically opens the first five file handles:

Handle	Name	Usual device connected	DOS device file name
0	Standard input	Keyboard	**Con**
1	Standard output	Display	**Con**
2	Standard error	Display	**Con**
3	Standard auxiliary	Serial port 1	**Aux**
4	Standard printer	Parallel port 1	**Prn**

These *standard* handles can be assigned differently. In fact, it's common to *redirect* standard input and output to data storage files, and standard printer to standard auxiliary. (A program cannot discover the *name* of a new input or output data storage file. But, as noted earlier, it *can* ascertain that the handle has been redirected, and even find the drive name.)

You can use file handles to request standard input/output operations: reading and writing, moving and finding the pointer, and closing the file. Data storage file input/output is always buffered: DOS reads and writes whole sectors at once (usually 512 bytes). Moreover, according to the **BUFFERS** command in your **Config.Sys** file, a number of the most recently read sectors are cached in memory for quicker repeated access. (DOS literature indicates that one buffer stores one sector. But some file storage devices—e.g., virtual disks—let you *select* sector size during installation, independent of the **BUFFERS** command. How this conflict is resolved isn't clear.) Although the DOS file buffer is associated with the handle, your programs cannot access it directly; you can't ascertain its location, size, or contents.

DOS associates with each file handle an *access* byte, which tells how the current program and others may access the corresponding file. (The access byte is *not* an attribute of the file itself: it is not retained once the file is closed.) Its format is shown in Figure 6.2.1. Turbo C Library header file **FCntl.H** defines constant macros as shown for requesting file access via **IO** functions. Inconsistencies in the access byte codes reveal a bad DOS design. Values of the **FCntl** constants (not shown) do not exactly parallel the codes.

When a program asks DOS for a file handle, it requests read and/or write access. A write access request will be denied if the file is read-only. The program may require that its child programs inherit the handle. (Child programs are those executed by the current one; this is discussed in Chapter 7.) Further, a program may request restrictions on access to this file via other file handles. It may in fact specify at most one of the

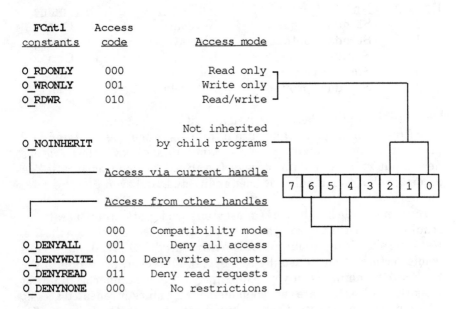

Figure 6.2.1 File access byte

access modes indicated by the **O_DENY...** constants. For these restrictions to apply, you must have executed previously the DOS memory resident utility **Share.Exe**. (The compatibility mode applies only to networked computers, and is beyond the scope of this book.) The default setting for the file handle access byte is 0000 0010: only the read/write access bit is set.

In addition to the DOS access byte, some of the Turbo C **IO** functions use and maintain an array **_openfd** of *file handle attribute* bytes, one for each of the 20 possible handles, whose layout is shown in Figure 6.2.2. The bits are self-explanatory, except for those indicating *text* and *binary* modes. Functions that use the file handle attribute byte apply a special translation process to text mode file handles: on input, <CR> characters are omitted from <CR><LF> pairs, and on output, <CR> is inserted before each <LF>. Moreover, these functions will set the **_O_EOF** bit and terminate input when they detect the <Ctrl-Z> end of file (EOF) character. Binary mode handles are subject to no such translations. Most of the functions that use the file handle attribute bytes refer to global variable **_fmode**, declared in header file **FCntl.H**, for the default setting if neither text nor binary mode is specified. Turbo C initializes this variable to **O_TEXT**, but you can change its value if you wish. Turbo C also appropriately initializes the attribute bytes for standard file handles 0..4; the others are set to zero.

Before describing individual **IO** functions in detail, it's helpful to consider their technique for reporting failure. Failures are perhaps more common in file handling than in any other programming context. When an **IO** function fails—for example, by attempting to read from a non-

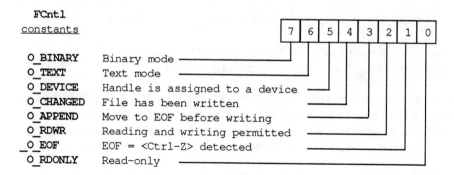

Figure 6.2.2 Turbo C file handle attribute byte

existent file, or to write on a read-only file—it usually signals failure by returning an invalid value. Sometimes no value is clearly invalid, so *all* the functions set the value of global variable **errno** (declared in header files **ErrNo.H** and **DOS.H**) to indicate success or the particular error. The zero value signifies success. You can either look up the corresponding error description **ErrNo.H** or execute **StdIO** function

void perror(char *S)

which outputs string **S**, then the **errno** description, to the standard error file handle. As demonstrated in Figure 6.2.3, you can use **S** to identify the location of the function that failed. You can gain access to the **errno** description string, without outputting it, via function

char *strerror(int N)

Just set **N** = **errno** before calling it. The **strerror** prototype is in header file **String.H**.

The next paragraphs describe in detail the most basic **IO** functions, and provide an overview of the entire family. Several of the functions are demonstrated together in the Figure 6.2.5 program **FileCas1.Dem**, discussed under the heading *Reading, writing, and closing files*. You will find an analogous program using the **StdIO** functions in Section 6.3.

Creating files

The first step in file handling is, of course, file creation. Among the functions **IO.H** provides for this service, these are the most useful:

int creatnew(char *FileName, int Attributes)
int creattemp(char *Name, int Attributes)

creatnew creates and opens a file with the given name, provided none already exists. It builds the DOS directory entry, with the specified attribute byte, and returns the file handle. Constants are defined in header file **DOS.H** for use in setting the **Attribute** parameter:

FA_RDONLY	FA_SYSTEM	FA_DIREC
FA_HIDDEN	FA_LABEL	FA_ARCH

These correspond to individual bits; you can combine them in a disjunction with the | operator. For example, you can create a read-only hidden file by setting

Attributes = FA_RDONLY | FA_HIDDEN

The DOS file handle access byte receives the default value, with only the read/write access bit set. You can write on the file until you close it, even though you may have designated it read-only! The Turbo C file handle attribute byte retains its initial zero value. If you attempt to create a file that already exists, **creatnew** will fail. Function **creattemp** is like **creatnew**, except that you specify a directory name. The function generates a file name different from those present in that directory, stores it in string **Name**, and creates the file. You're expected, but not required, to erase the file before your program terminates. (Use the Section 6.4 function **remove**.)

If you want to create a file and open it with file handle access and attribute bytes other than the default values, you should create it with **creatnew** or **creattemp**, close it, then open it with function **open** or **_open**, described in the next paragraph. **IO.H** includes two other file creation functions, **creat** and **_creat**. These are somewhat similar to **creatnew**. However, if a file with the specified name already exists, they will open it, perhaps emptying it in preparation for rewriting. Moreover, the access and attribute bytes are affected in complicated ways. It's safer to avoid those functions and separate clearly the operations of file creation and opening.

Opening files

The most appropriate **IO** function for opening an existing file is

int open(char *FileName, int Access)

The **Access** parameter specifies the requested DOS access and Turbo C file handle attribute bytes. It can be a disjunction of terms of the following types:

- At most one of **O_RDONLY, O_WRONLY, O_RDWR**;
- **O_NOINHERIT**;

- At most one of **O_DENYALL, O_DENYWRITE, O_DENYREAD, O_DENYNONE**;
- At most one of **O_BINARY, O_TEXT**;
- **O_APPEND**.

If successful, the function returns the file handle. When you open a file for reading, its pointer is located at the start. For writing, unless **O_APPEND** was specified, it's also at the start, and the file is emptied (truncated). However, when you open a file for appending, its data remains intact, and the pointer is positioned at the end before every write operation. If neither **O_BINARY** nor **O_TEXT** is specified, function **open** uses global variable **_fmode**, mentioned earlier, to determine the mode.

Another **IO** function, **_open**, is slightly lower level than **open**, and not really necessary. It ignores the Turbo C file handle attribute byte, always using binary mode and cannot use the **O_APPEND** access mode. Although these functions can be used to open—i.e., create and open—a new file, that's not advisable. Use the **access** function, described in the next paragraph, to ascertain existence of a file, and **creatnew** or **creattemp** to create and open one when necessary. You may find that neither of these allows you to specify the desired file or file handle attributes. In that case, close the file (as described later) and reopen it with **open**.

Program **Sharing.Dem** in Figure 6.2.3 demonstrates use of the file-sharing access bits. It opens its own **.Exe** file for write access via handle 5, restricting write access. Then no other handle can have write access; moreover, no other can restrict write access, because handle 5 has that access already. The program now opens the file for read access via handle 6, applying no further restrictions. Finally, it attempts to open the file for read access, restricting write access. This fails, as just predicted.

Finer control is possible in a file sharing context: You can *lock* a portion of a file, rather than the entire file, to prevent access from other handles while you're performing some update operation, then *unlock* it when you're done. Two **IO** functions are provided for this service: **lock** and **unlock**. Their use is beyond the scope of this book.

Two **IO** functions manipulate file handles in ways related to file creation:

int dup(int OldHandle)
int dup2(int OldHandle, int NewHandle)

dup returns a new handle, attached to the same device as the old one, with the same file handle access and attribute bytes, and with its pointer coupled to the old one. (That is, whenever the old pointer moves, the new one moves in the same way.) With **dup2**, you can specify the new handle; if currently open, it will be closed before the duplication. These functions can be used to update a file without closing it, and for input/output redirection. The former operation is described at the end of this section; the latter, in connection with executing child programs, in Chapter 7.

```
/****************************************************************/
/* Sharing.Dem      Demonstrate file sharing.  Open a file with*/
/*                  write access, denying write access from    */
/* other handles.  Open it again with read access, but no fur-*/
/* ther restrictions.  Try to open it a third time, denying    */
/*****************************  write access from other han-    */
                            /* dles.  This fails, because the*/
#include    <IO.H>         /* first one already has access. */
#include <FCntl.H>         /* You must execute the  DOS      */
#include <StdIO.H>         /* memory resident utility        */
                           /* Share.Exe  before this.        */
void main() {              /********************************/
  int H1,H2,H3;
H1 = open ("Sharing.Exe",O_WRONLY | O_DENYWRITE);
perror("Open for writing, denying others write access  ");
printf("Handle  %i\n",H1 );
H2 = open ("Sharing.Exe",O_RDONLY | O_DENYNONE );
perror("Open for reading, with no further restrictions ");
printf("Handle  %i\n",H2 );
H3 = open ("Sharing.Exe",O_RDONLY | O_DENYWRITE);
perror("Open for reading, denying others write access  ");
printf("Handle  %i\n",H3 ); }
```

Output
_____

```
Open for writing, denying others write access: Error 0
Handle  5
Open for reading, with no further restrictions: Error 0
Handle  6
Open for reading, denying others write access: Permission denied
Handle  -1
```

Figure 6.2.3 Program **Sharing.Dem**

Ascertaining and setting file and handle attributes

The Turbo C Library contains several functions that allow you to ascertain or set file and file handle attributes, and other properties associated with files, accessing them via the file name or handle. The chaotic organization of this set of functions is apparent from Figure 6.2.4, which lists some of their properties. Their prototypes are all in **IO.H**, except **fstat** and **stat**, which you will find in **Stat.H**. The latter two are particularly general. There is no need to consider any of these functions in great detail in this book, since their use is straightforward once you select the right one. You can find details in the Turbo C *Reference guide*, Reference [7]. For most of the properties listed, mnemonic constant macros are provided in **DOS.H, FCntl.H, IO.H,** or **Stat.H**.

Several of these functions merit brief comment. To check whether a file exists, use

int access(char *FileName, int Code)

with **Code** = 0. It returns 0 if the file exists, else -1. Next, it's useful to be able to change the time stamp recorded on a file, particularly when you want it to reflect the version number of a distributed software or data package. Use **setftime** to do that. It's also helpful sometimes to ascertain the drive on which a file resides, given its handle, in order to display instructions to the user. Since devices behave differently from data storage files, you may need to determine whether input or output is going to or coming from a device, in order to respond properly if DOS redirects it. Function **fstat** provides the last two services.

Functions **tell** and **lseek** can ascertain and set the file pointer relative to the file's start, end, or current pointer location. The file length calculations, as mentioned in the previous section, count the actual number of bytes. Function **filelength** does this by moving the pointer, ascertaining its location relative to the end, and restoring its previous position. **fstat** uses **filelength** for that service. Finally, function

int eof(int Handle)

returns 1 if the file pointer is at the end of the file, 0 if it's not, and -1 to indicate an error. First, it checks the Turbo C file handle attribute end-of-file bit. If that doesn't indicate that a <Ctrl-Z> end of file character has

Attribute /Property	Ascertain /Set	Name/ Handle	Function
Existence	Ascertain	Name	**access**
File attribute byte	Ascertain Ascertain Set	Name Name Name	**stat** **_chmod** **_chmod**
Read-only	Ascertain Ascertain Set	Name Handle Name	**access** **fstat** **chmod**
File time	Ascertain Ascertain Ascertain Set	Name Handle Handle Handle	**stat** **fstat** **getftime** **setftime**
Drive number	Ascertain	Handle	**fstat**
Length	Ascertain Ascertain Ascertain	Name Handle Handle	**stat** **fstat** **filelength**
Is a device?	Ascertain Ascertain	Name Handle	**stat** **fstat**
Text or binary?	Set	Handle	**setmode**
End of file?	Ascertain	Handle	**eof**
Pointer location	Ascertain Set	Handle Handle	**tell** **lseek**

Figure 6.2.4 Functions for ascertaining and setting file and file handle attributes and properties

been detected, then **eof** uses the same method as **tell** to check the position of the file pointer.

Reading, writing, and closing files

Two pairs of **IO** functions are provided for reading and writing files:

int _read(int Handle, void *Block, int N)
int   read(int Handle, void *Block, int N)
int _write(int Handle, void *Block, int N)
int   write(int Handle, void *Block, int N)

You specify the file handle, the memory block to input or output, and the number **N** of bytes to read or write. The functions return the number of bytes actually read or written, or -1 to indicate error. Functions **_read** and **_write** ignore the Turbo C file handle attribute byte, except that **_write** does observe its **O_APPEND** bit: if that is set, *all* write operations are done at the end of the file. Reporting the number of bytes read or written in text mode, **read** doesn't count end of file characters or the <CR> characters it deletes from the input, nor does **write** count characters it inserts. On detecting end of file, **read** sets the file handle **_O_EOF** attribute. Reading to end of file is never considered an error, but it may cause the returned number of bytes read to be less than **N**, the number requested. On the other hand, if **write** reports fewer bytes written than requested, the output medium is probably full.

Parallel to the DOS **Verify** command, Turbo C provides functions

int getverify(void)   void setverify(Code)

to ascertain or set the verification status. A return or **Code** value 0 indicates that verification is *off*; 1 signifies *on*. When verification is *on*, all disk and diskette output is verified to insure correctness. (This process is very time-consuming, so the default status is *off*.)

You can use **IO** function

int chsize(int Handle, long Size)

to change the size of a file that's open for writing. If you shorten it, you'll lose the data after the new end of the file; if you lengthen it, the function appends zeroes.

To close a file, use function

int close(int Handle)

This empties the DOS output buffer, updates the file's directory entry if necessary, clears the data structures associated with the handle, and releases the handle for later use. The related function **_close** is a little weaker: it ignores the Turbo C file handle attribute byte. Open files are automatically closed when a program terminates.

Sometimes, especially in a concurrent processing context, it's useful to empty an output buffer and update the directory information without closing the file. Moreover, in any context, closing and reopening it takes time. To flush the DOS file buffer without closing the file, use Turbo C TOOLS function

int flflush(int Handle)

Its implementation is interesting: it uses function **dup** to make a duplicate of the file handle, then closes that copy! Program **FileCas1.Dem** in Figure 6.2.5 demonstrates several **IO** functions. Execute it with command line

FileCas1 FileName Upper

to convert the specified file to upper case, or with last parameter **Lower** for lower case. The program uses functions

open tell read lseek write eof close

Another way to detect end of file is to compare the number of bytes read with that requested. That method fails in text mode because the program reads **N** bytes, deletes the <CR> characters, then returns the number of characters remaining—the number of bytes read *never* agrees with that requested! **FileCas1** could as well have been written with

_open _read _write _close,

ignoring the text/binary mode distinction altogether.

```
/*****************************************************************/
/* FileCas1.Dem     Demonstrate  IO  file handling functions  */
/*                  by converting a file to upper or lower     */
/*                  case.  The first command line parameter    */
/**************************************** names the file.  The*/
                                    /* second is  Upper  or*/
#include <CType.H>                  /* Lower.              */
#include    <IO.H>                  /*********************/
#include <FCntl.H>

#define BlockLength 1024            /* Can be anything.    */

void main(int   NParameters,        /* Not used.           */
          char *Parameter[]) {      /* File name, option.  */
  int  OptionIsLower,N,EndOfFile,I;
  int  F;                           /* File handle.        */
  long FP;                          /* File pointer.       */
  char Block[BlockLength];          /* Memory for  I/O.    */
OptionIsLower =
  (toupper(Parameter[2][0]) == 'L');
F = open(Parameter[1],O_RDWR);      /* Open file for  I/O. */
do {
    FP = tell(F);                   /* Remember position.  */
    N  = read(F,&Block,BlockLength);  /* N = how many read.  */
    EndOfFile = eof(F);             /* Remember EOF.       */
    for (I = 0; I < N; ++I)
      Block[I] = (OptionIsLower ?   /* Convert case.       */
        tolower(Block[I]) :
        toupper(Block[I]));
    lseek(F,FP,SEEK_SET);        /* Restore pointer position.*/
    write(F,&Block,N); }         /* Write converted text.   */
  while (!EndOfFile);            /* Repeat until end of file.*/
close(F); }
```

Figure 6.2.5 Program **FileCas1.Dem**

6.3 Stream Input/output

Concepts

Streams, standard streams
Stream buffering sometimes slows down file I/O
Creating and opening streams
Temporary files
Ascertaining and setting stream attributes
Controlling the stream buffer
Reading and writing streams
fseek must intervene between input and output
Pushing back an input character
Flushing and closing streams
Demonstration program **FileCas2.Dem**

The Turbo C **StdIO** functions provide file handling services with security and buffering features somewhat more powerful than the **IO** functions just described in Section 6.2. Their main benefit, however, is compatibility with many other C libraries. This section describes the functions in detail, and concludes with a demonstration program **FileCas2.Dem** analogous to program **FileCas1.Dem** in the previous section. With it you can compare usage of corresponding functions.

Streams

The additional functionality of the **StdIO** functions stems from their use of the **FILE** data structure defined in **StdIO.H**, which the C literature calls a *stream*. Here is its declaration:

```
typedef struct {
    short            level;      /* Used for buffering */
    unsigned         flags;      /* File status word   */
    char             fd;         /* DOS file handle    */
    unsigned char    hold;       /* ungetc character   */
    short            bsize;      /* Buffer size        */
    unsigned char    *buffer;    /* Turbo C i/o buffer */
```

```
unsigned char  *curp;      /* Used for buffering          */
unsigned        istemp;    /* Temporary file indicator */
  short         token; }    /* For checking validity       */
FILE;
```

Although your programs probably won't need to refer to the components of a **FILE** structure, a brief description will help you understand
the control that stream input/output provides in file handling. The **fd**
component is the DOS file handle for the open file. Since the five
standard handles 0..4 are always open, the Turbo C startup code
allocates and initializes *standard* streams corresponding to these handles.
StdIO.H defines

stdin stdout stderr stdaux stdprn

as pointers to these streams.

The **flags** component of a **FILE** structure is organized as shown in
Figure 6.3.1. **StdIO.H** provides macro constants for the individual bits.
Most are self-explanatory; some duplicate items in the Turbo C file
handle attribute byte described in the previous section. The **_F_BUF** bit
indicates when the stream provides buffering in addition to the DOS
buffer associated with the file handle. This is ordinarily the case; a
pointer to the stream buffer is stored in **FILE** structure component

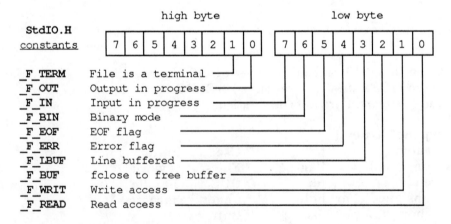

Figure 6.3.1 Turbo C **FILE** structure flags word

buffer, and its size in **bsize**. The default size is 512 bytes, but you can change that with function **setvbuf** described later in this section. If you use that service to allocate a buffer, it will set **flags** bit _F_BUF, so that function **fclose** will free the buffer when you close the stream. **FILE** structure Components **level** and **curp** store technical information concerning buffering.

flags bit _F_LBUF indicates whether line or full buffering is in effect. With either type, an input operation reads from the buffer unless it's empty. When the buffer is empty, an input operation will attempt to fill it from the file or device. Similarly, output is directed to the buffer, which is emptied to the file or device when it's full, or, if line buffering is in effect, when a <CR> is output. The **stdin** and **stdout** streams are ordinarily line buffered; the other standard streams are unbuffered. If you open a stream associated with a terminal device, it will be line buffered. Streams associated with data storage files are ordinarily fully buffered.

This book will not analyze stream buffering more deeply, for several reasons. First, the relevant Turbo C Library source code is classical spaghetti—just what programmers are cautioned against, because it's impenetrable. Second, the relationship between the stream buffer and the buffer associated with the DOS file handle is not clear. For example, the normal DOS buffer length is apparently 512 bytes, like the default stream buffer. Therefore, it seems that using a stream buffer may slow down input/output, contrary to claims in the Turbo C *Reference Guide*, Reference [7]. Ascertaining the effect of a different stream buffer size would require considerable experimentation, or else more information about DOS input/output than is easily obtainable. Moreover, the results would certainly depend on the application, and probably on the hardware, too.

The remaining **FILE** structure components are simple. **hold** sometimes stores a character that function **ungetc** (described later) has "pushed back" to the input. **istemp** identifies a temporary file, ordinarily created by function **tmpfile**, that must be destroyed when it's closed. Finally, **token** stores a code that identifies **FILE** structures created by **StdIO** functions. These functions will not handle structures with invalid **token** components.

This overview of the **FILE** structure shows that the main benefit of Turbo C stream input/output must lie in its compatibility with other C libraries. Gains in input/output efficiency can come only through exhaustive experimentation with particular applications and hardware.

Minor benefits are afforded by the pushback and temporary file features, which are not provided by the **IO** functions.

Before describing the **StdIO** stream input/output functions in detail, consider the error reporting system. Since the **StdIO** functions call the lower-level **IO** functions, the **IO** error reporting feature—global variable **crrno**—is active, and you can use functions **perror** and **strerror** to display and manipulate error messages, as demonstrated in the previous section. Like the **IO** functions, **StdIO** routines often return 0 to indicate success, or an invalid value to indicate failure. Two other **StdIO** functions,

int ferror(FILE *F)   void clearerr(FILE *F)

provide further services. The former returns a nonzero value just when the **_F_ERR** bit of the **flags** component of **F** indicates an error on that stream. Function **clearerr** clears this bit. (So does function **rewind**, described later.)

Creating and opening streams

The operations of creating and opening streams are combined in **StdIO** function

FILE *fopen(char *FileName, char *FileType)

String **FileType** consists of an access designator, possibly followed by a *mode* designator. The former is the letter **a**, **r**, or **w**, possibly followed by a **+**. The latter is **t** or **b**. The access designator tells the function what to do in case the file does or does not exist: see Figure 6.3.2. The mode designator indicates that the file handle should be opened in text or binary mode, as described in Section 6.2. If no mode is specified, global variable **_fmode** (declared in header file **FCntl.H**) determines the default mode. **fopen** is implemented as a call to an internal function **_openfp**, which sets up the stream buffer, then calls **IO** function **open** to open a file handle. Line buffering is used if **FileName** specifies a terminal device. **fopen** returns a pointer to the new **FILE** structure, or, to indicate an error, a null pointer.

If you use **fopen** to create a file, not realizing that one with the specified name exists already, you will destroy it inadvertently. Therefore,

Access designator	fopen actions	
	File exists	File does not exist
a	Open for appending only.	Create, open for appending only.
a+	Open for reading and appending.	Create, open for reading and appending.
r	Open for reading only.	Indicate error.
r+	Open for reading and writing.	Indicate error.
w	Empty the file, and open for writing only.	Create, open for writing only
w+	Empty the file, open for reading and writing.	Create, open for reading and writing.

Figure 6.3.2 fopen file access designators

you should check for existence—probably via function **access** described in the previous section—before using **fopen** to create a file. This situation often occurs when you need to create a temporary file in the current directory to hold intermediate results of some process. **StdIO.H** provides a function specifically for that purpose:

FILE *tmpfile(void)

This routine gets from function **tmpname** (described in Section 6.4) a file name of the form **TMP*.$$$** different from any in the current directory, then calls **fopen** to create and open it in binary mode for reading and writing. **tmpfile** returns a pointer to the **FILE** structure, having set its **istemp** component, so that the new file will be destroyed when it's closed. If you need access to the temporary file name, you'll have to perform these steps yourself, since you can't ascertain a filename through a handle or a stream.

The stream function analogous to **IO** function **dup2** is

FILE *freopen(char *FileName, char *FileType, FILE *F)

This closes stream **F**, then reopens it with the specified file, access, and mode. Its main use is in redirecting standard input/output for child programs, discussed in Chapter 7.

The following **StdIO** functions associate a stream with a file handle that's already open, and, conversely, return the handle associated with an open stream:

FILE *fdopen(int Handle, char *FileType)
int fileno(FILE *F)

Ascertaining and setting stream attributes

To ascertain and set most of the properties associated with files and file handles, you must rely on the **IO** functions already described in Section 6.3. The few **StdIO** routines of this sort are straightforward. Function

int feof(FILE *F)

returns a nonzero value just when the EOF bit in the **flags** component of **F** is set. **fseek** and **ftell** operate exactly like **IO** functions **lseek** and **tell**, except their first parameters are pointers to streams instead of file handles. (They make any necessary allowances for stream buffering, then call their **IO** counterparts. Functions **fgetpos** and **fsetpos** are variations of **fseek** and **ftell**, with different calling sequences. Function

int rewind(FILE *F)

calls **fseek** to move the file pointer to the start, then clears the error flag.

The most significant functions of this category are

void setbuf   (FILE *F, char *Buffer)
int setvbuf(FILE *F, char *Buffer,
            int Type, int Size)

To *disable* stream buffering for **F**, call **setbuf** with a null **Buffer** pointer. There are three ways to *set up* a stream buffer in addition to the DOS file buffer. First, you can allocate a buffer of length **BUFSIZE** (a **StdIO** constant macro with value 512), point to it with **Buffer**, and invoke **setbuf**. This will establish full buffering. Alternatively, you can allocate a buffer of any size, and call **setvbuf** with **Type** = _IOFBF or _IOLBF (**StdIO** constant macros) for full or line buffering. Finally, if you call **setvbuf** with a null **Buffer** pointer, it will use function **malloc** to allocate one for you, and set **Buffer** to point to it. In the last case, it will also set **flags** bit _F_BUF so that function **fclose** will free the buffer when you close the file. In other cases, you have the responsibility for freeing memory.

Reading and writing streams

StdIO.H provides a repertoire of stream input/output functions, each one analogous to a familiar keyboard or screen function or to the **read** or **write** function. In fact, several **StdIO** keyboard and screen functions simply perform stream input/output with the standard streams **stdin** and **stdout**. The stream functions are arranged in a hierarchy according to the structure of the input/output data, and are all based on **IO** functions **_read** and **_write**, as shown in Figures 6.3.3 and 6.3.4. The higher-level routines on the left call lower-level ones as indicated by the arrows. Except for these two, the functions whose names begin with the underscore character are not intended for execution by applications programs.

You invoke high-level functions **fscanf**, **vfscanf**, **fprintf**, and **vfprintf** just like their keyboard and screen counterparts **scanf**, **vscanf**, **printf**, and **vprintf**, using a pointer to the open stream as a new first parameter. Here are the corresponding pairs of string input/output functions:

Keyboard/screen	Stream input/output
char *gets(char *S)	**char *fgets(char *S, int N, FILE* F)**
int puts(char *S)	**int fputs(char *S, FILE* F)**

There is one minor lapse in correspondence between the calling sequences: **fgets** reads at most **N** - 1 characters. The two word-input/output functions

```
int getw(FILE *F)
int putw(int W, FILE *F)
```

have no keyboard/screen counterparts. Finally, the character input/output functions correspond closely:

```
int getchar(void)      int getc(FILE *F)
int fgetchar(void)     int fgetc(FILE *F)

int putchar(int Ch)    int putc(int Ch, FILE *F)
int fputchar(int Ch)   int fputc(int Ch, FILE *F)
```

fgetc and **getc** are identical, except the former is implemented as a call to **_fgetc**, after some attention to buffering, whereas the latter is a macro that mentions parameter **F** several times. Likewise, **putc** is a potentially dangerous macro. **fputc** is implemented as a function, and adjusts for line buffering. **getchar** and **putchar** are just macros that substitute **stdin** and **stdout** for **F** in calls to **getc** and **putc**. **fputchar** has the same relationship to **fputc**, but is implemented as a function. After some buffering details, **fgetchar** calls **_fgetc**.

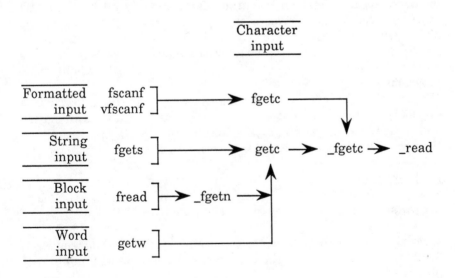

Figure 6.3.3 StdIO.H stream input functions

The **StdIO** block input/output stream functions are invoked like the corresponding **IO** functions **read** and **write**, but their calling sequences are slightly different:

int fread(void *Block, int Size, int N, FILE *F)
int fwrite(void *Block, int Size, int N, FILE *F)

Here, **Block** is a pointer to a memory region consisting of **N** items of the specified size. The functions return the number of items actually read or written. This may fall short of the number requested, if an error is encountered.

Although the Turbo C *Reference guide*—especially its description of **fwrite**—suggests that stream output can take place only at the end of a file, that is not true. As program **FileCas2.Dem** at the end of this section demonstrates, output occurs at the current location of the file pointer.

Because of the buffering technique, stream input and output operations must be separated by a call to **fseek** (or some function that invokes **fseek**).

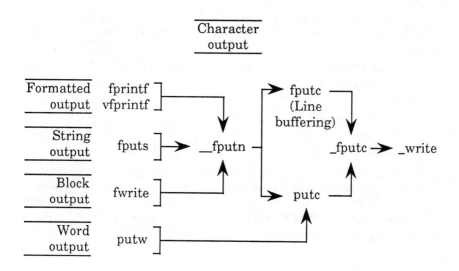

Figure 6.3.4 StdIO.H stream output functions

If you input a character from a stream, but decide you don't want to process it immediately, or if you simply want a certain character to appear as if it were the next input, you can use function

int ungetc(char Ch, FILE *F)

to *push back* the character. It's placed either in the stream buffer or in the **hold** component of its **FILE** structure, depending on buffering details. If the file pointer is moved, or **ungetc** called again, the character will be discarded. Otherwise, the next call to function **_fgetc** will retrieve it as though it were the next input from the stream.

Flushing and closing streams

Two sets of functions will flush a stream buffer or all open buffers, and close a stream or all open streams:

int fflush(FILE *F)   int flushall(void)
int fclose(FILE *F)   int fcloseall(void)

Flushing a buffer involves finishing any uncompleted output, then emptying the buffer and discarding any character that had been pushed back. Closing a file includes flushing its buffer, freeing it if it was allocated by **StdIO** functions, updating the file's directory entry, or destroying a temporary file created by function **tmpfile**, and freeing the **FILE** structure and other Turbo C and DOS structures associated with the file handle.

Demonstration program

Program **FileCas2.Dem** in Figure 6.3.5 demonstrates several **StdIO** stream functions. It performs exactly the same task as program **FileCas1.Dem** in the previous section, so you can compare the **IO** and **StdIO** techniques. Execute it with command line

FileCas2 FileName Upper

to convert the specified file to upper case, or with last parameter **Lower**
for lower case. The program uses functions

fopen ftell fread feof fseek fwrite fclose

```
/**************************************************************/
/* FileCas2.Dem     Demonstrate StdIO stream I/O functions*/
/*                  by converting a file to upper or lower   */
/*                  case. The first command line parameter   */
/************************************** names the file. The*/
                                      /* second is Upper or*/
#include <CType.H>                    /* or Lower.         */
#include <StdIO.H>                    /**********************/

#define BlockLength 1000              /* Can be anything.   */

void main(int   NoParameters,         /* Not used.          */
          char *Parameter[]) {        /* File name, option. */
  int  OptionIsLower,N,EndOfFile,I;
  FILE *F;                            /* I/O  stream.        */
  long FP;                            /* File pointer.       */
  char Block[BlockLength];            /* I/O  block.         */
OptionIsLower =
  (toupper(Parameter[2][0]) == 'L');
F = fopen(Parameter[1],"r+");         /* Open file for  I/O. */
do {
    FP = ftell(F);                    /* Remember position.  */
    N  = fread(&Block,1,              /* N = how many read.  */
      BlockLength,F);
    EndOfFile = feof(F);              /* Remember  EOF.      */
    for (I = 0; I < N; ++I)
      Block[I] = (OptionIsLower ?     /* Convert case.       */
        tolower(Block[I]) :
        toupper(Block[I]));
    fseek(F,FP,SEEK_SET);         /* Restore pointer position.*/
    fwrite(&Block,1,N,F);         /* Write converted text.   */
    fseek(F,  0,SEEK_CUR); }      /* Seek between out & in.   */
  while (!EndOfFile);             /* Repeat until end of file.*/
fclose(F); }
```

Figure 6.3.5 Program **FileCas2.Dem**

It could use either the default text mode—as here—or the binary mode, and could detect end of file either through function **feof** or by comparison of the number of items read with that requested. Unlike the **IO** version, the latter method had no problem with text mode. Note that an **fseek** call had to be inserted between the output and input operations, to maintain the buffering.

6.4 Directory manipulation

> **Concepts**
>
> Current drive
> Free space on a drive; removable media
> Volume label and time stamp
> Current directory
> Making, removing, and renaming directories
> Directory attributes and time stamp
> File name analysis, synthesis, and normalization
> Renaming a file; moving it to another directory
> Wild card searches
> Directory searches with the PATH string

This section is devoted to the remaining Turbo C and Turbo C TOOLS library functions involved in file input/output. These are mostly concerned not with individual files, but with directories and drives. Many are straightforward, paralleling familiar DOS commands. Others make available to your programs DOS techniques for handling **?** and * wild card characters in file names. Demonstration programs include a general file and directory renaming and redirection utility, and a directory search program that will produce statistics about disk files whose names match a specified wild card pattern.

Most of the directory manipulation routines report errors by returning an invalid or nonzero value and setting the **errno** constant. You can then ascertain the exact error by using functions **perror** and **strerror**, described in Section 6.2. The few exceptions are noted.

Drives and drive information

Paralleling DOS' usage of the **CD** command or the drive name to ascertain or set the current drive, the Turbo C Library provides functions

int getdisk(void)   int setdisk(int Drive)

Their prototypes are in header file **Dir.H**. You must set parameter **Drive** equal to 0,1... to specify **a:**, **b:**.... (Caution: other directory functions use 0 for the current drive and 1,2... for **a:**, **b:**....) Function **getdisk** is demonstrated by program **DiskInfo.Dem** in Figure 6.4.1. It isn't susceptible to error; **setdisk** simply ignores an invalid **Drive** parameter. Before calling **setdisk** with a possibly invalid **Drive**, you should invoke some other function—for example **getdfree**, considered next—that reports this error.

Function **setdisk** is supposed to return the total number of drives; however, its service is not reliable. First, it varies with the DOS version. In later versions, the number returned is at least five. Moreover, DOS enhancements may also change the value. When run under the author's *DESQview* system, **setdisk** reported 20 drives, although there were only five installed. Function **biosequip** also returns the number of diskette drives, but this is easily misinterpreted, since a single diskette drive can play both the **a:** and **b:** roles, some virtual disk device drivers masquerade as diskette drives, and some diskette device drivers identify themselves as fixed disks. These problems lie deeper than the Library functions: they reveal both bad PC and bad DOS design.

Other functions provide detailed information about drives. The most useful is

void getdfree(int Drive, struct dfree *D)

Set **Drive** = 0 for the current drive, or = 1,2... for drive **a:**, **b:**.... This function fills a structure of type **dfree**, which you must have previously allocated, with information from which you can determine the size of the medium, and the space currently free for use. You will find the function prototype and the structure definition in header file **DOS.H**. Here's the structure:

```
struct dfree {
  unsigned df_avail;  /* Number of available clusters.   */
  unsigned df_total;  /* Total number of clusters.       */
  unsigned df_bsec;   /* Bytes per sector.               */
  unsigned df_sclus; }/* Sectors per cluster.            */
```

Sectors and *clusters* are DOS disk space allocation units. (See Norton's book, Reference [30], for disk format details.) If you want the total or available space in bytes, you must multiply the factors given, taking care to cast their types to **unsigned long** or **real** lest you get overflow. To report an invalid **Drive** parameter, **getdfree** sets **D.df_sclus** = -1.

Most other functions that provide miscellaneous drive information are very technical, and rarely encountered in programs not specifically intended for managing disk details. Since they simply request BIOS or DOS services and report back the results, they are best considered in Chapter 8 under those headings. One of the data reported by **IO** function **ioctl** merits notice here: function call **ioctl(Drive,8)** returns an **int** value that is nonzero just when the **Drive** (specified as for **getdfree**) uses removable media. (Caution: some non-DOS diskette device drivers—for example, the author's Newport high-density system—return incorrect information to **ioctl**.) Program **DiskInfo.Dem** in Figure 6.4.1 demonstrates **getdisk**, **getdfree**, and **ioctl** by reporting the current drive and its statistics.

Volume labels

The Turbo C Library provides no functions for manipulating volume labels. Turbo C TOOLS fills the gap with three:

```
int flremvol(int Drive)
int flsetvol(int Drive, char *Label)
int flretvol(int Drive, char *Label,
                unsigned *Date, unsigned *Time)
```

The first removes any existing volume label on the specified **Drive** (0,1,2... for current, **a:**, **b:**...). The second installs the designated string as a new label; and the third reports the label and its date and time stamps. You must have allocated adequate space before calling **flretvol**. (**Label** requires 11 bytes for the label and one more for its trailing zero.) See the

```
/****************************************************************/
/* DiskInfo.Dem      Demonstrate functions  getdisk, getdfree  */
/*                   and  ioctl  service  8.  Display the cur- */
/***************************************** rent drive, indicate*/
                                        /* whether its medium  */
#include <StdIO.H>                      /* is removable, and   */
#include   <Dir.H>                      /* report its total and*/
#include   <IO.H>                       /* available space in  */
#include   <DOS.H>                      /* clusters and bytes. */
                                        /***********************/
void main() {
  struct dfree D;                       /* Defined in  DOS.H.  */
  unsigned long TotalBytes,AvailBytes;
  printf("The medium in  Drive %c:  is"
    "%sremovable.\n\n", getdisk() + 'A', /* Get drive letter.  */
      ioctl(0,8) ? " not " : " ");      /* Check removability: */
  getdfree(0,&D);                       /* 0 = current drive.  */
  TotalBytes = (unsigned long)          /* You cast the first  */
    D.df_total*D.df_bsec*D.df_sclus;    /* factors, and  C     */
  AvailBytes = (unsigned long)          /* casts the rest.     */
    D.df_avail*D.df_bsec*D.df_sclus;
  printf("Bytes/sector: %9u  Sectors/cluster: %2u\n",
    D.df_bsec ,D.df_sclus);
  printf("Total clusters:%9u  Available: %8u\n",
    D.df_total,D.df_avail);
  printf("Total bytes:  %9lu  Available: %8lu", /* l = long. */
    TotalBytes,AvailBytes); }
```

Output

```
The medium in Drive C: is not removable.

Bytes/sector:         512  Sectors/cluster:       4
Total clusters:     10863  Available:           955
Total bytes:     22247424  Available:       1955840
```

Figure 6.4.1 Program **DiskInfo.Dem**

Turbo C TOOLS manual, Reference [4], for the date and time stamp formats. **flsetvol** doesn't set the date/time information unless it creates a new volume label. If you want to change it to the current time, use **flretvol** to read the label, **flremvol** to remove it, then **flsetvol** to install a new label. If you want to change it to some other time, you'll have to save the current time, change it to the desired time, change the volume label as just described, then restore the correct time. (See Section 8.7 for DOS date/time services.) These functions return zero to report success.

Directories

You can ascertain or set the current directory on a drive via Turbo C Library functions

int getcurdir(int Drive, char *Name)
int chdir(char *Name)

To use **getcurdir**, set **Drive** = 0,1,2... for the current, **a:**, **b:**... drives. For **Name** you must allocate **MAXDIR** bytes—this is a macro constant defined in header file **Dir.H**, which also contains the function prototypes. **chdir** sets the current directory on the current drive if no drive is included in **Name**. If you include a drive identifier, it changes the current directory on that drive, but does *not* change the current drive. Both functions return zero to indicate success. A third function, **getcwd**, is an alternative to **getcurdir** with somewhat different features.

Parallel to the familiar DOS commands, Turbo C Library functions

int mkdir(char *Name)
int rmdir(char *Name)

will create a directory or remove one. They are subject to the same common sense restrictions as the commands.

DOS stores subdirectories (but not root directories) in the same format as data storage files. Therefore, like files, they have attribute bytes (see Section 6.1). DOS sets the *directory* attribute bit to identify a subdirectory. You can use function

int _chmod(char *Name, int Service)

with **Service** = 0 to return the attribute byte; **Name** can refer to a file or a subdirectory. With **Service** = 1 and an additional parameter, the same function will set the attribute byte:

int _chmod(char *Name, int Service, int Attribute)

However, you can't use _chmod to change the directory or volume label bits! You can set the read-only attribute of a subdirectory, but that seems to have no effect. A hidden or system subdirectory does not itself appear in directory searches or listings. The function prototype is in header file **DOS.H**, along with macro constants for the bits in the attribute byte.

Like files and volume labels, subdirectories have date/time stamps. Unfortunately, the Turbo C Library routines **getftime** and **setftime** that ascertain or set the date/time stamp of a file will not work with subdirectories. You can *read* the subdirectory date/time stamp as a byproduct of a wild card search, discussed later in this section. However, there is no easy way to set the stamp. This capability would be useful, for example, in preparing software for distribution, so that the directory time correlates with the version number. One unwieldy technique is at hand: reset the current date/time to the desired value, make a new directory with an appropriate name, copy to it all the required files, erase the old data, then restore the correct time. (See Section 8.7 for ascertaining and setting the current date/time.) There is a method that requires no file copying, but uses very low-level DOS services; it's discussed briefly in Section 8.5, in the context of FCB file handling.

To *rename* a subdirectory you can use function **rename**, the same one for renaming files, discussed later in this section. However, you *cannot move* a subdirectory as a unit from one directory to another. You could make a new subdirectory, copy the files, then erase the old data, but that wouldn't work if the old subdirectory itself had subdirectories. A general method requires a recursive subdirectory search, like the wild card search described at the end of this section.

Manipulating files and file names

Creating and destroying files were described in detail in Sections 6.2 and 6.3. Unlike the dangerous DOS command **erase**, you cannot use wild cards with Turbo C functions **unlink** or **remove** to erase multiple files at once. Ascertaining and setting their attribute bytes was also discussed in 6.2, and earlier in this section in the context of directory attributes. The only direct method in Turbo C for ascertaining or setting the file date/time stamp is through functions **getftime** and **setftime**, also discussed in 6.2. These functions require file handle parameters, so you have to open a file even to discover its date.

Function **fnsplit**, which parses a file name into drive, directory name, file name, and extension components, and function **fnmerge**, which reconstitutes it, were discussed in detail, with a demonstration program, in Section 3.8. Flaws were highlighted—particularly the functions' blind acceptance of invalid input. (Another function, **parsfnm**, performs a similar service; a vestige of DOS 1.1, it can't handle subdirectories.) All three prototypes are in header file **Dir.H**.

Turbo C TOOLS provides a function that *normalizes* a file name:

int flnorm(char *FileName, char *NormalForm, int *Last)

The following steps transform **FileName** to **NormalForm**: the function

- regards illegal characters as errors;
- converts all letters to lower case, and all slashes / to backslashes \;
- adds the current drive name if none is given;
- adds the name of the current directory on the specified drive;
- replaces the self-referential and parent directory names . and .. with their full names;
- eliminates any trailing colon: from a device name;
- truncates so that each part of the name—delimited by backslashes and/or the end—consists of one to eight characters, perhaps followed by a dot and a one- to three-character extension.

On completion, **Last** points to the last part of the name, and **flnorm** returns zero to indicate success, or 1 to indicate an illegal filename. Unless one of the DOS commands **Assign**, **Join**, or **Subst** is in effect, two filenames refer to the same file *if and only if* their normalized names coincide exactly. If you use **flnorm** first, **fnsplit** will yield correct results.

Two Turbo C functions generate names suitable for temporary files: **mktemp** and **tmpname**. The latter provides a name different from any in the current directory, which is used by function **tmpfile** to create a temporary file. **mktemp** uses a slightly different method. For details, consult the Turbo C *Reference guide,* Reference [7].

The **StdIO** function

int rename(char *OldName, char *NewName)

parallels the analogous DOS command somewhat, but enjoys both more and less capability. It will rename a subdirectory if the new name is in the same directory as the old, and rename a file even if the new name is in a different directory, as long as it's on the same drive. On the other hand, **rename** won't accept wild cards, and may unsuccessfully attempt to use the default drive with the new name unless you specify otherwise. (DOS command **Rename d:x y** will rename **d:x** as **d:y** regardless of the default drive.) The general utility program **NewName.Dem** in Figure 6.4.2 uses **rename**, and gets around the latter difficulty, but won't accept wild cards. That dangerous feat requires the wild card search technique, discussed later. This program could have been used as well to demonstrate **fnsplit** and **fnmerge**, but it was far simpler to do the necessary string manipulation directly.

```
/*********************************************************************/
/* NewName.Dem     Demonstrate function  rename.  Invoke this */
/*                 program like the  DOS  command.  It renames*/
/* a subdirectory if the new name is in the same directory,   */
/* and renames a file if the new name would be in a different */
/* directory, but on the same drive.  If the old file name    */
/* Parameter[1]  specifies a non-default drive but the new    */
/*************************************** name  Parameter[2]   */
                                      /* does not, then use   */
                                      /* the old drive with   */
#include  <StdIO.H>                   /* the new name, else   */
                                      /* rename  will fail    */
void main(int   NParameters,          /* after trying the de-*/
          char *Parameter[]) {        /* fault drive.         */
  char NewFile[100];                  /************************/
  int  K = 0;
if (((Parameter[1][1] == ':')         /* The:  means that     */
  && (Parameter[2][1] != ':'))) {     /* a drive name is      */
    NewFile[0] = Parameter[1][0];     /* specified.           */
    NewFile[1] = ':';                 /* NewFile  is a copy   */
    K = 2; }                          /* of the new file      */
strcpy(&NewFile[K],Parameter[2]);     /* name, perhaps with   */
if (rename(Parameter[1],NewFile)) {   /* the old drive.       */
  perror("rename  detected error"); }}
```

Figure 6.4.2 Program **NewName.Dem**

Directory searches

Two of the most powerful Turbo C Library functions are

int findfirst(char *FileName, struct ffblk *B, int Attribute)
int findnext(struct ffblk *B)

Together, they allow you to consider all entries of a specified directory that match a given file name or file name pattern containing wild card characters ? and *. You can also indicate whether or not to include in the search hidden or system files, volume labels, or subdirectories. The function prototypes are in header file **Dir.H**, along with the type definition

struct ffblk {
  char   ff_reserved[21];
  char   ff_attrib;
  unsigned   ff_ftime;
  unsigned   ff_fdate;
  long   ff_fsize;
  char   ff_name[13]; }

Records of this type are used to store information from the directory entry of a DOS file.

  findfirst determines from the current drive and directory and the **FileName** parameter a specified directory, and a file name pattern that may include wild cards. It returns via parameter **B** the first entry in the specified directory that matches the given pattern. The function returns zero to indicate success.

  The **Attribute** parameter determines whether or not **findfirst** will consider hidden or system files, volume labels, and subdirectories in its search. Its meaning is complicated due to an elaborate DOS convention:

* If **Attribute** = 0, the search is confined to *ordinary* files—these have hidden, system, volume label, and subdirectory bits 0.
* If any of the hidden, system, or subdirectory bits of **Attribute** is set, then the search is confined to files whose attribute bytes are any combination of the indicated bits (including the empty combination— i.e., ordinary files).

- If the volume label bit of **Attribute** is set, the search is confined to the volume label.

Directory search is not sensitive to the read-only or archive bits.

After a successful search, **findfirst** records its parameters **FileName** and **Attribute** in component **B.ff_reserved** of **ffblk** structure **B** for later use by **findnext**. The other components store the directory information for the *first* matching file. Function **findnext** can now continue the search, recording in the same manner the directory information for the *next* matching entry, if there is one, and setting up the **ff_reserved** component for yet another try. These functions return zero to indicate success; otherwise, they set global variable **errno**. When no (more) matching files are found, **errno = ENMFILE**, a macro constant defined in header file **ErrNo.H**.

In Figure 6.4.3 is program **WildCard.Dem**, which demonstrates these routines. This program searches the directory tree, starting at a given file name, for a specified wild card pattern. It outputs the names of the initial file and all subdirectories searched, indenting to show tree structure. Finally, it tallies the number of matching files, and the total number of bytes. The program employs a recursive function **Process** that will consider the initial file name or search a subdirectory. The main program merely sets the initial output indentation, reads the specified directory and wild card pattern, and writes the final tallies. Note that it does not check for invalid input—that is left to various Turbo C routines.

Several features of procedure **Process** need further explanation. This routine searches a directory **FileName** for names with wild card pattern **Quest**, and invokes itself recursively to search all subdirectories. It returns the numbers of files and bytes found. On its first invocation, **FileName** is the name specified by the user; it might be an ordinary file or a root directory, instead of a subdirectory. Therefore, some initial steps are necessary to determine which. **findfirst** provides this service. Essentially, **Process** searches the current directory for **FileName**. (The first entry of every subdirectory S is a subdirectory **.** whose name field contains the name of S.) If a *file* is found, the result is determined immediately. With a subdirectory, **Process** prepares for the wild card search. If **FileName** is a *root directory,* however, **findfirst** will report failure, because root directories have no self-referential subdirectories. This situation is distinguishable from bonafide failures because here the last character of **FileName** is a colon or backslash. Once **FileName** is determined to be a directory of one sort or the other, **Process** makes a

```
/*************************************************************/
/* WildCard.Dem    Demonstrate functions  findfirst  and    */
/*                       findnext.  Search the directory tree, */
/*********************** starting at a specified file name, */
/*                 /* for a given wildcard pattern.  Out-*/
#include <General.H>    /* put the names of the initial file */
#include   <CType.H>    /* and subdirectories processed.  In- */
#include     <Dir.H>    /* dent to show the tree structure.   */
#include     <Dos.H>    /* Tally the number of matching files */
#include   <StdIO.H>    /* and their total length.            */
                        /*************************************/

int Indent = 2;

void Process(char *FileName,        /* This recursive rou- */
             char *Quest,           /* tine processes the  */
             int  *Files,           /* initial file name,  */
             long *Bytes) {         /* and subdirectories  */
  int          Code;                /* below.              */
  struct ffblk Info;
  char         Ch;
  char         Directory[MAXPATH];
  int          MoreFiles;
  long         MoreBytes;                /* Indent shows   */
printf("%*s%s\n",Indent,"",FileName);    /* depth.         */
*Files = *Bytes = 0;                     /* Start tallies. */
Code = findfirst(FileName,&Info,FA_DIREC); /* Get directory */
                                         /* information.   */

if (Code) {
  Ch = FileName[strlen(FileName)-1];  /* findfirst has just */
  if (Ch == ':' || Ch == '\\')        /* failed, either be- */
      Info.ff_attrib = FA_DIREC;      /* cause it was search-*/
    else {                            /* ing a root directory*/
      puts("No file found.\n");       /* for its own name, or*/
      return; }}                      /* for some other     */
                                      /* reason.            */
if (Info.ff_attrib != FA_DIREC) {     /* Ordinary file.  Just*/
  *Files = 1;                         /* return its size.   */
  *Bytes = Info.ff_fsize;
  return; }
```

Figure 6.4.3 Program WildCard.Dem (*Continue on next page*)

```c
  getcwd(Directory,MAXPATH);          /* If you arrive here,  */
  chdir(FileName);                    /* FileName  is a di-   */
                                      /* rectory.  Change to  */
  Code = findfirst(Quest,&Info,0);    /* it, saving current   */
  while (Code == 0) {                 /* one.  Search for or- */
    ++*Files;                         /* dinary files match-  */
    *Bytes += Info.ff_fsize;          /* ing the pattern, and */
    Code    = findnext(&Info); }      /* update the tallies.  */
  Code =                              /* Consider all subdi-  */
    findfirst("*.*",&Info,FA_DIREC);  /* rectory entries ex-  */
  while (Code == 0) {                 /* cept the self-       */
    if (Info.ff_attrib == FA_DIREC    /* referential . and    */
      && Info.ff_name[0] != '.') {    /* parent ...           */
        Indent += 2;                  /* RECURSION!  Increase */
        Process(Info.ff_name,Quest,   /* Indent  to show      */
          &MoreFiles,&MoreBytes);     /* greater depth.  Pro- */
        Indent -= 2;                  /* cess subdirectory.   */
        *Files += MoreFiles;          /* Restore former       */
        *Bytes += MoreBytes; }        /* indentation.         */

    Code = findnext(&Info); }         /* Continue the search. */

  chdir(Directory); }        /* Return to original directory. */

  void main () {                      /* Note:  this program  */
    int  Drive,Files;                 /* remembers the cur-   */
    char FileName[MAXPATH],           /* rent drive, changes  */
      Quest[MAXPATH];                 /* it if required, then */
    long Bytes;                       /* restores it.         */
  Drive = getdisk();
  printf("Search the directory tree starting at     ");
  gets(FileName);
  if (FileName[1] == ':')
    setdisk(toupper(FileName[0]) - 'A');
  printf(
    "Search for files matching this pattern:  ");
  gets(Quest);
  printf("Processing directories:\n");
  Process(FileName,Quest,&Files,&Bytes);
  printf("Number of files found = %d \n",Files);
  printf("Total number of bytes = %ld\n",Bytes);
  setdisk(Drive); }
```

Figure 6.4.3 (*Continued*) Program **WildCard.Dem**

note of the current directory, then switches to directory **FileName** to make the wild card search.

The search is carried out in two stages. The first uses **findfirst** and **findnext** in a straightforward way to find and tally all files in directory **FileName** matching the pattern **Quest**. The next stage searches **FileName** for all subdirectories, and invokes **Process** recursively on each one. To keep track of depth in the directory tree, the indentation is incremented just before the recursive call, and restored afterward.

The second stage of this search is a good example of a general search where processing the selected files is governed by some condition—in this case, the subdirectory attribute. You could imitate this technique to modify the first stage to tally only files altered since some date, or satisfying some other condition.

Figure 6.4.4 shows the formats of the **ff_time** and **ff_date** components of the **ffblk** structure. It's simple to pull these apart and analyze them. Since the bit fields are in the proper order, you don't even have to disassemble them to compare the times and/or dates of different directory entries. Moreover, since you can set the **Attribute** parameter so that functions **findfirst** and **findnext** will find subdirectories and volume labels, you can use them to ascertain directory and label time and date stamps. You can set these stamps as well, but that requires techniques discussed later in Chapter 8.

There is one additional complication. **findfirst** obtains directory information by changing a DOS pointer, the Disk Transfer Address (DTA), to point to the **ffblk** structure. DOS then places the information in that structure. The DTA must remain set during the directory search. However, it is used by various DOS services. Therefore, before you call **findfirst** or **findnext**, you should push onto your stack the current DTA value, then pop it back when the function returns. Otherwise, if your program interrupts another, it could disrupt a DOS service.

ff_time			**ff_date**		
Bits	Content		Bits	Content	
0..4	Seconds/2	(0 - 29)	0..4	Day	(1 - 31)
5..10	Minutes	(0 - 59)	5..10	Month	(1 - 12)
11..15	Hours	(0 - 23)	11..15	Year - 1980	

Figure 6.4.4 **struct ffblk** time and date formats

(**WildCard.Dem** is gambling that it's the only game in town.) Similarly, you must hope that any software that interrupts yours is equally polite. Turbo C functions ***getdta** and **setdta** are provided for this purpose. Consult the *Reference guide,* Reference [7], for details.

One final routine, not related to wild card searches, should be mentioned in this section. Function

char *searchpath(char *FileName)

will attempt to locate a file by following the DOS environment **PATH** string. If it succeeds, it returns a pointer to the full file name; else it returns a null pointer. Its prototype is in header file **Dir.H**. You needn't allocate space for the full name: the function uses a global data area that's overwritten by each invocation. **searchpath** is not restricted to searching for executable files; thus, your program can use it to find any file. A good project would be to modify it to follow a specified DOS environment string formatted like **PATH**. Then your software could have its own private, limited version of the troublesome DOS **Append** command.

7

Memory Management and Program Execution

Contents

7.1 PSP and environment
7.2 Memory management
7.3 Executing and communicating with other programs
7.4 Program termination

Memory management and program execution are related concepts, not so much because of their logic, but because you must often pay careful attention to memory management when you write a program that will execute another one. In fact, that is by far the most common situation where you'll encounter memory management questions. Making your program execute another one—a *child* program—involves memory management in two ways: allocating memory for the child, and using memory resources to communicate information between parent and child. If all goes smoothly, you may not need to use your knowledge of memory management details. Turbo C Library functions and DOS will take care of those for you. However, if a program execution or interprogram communication strategy fails, misunderstanding memory management concepts may be the cause, and analyzing memory allocation details may provide the cure.

This chapter starts with a discussion of two memory areas that DOS associates with your program: its *environment* and *Program Segment Prefix* (PSP). The former is a medium for communicating small amounts of information from parent program to child. The PSP contains a few items vital to proper execution of your program—for example, the segment address of the environment. Both areas play major roles in DOS' memory allocation scheme, because it initially allocates two memory blocks to each program: the environment and the code block, which begins with the PSP.

Next, the chapter discusses DOS' memory allocation technique in detail, and presents a routine that will produce a memory map giving information about all the blocks allocated at any time. You can use this to gain information about the memory allocated to resident software, for example.

Section 7.3 covers program execution techniques. In itself, execution is not difficult. The interesting questions come in arranging interprogram communication. Demonstration programs are included that can communicate on a large scale by sharing a memory buffer, and that use the environment and the program command line to communicate small amounts of data, like the buffer address. Examples show how to do this and return control to the parent when the child terminates, and how to *chain* to a child program that never returns to the parent.

A related technique is the execution of DOS commands. Section 7.3 shows how to execute any DOS command via the Turbo C Library function **system**. Actually, this routine works by executing a secondary copy of the DOS command processor (usually **Command.Com**) as a child program.

One use of **system** is to implement interprogram communication by redirecting a child program's standard input/output. However, that method is inefficient because of the overhead involved in locating and executing the command processor. Section 7.3 concludes with some examples showing how your program itself can redirect file handles—in particular, a child program's standard input/output—without incurring this overhead.

The chapter concludes with a short section detailing several methods for terminating Turbo C programs. You can pass an **ErrorLevel** code to DOS, register and execute Turbo C exit functions, and produce various messages explaining abnormal terminations.

7.1 PSP and environment

Concepts

Program segment prefix (PSP)
Environment inherited from parent program
Function **main** parameters
Turbo C environment array
Locating the environment and program name for a given PSP

When DOS loads a program, it allocates two blocks of memory: that occupied by the program itself, and a block for the environment it inherits from its parent program (usually the DOS command processor **Command.Com**). The program block begins with the Program Segment Prefix (PSP) in its first hex 100 bytes. One item in this record is the segment address of the inherited environment. The environment and PSP are discussed in detail in this section. The environment was introduced earlier, in Section 3.9; more detail is required now because of its role in spawning child programs.

Program Segment Prefix (PSP)

Although it's mostly a relic of DOS' predecessor, the CP/M operating system, the PSP contains several items important to programmers. The Turbo C startup code stores the PSP segment address in global variable **unsigned _psp**, declared in header file **StdLib.H**. Figure 7.1.1 shows the exact offsets within the PSP where various data are found. Several items require explanation.

The word at offset 2 contains the segment address of the first paragraph after the program's allocated memory block. That paragraph may be free or may be allocated to some other program. A program can use this feature to ascertain how much memory it's been allocated.

Four-byte fields at offsets a, e, and 12 contain segment:offset addresses of routines (usually DOS routines) that handle three abnormal situations:

offset	routine
a	Program termination
e	Ctrl-Break keystroke
12	Critical error

(*A critical error* is something like printer out of paper or diskette drive door open.) These are, in fact, the routines that were assigned to handle such situations before your program was loaded. Your program may change the interrupt vectors DOS uses to find them, in order to substitute your own custom services. To be able to restore the vectors to their original states when your program terminates, DOS keeps copies in the PSP. *Do not disturb them!* (More information about these concepts is given in Section 8.9.)

The word at offset 2c contains the segment address of the program's inherited environment. Near the environment is stored the full file name of your program. These matters are discussed in detail later in this section.

Offset (hex)	Length (dec)	PSP Field
0	2	**Int 20** instruction (CP/M relic)
2	2	First segment address after allocated memory
4	1	Reserved
5	5	Call instruction (CP/M relic)
a	4	DOS terminate routine address
e	4	DOS user break routine address
12	4	DOS critical error routine address
16	22	DOS work area
2c	2	Segment address of inherited environment
2e	34	DOS work area
50	3	**Int 21** and far return instructions (relics)
53	2	Reserved
55	7	FCB #1 extension
5c	9	FCB #1 *and* formatted command line parameter #1
65	7	FCB #2 extension
6c	9	FCB #2 *and* formatted command line parameter #2
80	128	Command line parameters *and* Disk Transfer Area

Figure 7.1.1 PSP format

The fields at offsets 55, 5c, 65, and 6c were intended mainly for the File Control Block (FCB) file handling mechanism used before DOS 2.0 appeared. They must be maintained, to permit execution of programs written according to the earlier standard. Since FCBs are never needed until after your program has gained control, DOS stores here the first two command line parameters, as though they consisted of drive names followed by file names (with no subdirectories involved). Drive names **a:**, **b:**,... are coded as bytes 1, 2,..., and file names are converted to upper case. Even this feature is obsolete, because it doesn't handle subdirectories.

Offset 80 contains the length n of the entire command line parameter string, starting with the separator following the program name. The next n bytes contain this string, verbatim, except that any standard input/output redirection specifications are omitted. The length of this field is the source of DOS' 128-character limit on command line parameters. The Turbo C startup code obtains from this area the values of the corresponding command line parameter arguments for function **main**, described in Section 3.9. If you need information from this field, you should obtain it, as the startup code does, before your program does any disk input/output, because DOS may use the field later as a Disk Transfer Area (DTA). A DTA is a buffer for storing information between requests for certain DOS file directory services.

(Redirection, mentioned in the previous paragraph, is carried out by **Command.Com** before it loads a program. A program has no easy way to know whether redirection is in effect. Using methods described in Chapters 6 and 8, however, you can test for some file properties—for example, the drive name—inappropriate for standard input/output. If such a property holds, redirection is in effect.)

At offsets 0, 5 and 50 are binary codes for instructions once needed by CP/M. They have little present use.

Inherited environment; program name

When loaded by DOS, a program inherits a copy of its parent's environment. This memory block contains strings specifying the current path, the prompt, the location of the DOS command processor, and other data the parent program may want to communicate. Its role as a communication channel when one program executes another is described in Section 7.3. The inherited environment always starts on a paragraph boundary; its segment address is found at offset 2c in the PSP.

As noted already in Section 3.9, the environment consists of a sequence of ASCII Z-strings, terminated by a null string, whose sole entry is its trailing zero. You can list the strings in the DOS command processor's environment at any time by executing DOS command **Set**.

For ease in manipulation, the Turbo C startup code copies the inherited environment strings into an array, to which functions

char *getenv(char *Variable)
int putenv(char *Variable)

provide access. You'll find a demonstration program for the first function in Section 3.9. The initial address of the environment array is contained in the third function **main** parameter, and in global variable

extern char* environ[ ]

declared in header file **DOS.H**. The first address is reliable only until **putenv** alters the array. If it must relocate the array to add a new string or lengthen an existing one, **putenv** will update **environ[ ]** but not the **main** parameter. Program **Malaysia.Dem** in Figure 7.1.2 demonstrates all these environment array features: it displays the array location, verifies that no strings with given names are present in the array, adds two strings, displays them, then verifies that **environ[ ]** has changed but not the third **main** parameter. Section 7.3 will show how the environment array is used to communicate information to a spawned program.

Because of its role in program spawning and memory allocation, you may need to locate the environment of the program that occupies a specified memory block: that is, given the segment address of a PSP, find that of the corresponding environment. (The last paragraph was concerned with the environment *array* of the current Turbo C program, not with the environment of a program in another memory block.) Function

unsigned EnvSeg(unsigned PSP)

in Figure 7.1.3 does that easily, using the environment segment address stored at **PSP** offset 2c. For simple, consistent use of far pointers, this function is designed for compiling with a large data model—for example, the compact memory model. It's used in later demonstration programs.

```
/*****************************************************************/
/* Malaysia.Dem     Demonstrate  Turbo C  environment array    */
/*                  features.  Verify that strings  B  and  C */
/* do not occur in the array.  Give them values, and verify    */
/* that the array address in global variable  environ  may     */
/*********************************** change, but the third      */
                                   /* main  parameter does not.*/
#include <General.H>              /**************************** */

void DisplayEnv(char *V) {         /* Display a specified envi-*/
  char *Value;                     /* ronment entry or indicate*/
Value = getenv(V);                 /* that it's not present.   */
if (Value == NULL)
    printf("String  %s  is  not  in the environment array.\n",V);
  else
    printf("%s=%s  is in the environment array.\n",V,Value); }

void main(int Param1, char *Param2[], char *Param3[]) {
DisplayEnv("B");
DisplayEnv("C");
printf(" Parameter 3 , environ = %p , %p .\n",Param3,environ);
printf("Having set string B ,  putenv  returned  %d .\n",
  putenv("B=BANANA  TREES"));
DisplayEnv("B");
printf(" Parameter 3 , environ = %p , %p .\n",Param3,environ);
printf("Having set string C ,  putenv  returned  %d .\n",
  putenv("C=COCONUT PALMS"));
DisplayEnv("C");
printf(" Parameter 3 , environ = %p , %p .\n",Param3,environ);}
```

Output

```
String  B  is  not  in the environment array.
String  C  is  not  in the environment array.
Parameter 3 , environ = 0522 , 0522 .
Having set string B ,  putenv  returned  0 .
B=BANANA  TREES  is in the environment array.
Parameter 3 , environ = 0522 , 0522 .
Having set string C ,  putenv  returned  0 .
C=COCONUT PALMS  is in the environment array.
Parameter 3 , environ = 0522 , 052E .
```

Figure 7.1.2 Program Malaysia.Dem

Beginning at the third byte after the inherited environment is another ASCII Z-string containing your program's complete file name, starting with its drive. The Turbo C startup code points the initial entry of the second function **main** parameter to this name. Function **ProgName** in Figure 7.1.3 provides a more general service: given a PSP segment address, it returns a pointer to the full program file name. You can use it to ascertain what program is stored in a given memory block. **ProgName** uses **EnvSeg** to find the environment, then steps to its end, and three bytes beyond, to find the name. It's demonstrated in Figure 7.2.5 in the next section.

```
/*****************************************************************/
/* Env&Prog.C     Functions EnvSeg and ProgName . Given a */
/*              PSP  segment address, these return the cor- */
/* responding environment segment address, and a pointer to   */
/* the program file name.  Compile with a large data model.   */
/*****************************************************************/

#include <DOS.H>

unsigned EnvSeg(unsigned PSP) {    /* Return the segment ad- */
   unsigned *EnvSegPtr;            /* dress of the environment */
EnvSegPtr = MK_FP(PSP,0x2c);       /* of the program with the */
return *EnvSegPtr; }               /* specified PSP  segment. */

char *ProgName(unsigned PSP) {     /* Return the name of the */
   char      *P;                   /* program with the speci- */
   unsigned  I;                    /* fied PSP segment. */
P = MK_FP(EnvSeg(PSP),0);
for (I = 0; (P[I] != 0) || (P[I+1] != 0); ++I);
return P+I+4; }
```

Figure 7.1.3 Functions **EnvSeg** and **ProgName**

7.2 Memory management

Concepts

DOS memory blocks
Memory control blocks (MCBs)
Memory Control Blocks Destroyed message
Function **MemryMap**
Turbo C Library memory management routines

Occasionally, you'll need to allocate and manage memory blocks outside the one occupied by your program. This section describes first the DOS memory management system, then shows how to manipulate it with Turbo C Library functions. A function is provided that will construct a map of the memory allocated to the calling program and other software currently resident in memory. This is used later to analyze the effect of the memory management functions. It can also help you solve some of the puzzles that arise when memory resident programs contend for memory resources.

Memory blocks

DOS allocates memory in contiguous *blocks,* each owned by a resident program. Every program owns at least two: the block that its code occupies, and its environment segment. These are allocated to the program at the request of the DOS program execution service. Officially they are owned by the first block, which starts with the PSP. Thus, a PSP block owns itself. You can use Turbo C TOOLS function

unsigned mmsize(void)

to ascertain the size (in paragraphs) of your program's PSP block. Usually, the corresponding environment block immediately precedes the PSP block.

When DOS loads a program, it allocates the first block it finds that is large enough. Usually, this results in the program gaining control of *all* available memory. Well-behaved **.Exe** programs can avoid this overallocation in several ways. For example, a Turbo C program immediately releases to DOS any part of its allocation that it doesn't need. Programs that do not observe this protocol may prevent DOS extensions from loading other software for concurrent execution. (Unfortunately, all .Com programs are ill-behaved—they cannot control their memory allocation. See the *MS-DOS encyclopedia,* Reference [28], Article 4, for detailed information on this subject.)

A program can request more memory by specifying to the DOS allocation service the amount needed. DOS will allocate the first free block it finds that is large enough, and indicate the starting address of the block. It is also possible to change the size of an allocated block, and to free it, returning it to DOS for reallocation. Before turning to details of the allocation process, it's helpful to study DOS' technique for managing memory blocks.

Memory Control Blocks (MCBs)

DOS organizes all memory at its disposal into *free* blocks, *allocated* blocks, and *control* blocks. These are disjoint and contiguous. Each block begins on a paragraph boundary, so that its location can be specified simply by its segment address.

Each free or allocated block is immediately preceded by a *Memory Control Block* (MCB) that specifies its ownership and length. An MCB is one paragraph (sixteen bytes) long; its structure is shown in Figure 7.2.1. The first byte is a *signature,* character M or Z. Signature Z distinguishes the block with highest address; this one always extends to the end of standard memory. If DOS looks at a paragraph just before or after a free or allocated block, expecting MCB information, and finds in its first byte something different from a signature, it assumes that its memory allocation scheme has been corrupted, writes the message

Memory Control Blocks Destroyed

and crashes so severely that a warm boot is required. When a program writes to memory beyond its allocated block, it is very likely to overwrite the next MCB. DOS will crash the next time it tries to allocate memory— probably when it tries to load a program. That is why you must observe DOS protocol when writing outside your program's originally allocated block.

The word at MCB offset 3 indicates the length, in paragraph units, of the corresponding free or allocated block (not including the MCB). Bytes 5 to 15 are not used. If the block is free, then the *ownership* word at offset 1 is zero. If allocated, it's the segment address of the owning program's PSP. Figure 7.2.1 shows the memory block structure resulting from a total of three blocks, the first owning the third, and the second unallocated. (There are rarely this few.)

When DOS loads a program, it allocates two blocks—the environment block, then the program block itself. The latter always owns the former. The initially allocated program block is usually the final block with signature Z extending to the end of standard memory. However, as with Turbo C programs, a program's first action may be to release to DOS all memory beyond what is really needed. With such a program you cannot verify the initial allocation, because excess memory is freed before you

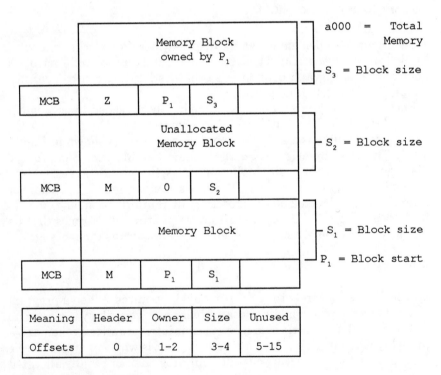

Figure 7.2.1 Memory blocks

gain control. When a program terminates properly using DOS, these two memory blocks are freed. A program may request additional memory blocks from DOS, alter their size if necessary, and release them once they've served their purpose.

Function MemryMap

In Figure 7.2.6 is a tool, function **MemryMap**, that is useful both in illustrating memory management and analyzing puzzling situations arising with memory resident software. It was executed by demonstration programs in three different situations, producing the outputs in Figures 7.2.2 to 7.2.4.

Block Address	Length	Owner PSP	Owner Name
0973	0b16	0008	?
148a	00d3	148b	
155e	0003	0000	Free
1562	000a	148b	
156d	0005	1574	C:\POPALARM.EXE?
1573	03ca	1574	C:\POPALARM.EXE?
193e	0006	1946	C:\APPEND.EXE
1945	0113	1946	C:\APPEND.EXE
1a59	0007	1a62	C:\FASTOPEN.EXE
1a61	00da	1a62	C:\FASTOPEN.EXE
1b3c	0007	1b45	C:\PUSH&POP.COM
1b44	0491	1b45	C:\PUSH&POP.COM
1fd6	0007	1fdf	C:\SUPERSPL.COM
1fde	0182	1fdf	C:\SUPERSPL.COM
2161	0006	2169	C:\NLSFUNC.EXE
2168	009a	2169	C:\NLSFUNC.EXE
2203	0006	0000	Free
220a	016e	220b	C:\SHARE.EXE
2379	0007	2382	C:\turboc\work\MAPTEST1.EXE
2381	0340	2382	C:\turboc\work\MAPTEST1.EXE
26c2	793d	0000	Free

Figure 7.2.2 Output from program **MapTest1.Dem**, executed from the DOS prompt

For Figure 7.2.2, a one-line demonstration program

void main() { MemryMap(); }

in file **MapTest1.Dem** was compiled, then executed directly from the DOS prompt. **Command.Com** was its parent. The output shows memory blocks owned by the following resident software:

- DOS, evidently **Command.Com**
- *PopUp Alarm Clock,* by Bellsoft, Inc. This puts a neat clock in a screen corner, and provides a time stamp for memos and drafts.
- The DOS **Append, FastOpen, NLSFunc**, and **Share** utilities.
- A custom utility **Push&Pop** for remembering and retracing current directory changes.
- *SuperSpool,* a print buffer by AST Research, Inc.
- **MapTest1.Exe**

(In order to show all these memory resident utilities, the author disabled the *DESQview* system normally used to produce this book. It does its own, more complicated, memory management.) The shorter blocks are the corresponding environments. The **?** marks indicate that a block called a PSP departs from the usual PSP format. For **POPALARM** the departure is minimal, and the PSP is easily recognized. However, in initial block 0973, the "PSP" block is unintelligible. Apparently DOS does something special with its first block. Ownership of the PSP block at 148b is not clear; inspection of its FCBs indicated that it had been used with the DOS **Replace** utility when **AutoExec.Bat** was executing. The program filename field after its environment at 1563 had been cleared to zeroes. The last block, at segment 26c2, is free, indicating that **MapTest1** did release its excess memory allocation.

Immediately after producing Figure 7.2.2, the author moved some Turbo C Library files using the DOS **Replace** utility and loaded the Turbo C compiler. The following version **MapTest2.Dem** of the demonstration program was compiled and run via the integrated environment:

```
#include <StdIO.H>   /* For stdout */
void main() {
  freopen("MapTest2.Out","a",stdout);
  MemryMap(); }
```

This used function **freopen** (see Section 6.3) to redirect standard output to a file for inclusion in the manuscript. The output, shown in Figure 7.2.3, is like that in the previous figure through block 2203. For some reason, DOS released the **Share.Exe** block 220a and reallocated it to **Replace.Exe**. It's not clear whether the latter is now memory resident (if so, it has no environment block) or if DOS neglected to release its block. The Turbo C compiler **TC.Exe** is present, followed by its offspring, **MapTest2**.

Finally, the integrated environment **File/OS** shell command was executed to regain access to the DOS command processor. The latter was then used to rerun **MapTest1.Exe**. The Turbo command really loads a new copy of the command processor as child of Turbo C, which then spawns **MapTest1** as its own offspring. The output, in Figure 7.2.4, agrees with Figure 7.2.2 through block 2168. Some process is using the blocks at 2203, 6245, and 6319, and has corrupted its program file name. The block formerly allocated to **Replace** has been freed and reallocated to the new **Command.Com**. There's no way to tell from this output that the latter—not the compiler—is parent of the **MapTest1.Exe** program.

Figure 7.2.5 shows the **MemryMap** source code. If you only wanted to see memory blocks allocated by your program and its descendants, **MemryMap** could simply find the beginning of the current PSP at segment address **_psp**, back up one paragraph to its MCB, then follow the MCB chain to the block with signature Z at the end of installed memory. However, this strategy won't map the blocks allocated *before*

Block Address	Length	Owner PSP	Owner Name
:	:	:	:
2168	009a	2169	C:\NLSFUNC.EXE
2203	0006	0000	Free
220a	016e	220b	D:\REPLACE.EXE
2379	0004	148b	
237e	0007	2387	C:\TURBOC\WORK\..\TC.EXE
2386	3ebe	2387	C:\TURBOC\WORK\..\TC.EXE
6245	0007	624e	C:\TURBOC\WORK\MAPTEST2.EXE
624d	03c0	624e	C:\TURBOC\WORK\MAPTEST2.EXE
660e	39f1	0000	Free

Figure 7.2.3 Output from program **MapTest2.Dem**, executed by the Turbo C integrated environment **Run** command

Block Address	Length	Owner PSP	Owner Name
:	:	:	:
2168	009a	2169	C:\NLSFUNC.EXE
2203	0006	6246	ATH=
220a	016e	220b	C:\COMMAND.COM
2379	0004	148b	
237e	0007	2387	C:\TURBOC\WORK\..\TC.EXE
2386	3ebe	2387	C:\TURBOC\WORK\..\TC.EXE
6245	00d3	6246	ATH=
6319	000a	6246	ATH=
6324	0007	632d	C:\turboc\work\MAPTEST1.EXE
632c	0340	632d	C:\turboc\work\MAPTEST1.EXE
666d	3992	0000	Free

Figure 7.2.4 Output from program **MapTest1.Dem**, executed from the copy of **Command.Com** loaded by the Turbo C integrated environment **File/OS** command

your program was loaded. You have to backtrack from a known MCB, checking each paragraph to see if it has an MCB signature. If so, **MemryMap** checks the MCB size field to see if it records the correct number of bytes since the previous MCB. It's possible, but unlikely, that these numbers agree by chance. Without deciphering the machine language of the DOS memory allocation routine, there's no *certain* way

```
/****************************************************************/
/* MemryMap.C    Function MemryMap: report all  DOS  memo- */
/*               ry control blocks and their owners.  Compile*/
/***************************************** this with a large   */
                                        /* data model.        */
#include  <General.H>                   /*********************/

#define Int20 0x20cd                    /* First byte of most */
                                        /* PSPs.              */
void MemryMap() {
  unsigned  S,GoodS,i,Found,Question;
  char      *MCB,*Name;
  unsigned *Owner,*Size,*OwnersPSP;
```

Figure 7.2.5 Function **MemryMap** (*Continue on next page*)

```
                                       /* Current  MCB  is    */
S = _psp - 1;                          /* just before  PSP.   */
do {                                   /* Look for segments    */
    GoodS = S;                         /* beginning with  MCB */
    for (i = Found = 0;                /* identifier  'M'  and*/
        (S != 0) && !Found; ++i) {     /* with size field =   */
        MCB = (char *) MK_FP(-S,0);    /* distance to previous*/
        Owner = (unsigned *) MK_FP(S,1);  /* GoodS  = seg- */
        Size = (unsigned *) MK_FP(S,3);   /* ment address of*/
        Found = ((*MCB == 'M')            /* a known  MCB.  */
            && (*Size == i)); }}       /* Stop at segment  0  */
  while (S != 0);                      /* (not a  GoodS ).    */

printf("%s\n","      Block         Owner            ");
printf("%s\n","Address  Length     PSP  Owner Name");

S = GoodS;                             /* Go back to the last */
do {                                   /* GoodS,  then look   */
    MCB   = (    char *) MK_FP(S,0);   /* at all  MCBs.       */
    Owner = (unsigned *) MK_FP(S,1);   /* Pointers to segment */
    Size  = (unsigned *) MK_FP(S,3);   /* addresses.          */
    printf("  %04x    %04x   %04x  ",  /* Display MCB  seg-   */
       S,*Size,*Owner);                /* ment address and    */
    Question = 0;                      /* contents.           */
    if (*Owner == 0)                   /* Unowned blocks are  */
        Name = "Free";                 /* free.               */
      else {                           /* Before 3.30,  DOS   */
        if (EnvSeg(*Owner) == 0)       /* owned some blocks   */
            Name = "DOS";              /* with no environment.*/
          else {                       /* You need that to get*/
            Name = ProgName(*Owner);   /* the program name.   */
            if (Name == EmptyStr)      /* Maybe  DOS  craves  */
               Name = "DOS"; }         /* anonymity.          */
        OwnersPSP =                       /* Call attention */
           (unsigned *) MK_FP(*Owner,0);  /* to blocks that */
        Question =                        /* don't begin the*/
           (*OwnersPSP != Int20); }       /* usual way.     */
    printf("%s",Name);
    if (Question) printf("%c",'?');
    printf("\n");
    S = S + *Size + 1; }          /* Step to the next  MCB.  The  */
while (*MCB == 'M'); }            /* last one starts with  Z ≠ M. */
```

Figure 7.2.5 *(Continued)* Function **MemryMap**

of finding the beginning of the MCB chain.

When **MemryMap** has seemingly found the beginning of the MCB chain, it reverses direction and steps through to the end. Ownership of the memory block following an MCB is determined as follows: if the ownership field is zero, the block is free. Otherwise, it's the segment address of the owner's PSP. Function **EnvSeg**, described in the previous section, extracts the environment segment address from the PSP. If this is zero, the owner is apparently DOS. Otherwise, function **ProgName**, also described in Section 7.1, provides the owner's name. If that's the empty string, the likely owner is DOS. If the first word of a supposed PSP block is not the usual **Int 20** instruction, **MemryMap** writes a **?** to indicate that its output may be questionable.

Turbo C Library memory management routines

Three Turbo C Library routines give you some control over the memory allocation process. To allocate a memory block to your program, execute

int allocmem(unsigned N, unsigned *Segment)

Specify the amount of memory required via parameter **N**, in paragraph units. If DOS can accommodate your request, **allocmem** sets **Segment** equal to the segment address of the block, and returns -1 to indicate success. Otherwise, the function returns the size of the largest block available, but doesn't actually allocate any memory. To release a block to DOS for later reallocation, use function

int freemem(unsigned Segment)

Set **Segment** equal to the address returned by **allocmem** when the memory was allocated. This function returns zero to indicate success. To alter a block allocated to your program, execute function

int setblock(int Segment, int N)

This requests that the block with specified segment address be changed to **N** paragraphs. The **setblock** return value is like that of **allocmem**. In addition to setting their return values, these three functions report errors by setting global variable **errno**, declared in header file **DOS.H**.

You'll also find there the three function prototypes.

You can use function **MemryMap** to demonstrate the memory management routines. For example, program **Mem.Dem** in Figure 7.2.6 calls **allocmem** and **freemem** to allocate two memory blocks and free one, then invokes **MemryMap** to display the resulting "hole" that's hex 10 paragraphs long.

```
/*****************************************************************/
/* Mem.Dem      Use  MemryMap  to demonstrate functions     */
/*              allocmem  and  freemem.  Compile this with the */
/***************************************** same model as       */
                                  /* MemryMap.C .         */
#include <General.H>              /*********************/

void main() {
  unsigned A,B;
allocmem(0x10,&A);
allocmem(0x20,&B);
freemem(A);
printf("10  and  20  paragraph segments  A,B = %x,%x\n"
  "were allocated and  A  released.\n\n",A,B);
MemryMap(); }                                         /* See? */
```

Output

```
10  and  20  paragraph segments  A,B = 7315,7326
were allocated and  A  released.

      Block         Owner
Address  Length   PSP  Owner Name
  2f9a    00d3    2f9b
  306e    000a    2f9b
  3079    0004    2f9b
  227e    0006    3086  C:\TURBOC\WORK\..\TC.EXE
  3085    3f87    3086  C:\TURBOC\WORK\..\TC.EXE
  700d    0005    7014  C:\TURBOC\WORK\MEM.EXE
  7013    0300    7014  C:\TURBOC\WORK\MEM.EXE
  7314    0010    0000  Free
  7325    0020    7014  C:\TURBOC\WORK\MEM.EXE
  7346    3489    0000  Free
```

Figure 7.2.6 Program **Mem.Dem**

7.3 Executing and communicating with other programs

Concepts

Interprogram communication
Spawning a child program
Program chaining
Executing DOS commands
Input/output redirection and restoration

When you're writing a Turbo C program to execute other software, particularly if the source code is unavailable or in another language, communication between programs may be a major problem. This chapter will discuss communication techniques first, then the actual methods for executing other programs. These are demonstrated by two Turbo C programs that use a variety of communication channels. Your ability to execute software other than your own Turbo C programs will depend on its communication requirements and the extent to which it provides access to methods like these. The section concludes with some special considerations for executing DOS commands, and a general discussion of standard input/output redirection as an interprogram communication tool.

When one program executes another, terminology is needed to distinguish the two. This section will speak of *a parent program executing a child program*—in spite of the gruesome imagery.

Communication between programs

Interprogram communication can be separated into large scale and small. You must communicate large amounts of data via memory buffers or files. The memory buffer can be an array in the parent program, provided the child's program block does not overlay the parent's. If that's a problem, the parent can use function **allocmem** to obtain from DOS a new block to use as a buffer. In either case, parent must communicate to child the buffer's segment address.

If the child program uses DOS standard input/output, the parent can *redirect* that to files of its own choice. Three input/output redirection techniques are described at the end of this section, with demonstration programs.

Otherwise, to use a file for interprogram communication, the parent may simply place the appropriate data there and send the file name. Alternatively, it may leave the file open and indicate the handle. (When the child is loaded for execution, it receives duplicates of the parent's file handles—unless the parent indicated otherwise when it opened its files.) In this situation, parent's file pointer is coupled to child's. When the child terminates, its handle is closed, but the parent's remains open. The child inherits only the file handles and associated DOS information. No Turbo C file handle attributes or stream structures are passed on.

Since standard memory manipulation and file input/output techniques are available, the large-scale interprogram communication problem really reduces to two problems: input/output redirection and small-scale communication. The latter includes sending from parent to child a memory buffer location, file name, or file handle, and perhaps some format details.

For small-scale communication, there are three channels, already discussed in Sections 3.9 and 7.1:

Command line parameters
Environment strings
ErrorLevel variable

Command line parameters and environment strings can be accessed via the parameters of function

void main(int ParamCount,char *Param[],char *E[])

You may select the parameter names—their positions determine their function. **ParamCount** is always one greater than the number of parameters in the command line that executed your program, and specifies the size of the array **Param** of command line parameter strings. **Param[0]** is the full program file name, and **Param[1]..Param[ParamCount]** are the strings (that is, pointers to the corresponding character arrays). DOS standard input/output redirection indicators are not included.

The last function **main** parameter—**E** in the previous paragraph—is another array of string pointers, the last of which is null. When your program is executed, it inherits an environment from its parent, from which Turbo C builds array **E**. Turbo C preserves **E** as a record of your inherited environment; you should not disturb it. For your convenience, Turbo C makes a working copy of **E** called **environ**, a global variable declared in header file **DOS.H**. Preparing to execute your own child program, you may want to alter this array, because Turbo C and DOS can build your child's environment from it during spawning. Turbo C Library functions **getenv** and **putenv**, described in Section 7.1, are provided for inspecting and altering **environ**. For convenience and safety, you should use only these functions for those tasks. As you add strings to this array, **putenv** may have to move it to obtain contiguous memory space; it keeps the variable **environ** up to date. Of course, the function **main** parameter **E** doesn't change, because it preserves the record of your own inherited environment. When you spawn a child program, it inherits an environment *constructed* from yours. It has no access to its parent's environment, so cannot disrupt it—a situation quite unlike ordinary life.

Thus, the command line and the environment are small-scale, one-way communication channels from parent to child programs. The only reverse channel is even narrower: if you declare **main** as **int main(...)** it can return a value. This becomes either the return value of the Turbo C function that executed your program, or the DOS **ErrorLevel** variable that you can inspect with **DOS** batch program command **if ErrorLevel....** (Evidently, you can return any sixteen bit value, but DOS only recognizes the low byte.)

These three small-scale communication techniques are severely limited by their overall size. In addition, since command line parameters and environment strings are manipulated as ASCII Z-strings, numerical information must be encoded in them as numerals of some kind. (Otherwise a NUL character representing the number zero would be interpreted as the end of a parameter or environment string.) All these techniques are demonstrated in programs **Spawn.Dem** and **Child.Dem** later in this section.

Spawning a child program

In systems programming (though rarely in biology) *spawning* is equivalent to executing one's child. Suites of related Turbo C Library **spawnl..** and **spawnv..** functions provide that service. Here are their names, and prototypes of the second suite:

spawnl	int spawnv (int Mode, char *Program, char *Param[])
spawnle	int spawnvp (int Mode, char *Program, char *Param[])
spawnlp	int spawnve (int Mode, char *Program, char *Param[], char *Environ[])
spawnlpe	int spawnvpe(int Mode, char *Program, char *Param[], char *Environ[])

All the prototypes are in header file **Process.H**. To use these functions you specify a file name of a **Program** to run. They search first for the exact name specified, then add **.Com** if neither dot nor extension was included, and finally search for an **.Exe** file if no match has been found yet. (You cannot use this technique to execute a **.Bat** file. A method for that is described later in this section.) The functions search the specified directory and/or drive, or if either of those was omitted, the current one. The functions with names containing **p** after **spawn** search also the directories specified by the **PATH** string in the parent's inherited environment. (The functions ignore the environment arrays Turbo C makes.) Contrary to the Turbo C *Reference guide,* Reference [7], these functions don't search a root directory unless it's current or in the **PATH**.

For the **Mode** parameter you may select from two macro constants defined in **Process.H**: **P_WAIT** and **P_OVERLAY**. For spawning, always use the former. Overlays are discussed later in this section under the heading *Program chaining.*

If the letter **e** occurs in the **spawn..** function name, specify as its last parameter an environment array **Environ** in the Turbo C format for the third function **main** parameter. The **spawn..** function will construct the child's inherited DOS environment from the array. The easiest way to use this feature is to invoke function **putenv** to change the parent program's environment array as required, then pass global variable **environ** as the last **spawn..** parameter. If you pass an array whose initial entry is a null pointer, the child will inherit an exact copy of the parent's environment.

The difference between corresponding **spawnl..** and **spawnv..** functions names is best illustrated by an example. Suppose you want to execute program **P** with command line parameters **P1** and **P2**. You can use either of the following program fragments:

```
char *Child;               char *V[4];
Child = "P";               char *Child;
spawnl(Mode,Child,         Child = "P";
  Child,                   V[0] = Child;
     "P1","P2",            V[1] = P1; V[2] = P2;
        NULL);             V[3] = NULL;
                           spawnv(Mode,Child,V);
```

The principal difference is that you don't need to know the number of command line parameters for **P** when you write the code that invokes the **spawnv..** functions. Where those require a single array of N string pointers with the last one null, the **spawnl..** functions require N separate string pointers with the last null. The first of these strings should repeat the name of the child program, even though that's already been specified by the previous parameter. (This is apparently another example of the Turbo C Library's insuring portability of bad design. (Although the Turbo C *Reference guide,* Reference [7], suggests that the second occurrence of the pointer to the child program name is ignored, the author tried using a null pointer and caused a crash.)

To report success, the **spawn..** functions return the **ErrorLevel** value from the executed program. To report failure, they return -1 (not a valid **ErrorLevel** value) and set global variable **errno** appropriately.

In Figures 7.3.2 and 7.3.3 are two programs, **Spawn.Dem** and **Child.Dem,** that demonstrate techniques described in this section. **Spawn** allocates a memory buffer, writes a message there, places in an environment string the hex numeral for the buffer's segment address, then executes **Child.Exe** with the environment string name as a command line parameter. **Child** then must read the parameter, extract the numeral from the environment string, convert it to the corresponding segment address, and read the message. It places a reply in the buffer then terminates, setting the **ErrorLevel** value. Once the parent **Spawn** regains control, it reads **ErrorLevel** and the message. (Of course it already knows where the buffer is.) The programs report all events as they happen; their output is shown first, in Figure 7.3.1. To simplify handling pointers, both programs were designed for compiling with a large data model.

```
Parent has set
   Message              Child, you come back here!
   Command line         MESSAGEAT
   Environment string   MESSAGEAT=3609
and will now spawn      Child.Exe

Her child  C:\TURBOC\WORK\CHILD.EXE  has seen
   Command line         MESSAGEAT
   Environment string   MESSAGEAT=3609
   Message              Child, you come back here!
and has now set
   Message              Coming, Mother!
   ErrorLevel           12

The parent has regained control, and sees
   Message              Coming, Mother!
   ErrorLevel           12
```

Figure 7.3.1 **Spawn.Dem** and **Child.Dem** output

```
/****************************************************************/
/* Spawn.Dem     Demonstrate techniques for spawning and com- */
/*               municating with a child program.  Use memory */
/***************************************** for sending mes-     */
                                        /* sages, an environ-  */
#include <General.H>                    /* ment string to spec-*/
#include <Process.H>                    /* ify the memory loca-*/
                                        /* tion, and the com-  */
void main() {                           /* mand line to identi-*/
  char    *Param1;                      /* fy the string.  Re- */
  unsigned Segment;                     /* port events as they */
  char     SegmentHex[5];               /* happen.  Compile    */
  char     EnvString[80];               /* this with a large   */
  char    *Message;                     /* data model.         */
  char    *Child;                       /***********************/
  int      ErrorLevel;
if (allocmem(0x10,&Segment) != -1) {       /* Allocate memory*/
  perror("Function  allocmen  failed");    /* for the message*/
  return; }                                /* buffer.  Build */
sprintf(SegmentHex,"%04x",Segment);        /* an environment */
```

Figure 7.3.2 Program **Spawn.Dem** (*Continue on next page*)

```
Param1 = "MESSAGEAT";                              /* string incor-  */
strcpy(EnvString,Param1);                          /* porating the   */
strcat(EnvString,"=");                             /* hex numeral for*/
strcat(EnvString,SegmentHex);                      /* its segment    */
putenv(EnvString);                                 /* address.       */
Message = MK_FP(Segment,0);
strcpy(Message,"Child, you come back here!");      /* Write a        */
Child = "Child.Exe";                               /* message.       */
printf("Parent has set             \n"
       "   Message          %s   \n"               /* Report.        */
       "   Command line     %s   \n"
       "   Environment string  %s=%s\n"
       "and will now spawn   %s \n\n",
  Message,Param1,Param1,getenv(Param1),
     Child);
ErrorLevel = spawnle(P_WAIT,       /* Spawn a child, passing   */
  Child,                           /* the prepared environment,*/
     Child,                        /* and using a command line */
       Param1,                     /* parameter to identify the*/
          NULL,                    /* environment string.      */
             environ);
printf("The parent has regained control, and sees\n"
       "   Message          %s\n"
       "   ErrorLevel       %i\n",                 /* Report   */
  Message,ErrorLevel); }
```

Figure 7.3.2 *(Continued)* Program **Spawn.Dem**

Program chaining

While program **Spawn.Dem** executed its child program **Child.Dem**, it remained resident in memory, and resumed control once **Child** terminated. Sometimes this behavior may be undesirable, especially if it's not really necessary to return control to the parent once the child is running. In that case, having both programs resident may waste a scarce memory resource. You can avoid that by invoking a **spawn..** function with first parameter **P_OVERLAY**. (This macro constant is defined in header file **Process.H**.) In this case, the child is simply loaded into the parent's memory block, starting just after the PSP. If the block is too small, it will be extended if possible. Control is passed from parent to child via a jump instruction, hence there's no return to the parent. (Since the jump

```
/************************************************************/
/* Child.Dem     Demonstrate techniques for communicating with*/
/*               a parent program.  Receive and send messages */
/************************************ via a memory buffer.     */
                                   /* Read an environment      */
#include <General.H>              /* string to ascertain the  */
                                   /* buffer location, and a   */
int main(int    ParamCount,       /* command line parameter to*/
         char *Param[]) {         /* determine the string     */
  char    *Program;               /* name.  Report what's hap-*/
  char    *SegmentHex;            /* pening.  Compile this     */
  unsigned Segment;               /* with a large data model. */
  char    *Message;               /***************************/
  int      ErrorLevel = 12;

Program     = Param[0];           /* Program name for report. */
SegmentHex = getenv(Param[1]);   /* Param[1]  names the en-   */
sscanf(SegmentHex,"%x",           /* vironment string with the*/
  &Segment);                      /* hex numeral for the mes- */
Message     = MK_FP(Segment,0);   /* sage segment address.    */

printf("Her child %s  has seen      \n"      /* Report.          */
       "  Command line         %s  \n"
       "  Environment string %s=%s\n"
       "  Message             %s  \n",
  Program,Param[1],Param[1],SegmentHex,Message);

strcpy(Message,"Coming, Mother!");           /* Send a reply.   */

printf("and has now set            \n"       /* Report again.  */
       "  Message             %s  \n"
       "  ErrorLevel          %i \n\n",
  Message,ErrorLevel);
return ErrorLevel; }
```

Figure 7.3.3 Program **Child.Dem**

instruction is itself in the parent's block and will be overlaid by the incoming child, the **spawn..** function must copy part of itself to some safe location, then jump to the copy. The copied code loads the child program, then makes that final jump.) The child inherits the parent's PSP, modified to reflect the new command line. Its environment pointer at offset 2c points to a new environment segment constructed as specified by the invocation of the **spawn..** function.

You can construct a demonstration of this chaining technique by modifying program **Spawn.Dem** slightly. Change **spawnle** parameter **P_WAIT** to **P_OVERLAY**. The communication works as before, except that the modified **Spawn.Dem** never regains control, hence never writes her final report.

The Turbo C Library includes **exec..** function suites with names and calling sequences like the **spawn..** functions, except they have no **Mode** parameter. They function exactly like the corresponding **spawn..** functions with **Mode = P_OVERLAY**.

Use of the word *overlay* in the last three paragraphs is misleading. The technique you see here is properly called program *chaining*, and falls far short of the general overlay management systems included with many high-level language compilers.

Executing DOS commands

If you want your program to execute DOS commands, you must realize that there are several kinds:

- Commands to execute **.Com** and **.Exe** program files.
- DOS external commands, like **Format**. These are really commands to execute separate **.Com** or **.Exe** utility program files shipped with DOS.
- DOS internal commands, like **Dir**.
- Commands to execute **.Bat** program files. These consist of sequences of lines, each one a DOS command.

Commands to execute **.Com** and **.Exe** programs, including the DOS utilities, are handled by a DOS service, invoked by the Turbo C **spawn..** and **exec..** functions described earlier. In fact, even when you enter such a command directly from the keyboard, the DOS command interpreter **Command.Com** calls on this service after finding that it can't execute the command directly. On the other hand, the program execution service can't execute *internal* commands or batch programs directly; neither can the **spawn..** or **exec..** functions. Instead, you may use function

int system(char *Command)

Its prototype is in header file **StdLib.H**. The parameter is simply the desired DOS command. One problem with this function is its return value, which seems unpredictable. It is discussed later.

Various one-line demonstration programs for function **system** are obvious: for example,

void main() {system("Dir d:"); }
void main() {system("ChkDsk d:"); }

A more substantial example results from modifying program **Spawn.Dem** in Figure 7.3.2. In place of the lines on the left, insert those on the right:

```
char    *Child;           char     Command[80];
   :                         :
   :                      strcpy(Command,"Child ");
Child = "Child.Exe";      strcat(Command,Param1);
printf("Parent has set... printf("Parent has set \n"
   :                         "  Message             %s \n"
   :                         "  Environment string %s=%s\n"
   :                         "and will now execute %s \n\n",
   :                      Message,Param1,getenv(Param1),Command);
ErrorLevel = spawnle(...  ErrorLevel = system(Command);
```

The new code sets up and executes the DOS command

Child MESSAGEAT

Everything works as in the original **Spawn.Dem** except **ErrorLevel**. Compiling the resulting program with the compact memory model, the author encountered a bug involving interplay between the last two **printf** parameters and function **system**. He couldn't fix that, but the program ran properly with the huge model.

Another program, demonstrating the use of function **system** with standard input/output redirection, is described later in connection with Figure 7.3.4.

Executing internal DOS commands via function **system** almost involves recursion. You probably execute the parent program from the DOS prompt: the command interpreter is running, and invokes the DOS program execution service to run your program, which calls function **system**. The function *should* be able to pass the specified DOS command directly to the command interpreter, which is already resident. However, the usual interpreter **Command.Com** is not reentrant: it cannot be invoked recursively that way. Therefore, **system** must build a command line parameter consisting of the signal /C followed by your command, and call the program execution service to run the command interpreter with that parameter. This loads a so-called *secondary copy* of the interpreter, which strips off the /C signal and processes your command. Of course, **system** must be able to locate the interpreter—for this it uses the file name specified by the **COMSPEC** string in your program's environment. The next problem is that **system** must secure enough memory to duplicate the parent program's environment for the command interpreter, and enough to load the interpreter itself.

Function **system** returns -1 to indicate failure if it can't locate the command interpreter or can't allocate sufficient memory. Otherwise, according to the Turbo C *Reference guide,* Reference [7], it returns the **ErrorLevel** value set by the command interpreter. Unfortunately, this value is not documented anywhere.

Standard input/output redirection

Interprogram communication becomes particularly easy if the child program uses the DOS standard file handles for input/output. The parent can redirect those to its own files, and thus prepare the input and inspect the output. Clearly, you can implement redirection by providing the proper command line parameter for function **system**, since it can execute *any* DOS command. This elementary technique is described later as an alternative to program **FReopen** in Figure 7.3.4. The problem with using **system** is the excessive time and memory overhead required to load and execute a secondary DOS command processor.

Redirection is possible with the **spawn..** and **exec..** functions, but not really straightforward. (By definition, it *couldn't* be!) The problem is that redirection is normally performed by the command processor **Command.Com**, not by the DOS program execution service. Functions **spawn..** and **exec..** are more efficient than **system** precisely because they use just the execution service. Thus, if you want redirection, you must do it yourself. The simplest way is to use **StdIO** function

FILE *freopen(char *FileName, char *Type, FILE *F)

F must be an open stream; **freopen** substitutes the file with the specified **FileName** for the one currently associated with **F**. In the process, it

```
/*****************************************************************/
/* FReopen.Dem    Demonstrate  I/O  redirection via function  */
/*                freopen.  Write a random array to a tempo-  */
/* rary file, and generate another temporary file name.  Exe- */
/* cute the  DOS  Sort  utility with its  I/O  redirected to  */
/* the temporary files.  Read its output, display the original*/
/*********************************** and sorted data, and     */
                                  /* erase temporary files.   */
#include <General.H>             /***************************/
#include <Process.H>
#define N 5                       /* Array size.            */
#define Template "d:\XXXXXX"      /* For temporary file names.*/

void main() {
  char   Temp1[15],Temp2[15];         /* Open temporary file */
  FILE *F;                            /* Temp1  first to make*/
  int    I,X[N],Y;                    /* a directory entry,  */
                                         /* else  mktemp     */
  strcpy(Temp1,Template);  mktemp(Temp1);   /* will generate */
  F = fopen (Temp1,"a");                    /* Temp2 = Temp1. */
  strcpy(Temp2,Template);  mktemp(Temp2);
  for (I = 0; I < N; ++I)                  /* Make random ar-*/
    fprintf(F,"%5d\n",X[I] = rand());      /* ray and write  */
  fclose(F);                               /* temporary file.*/

  freopen(Temp1,"r",stdin);           /* Redirect standard   */
  freopen(Temp2,"w",stdout);          /* input/output.       */

  spawnlp(P_WAIT,"Sort","Sort",NULL);   /* Execute  Sort  (on */
                                        /* the  DOS  PATH).   */
  freopen("CON","a",stdout);          /* Restore  standard   */
  freopen("CON","r",stdin);           /* input/output.       */

  printf("Executed  Sort  with  i/o   \n"     /* Report      */
         "redirected to temporary files \n\n");  /* header.  */
  printf("Random  Sorted    \n");
  printf("Array    Array  \n\n");
  F = fopen(Temp2,"r");                /* Read and display    */
  for (I = 0; I < N; ++I) {            /* Sort  output, along-*/
    fscanf(F,"%d",&Y);                 /* side original data  */
    printf("%5d     %5d\n",X[I],Y); }  /* for comparison.     */
```

Figure 7.3.4 Program **FReopen.Dem** (*Continue on next page*)

```
fclose(F);
remove(Temp1);   remove(Temp2); }          /* Clean up.               */
```

Output

```
Executed Sort with i/o
redirected to temporary files

Random  Sorted
Array   Array

  346      130
  130      346
10982     1090
 1090    10982
11656    11656
```

Figure 7.3.4 (*Continued*) Program **FReopen.Dem**

closes **F** and reopens it with the new file. Program **FReopen.Dem** in Figure 7.3.4 demonstrates this technique. It sorts an array **X** by writing it to a temporary file with name **Temp1** generated by function **mktemp**, then invoking the DOS **Sort** utility with standard input redirected to **Temp1** and output to another temporary file **Temp2**. Finally, the parent program restores its former standard input/output, reads **Temp2**, erases the temporary files, and resumes processing the array.

Besides the comments in the **FReopen.Dem** source code itself, some other points are important. First, function **mktemp** constructs file names **d:\AA.AAA** and **d:\AA.AAB**, unless these are already present in **d:**. Second, the program closes file **F** after writing it. This file is invisible to the child except via standard input. Moreover, when **freopen** opens it as the standard input file, it repositions the file pointer at the start, for the child's use. Finally, the program restores the former standard input/output arrangement by using **freopen** to associate with it the standard file **CON**—the console. If **FReopen.Dem** had been executed *itself* with redirected input or output, it *could not know* the actual file name, and this whole technique would fail. If that's a possibility, you'll have to use the lower-level **dup..** functions, discussed later in this section.

An earlier paragraph mentioned the possibility of implementing redirection in a more elementary but less efficient way via function **system**. You can easily modify program **FReopen.Dem** to use that technique. Simply declare a sufficiently long character array **Command[]**, and substitute for the **FReopen.Dem** fragment on the left the commands on the right:

```
freopen (Temp1,"r",stdin);            strcpy (Command, "Sort <");
freopen (Temp2,"w",stdout);           strcat (Command,Temp1);
spawnlp (P_WAIT,"Sort","Sort",NULL);  strcat (Command," >");
freopen ("CON","a",stdout);           strcat (Command,Temp2);
freopen ("CON","r",stdin);            system (Command);
```

The string manipulation functions merely construct the DOS command

Sort <d:\AA.AAA >d:\AA.AAB.

As mentioned earlier, you might need to implement standard input/ output redirection with lower level redirection functions

int dup(int Handle)   int dup2(int Handle,
int NewHandle)

These have prototypes in header file **IO.H**. Their use is considerably more delicate. Function **dup** returns a new file handle—the next one available—associated with the same open file, file pointer, and access mode as the specified **Handle**. Function **dup2** performs essentially the same task, but you may specify the new handle; if it's open, **dup2** will close it before proceeding. These functions just code your request into assembly language and pass it on to DOS. It's an easy task for DOS: the programs' pointers to DOS' file handles are simply adjusted. However, this can have complex effects on your programs. Figure 7.3.5 demonstrates the **dup..** functions through program **Dup.Dem**, a modification of Figure 7.3.4 program **FReopen.Dem**. The programs perform the same computation; their output is identical.

As with the earlier program, there are some important points to consider. First, **StdIO** function **fileno** provides the file handle parameters that **dup2** requires. This step wouldn't have been necessary had **Dup.Dem** used lower-level **IO.H** file handling functions to prepare the temporary files. Second, the **rewind** call preceding redirection is absolutely necessary. The child program inherits the file handles *with their*

```
/*****************************************************************/
/* Dup.Dem     Demonstrate  i/o  redirection via functions    */
/*             dup  and  dup2. This works like FReopen.Dem    */
/**********************************  except that these func-   */
                                 /* tions are used in place    */
#include <General.H>             /* of  freopen,  and there    */
#include      <IO.H>             /* is more file handle        */
#include <Process.H>             /* overhead.                  */
#define  StdIn      0            /***************************** */
#define  StdOut     1
#define  N          5            /* Array size.               */
#define  Template "d:\XXXXXX"    /* For temporary file names.*/

void main() {
  char    Temp1[15],Temp2[15];
  FILE    *F1,*F2;                        /* Open temporary */
  int     I,X[N],Y;                       /* file Temp1     */
  int     Handle1,OldStdIn;               /* first to make  */
  int     Handle2,OldStdOut;              /* a directory en-*/
                                          /* try, else      */
  strcpy(Temp1,Template);  mktemp(Temp1); /* mktemp will    */
  F1 = fopen(Temp1,"w+");                 /* generate       */
  strcpy(Temp2,Template);  mktemp(Temp2); /*   Temp1        */
  F2 = fopen(Temp2,"w+");                 /*     = Temp2.    */
  for (I = 0; I < N; ++I)                 /* Make random ar-*/
    fprintf(F1,"%5d\n",X[I] = rand());    /* ray and write  */
  rewind(F1);                             /* file Temp1.    */

  Handle1   = fileno(F1);            /* Redirect standard  */
  OldStdIn  = dup(StdIn);            /* input.             */
  dup2(Handle1,StdIn);
  Handle2   = fileno(F2);            /* Redirect standard  */
  OldStdOut = dup(StdOut);          /* output.            */
  dup2(Handle2,StdOut);

                                     /* Execute  Sort  (on */
  spawnlp(P_WAIT,"Sort","Sort",NULL); /* the  DOS  PATH).  */

  dup2(OldStdIn ,StdIn);            /* Restore standard   */
  dup2(OldStdOut,StdOut);           /* input/output.      */

  printf("Executed  Sort  with  i/o      \n"      /* Report */
         "redirected to temporary files \n\n");   /* header. */
```

Figure 7.3.5 Program **Dup.Dem** (*Continue on next page*)

```
printf("Random   Sorted    \n");
printf("Array    Array  \n\n");
rewind(F2);                              /* Read and display     */
for (I = 0; I < N; ++I) {                /* Sort  output, along-*/
   fscanf(F2,"%d",&Y);                   /* side original data   */
   printf("%5d    %5d\n",X[I],Y); }      /* for comparison.      */
fclose(F1);   remove(Temp1);             /* Clean up.            */
fclose(F2);   remove(Temp2); }
```

Figure 7.3.5 (*Continued*) Program **Dup.Dem**

pointers. It doesn't reopen them, so without **rewind** its standard input pointer would be at the end of the file, not the start. Moreover, according to the Turbo C *Reference guide,* after the write operation in the parent program, a subsequent read may fail—even one in a child program—unless some function that calls **lseek** intervenes, like this **rewind.** *That* is real delicacy! Third, program **Dup.Dem** doesn't close its handles **F1** and **F2** before spawning **Sort.Exe**; for neatness and safety, you should, then reopen **F2** after the child returns, unless you *want* the **F1** and **F2** pointers to reflect the child's actions. Finally, note that unlike higher level function **freopen, dup2** requires only the previous file handles, not the file names, to restore standard input/output to its previous state. Thus, unlike **FReopen.Dem**, program **Dup.Dem** will work even if its own standard input/output has been redirected.

7.4 Program termination

Concepts

Normal termination
Checking for assignments via null pointers
Registering and executing exit functions
Abnormal program termination
Assertions

This short final section describes several Turbo C techniques for terminating programs. It outlines in detail the normal termination process, then considers two functions intended to provide information if a program terminates abnormally, either during a production run or during development.

Normal termination

There are three common normal termination techniques. First, you can do nothing at all—that is, finish executing the last statement in your program. Second, you can execute a statement like **return ErrorLevel**. Third, you can execute Library function

void _exit(int ErrorLevel)

(A fourth, higher-level, alternative is discussed later.) Exactly how these methods are related is not documented, even in the Turbo C Library source code. However, some detective work leads to the following tentative conclusions. First, doing nothing is equivalent to executing **return 0**.

Second, executing any **return** statement sets up the function **main** return value as documented in the Turbo C *User's guide,* Reference [8]. Then **_exit** is called. There's no point in returning a value longer than two bytes, because **_exit** won't pass it on. Returning a two-byte **ErrorLevel** value is equivalent to executing **_exit(ErrorLevel)**.

Function **_exit** restores interrupt vector 0 to the value it had before your program was loaded. The Turbo C startup code had redirected it to point to a floating point arithmetic error handling routine. (Section 8.9 discusses these concepts.) Next, **_exit** uses a check sum to see if the Turbo C copyright message at the beginning of the Data Segment is intact. If it has been altered since your program started, you probably made an invalid assignment via a null pointer. In that case, **_exit** outputs the message

Null pointer assignment

via the standard error file handle (usually the screen). In any case, **_exit** returns to the DOS program execution service. DOS then closes all the program's open file handles, copies the program termination address from the PSP to interrupt vector 22, releases all the program's allocated memory, and returns to the calling program via vector 22.

You can implement a higher-level exit protocol via function

void exit(int ErrorLevel)

This routine will execute in sequence up to 32 "registered" *exit functions,* then call **_exit(ErrorLevel).** An exit function must have type **atexit_t,** defined as follows:

typedef void (* atexit_t)(void)

You register an exit function **F** by executing function

int atexit(atexit_t F)

There is no way to "unregister" an exit function. You'll find both the **atexit** prototype and the **atexit_t** definition in header file **StdLib.H.**
Prototypes for functions **_exit** and **exit** are in header file **Process.H.** The source code for the former is embedded in the Turbo C startup code in Library file **C0.Asm**. The Turbo C *Reference Guide* suggests that **_exit** does not close any files, but **exit** does. The first part of this statement is not true. The latter function calls the former, which returns to DOS, which closes all open files.

Abnormal termination

The Turbo C Library provides two functions for handling abnormal terminations: **abort** and **assert**. The latter is specially designed for program development. Function

void abort(void)

on the other hand, is very simple: it simply outputs the message

Abnormal program termination

via the standard error file handle, then calls **_exit(3)**. The choice of magic number **3** is not explained. The prototype for **abort** is in header file **StdLib.H**; its source code is embedded in the startup code in Library file **C0.Asm.**

Header file **Assert.H** defines function

void assert(int Test)

as a macro. If **Test** is zero, **assert** outputs via the standard error file handle the message **Assertion failed:** followed by the **Test** value, the name of the source code file containing the **assert** statement, and its line number within the file. Then **assert** calls **abort**. This is intended for use during debugging. In fact, if you place directive **#define NDEBUG** before **#include <Assert.H>** in your program, the preprocessor will cause the **assert** statement to be ignored.

8

Interrupt Services

Contents

This long chapter on interrupt services is possibly the most important in the book. That is certainly true if your main goal is to learn the principles underlying the techniques developed in earlier chapters for screen, keyboard, and file input/output, memory management, and program execution: they are all based on BIOS and DOS interrupt services. This chapter is also essential for understanding programming techniques for memory resident software: memory resident programs *are* interrupt service routines. Finally, several areas, like printer services, comparable to those covered in earlier chapters, are considered here because they are based on interrupt services but don't merit chapters of their own.

Sections 8.1 and 8.3 are devoted to interrupts in general. The first describes the basic concept, contrasting it with other methods of transferring control between routines. Section 8.3 shows how to execute interrupts using Turbo C or **Debug**. Section 8.2 intervenes, giving a catalog of the PC interrupt vectors—the address locations that give access to hundreds of BIOS and DOS program services. These are used to provide examples for Section 8.3.

Sections 8.4 and 8.5 describe most of the BIOS and DOS interrupt services. Most of these are made more accessible to Turbo C programs through functions in its Library and the Turbo C TOOLS package, and have been discussed in earlier chapters in that guise. Therefore, it was possible to avoid repeating much of the detailed descriptions of these services. Four categories of interrupt services are described separately in Sections 8.6 to 8.9: printer, clock/calendar, serial communications, and error recovery. This organization was suggested either by the extra amount of discussion required, or, particularly in 8.7, by the inadvisability of considering related BIOS and DOS services separately.

8.1 What is an interrupt?

Concepts

Jumps
Procedure calls
Interrupts
Flags register
Interrupt priority classes
Single stepping
8259A interrupt controller chip

As an experienced programmer, you are familiar with various ways of dividing a programming project into smaller modules, or *processes*, and transferring control from one to another. A process can be as small as a few machine language instructions, or as large as a family of programs. Because of this variance, it is easiest to analyze modularization techniques by concentrating on methods for transferring control. Three mechanisms are most common: *go to, procedure call,* and *interrupt.* This chapter's goal is for you to understand the last type thoroughly. A first step is to see how it differs from the others.

Jumps

When you execute a *go to,* you have no intention to return whence you came. You must ascertain the address of the destination process, but it never needs to know yours. The usual machine language implementation of a go to is a *jump* instruction. (There are also *conditional* jumps, which transfer control only if some condition is valid.) For the Intel 8086 CPU family there are several types of jumps, with different ways for determining the destination address. Once that has been calculated, the transfer is effected simply by putting the destination segment and offset into the CS and IP (*Code Segment* and *Instruction Pointer*) registers. The 8086 always uses these registers to find its next instruction.

Chaining from program A to program B, discussed in Section 7.3, is a type of *go to* in a larger context. Program A disappears after the transfer, because B is not expected to return.

Procedure calls

When control is transferred by a *procedure call,* the destination process, or *procedure,* is expected to return to the next step in the original process, or *caller.* This is a particularly useful device for processes that carry out details required in various contexts. A routine that governs overall project organization can invoke their services when necessary, proceeding in sequence. The caller knows the procedure addresses, but the latter are not expected to have direct knowledge of the return addresses in the caller.

Some systems implement a weak form of procedure call just using *go to* transfers. The caller stores the procedure *parameters* (its input/output) and the return address in some *fixed* location known to the procedure, and the latter uses that information to finish its task and return. The problem with this approach is that it prevents a procedure from calling itself, or two from calling each other. Although such *recursive* algorithms are often useful—there are examples in Sections 3.5, 3.7, and 6.4—under this convention they result in endless loops or other sorts of crashes. Unfortunately, portions of DOS use this type of procedure call, and thus create major difficulties for memory resident applications programs, described in Chapter 9.

The *stack* concept was invented to facilitate programming recursive procedures. It has several benefits:

- A stack provides a system for distinguishing the return addresses for nested invocations of the same procedure, thus avoiding the endless loop just mentioned.
- It provides separate workspaces for these invocations, as required by recursive algorithms.
- More generally, it lets you preserve the essentials of your machine's state at the time of the call, so that you can restore them upon return.

The 8086 implements procedure calls with *call* and *return* instructions. When Program A calls Procedure B to perform some task using parameters P and Q, the machine language looks something like this:

Program A   1) *Push* onto the stack various data and register values needed later that procedure B might alter.
                     2) *Push* onto the stack parameters Q and P.
                     3) *Call* procedure B.

(Step 1 may be redundant. B should do this service if possible, and its documentation should warn you if A must be extra careful.) The *call* stacks the address CS:IP of the next instruction in A, then places B's address in CS:IP. Execution therefore proceeds with the first instruction in B:

Procedure B   4) If B will change values of any registers commonly used by callers, it should stack them for later restoration.
                     5) B sets up its workspace on the stack.
                     6) B performs its task, using the parameters and workspace on the stack, and places in the appropriate stack locations any parameter values that it must return to A.
                     7) B executes *pop* instructions to clear its workspace from the stack. Now the return address is atop the stack, with the parameters jut below.

8) B executes a *return* instruction.

The *return* instruction pops the return address into CS:IP, so execution proceeds as desired in Program A:

Program   9) A pops parameter P, then Q, and any other vital information it saved on the stack.

The stack has now been returned to its state before Step 1), and A proceeds in sequence.

If you know that CS does not need to change during the transfer, you can use *near* call and return instructions that only push and pop register IP. Otherwise, you must use the slower *far* call and return.

Clearly, you can implement procedure calls gracefully using push-pop and call-return instruction pairs. Parameters, return addresses, and workspaces are associated with particular procedure *invocations,* not with a procedure itself, so the mechanism is general, and permits recursion.

The procedure invocation protocol just described permits use of a variable number N of parameters. If the first parameter contains the number N-1 of parameters following, the procedure can inspect it first, and use it in a loop that reads the other parameters. Some software systems don't reverse the order when they push parameters, hence don't have the capacity to vary N.

Interrupts

Often in practice a process A needs the services of a procedure B, but does not know its address. For example, A may have detected a <Ctrl-Break> keystroke, and knows that this needs special handling. But different <Ctrl-Break> handlers may be in effect at different times. It's not practical to load the current handler always at the same address—that would require too much shuffling, as well as reservation of enough space to accommodate the largest conceivable handler, even when it's not in service.

The *interrupt* method of transferring control provides a solution. It's somewhat like a procedure call, except it finds the *address* of the destination procedure in a specific location, called an *interrupt vector.*

The procedure is called an *interrupt service routine (ISR)*. For the previous example, Process A merely needs to know which interrupt vector is used to direct it to the <Ctrl-Break> ISR currently in service.

Intel 8086 family CPUs have 256 different interrupt instructions **Int 0** to **Int ff**. Interrupt vector **n** corresponding to interrupt **Int n** occupies the same four bytes in any 8086 machine:

	Interrupt vector n	
Address	Content:	ISR address
0000:4n	Offset	low byte
0000:4n+1	Offset	high byte
0000:4n+2	Segment	low byte
0000:4n+3	Segment	high byte

The vectors thus occupy the first 1K = hex 400 bytes of memory.

At first, you might expect that a return instruction is appropriate for transferring from an ISR back to the interrupted process. However, a special *interrupt return* instruction **IRet** is required, as described later.

Interrupts tend to occur unexpectedly in delicate situations requiring meticulous attention to preserving the status of the interrupted program for restoration when it resumes. Using the stack to preserve register values was described earlier. In certain circumstances involved with interrupt processing, stacking the registers mentioned so far in this book does not preserve enough information. The 8086 machines have an additional Flags register that interrupts treat specially. It will be described in detail later.

Here is the precise action of instruction **Int n**:

- Push the Flags register onto the stack.
- Turn off the Flags register IF and TF bits.
- Execute a far call to the procedure whose address is in interrupt vector **n**.

Now you can infer what the interrupt return instruction **IRet** must do:

- Execute a far return.
- Pop the stack into the Flags register.

When an interrupt instruction occurs explicitly in a program, it is called a *software* interrupt. In certain situations, usually involving an error condition or a service demand by peripheral equipment, the CPU can execute an interrupt automatically after the current instruction is completed. That is called a *hardware* interrupt. The distinction is important and delicate. For example, executing instruction **Int 0** in a program results in a software interrupt. But if that action is triggered automatically by an attempted division by zero—its intended use—it is a hardware interrupt. The IF and TF bits just mentioned help control hardware interrupts. Clearly, an event that triggers a hardware interrupt can occur while an earlier one is being serviced; in fact, two or more can occur simultaneously. Therefore, interrupt processing involves priority conventions and hardware to implement them. These considerations are discussed later.

Flags register

The Flags register consists of two bytes, of which eleven bits, or *flags*, have special uses in all 8086 family CPUs. (Some others are used in the 80286.) The format is shown in Figure 8.1.1. Most flags are used principally to indicate arithmetic conditions, as their names suggest. Some of those occasionally indicate DOS errors of various other types. The direction flag DF controls the direction of operation (forwards or backwards) of some string manipulation instructions. The two flags of

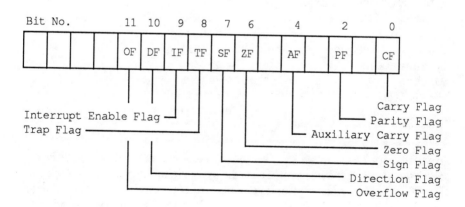

Figure 8.1.1 Flags register

interest in this chapter are the Interrupt Enable and Trap Flags IF and TF. The Trap Flag is used only with instruction **Int 1** to implement the single-step trace feature of a debugger. It is of interest here because it figures in interrupt prioritization, discussed later.

Several machine language instructions involving the Flags register are important for interrupt handling. Instructions **Sti** and **Cli** turn IF on and off. This enables or disables certain hardware interrupts. The only way to modify TF is to push the Flags register onto the stack with instruction **PushF**, modify the TF bit in the stacked copy, then use instruction **PopF** to pop the modified word back into the register.

The Turbo C Library provides two functions that simply execute machine language instructions **Cli** and **Sti**:

void disable(void)
void enable(void)

They are defined as macros in header file **DOS.H**.

Interrupt priority classes

To establish which ISR has priority when two interrupt services are demanded at once, interrupts are divided into several classes, as follows.

Interrupt priority classes

8086	80286
Software, Exception	Software, Exception
Non-maskable	Single step
Maskable	Non-maskable
Single step	Processor extension segment overrun
	Maskable

An interrupt has priority over all those in lower classes. There is only one class *within* which two members ordinarily vie for service: the maskable interrupts. (A rare exception is the non- maskable class.) Prioritization for the 80286 differs from that for earlier CPUs. Details of priority implementation are discussed later. First, it's necessary to describe the various classes.

Software interrupts are those caused by explicit **Int n** instructions in programs, and by the conditional interrupt instruction **IntO**, which executes **Int 4** if the Overflow Flag bit OF is on.

Exceptions are hardware interrupts triggered by error conditions encountered by certain instructions. For the 8086 there is only one type of exception: certain errors detected by division instructions trigger **Int 0**. (These are usually attempts to divide by zero.) For the 80286 there are several, detailed in Section 8.2. 80286 exception interrupts execute slightly differently from the 8086: the stacked return address is not the address of the *next* instruction, but that of the *current* one. That makes it possible for the exception ISR to determine which instruction failed. With the 8086 that is difficult because various division instructions differ in length.

Since the CPU executes only one instruction at a time, no two software or exception interrupts can ever request service simultaneously.

One of the lines connected to the 8086 is devoted to the *non-maskable* interrupt (NMI). Its name indicates that it cannot be disabled easily. A signal on the NMI line causes hardware Interrupt 2. According to the Intel design, this interrupt should be used only for the most urgent service requests. On the PC it occurs on certain parity errors, but design integrity was compromised by using it as well to report some 8087 Numeric Coprocessor errors. On the PC/AT it's triggered only by parity errors. Apparently, one NMI can occur while another is being serviced. If you need to prevent this, you can disable the NMI by outputting zero to CPU port hex a0, and reenable it by outputting hex 80. On the PC/AT, this may not be necessary, because occurrence of an NMI inhibits any further NMIs until an **IRet** instruction is executed.

Maskable interrupts are used by external devices to request CPU service. For example, the keyboard processor uses a maskable interrupt to signal the BIOS to process a keyboard event. (See the discussion of the keyboard buffer in Section 5.2.) If you are using an interrupt driven communication program, arrival of a byte in a serial port triggers a maskable interrupt. The corresponding ISR inspects the port for possible error conditions, and normally places the byte in a buffer in memory for the program to process as appropriate.

Clearly, an event that triggers an exception, the NMI or a maskable interrupt can occur while a previous one is being serviced; two such events could even occur simultaneously. Competition within these classes is handled by the *interrupt controller chip* through a masking process described later.

Maskable interrupts can occur only when the interrupt enable flag IF is on. Programs frequently use instruction **Cli** to turn off IF during certain housekeeping tasks that would cause inconsistent information to be recorded if they were interrupted.

An 80286 *processor extension overrun exception* occurs if an 80287 Numeric Coprocessor attempts to access a multi-byte operand that would either wrap around from the end of a segment to its beginning, or else overlap from the end of one segment to the beginning of the next. This probably indicates a programming error that would go undetected in the 8086, which always assumes that wrap-around is intended.

The *single step* interrupt, hardware Interrupt 1, is used by debuggers to let you step through your program, one instruction at a time. It's controlled by the Trap Flag TF. When TF is on, Interrupt 1 will occur after the current instruction, unless a higher priority interrupt occurs before the current instruction completes its execution. With the 8086, any hardware interrupt takes priority over the single step, but in the 80286, only exceptions do.

Single stepping

Although not directly applicable to Turbo C programming, details concerning the single-step interrupt are described here, because they illustrate the operation of interrupt priority classes.

Preparing to single-step your program, a debugger turns TF on, which will trigger Interrupt 1 after your first instruction is completed. When that occurs, the Flags register is pushed onto the stack automatically and TF is turned off. In the stacked copy of the Flags, the TF bit remains on. The single-step service routine, part of the debugger, reports how your first instruction affected the registers, and outputs a disassembled version of your next instruction (its address lies atop the stack). The ISR is not itself single-stepped, because TF is off. When the ISR has completed its task, its return **IRet** instruction pops the stack into the Flags register, which turns TF on again. Your next instruction executes, in single step mode.

The change in single-step interrupt priority from the 8086 to the 80286 corrects a problem with the earlier CPU. On the 8086, no ISR can be single-stepped, because an interrupt instruction always turns TF off. (It is turned on again when the corresponding **IRet** pops the stack into the Flags register.) In fact, you don't want to single-step the Interrupt 1 service routine itself, nor service routines for hardware interrupts triggered by external events during debugging. However, you might want to analyze or debug an interrupt service routine by invoking it with a software interrupt.

The 80286 prioritization makes this possible: the debugger's single step ISR merely has to turn on IF and turn on the TF bit in the copy of the Flags register that its interrupt instruction saved on the stack. When a software interrupt is single-stepped, it is executed first, followed immediately by the single-step interrupt. Therefore, the single-step ISR is executed before even the first instruction of the software ISR, and turns TF back on as it returns to the software ISR. In the case of a lower-priority interruption, the single step interrupt occurs first, followed by the hardware interrupt as soon as IF is turned on. The hardware interrupt executes at normal speed because TF does not come on until the single step ISR is finished.

Unfortunately, this scheme single-steps exception ISRs as well as software ISRs. Here is a puzzle: how can a single step ISR distinguish this situation from the first scenario just described and switch to full speed?

8259A Interrupt Controller Chip

Each external device that uses a maskable interrupt to request CPU service is connected to one of the *interrupt request lines* IRQ0 to IRQn on the system bus. These correspond to some of the gold strips on the expansion board connectors that you plug into motherboard slots. In the PC, there are eight IRQ lines. That number has proved inadequate for the variety of peripheral equipment in common use, so capacity was expanded in the PC/AT to fifteen. The IRQ lines are all serviced by an Intel 8259A *programmable interrupt controller* chip. (In the PC/AT, two 8259As are installed. The IRQ2 line connects them, and is not available for external use.)

During the initialization part of the boot process, the BIOS sets the controller's priorities for servicing requests on the various IRQ lines. In fact, priorities are assigned in reverse numerical order. IRQ0 has highest priority—it connects with the timer chip. The BIOS also informs the controller which interrupt vectors correspond to the IRQ lines, and it initializes the vectors to point to the appropriate BIOS ISRs. The BIOS uses **In** and **Out** instructions to communicate with the controller via certain CPU ports.

When the controller determines that a maskable interrupt request should be honored, it sends a signal to the CPU. The CPU will honor such an interrupt only if IF is on. Programs frequently use instruction **Cli** to turn off IF during certain housekeeping tasks that would cause inconsistent information to be recorded if they were interrupted. It should be turned on whenever feasible. Otherwise, timing and communications processes, for example, could be disrupted. When the CPU does honor a maskable interrupt request, it sends an acknowledgement back to the controller.

The interrupt instructions all turn IF off, to enable ISRs to do noninterruptible housekeeping first. (If interrupts didn't turn off IF, an ISR might not get a chance to execute even a single **Cli** before it is itself interrupted!) ISRs should use **Sti** to turn IF on as soon as possible, thus enabling higher priority maskable interrupts. Of course, an ISR can always be interrupted by the NMI or an exception interrupt, and it can execute software interrupts.

It is the interrupt controller's job to ensure that maskable ISRs are interrupted only by higher priority requests. To this end, it has a *Service Register* with one bit for each IRQ line. When the CPU acknowledges that it's honoring an interrupt request, the controller turns on the appropriate service register bit. Since an ISR can be interrupted by higher-priority interrupts, several service register bits may be on, but the one with highest priority always indicates the currently executing ISR. By inspecting the Service Register, the controller can determine whether to honor an incoming request on an IRQ line immediately, or to wait until a higher priority ISR is finished.

Somehow, the interrupt controller must be informed that a maskable ISR has completed its task. Otherwise, no lower priority interrupt request would ever again be honored! There is no automatic way for the CPU to do it; the ISR itself must take care of this detail, by sending a byte called an *End of Interrupt* (EOI) signal to the controller via a CPU port. The PC and PC/AT use port hex 20, and the EOI signal is also hex 20.

The 8259A interrupt controller chip is programmable, and can be set up to handle interrupts in many ways other than the standard PC scheme just described. For more information, consult the Intel *Microsystem components handbook,* Reference [17, pp. 2-89 ff.], the PC *Technical reference* manual [20], and the books by Eggebrecht [11, Ch. 9] and Sargent and Shoemaker [33, Section 6.4].

8.2 Interrupt vectors

Concepts

Map of interrupt vectors
How are the vectors initialized?
Displaying their current values

In Section 8.1 you saw how a program can use the interrupt mechanism to invoke a service routine when neither process knows the location of the other. This is the usual way to obtain common services provided by the BIOS, DOS, or other system software, usually written independently of your application. The service routine address is placed in one of the 256 interrupt vectors. Its documentation defines which vector is used, and exactly how its parameters are to be passed. Generally, CPU registers are used for both input and output parameters. Precise details of parameter format and service routine side effects must be documented.

To avoid conflicts between interrupt vector assignments by various software packages, IBM established a partly successful allocation of the vectors. In overall numbers, the allocation can be summarized as follows:

Number of vectors	Who determines their use
12	8086, 80286
28	BIOS
32	Peripheral equipment
32	DOS
113	BASIC
39	Custom software
256	

The scheme is flawed; there are still overlaps, and some of the above numbers are only approximate. In the original 8086 design, Intel reserved the 32 vectors hex 00 to 1f to provide services for various conditions arising in that CPU and later models. Five of these are actually used in the 8086 and twelve in the 80286. Unfortunately, before the 80286 was announced, IBM had already begun to use some of those twelve and all of the remaining twenty for the PC BIOS. The result is a mess for a systems programmer to sort out. For example, if a PC/AT 80286 CPU encounters a **Bound** instruction exception—an index out of range—it will execute hardware Interrupt 5. Unless corrected by very sophisticated software, the effect will be execution of the PC/AT BIOS Interrupt 5 service routine, designed to service the <Shift-PrtSc> keystroke. Thus, an index-out-of-range error causes the screen to be printed (or crashes, if you have no printer attached)! The problem can be solved only by redirecting interrupt vector 5 to a custom ISR whose first task is to determine which condition caused the interrupt. How to determine that is a fine puzzle.

Figure 8.2.1 details the interrupt vector allocation. Sections 8.4 and 8.5 will describe many of the BIOS and DOS service routines mentioned in the figure. From here on, *all interrupt numbers are given in hexadecimal notation.*

In the original PC *Technical reference* manual, IBM listed vectors 40..7f as not used. Various software developers then began using them for custom software. With the appearance of the PC/AT, IBM decided to use most of them either for the PC/AT BIOS or other peripheral equipment. Some unlucky software, of course, began to experience conflicts with hardware demands for these vectors. Software designers can get around this problem with a software installation procedure that allows the user to specify which interrupt vectors are to be used. (Presumably there are some left.) Unfortunately, this assumes an unreasonably high level of user sophistication. Some manufacturers of popular interrupt driven software have attempted to develop standards to avoid these conflicts.

It's not clear why so many vectors are used by BASIC. Perhaps that simply reflects poor programming practice. A cursory inspection with the BASIC **Peek** function revealed that vectors 80..85 had never been initialized, but 86..f0 were actually in use. About half of the latter set all contained copies of the same pointer, so it's likely that they aren't in *actual* use, either. All the BASIC vectors are available for custom use, provided BASIC will never be executed simultaneously.

During the bootstrap process, the BIOS initializes all interrupt vectors to zero, then sets vectors 00..1c to point to various ISRs in the BIOS itself. In vectors 1d..1f it stores addresses of three tables used by the ISRs: parameters describing the display adapter, diskette drives, and the dot matrices for the Color/Graphics Adapter characters with ASCII/IBM codes 128..255. After this initialization, the BIOS checks whether any adapters are installed with custom BIOS chips. It transfers control to each of these in turn to execute custom testing and initialization routines. A custom BIOS may initialize other vectors. On the author's

Interrupt Vectors	Brief Description
00..1f 00..04 05..09, 0d,10	Reserved by Intel to service conditions arising in CPU Used by Intel in the 8086 and 80286 Used by Intel in the 80286
05,10..1c 08..09 1d..1f	Used by BIOS to service various software interrupts Used by BIOS to service hardware interrupts from timer, keyboard controllers Used by BIOS to store addresses of some vital tables
20..3f 20:.28,2f	Reserved by DOS to service various software interrupts Officially used by DOS 3.3

40..5f
 	
42..44
4a
	Originally termed unused. Now reserved for peripheral
	  equipment support. Some are used by the PC/AT disk
	  controller BIOS
	Used by Enhanced Graphics Adapter BIOS
	Used by PC/AT for real-time clock alarm service

60..6f	Unallocated. Available for custom use. 67 is used by Lotus/Intel/Microsoft/AST expanded memory management
70..77	Used by PC/AT BIOS to service various interrupts from peripheral hardware.
78..7f	Unallocated. Available for custom use
80..85	Used by BASIC (?)
86..f0	Used by BASIC interpreter
f1..ff	Unallocated. Available for custom use

Figure 8.2.1 Interrupt vector map

system, for example, vectors 40 and 41 are initialized and 0d altered; 0d and 41 then point to custom fixed disk BIOS routines with segment address c800, and vector 40 to a disk service routine in the PC BIOS.

When it has finished its bootstrap testing and initialization, the BIOS searches for an operating system bootstrap routine. If it fails, control is transferred to ROM BASIC. Otherwise, the BIOS loads and transfers control to the operating system bootstrap. That program loads the rest

```
/*****************************************************************/
/* IV.Dem     Display all interrupt vectors.                  */
/*****************************************************************/

#include <General.H>

void main() {
  int I,J,K;
  void far * far *L;
printf("Interrupt vectors\n\n");
for (I = 0; I < 64; ++I) {                    /* Output in four */
  for (J = 0; J < 4; ++J) { K = 64*J + I;   /* columns.        */
    L = MK_FP(0,4*K);
    printf("%02x %Fp     ",K,*L); }
printf("\n"); }}
```

Figure 8.2.2 Program **IV.Dem**

of the operating system and performs its own initialization. During this process, DOS sets its own interrupt vectors 20..3f and alters several others previously set by the BIOS. For example, the BIOS originally sets the divide exception interrupt vector 0 to point to a dummy ISR, which merely sends an end of interrupt signal to the controller chip. This vector is changed to point to a DOS routine, which prints the error message **Divide overflow**. DOS 3.3 places in vectors 28,2a-2d,31-3f pointers to a dummy service routine containing a single **IRet** instruction. It's not currently using those vectors, except for vector 28. DOS executes **Int 28** when it's waiting for keyboard input. Programmers are invited to write custom ISRs for this interrupt, to execute certain routines that must take advantage of DOS' inactivity. See Section 9.4 for further discussion.

The only way to determine how the PC and custom BIOS originally sets the interrupt vectors is to read the assembly language listings. Even then, you may have to use a debugger to match those to the code actually in your ROM, which may be a different version. To verify how DOS adjusts the vectors, use the debugger to inspect the vectors themselves. *Caution:* the debugger has an opportunity to change the vectors from the DOS setting before you see them! You can check the BASIC vectors by using its **Peek** function.

Other software alters the interrupt vectors, too. For example, every Turbo C program changes vector 0 to point to its own divide exception

ISR, which outputs the message **Divide error** via the standard error file handle and terminates the program with **ErrorLevel** = 3. To inspect the vectors as set by Turbo C, DOS, and any memory resident software currently installed, you may want to use program **IV.Dem** listed in Figure 8.2.2. Compile it to an **.Exe** file and run that to eliminate any settings specific to the compiler. By running **IV.Dem** before and after installing a memory resident program, you can determine the latter's effect on the interrupt vectors.

8.3 Executing Interrupts

Concepts

Executing interrupts with **Debug**
Using Interrupt 18 to enter ROM BASIC
Using Interrupt 19 to reboot
Turbo C Library functions for executing interrupts

In the last two sections you have seen how interrupts can provide services for your programs. Included in the BIOS and DOS are about two hundred service routines that give you command over PC hardware. Clearly, they were written independently of your software, and in different systems the service routines will have different locations. Moreover, some of the services must respond to conditions arising in equipment external to the CPU, like the keyboard and the system clock. Therefore, the interrupt mechanism is appropriate for transferring control to and from the service routines.

In a higher-level language like Turbo C, the usual mechanism for invoking a subprogram and regaining control is the procedure call, not the interrupt. More closely involved with hardware features like registers, interrupts have been regarded as lower-level language concepts. They have not been accepted as an integral part of a higher-level language. However, because interrupt services are so useful, many software toolkits, like the Turbo C Library, incorporate routines that permit you to execute any specified interrupt. This section shows how to use those features. It starts one level lower, with some assembly language, to give a better idea of what's happening.

You will see that even the Turbo C interrupt feature is tedious to use, and will quickly appreciate the benefits gained by building higher level routines around the interrupts, so that application programs can access interrupt services with minimal concern for machine language detail. Most of the Turbo C Library functions described in earlier chapters do just that for the interrupts necessary to obtain BIOS and DOS services.

Sections 8.4 and 8.5 describe the BIOS and DOS services in some detail, and correlate them with Library routines discussed earlier. There you will find close analysis of some source code to see how routines like these actually use the methods of the present section.

How can the assembly language technique for invoking an interrupt service routine be illustrated effectively in a book that aims to avoid assembly language detail? One handy tool is the **Debug** program distributed with DOS. It is not a very powerful debugger, but you have it, and it is sufficient for the task. It will be used to obtain some BIOS and DOS services. Simple examples are chosen to enable you to see the essentials clearly.

The first example is BIOS Interrupt 18. The corresponding ISR invokes ROM BASIC. You rarely use this BASIC directly, because it is weak compared with the BASICA software that comes with DOS. If your PC has no fixed disk, then you can enter ROM BASIC by booting with no DOS diskette. After searching for one, the BIOS bootstrap gives up and executes **Int 18** If you have installed DOS on a fixed disk, the only way you can easily invoke ROM BASIC is through this interrupt.

Warning! Once there, you can't leave! The normal way to exit from BASIC is its **System** command, but that is inoperative in ROM BASIC. This is the first software installed, and it cannot expect that there is a system to return to. The only exit is to reboot. Don't execute **Int 18**unless you have saved on permanent storage any files you may have temporarily stored on a virtual disk!

An assembly language program to illustrate the ROM BASIC interrupt consists of a single line: the instruction **Int 18** The script in Figure 8.3.1 shows you how use the DOS debugger to write and execute this program. Its outputs are in normal typeface; your inputs are in **boldface**.

You can assemble this little program to a file **Int_18.Com** by following the script in Figure 8.3.1 up through the assembly, then executing **Debug** commands **N** to name the file, **R** to set BX,CX = 0000,0002—two words giving the number of bytes to write—and command **W CS:0100**to

Script	Comments
Debug	Execute the debugger program.
-A	The hyphen is its prompt. Enter the command to Assemble.
35F5:0100 **Int 18**	Offset 100 in the code segment. This leaves room for the PSP.
35F5:0102	Enter <CR> to terminate assembly.
-G	Enter the command to Go. This executes the program just assembled.
	Now you have entered ROM BASIC, and you can't return.

Figure 8.3.1 Debug script to enter ROM BASIC

write the indicated number of bytes on the specified file, beginning at offset 0100 in the code segment. Execute it like any other **.Com** file.

Another one line program is interesting to try. Use **Int 19** in place of **Int 18**. If you have no device drivers listed in your **Config.Sys** file, you will reboot DOS, skipping the initializations performed by the BIOS when it detects the <Ctrl-Alt-Del> keystroke. When you turn on the machine, the BIOS sets interrupt vector 19 to point to its routine that reads and executes an operating system bootstrap program. This may be immediately changed during custom disk controller BIOS initialization to point to a routine that reads the bootstrap from drive **c:**. During the DOS bootstrap process, the vector is changed again to point to a DOS routine, apparently to give DOS greater control over the reboot process. DOS performs some chores, but invokes the disk controller BIOS to read the bootstrap program.

Some authors have suggested using **Int 19** to reboot after changing the BIOS record of the amount of memory installed, and perhaps **Config.Sys** and/or **AutoExec.Bat**, to reconfigure the machine to suit your application. Of course, the new **AutoExec.Bat** would have to restart your program. No data stored in memory would be lost, except what is overwritten by DOS, device drivers listed in the new **Config.Sys**, or programs executed by the new **AutoExec.Bat**. However, if the new **Config.Sys** lists any device drivers, this probably won't work, because some device drivers— the DOS virtual disk driver **VDisk.Sys**, for example—apparently expect to find the interrupt vectors as set originally by the BIOS, not as altered by software prior to your **Int 19**. The symptom is a hung machine. How to avoid this problem is a puzzle.

Any example that does not intentionally end catastrophically like the last two must have a termination instruction, else it will continue executing whatever happens to be in memory following its last instruction. The simplest way to terminate a program of this sort is to invoke the DOS Interrupt 20 program termination service. *Caution!* This is *no longer* the recommended way to end an assembly language program; it is used here to shorten the examples. You should try another one-line program consisting of this interrupt alone. Nothing happens—of course.

The second sample **Debug** script, in Figure 8.3.2, invokes a DOS Interrupt 21 function to change the current drive. To obtain this service, place function number e in register AH (the high-order byte of register AX), the new drive designation in DL (the low-order byte register DX),

Script	Comments
C>	DOS prompt. Current drive is **c:**.
Debug	Enter the debugger.
-A	Assemble.
35f5:0100 **Mov AH,0e**	Function number to AH.
35f5:0102 **Mov DL,03**	Drive code to DL. 03 means **d:**.
35f5:0104 **Int 21**	DOS function call interrupt.
35f5:0106 **Int 20**	DOS program termination interrupt.
35f5:0108	Enter <CR> to terminate assembly.
-G	Go.
	Blank line.
Program terminated normally	This is an internal **Debug** message.
-Q	Quit
D>	Current drive is **d:**.

Figure 8.3.2 **Debug** script to change current drive

and execute the interrupt. The drive designations are hex 0, 1, 2,... for **a:**, **b:**, **c:**,.... . Finally, terminate with **Int 20**, as just described.

If you want to assemble the program in Figure 8.3.2 to a **.Com** file, you need its length for entry into register CX. That is given by the **Debug** assembler prompts: 0108 - 0100 = 8 bytes.

The previous examples show how some simple interrupts are executed in machine language. How can you do it with Turbo C? You have several options. The first is to execute function

void geninterrupt(int N)

which is defined as a macro in header file **DOS.H**. This routine simply executes interrupt **N**. To secure an interrupt service, you almost always have to move some input parameters into the CPU registers before executing the interrupt, and remove results from the registers afterward. (Interrupts 18 to 20, discussed earlier, are rare exceptions.) Function **geninterrupt** has no direct provision for manipulating any registers. You must use the corresponding Turbo C pseudo-variables, as in the Figure 8.3.3 demonstration program **GenInter.Dem**. This corresponds to the **Debug** script in Figure 8.3.2, executing DOS Interrupt 21 Function e to change the current drive to **d:**. The problem with **geninterrupt** is unreliability of the pseudo-variables. There is no way to guarantee that registers will retain their values during a succession of pseudo-variable assignments before or after a **geninterrupt** invocation.

There are three Library functions more reliable for executing interrupts: **int86x**, **int86**, and **intr**. Their differences lie in the way you prepare and

```
/******************************************************************/
/* GenInter.Dem     Demonstrate function  geninterrupt,  us-  */
/****************************** ing it to invoke  DOS  Inter- */
                           /* rupt  21  Function  e  to         */
#include <DOS.H>           /* change current drive to  d:.      */
                           /*********************************** /
void main() {
_AH = 0x0e;                          /* AH = function no.    */
_DL = 0x03;                          /* DL = drive no.       */
geninterrupt(0x21); }                /* Execute  Int 21.     */
```

Figure 8.3.3 Program **GenInter.Dem**

obtain input and output parameter values. Functions **int86x** and **int86** use several data structures defined in header file **DOS.H**. The first one is designed to store values en route to and from the segment registers; function **segread** is provided to manipulate it. Here are the structure definition and prototype, from **DOS.H**:

struct SREGS { unsigned int es,cs,ss,ds; }
void segread(struct SREGS *SegReg)

Function **segread** simply copies the values of the four segment registers into the corresponding structure **SegReg** items.

DOS.H defines three more structures to accommodate values en route to and from the other registers:

struct WORDREGS { unsigned int
  ax,bx,cx,dx,si,di,cflag,flags; }
struct BYTEREGS { unsigned char
  al,ah, bl,bh, cl,ch, dl,dh; }
union REGS { struct WORDREGS x;
        struct BYTEREGS h; }

The **REGS** union reflects the frequent use of the first four sixteen-bit registers as pairs of eight-bit registers:

	low byte	high byte
x.ax =	h.al	h.ah
x.bx =	h.bl	h.bh
x.cx =	h.cl	h.ch
x.dx =	h.dl	h.dh

Item **cflag** of the **WORDREGS** structure is intended to reflect the value of the carry flag in item **flags**: **cflag** is zero just when the flag is not set. This one flag receives special treatment because DOS frequently sets it to indicate an error condition. (This has nothing to do with its use in arithmetic operations—from which its name is derived.)

DOS.H also contains the prototypes

int int86(int N, union REGS *In, union REGS *Out)
int int86x(int N, union REGS *In, union REGS *Out,
       struct SREGS *SegReg)

Function **int86x** sets register values from structures **In** and **SegReg** as follows:

From structure	To registers
In	AX,BX,CX,DX,SI,DI
SegReg	DS,ES

Then it executes instruction **Int N**, and reads the resulting register values into structures **Out** and **SegReg**:

From registers	To structure
AX,BX,CX,DX,SI,DI,Flags	**Out**
DS,ES	**SegReg**

Unless some precaution is taken, this process could result in a DS value on return from **int86x** different from that on entry, which would keep Turbo C from finding global data. Fortunately, that does *not* happen: **int86x** pushes and pops DS around the interrupt, so that the original DS value is restored on return. The assembly language source code for this function is rather delicate, not just because it has to access so many registers, but also because it must *construct* the interrupt instruction. (**Int N** does not take N as a parameter; rather, it is a single instruction with **N** built into its machine language code.) For some reason, Interrupts 25 and 26, which DOS uses to control disk input/output, must be handled specially. After returning from the interrupt, **int86x** copies register AX into global variable **_doserrno** (defined in **DOS.H**). Many DOS interrupt services set the carry flag to indicate error, and in that case return an error code in AX. This **int86x** action may be inappropriate if the interrupt service routine does not observe the DOS convention. Finally, **int86x** returns the value of register AX.

Function **int86** is a simplified version of **int86x**, for use when the request for the desired interrupt service does not use special settings of the segment registers. Its source code consists of a call to **segread** to load structure **SegReg**, then a call to **int86x**.

The remaining Turbo C Library interrupt function

void intr(int N, struct REGPACK *Reg)

uses a slightly different structure, defined, with the function prototype, in **DOS.H**:

struct REGPACK {
  unsigned r_ax,r_bx,r_cx,r_dx;
  unsigned r_bp,r_si,r_di,r_ds,r_es,r_flags; }

This works like **int86x**, except

- the same structure is used for input and output parameters;
- **_doserrno** is not set;
- no value is returned;
- **intr** doesn't change the value of the Flags register.

Before executing the specified interrupt, functions **int86x** and **intr** load all the registers from their **REGS** or **REGPACK** parameters; **int86** loads all but the segment registers. If you don't store appropriate values in these structures before executing the functions, the registers will receive garbage values. This could be a problem if an interrupt service routine makes an assumption about some register but doesn't document it. You should opt for safety by not using **int86x** when **int86** will suffice,

```
/******************************************************************/
/* ROMBASIC.Dem    Go to  ROM  BASIC.  To exit, you must    */
/*                 reboot!                                   */
/******************************************************************/

#include <DOS.H>

void main() {
  struct REGPACK R;                 /* Required, but not used.  */
  R.r_ds = _DS;  R.r_es = _ES;      /* You crash without these. */
  intr(0x18,&R); }
```

Figure 8.3.4 Program **ROMBASIC.Dem**

and by explicitly loading the two segment register components **r_ds** and **r_es** of the **REGPACK** structure whenever you use **intr**.

The Turbo C version of the one-line **Debug** script for entering ROM BASIC is program **ROMBASIC.Dem** in Figure 8.3.4. Remember, you can't exit from ROM BASIC without rebooting, so before testing this program, save in permanent storage any important files you have temporarily placed on a virtual disk!

Program **To_D.Dem** in Figure 8.3.5 is a more typical example—a Turbo C version of the **Debug** script in Figure 8.3.2 that changes the current drive to **d:**. Here the **REGPACK** parameter plays an essential role. As noted in connection with Figure 8.3.3 program **GenInter.Dem**, this technique is more robust than using function **geninterrupt** with pseudo-variables.

ROMBASIC.Dem and **To_D.Dem** are unrealistically simple examples. Using interrupt services generally involves tedious **REGPACK** parameter encoding before the interrupt, and decoding afterward to inspect the results. This requires detailed knowledge often available only in the PC *Technical reference* manual, or the *MS-DOS encyclopedia*, References [20,28]. Most routines of this sort that you will need are provided by the Turbo C Library, which takes care of much of the detail for you. The next two sections will provide realistic examples of the use of interrupt services, comparable to the Library routines. The Library provides several functions specifically for executing Interrupt 21; they are described in Section 3.5.

```
/*******************************************************************/
/* To_D.Dem      Demonstrate function  intr,  using it to exe- */
/****************************** cute  DOS  Interrupt 21    */
                             /* function  e  to change the */
#include <DOS.H>             /* current drive to  d:.      */
                             /*****************************/
void main() {
  struct REGPACK R;
  R.r_ax = 0x0e00;                     /* AH = function no.    */
  R.r_dx = 0x0003;                     /* DL = drive no.       */
  intr(0x21,&R); }                     /* Execute  Int 21.     */
```

Figure 8.3.5 Program **To_D.Dem**

8.4 BIOS interrupt services

Concepts

Overview of BIOS interrupt vectors
Equipment and memory services
Screen services
Example Turbo C TOOLS routine **scattrib**
Keyboard services
Accessing the BIOS data area
Disk, cassette, and joystick services
Interrupt vectors reserved for custom services
Redirected PC/AT maskable interrupt vectors
Breakpoints
80286 exceptions

This section describes in some detail the interrupt services offered by the BIOS. Besides the interrupt vectors that actually provide access to BIOS services, a few are reserved for services that may be provided by custom software. Because the BIOS must deal with overall system organization, these are described here as well. Figure 8.4.1 is an overview of the BIOS interrupt vector organization. Some vectors are used for several services, perhaps unrelated to each other, hence occur more than once in the figure. You select the service by placing a code in register AH before executing the interrupt. That level of detail is not shown here, but is included in later discussions. The discussions indicate clearly which services are peculiar to the PC/AT.

Many Turbo C Library and Turbo C TOOLS functions serve as bridges between your programs and the BIOS. Most of these have already been discussed in earlier chapters. They allow you to specify BIOS service request parameters and receive any resulting information in formats convenient for a C program. The functions translate your parameter values into proper form for BIOS service requests, execute the appropriate interrupt, and translate any information returned from the BIOS service back into the C format. The BIOS service request parameters and return values are usually transmitted as codes in various registers. As the BIOS services are described in this section, any corresponding Turbo C Library and Turbo C TOOLS functions are indicated. One of the latter, as well as a new function, are described in detail. With these examples and an understanding of the BIOS, you should be able to write such tools yourself.

The BIOS printer, clock/calendar, and serial communications services are discussed separately in Sections 8.6 to 8.8.

Software interrupt service		Related hardware interrupt services	
Int	Request	Int	Origin of request
11,12 15	What equipment is installed? PC/AT extended memory		
15	PC/AT protected mode memory move		
10	Screen service		
16	Keyboard service	9	IRQ1 = keyboard controller
13	Disk service	e,76	IRQ6, 14 = disk controller
15	Cassette service (not on PC/AT)		
15	Joystick service (PC/AT)		
5,17	Printer service		
1a 15 1c	Timer service PC/AT only Reserved for custom use	8 70 4a	IRQ0 IRQ8 = PC/AT real time clock PC/AT real time clock alarm
		a,d,f 71-74 75 77	IRQ2, 5, 7 IRQ9-12 (PC/AT) Reserved for IRQ13 = PC/AT 80287 IRQ service IRQ15 (PC/AT)
14	Serial port service	b c	IRQ3 = COM2 Reserved for IRQ4 = COM1 port service
		2	NMI = Parity failure, 8087
1b,3 4,15	Ctrl-Break, Breakpoint IntO, PC/AT multitasking	1	Single step (TF flag)
		0 5-10,d	Divide instructions Exceptions 80286 instructions

Figure 8.4.1 BIOS interrupt vectors

Equipment and memory services

During the bootstrap process, the BIOS surveys the equipment and installed memory, and records that data in a reserved part of memory called the *BIOS data area*. Some of this information is obtained merely by reading various PC switch settings. On the PC/AT, some of the switches take the form of particular bits in nonvolatile CMOS memory. Sometimes, especially with the PC/AT memory, the equipment is actually checked to verify the switches.

Three BIOS interrupt services give you access to the equipment information. The first, Interrupt 11, returns in register AX information about diskette drives, game, serial, and parallel ports, numeric coprocessor, and motherboard RAM. The format is shown in Figure 8.4.2. Some of this data is relevant only for early model PCs. You may recognize the pattern in bits 0-7 as the settings for Switch 1 on the PC motherboard.

Interrupt 12 returns in AX the amount of conventional memory, in 1K units, occupying segments 0000 through 9000. Turbo C Library function **biosmemory**, described in Section 2.2, returns this value. On the PC/AT, Interrupt 15 Service 88 returns in AX the amount of extended

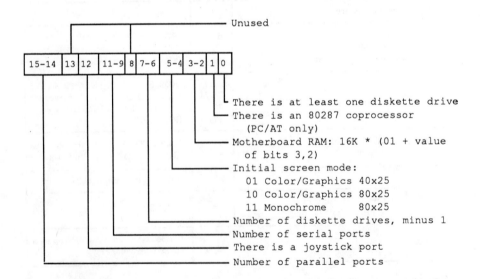

Figure 8.4.2 Equipment information returned by Interrupt 11

memory, in 1K units. No Turbo C Library or Turbo C TOOLS function provides this information; the new function **ExtMem** in Figure 8.4.3 converts it to a format that your programs can use.

The equipment and memory verification Interrupts 11, 12, and 15 (Service 88) all operate by reading data previously placed in memory, not by making fresh surveys. Thus, they can return incorrect information if some other program has changed the stored values.

One further service, available on the PC/AT only, falls in the memory category. Invoking Interrupt 15 Service 87, with various registers set properly, moves a block of data from one place to another in protected mode. You specify twenty-four bit source and target addresses and the number of bytes to move. The ISR places the CPU in protected mode, moves the data, and reenters real mode. (The last is quite a feat, requiring rebooting the CPU!) This feature is most commonly used to move data between conventional and extended memory. A versatile routine, providing an interface between a higher-level language and the BIOS code, is described in detail in Section 10.4 of the author's earlier book, Reference [34]. Although it's written in IBM Pascal, you could convert it easily to Turbo C. The routine automatically takes care of an unpleasant task for you: constructing a complicated global descriptor table required by the 80286 for protected mode operation. Understanding that requires a knowledge of 80286 architecture, which is beyond the scope of this book.

```
/**************************************************************/
/* ExtMem.C    Function ExtMem:  return the amount of ex-   */
/*             tended memory installed, in  1K  units, by re-*/
/****************************************** questing  PC/AT   */
                                          /* BIOS  Interrupt 15 */
#include <DOS.H>                          /* Service 88.  In-  */
                                          /* clude  DOS.H  before*/
unsigned ExtMem(void) {                   /* this code.        */
  struct REGPACK R;                       /**********************/
R.r_ds = _DS;
R.r_es = _ES;
R.r_ax = 0x8800;
intr(0x15,&R);
return R.r_ax; }
```

Figure 8.4.3 Function **ExtMem**

Screen services

The rich selection of screen services offered by the BIOS Interrupt 10 service routine is outlined in Figure 8.4.4. For your convenience, some additional services of the BIOS on the EGA board are also included. You select the particular service by placing its service number in register AH before executing the interrupt. The services fall into several categories, which are grouped together in the figure. The corresponding service numbers are not necessarily closely related. Using a particular service requires encoding and/or decoding various parameters in other registers. For most of the services, the Turbo C TOOLS package provides routines to take care of that—they were discussed in detail in Section 4.3. The figure also shows the correspondence between those routines and the BIOS services.

The various screen services are described next, in some detail. For complete information, consult the BIOS listings in the PC and video adapter *Technical reference* manuals, References [20] and [21]. The source code of one of the Turbo C TOOLS routines is analyzed later as an example of the use of these services.

Although the PC can accommodate two displays—usually one for graphics and one for text—you can interact with only one at a time, the *current* display. This is determined by the BIOS adapter *mode*. The first category of services—AH = 0 or f—set or ascertain the mode. One Monochrome Adapter mode is available, and seven Color/Graphics modes. An EGA board can emulate all these, and offers seven more with additional colors or higher resolution. You set a mode by entering its code number (from the *Technical reference* or Turbo C TOOLS manual) into register AL, placing service number 0 in AH, and executing **Int 10**. If two adapters are installed, the appropriate one is selected. To ascertain the current mode, merely request Service f the same way; the mode number is returned in AL. For convenience, the number of text columns on the screen is returned in AH. Because of differences in the adapters, switching between modes is no trivial matter. Turbo C TOOLS contains several routines that work together to make that easier.

Some modes permit you to store and display several alternate text *pages. Caution:* many display controllers compatible with the IBM controllers provide more pages; but the BIOS supports only pages available on the IBM controllers. Using this feature requires the concepts of *active* and *current* page. The *active* page is the one now visible. The *current* page is the one now addressed by a screen service. It's

Interrupt 10 screen services			T = Text G = Graphics E = EGA P = Can specify affected page	
Service		AH=	Turbo C TOOLS routines Comments	
Adapter mode Set	TGE	0	**scnewdev**	
Ascertain	TGE	f	**scmode**	
Active page Set	TGE	5	**scapage**	
Ascertain	TGE	f	**scmode**	
Cursor mode Set	T E	1	**scpgcur**	
Ascertain	T E	3	**sccurst**	
Cursor Set	T EP	2	**sccurset** (Top, Left) = (0, 0)	
location Ascertain	T EP	3	**sccurst**	
Read attribute and character at the cursor.	TGEP	8	**scread**	
Write copies of an attribute and character at the cursor.	TGEP	9	**scattrib** Analyzed in this section	
Write copies of a character at the cursor.	TGEP	a	**scwrite**	
Write a character in TTY fashion at the cursor.	TGEP	e	**scttywrt**	
Write a string in TTY fashion at the cursor.	TGEP	13	BIOS: PC/AT, EGA only Option to move cursor	
Scroll active page up/down.	TGE	6/7	**viscroll viscroll**scrolls any page	
Ascertain light pen location.	TGE	4		
Set border color.	TG P	b	**scborder**	
Set palette.	G	b	**scmode4**	
Set EGA palette registers.	E	10	**scblink scborder scpall scpalett**	
Read/write a dot.	G	d/c	**grptread grptwrit**	
Select EGA character set.	E	11	**scnewdev**	
Return EGA information.	E	12	**scequip** Set BL = 10	
Select alternate EGA PrtSc routine.	E	12	Set BL = 20	

Figure 8.4.4 Interrupt 10 screen services

common to build or modify a current page that's not active, then switch active pages to display it in finished form. Two screen services set or ascertain which page is active. Service 5 sets it: place the page number in AL before executing the interrupt. Service f, already mentioned, returns the active page in BH.

The cursor is a small item, but close attention is required to use it effectively. The BIOS provides cursor service in text modes only. You can control its *shape* as well as its location. The next category of screen services is concerned with the shape. You can set this with Service 1 by placing a code in register CX as shown in Figure 8.4.5. Service 1 affects the cursor on the active (visible) page only. The scan line numbers used to describe the cursor shape refer to the vertical dimension of the character dot matrix. The Monochrome and EGA boards provide a character set with scan lines 0 at the top through 13 at the bottom; on the Color/Graphics Adapter, the lines are numbered 0..7. The cursor is a solid block extending from the top through the bottom lines entered in CX. Various strange effects occur when the top number is larger than the bottom, or either exceeds the current adapter's range. The BIOS attempts to compensate for the different numbers of scan lines when software written for one of the adapters is used with another, but that is not always successful. You have probably noticed the effect: after switching modes, the cursor suddenly disappears or climbs to the middle of the text line. (There would have been less susceptibility to error had the designers simply numbered the scan lines from bottom to top!)

As shown in Figure 8.4.5, CX bit 13 turns the cursor on or off. When the cursor is on, it always blinks; you cannot control that.

Service 3 returns the cursor shape in CX exactly as shown in Figure 8.4.5. Often you need to ascertain the dimensions, because it's polite to

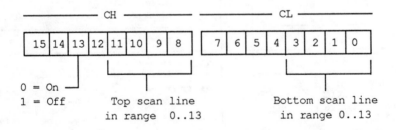

Figure 8.4.5 Defining cursor shape

restore the cursor's previous appearance if you change it for your application. To turn off the cursor, for example, you should use Service 3 to ascertain the shape, store that somewhere for later restoration, turn off bit 13, then request Service 1. Turning the cursor on or changing its shape requires a similar two-step process.

Turbo C TOOLS includes functions **scpgcur** to turn the cursor off or on and set its shape, **sccurst** to ascertain its location and dimensions, and **sccurset** to set its location.

BIOS screen Services 2 and 3 allow you to set or ascertain the cursor position for any page. Their coordinate system, which is also used by the corresponding Turbo C TOOLS functions **sccurset** and **sccurst**, locates position (0,0) at the top left corner. These routines allow you to work with any page, whereas the Turbo C Library functions **gotoxy**, **wherex**, and **wherey** only apply to Page 0. The Library functions assign coordinates (1,1) to the top left corner, and, like other **ConIO** functions, respect a current screen window.

Screen Services 8, 9, and a form the basis of Turbo C TOOLS functions **scread**, **scattrib**, and **scwrite**, which read a character, write copies of a character/attribute pair, or write copies of a character, at the cursor location. The last of these preserves existing screen attributes. The ASCII/IBM character codes, as well as screen attributes, are described in Section 4.2 and Appendix C. The BIOS routines require you to specify the page. Turbo C TOOLS maintains a global variable **b_curpage**, declared in header file **BScreens.H**, to reflect the page you're working on.

Figure 8.4.6 reproduces the source code for **scattrib**, edited somewhat to conform to this book's style conventions. Notice that it uses screen Service 9 directly, taking the page number from the global variable just mentioned. This practice is typical of the Turbo C TOOLS routines in guarding against invalid parameter values. Function **utnybbyt** is a Turbo C TOOLS macro, mentioned in Section 2.4.4, that assembles a byte from its low and high nybbles.

Screen Service e writes a character in TTY fashion with a specified foreground attribute, using the existing background attribute, at the cursor location on a specified page. In the PC/AT and EGA BIOS, Service 13 extends this to write a string. The string may consist of just characters, or character/attribute pairs, and you have the option of moving the cursor to its end. The corresponding Turbo C TOOLS function **scttywrt** uses Service e only.

```
/*************************************************************/
/* ScAttrib.C    Function  scattrib:  write  N  copies of   */
/*               character  Ch  on the current display page */
/* with the specified Foreground  and  Background  attri-   */
/* butes, starting at the current cursor location.  The func- */
/* tion always returns  0  and never moves the cursor.  Unex- */
/* pected results may occur if you write beyond the end of the*/
/* screen, or beyond the end of the current text row in graph-*/
/* ics mode.  This function will not scroll the screen.     */
/*****************************                               */
                        /*    Version 5.00   (C) Copyright  */
                        /*    Blaise Computing Inc.         */
#include      <DOS.H>    /*    1983, 1987                    */
#include <BScreens.H>         /*********************************/

int scattrib(int Foreground,Background; char Ch; unsigned N) {
  union REGS In,Out;
if (N) {
  inregs.h.ah = 9;
  inregs.h.al = Ch;
  inregs.h.bh = (unsigned char) b_curpage;
  inregs.h.bl = (unsigned char) utnybbyt(Background,Foreground);
  inregs.x.cx = N;
  int86(0x10,&In,&Out);  }
return 0; }
```

Figure 8.4.6 Function scattrib

Screen Services 6 and 7 scroll a rectangular region of the active (visible) page up or down N lines. You must place the coordinates of its top left and bottom right corners in registers CH,CL and DH,DL; N in register AL; and the attribute byte for the new blank area in BH. If you specify N = 0 you will clear the region. The corresponding Turbo C TOOLS routine viscroll is slightly more general: it will scroll whatever page is current.

For the Color/Graphics Adapter and EGA, screen Service 4 returns the light pen position. The value AH = 0 signals that the pen is not active. Otherwise, the character row and column position (in text or graphics mode) is returned in registers DH,DL. In graphics mode the pixel row is returned in CH, and an approximate pixel column in BX. There is no corresponding Turbo C Library or Turbo C TOOLS routine; writing one would be an easy exercise.

Screen Service b is concerned mainly with the graphics color palette. However, one feature is useful for Color/Graphics Adapter text modes. If you set BH = 0 and BL equal to one of the color numbers defined in Section 4.2, the interrupt service will set the screen border accordingly. Turbo C TOOLS function **scborder** is based on this service.

The remaining screen services are concerned entirely with graphics or the EGA, and thus lie beyond the scope of this book. You can find more information on graphics programming with the Color/Graphics adapter, using mostly the BASICA language, in the book by Waite and Morgan, Reference [36]. For information on the EGA, consult its *Technical reference* manual, Reference [21]; some articles by Petzold, Reference [32]; and the book by Kliewer, Reference [23].

Keyboard services

In Section 5.2 you saw how the BIOS processes keystrokes and makes them available to your software. Each keyboard event—touching or releasing a key—causes the keyboard processor to request interrupt service via line IRQ1. The only line with higher priority is timer line IRQ0. In response to this request, the controller will signal the CPU to execute hardware Interrupt 9. The BIOS Interrupt 9 service routine **KB_INT** analyzes the keystroke and acts accordingly. Of concern here are the shift and toggle keystrokes, which it records in a word in the BIOS data area called **KB_FLAG**, and ordinary keystrokes with ASCII/IBM or Extended ASCII codes, for which it stores entries in a fifteen word queue, the keyboard buffer. Buffer entries consist either of the one byte ASCII/IBM code and a scan code byte precisely identifying the key, or else a zero byte and the Extended ASCII keystroke code. The former convention is used, for example, to tell which key entered the digit 8; the latter, to identify a keystroke like <Alt-F10>. These codes are tabulated in Appendix D.

The BIOS Interrupt 16 service routine provides three services giving your programs direct access to the keyboard buffer and the data in **KB_FLAG**. You select a service by placing its number in AH before executing **Int 16.**

Service 0 moves one keystroke code from the buffer to registers AH,AL, waiting if the buffer is empty. AL receives the ASCII/IBM code or zero, and AH the scan or Extended ASCII code. This service corresponds exactly to Turbo C TOOLS function **kbgetkey**. If you merely want to determine whether the buffer is empty, and inspect it if not, you can use Service 1, which corresponds to Turbo C TOOLS function **kbready**. Service 1 sets Flags register bit ZF to indicate that the buffer is empty; if not, it copies the keystroke code into AH,AL just like Service 0, but does not remove it from the queue. The two Turbo C TOOLS functions were described in Section 5.3.

Service 2 returns the low-order byte of **KB_FLAG** in the AL register. Unfortunately, additional interesting information of this sort is recorded in the high-order byte, which is ignored. All the bit definitions are indicated in Figure 8.4.7. To gain access to the high order byte information, you must read the word **KB_FLAG** directly from memory—its address is 0000:0417. Using this method, Turbo C TOOLS function **kbstatus** returns a C structure of type **KEYSTATUS** that records all these bits. (See Section 5.3.) Of course, this function is not portable. A clone BIOS may store the information in a different location.

Five further Turbo C TOOLS keyboard routines access the BIOS data area directly, simply because it's not practical to do otherwise. Function **kbset**, complementing **kbstatus**, lets you set all the bits in **KB_FLAG**. Function **kbqueue** reports the length and empty positions left in the keyboard buffer, **kbflush** empties it, and **kbplace** places a keystroke code there so that some other program will think it came from the keyboard. A more complicated function, **kbstuff**, will place a whole string in the buffer. These last four routines use the following items in the data area:

BIOS Name	Address	Content
BUFFER_HEAD	0000:041a	Pointer to current head of queue
BUFFER_TAIL	0000:041c	Pointer to current tail of queue
KB_BUFFER	0000:041e	15 word queue + one word overhead
KB_BUFFER_END	0000:043e	First address after end of buffer

Disk, cassette, and joystick services

Somewhat like the keyboard handling system, the BIOS disk control system uses both hardware and software interrupts. Hardware Interrupts e and 76 respond to requests for service on lines IRQ6 and IRQ14.

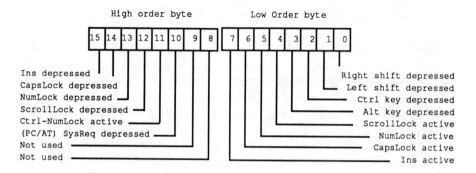

High order byte   Low Order byte

| 15 | 14 | 13 | 12 | 11 | 10 | 9 | 8 | 7 | 6 | 5 | 4 | 3 | 2 | 1 | 0 |

Ins depressed
CapsLock depressed
NumLock depressed
ScrollLock depressed
Ctrl-NumLock active
(PC/AT) SysReq depressed
Not used
Not used

Right shift depressed
Left shift depressed
Ctrl key depressed
Alt key depressed
ScrollLock active
NumLock active
CapsLock active
Ins active

Figure 8.4.7 BIOS **KB_FLAG** (0000:0417)

(IRQ14 exists only on the PC/AT.) Software Interrupt 13 provides a number of services to programs. There the similarity ends. First, the BIOS services are low level, and normally not invoked directly by application programs. Your programs ordinarily use DOS disk services, and DOS issues the appropriate **Int 13** service requests. Second, disk equipment is not standard, and a disk controller normally contains a custom BIOS that extends the PC BIOS. It may use other interrupts in addition to e and 76 for servicing hardware demands. This type of programming is for specialists, and is not considered further here.

The original PC could control a cassette drive, and programs could obtain cassette services through Interrupt 15. This feature was hardly ever used. In fact, the author recalls more references to the use of cassette services to control other kinds of equipment attached to the cassette port than to the use of the cassette drive *per se*. Cassette support has been eliminated from later models.

The PC/AT ISR 15 does provide several joystick control services. Executing **Int 15** subservice 84 with DX = 0 returns to AL four Game Adapter switch values. With DX = 1, it returns in registers AX,BX,CX,DX the x,y values for joysticks A,B in the order Ax,Ay,Bx,By. Consult a Game Adapter manual for further information. It would be an easy exercise to develop some Turbo C routines to provide convenient access to these services on a PC/AT. You could also follow the outline of the PC/AT ISR 15 to develop Turbo C tools that work on earlier PC models. Because of the design of the Game Adapter, that would require use of timer services described in Section 8.7.

Interrupt vectors reserved for custom services

A few interrupt vectors are reserved for custom ISRs; the BIOS provides only rudimentary services, if any. These are generally hardware interrupts, and fall into several categories.

First, certain vectors correspond directly to the IRQ lines connected to the interrupt controller chip. You have already encountered, for example, the Keyboard Hardware Interrupt Vector 9 corresponding to IRQ1. The complete list is shown in Figure 8.4.8. The only other service routines of this nature provided by the BIOS are the Timer Interrupt 8 and 70 service routines described in Section 8.6. The latter is found only in the PC/AT.

In the PC/AT, the IRQ2 line connects the two interrupt controller chips. If you are converting from the PC to the PC/AT an interrupt driven system that used PC line IRQ2, it will be connected to IRQ9 on the PC/AT. The corresponding Interrupt Vector 71 will be set automatically to point to the Interrupt a routine that formerly served IRQ2 requests.

An interrupt request on the NMI line triggers hardware Interrupt 2. The BIOS Interrupt 2 service routine prints the dreaded **PARITY CHECK 2** message and crashes. On the PC, certain 8087 Numeric Coprocessor errors also trigger this interrupt, hence software that uses the 8087 must redirect Vector 2 to its own ISR. That routine must determine the cause and act appropriately. On the PC/AT, 80287 coprocessor errors trigger IRQ13 requests. Therefore the corresponding Interrupt Vector 75 is automatically set to point to the Interrupt 2 routine that formerly serviced NMI requests.

PC and PC/AT			PC/AT only		
Int	IRQ	Use	Int	IRQ	Use
8	0	Timer	70	8	Real time clock
9	1	Keyboard	71	9	
a	2		72	10	
b	3	COM2:	73	11	
c	4	COM1:	74	12	
d	5		75	13	80287
e	6	Disk	76	14	Disk
f	7		77	15	

Figure 8.4.8 IRQ lines and corresponding interrupts

When it detects a <Ctrl-Break> keystroke, the BIOS keyboard Interrupt 9 service routine executes software Interrupt 1b, and places the word 0000 in the keyboard buffer. The BIOS ISR 1b does nothing, but other software systems are invited to redirect the vector to their own routine to help handle user breaks. In fact, DOS redirects the vector to a routine that sets a flag used later when DOS detects the 0000 code in the keyboard buffer. See Section 8.9 for details.

As you saw in Section 8.2, hardware Interrupt 1 is triggered by Flags register Trap Flag bit TF. A debugger directs the corresponding vector to its single step routine. The *breakpoint* Int 3 instruction is just one byte long. A debugger directs Vector 3 to its breakpoint routine. Then it can replace the first byte of any instruction in your program by a breakpoint interrupt. Its breakpoint routine normally stops temporarily and displays a status report, enabling you to check on the progress of your program. Then it restores the original instruction, returns to it, and continues.

The conditional interrupt instruction IntO executes Interrupt 4 if the Flags register Overflow Flag bit OF is set. Software systems must provide a corresponding ISR. In fact, DOS redirects Vector 4 to its own routine. It's not clear what that does: a two line program consisting of Int 4 and the DOS terminator Int 20 has no visible output.

The *exceptions* form a final category of interrupts reserved for special services. These are hardware interrupts triggered by various internal CPU conditions, usually programming errors. Software systems are expected to provide corresponding ISRs. Only one occurs in the 8086: the divide exception, Int 0. The BIOS Int 0 service routine does nothing, but DOS redirects Vector 0 to its own ISR that prints **Divide overflow** and stops. Turbo C programs redirect it again to the Turbo C error reporting system.

The situation is complicated with the PC/AT, because its 80286 CPU has eight exceptions, and all but the divide exception use interrupts already claimed by various BIOS services. Here is the complete list:

80286 real mode exception interrupts

Int 0	Divide error	Int 7	Processor extension not available
Int 5	Bound instruction range exceeded	Int 9	Processor extension segment overrun
Int 6	Invalid op code	Int 10	Processor extension error
Int d	Segment overrun	Int 8	LIDT instruction error

Segment overrun exceptions occur if an instruction tries to access a word whose low-order byte has segment:offset address of the form S:ffff. (Is the high order byte at (S+1):0000 or—as expected by the 8086—at S:0000?) The *processor extension* exceptions occur only while using an 80287 Numeric Coprocessor, and the **LIDT** exception only when switching to protected mode. DOS provides an ISR *only* for the divide error exception. If your software might encounter any of the other situations, it must provide custom ISRs. The BIOS already uses some of these interrupts for various services. Thus, if you don't provide custom ISRs and exceptions do occur, they will invoke the wrong services! For more information about exceptions, consult the Intel *iAPX 286 programmer's reference manual,* Reference [16], Chapter 5.

Further topics

Several BIOS interrupt services remain to be discussed. Printer services offered via software Interrupts 5 and 17 are described together with DOS printer services in Section 8.6. Timer services for Interrupts 8, 15, 1a, 1c, 4a, and 70 are described together with DOS clock services in Section 8.7. Interrupt 14 serial communications services are considered with similar DOS services in Section 8.8. Two ISRs with no return have already been considered as examples in Section 8.3—the ROM BASIC and operating system bootstrap Interrupts 18 and 19. There is yet another one-way interrupt, Interrupt 15 Service 89, which provides a convenient way to place a PC/AT in protected mode. More information on protected mode operation is available in the author's earlier book, Reference [34]. Once in protected mode, no BIOS services are provided, and you cannot return to real mode without rebooting the machine!

8.5 DOS interrupt services

Concepts

DOS interrupt vectors
DOS function calls
Determining the DOS version
Setting and inspecting interrupt vectors
International services
Standard input/output services
File input/output services
Memory management and program control

DOS provides interrupt services at a generally higher level than the BIOS. Except for a few error handlers already noted in Section 8.4, DOS provides only software interrupt services. For maximum portability, your programs should use the DOS services—they are available on any machine that runs DOS. In many cases, however, you will have to use BIOS routines because you need a service that DOS doesn't provide, or a faster one.

The DOS interrupt services are organized differently from the BIOS services. Although Vectors 20..3f are all reserved for DOS, most of its services are delivered as subservices of Interrupt 21, and termed DOS function calls. The Turbo C Library provides four functions specifically for executing this interrupt: **bdos**, **bdosptr**, **intdos**, and **intdosx**. Their prototypes are in header file **DOS.H**. The first two are redundant and hard to document, and will not be discussed further. Here the others' prototypes:

int intdos(union REGS *In, union REGS *Out)
int intdosx(union REGS *In, union REGS *Out,
 struct SREGS *SegReg)

Use them just like the more general functions **int86** and **int86x**, described in the previous section. Function **intdosx** is written in assembly language; **intdos** is implemented as a call to **intdosx** preceded by a call to **segread** to set the **SegReg** parameter.

Figure 8.5.1 is an overview of the use of the various interrupts, indicating the category of service. Services in the *Programs* category are

Int	Service	Category
20	Terminate	Programs
21	Function call	
22	Terminate address	Programs
23	User break	ISRs
24	Critical error	ISRs
25-26	Read/write	Low level disk
27	Stay resident	ISRs
28	Idle	ISRs
29-2e	Reserved for future	
2f	Printer	Printer
30-3f	Reserved for future	

Figure 8.5.1 DOS interrupts

described later in this section. *Printer* services are detailed in Section 8.6, and services designed specifically for installing custom *ISRs* are described in Chapter 9. Like BIOS Interrupt 13, the *low-level disk* services address the disk by sector, ignoring the directory tree, and are not really intended for use by application programs. Ordinarily, you use instead the DOS directory and file handle function calls described later.

Figure 8.5.2 shows the approximately one hundred DOS function calls. These services are obtained by placing the function number in AH, setting other registers with the appropriate parameter values, and

Function	Category	Function	Category	Function	Category	Function	Category
0	Programs	21-24	FCB	35	Vector	55	?
1-2	Standard I/O	25	Vector	36	File I/O	56-57	File I/O
3-4	Serial I/O	26	Programs	37	?	58	Memory
5	Printer	27-29	FCB	38	International	59	Error
6-c	Standard I/O	2a-2d	Timer	39-47	File I/O	5a-5c	File I/O
d-e	File I/O	2e-2f	File I/O	48-4a	Memory	5d	?
f-17	FCB	30	Version	4b-4d	Programs	5e-5f	Network
18	?	31	ISRs	4e-4f	File I/O	60-61	?
19-1a	File I/O	32	?	50-51	ISRs	62	Programs
1b-1c	FCB	33	Programs	52-53	?	63	International
1d-20	?	34	ISRs	54	File I/O		

Figure 8.5.2 DOS function calls

executing Interrupt 21. This book always gives the function number in hex. The function calls are organized in categories just like the DOS interrupts. In the figure, the category designation ? indicates that the function call may be used internally by DOS but is not documented. Although sleuthing might reveal the purposes of some of these, using them is hazardous because they could be changed without notice at any time. A few functions, concerned with networks, are beyond the scope of this book, and will not be mentioned again.

The remaining DOS interrupt and function call categories are discussed later in this order:

Version	Determining the DOS version.
Vector	Inspecting and setting interrupt vectors.
International	These allow you to set and determine country dependent notation conventions.
Standard I/O	Redirectible keyboard and screen I/O.
FCB	Obsolete file manipulation services.
File I/O	The current file technique using file handles.
Memory	Memory management.
Programs	Program execution and termination.
Printer	Discussed in Section 8.6.
Timer	Discussed in Section 8.7.
Serial I/O	Discussed in Section 8.8.
Error	Diagnosing and servicing errors from other DOS interrupts and function calls—discussed in Section 8.9.
ISRs	Services for installing custom ISRs, discussed in Chapter 9.

Two of the categories, *Version* and *Vector*, should be discussed immediately, because only a few very simple services are involved. Function 30 returns in AL,AH the major and minor numbers of the version of DOS in use—for example, AL,AH = 3,1 for DOS 3.1. (For versions earlier than 2.0, AL = 0 and AH is meaningless.) The Turbo C startup code executes this function and stores the numbers in the high and low bytes of global **int** variable **_version**; the individual bytes are also available as global **char** variables **_osmajor** and **_osminor**. These are all defined in header file **DOS.H**.

Functions 25 and 35 allow you to set and inspect an interrupt vector, as follows:

Function	Interrupt Service	number in	ISR address in
25	Set vector	AL	DS:DX
35	Get vector	AL	ES:BX

Although these tasks are simple enough to do yourself, the DOS ISRs take care of details like insuring that you change a vector without being interrupted while it is in an inconsistent state. You might neglect this precaution otherwise. Two Library functions let you obtain these two services directly from Turbo C programs:

void interrupt(*getvect(int N)) ()
void setvect(int N, void interrupt (*ISR) ())

The Turbo C **interrupt** type applies to functions that use the registers for transmitting parameters and return via an **IRet** instruction. They are used for implementing ISRs, and are mentioned again in Chapter 9. Function **getvect** accepts an **int** parameter **N**—an interrupt number— and returns a pointer to the corresponding **interrupt** function. **setvect** accepts an interrupt number **N** and a pointer **ISR** to an **interrupt** function; it places the pointer in interrupt vector **N**. Prototypes for these functions are in header file **DOS.H**. Each is a short assembly language program. Chapter 9 is devoted to Turbo C TOOLS techniques. To maintain consistency with other software, that package does not use type **interrupt**, hence it must provide its own feature equivalent to **setvect** and **getvect**.

International services

Since DOS is marketed internationally, it makes a polite effort to report the date and time using notational conventions appropriate to the country selected by the user. (Otherwise, users would always have to think about whether 9/7/86 means the seventh of September or the ninth of July, and whether 08:00 might be an evening hour or not.) DOS makes these conventions available to your programs, as well as some other conventions involving currency, etc., through Function 38. DOS 3.3 knows the conventions of fifteen countries. They are identified by their international telephone codes, and listed in Section 3.8. You can set the

```
/****************************************************************/
/* CtryInfo.C     Function CtryInfo:  fill  *C  with formats */
/*                specified by country  Code.  Include header */
/****************************************** file  DOS.H  before */
                                         /* this.  Before invok-*/
#include <DOS.H>                         /* ing  CtryInfo,  you */
                                         /* must run the  DOS   */
void CtryInfo(unsigned Code,             /* utility  NLSFunc.   */
       struct country *C) {              /************************/
  struct SREGS S;
  union  REGS  R;
segread(&S);
S.ds  = FP_SEG((struct country far *) C);  /* Address of  C  */
R.x.dx = FP_OFF((struct country far *) C);  /* in  DS:DX.     */
R.h.ah = 0x38;                             /* Function 38.   */
if (Code < 0xff)                           /* Country code in*/
   R.h.al = Code;                          /* AL,  or in  BX */
  else {                                   /* if it's too    */
    R.h.al = 0xff;                         /* big.           */
    R.x.bx = Code;  }
intdosx(&R,&R,&S);  }                      /* DOS  function. */
```

Figure 8.5.3 Function CtryInfo

current country during booting by including a **Country** line in your **Config.Sys** file. Code 0 then designates whatever country is current. If you will need Function 38 access later to conventions for other countries, you must execute the DOS **NLSFunc** utility—perhaps through your **AutoExec** program—to load the required data.

The Turbo C Library makes Function 38 services accessible to your programs through function **country**, described in detail in Section 3.8. Unfortunately, in Version 1.5, it doesn't work for country codes larger than 254. In Figure 8.5.3 is a function **CtryInfo** that does. The description in this section includes the Function 38 details; you may refer to Section 3.8 for some information already presented in connection with function **country**.

You can set the current country through software by using Function 38. The same function allows you to ascertain the current country as well as detailed information about notation. Each Function 38 service uses register AL to transmit the country code if it's less than 255 = hex ff; otherwise, AL = ff and BX contains the code. To *set* the current country, put DX = ffff. To *ascertain* what country is current, set AL = 0; the code is returned in BX. To gain access to the notation conventions, place a country code in AL or BX as just explained, and in DS:DX the segment:offset address of a 34 byte memory area where DOS will store a record of the notation. Its format is mirrored in the C data structure **struct country** defined in header file **DOS.H** and already described in detail in Section 3.8. If an error occurs, DOS sets the Carry Flag CF, and returns an error code in AX. You can analyze that using techniques described in Section 8.9.

In Figure 8.5.3 is a function **CtryInfo** that fills a C data structure of the type just mentioned with the format data for a country with a specified code. A program can call this function, then use the structure to produce output like that shown in Section 3.8 for the United States and France.

There are two more very minor international features of the DOS interrupt services. The **struct country** component **co_case** is the address of a country dependent routine to convert lower case ASCII/IBM codes to upper case, and Function 63, available only in MS-DOS Version 2.25, has something to do with Japanese and Korean character sets.

Standard input/output services

The DOS functions include a number of services for the standard input/output file handles (described in Section 6.2). These are normally associated with keyboard and screen, but can be redirected at execution time. The various routines exhibit curious combinations of features, with no apparent logical pattern. The available features were probably just those that were most convenient for writing the DOS command processor. Figure 8.5.4 gives an overview. As indicated, some of the routines check for the user break keystrokes <Ctrl-Break> and ^C, and execute DOS Interrupt 23 if one is detected. Others do not, unless the DOS **Break** switch is on. Most routines input or output single characters only, but there is one string input and one string output service. Some of the input routines echo keyboard input on the screen, others do not. Some wait for keyboard input if necessary, others merely inform you when none is available. Function 6 provides an *input* service if you set DL = ff; it *outputs* any other value of DL. Function c is a compound

			Registers	Comments
		B = User breaks checked S = String I/O X = Input echoed E = User may edit input W = Wait if necessary		
I N P U T	1	B X W	AL	Basis of getche.
	6 (DL=ff)		AL,ZF	Sets ZF = 1 if no input is available.
	7	W	AL	Basis of getch.
	8	B W	AL	
	a	BSXEW	DS:DX	DOS buffered keyboard string input. Basis of cgets.
	b	B	AL	Sets AL = ff if input is ready; else AL = 0.
	c			Flush and do function in AL.
OUT- PUT	2	B	DL	
	6 (DI≠ff)		DL	
	9	BS	DS:AX	String terminator is $.

Figure 8.5.4 DOS standard I/O functions

service: it flushes the input buffer, then executes whichever of Functions 1, 6, 7, 8, a that you specify in AL. (The latter function may require that you set other registers.) Function 9 is rarely used because it regards any $ in the output string as a terminator. (It should have used the NUL character.)

As indicated in Figure 8.5.4, three of the standard input/output functions underlie the Turbo C Library console input functions **getche**, **getch**, and **cgets**. You may find other DOS standard I/O functions useful because they offer just the combination of services that you need, or because you require portability to other computers. On the other hand, as mentioned in Section 5.1, DOS keyboard input is not robust. Moreover, the screen output services are often unacceptably slow. Finally, executing DOS functions is sometimes hazardous in memory resident programs—that is discussed in Chapter 9.

File input/output services

DOS provides many functions for manipulating the directory/file system. These are described here using a top-down classification: functions that affect the entire system, a medium in a given drive, a directory on the medium, and a file in that directory. Generally, the functions form the basis of Turbo C Library functions described in Sections 6.2 and 6.4. Use of those routines is recommended, because they perform automatically the tedious function parameter encoding and decoding. Therefore, few of the parameters will be described in detail. Earlier in this section it was noted that DOS Interrupts 26 and 27 provide low-level disk services. Since these address the disk in terms of sectors, not files, they are not really intended for use by applications programs. A number of functions implement the FCB (File Control Block) file manipulation system that became obsolete with DOS 2.0. These are all designated FCB in Figure 8.5.2. Neither the low level services nor the FCB functions are described in this book.

Function d *resets* the entire disk system, flushing all buffers. This merely ensures that data written by other function calls has actually been recorded on the medium; it does not update directory entries or otherwise affect the directory/file system. Functions 2e and 54 set or ascertain the status of the DOS *verification* switch: AL = 0,1 indicates off, on. This switch can also be set by the DOS command **Verify**; when it is on, all disk writes are immediately verified by subsequent reads. Under normal conditions, the switch remains off, because disk writes are reliable and verification is extremely time-consuming. These two functions underlie the Turbo C Library routines **getverify** and **setverify**.

Functions e and 19 set and ascertain the *current drive*. To invoke the former, place the drive number in register DL: 0, 1, 2... stand for **a:**, **b:**, **c:** .... The latter function returns the current drive in AL. Function e also purports to return in AL *how many* drives are installed, but this report is usually incorrect. These two functions underlie Turbo C Library routines **getdisk** and **setdisk**.

Functions 1b and 1c are obsolete, both replaced by Function 36, which returns some valuable *information about a medium*. If you place in DL the drive number, this function will return the following data:

AL sectors per cluster,
CX bytes per sector (512 on standard PC media),
BX unoccupied clusters,
DX clusters on medium.

For this function and others where the notion of current drive is used, 0, 1, 2... stand for the current drive, **a:**, **b:**, ... If the drive specification is invalid, the function returns AX = ffff. A *cluster* is the smallest unit of disk space allocated to a file; it varies from medium to medium. From this information you can determine the available space in bytes: BX * AL * CX. Function 36 is the basis of Turbo C Library routine **getdfree**.

You can use Functions 3b and 47 to set and ascertain the *current directory*. For the former, DS:DX must point to an ASCII Z-string specifying the directory name. If this includes a drive name, then the current drive will be changed as well. Thus, to change the current directory on a non-current drive, you must first ascertain the current drive with Function 19, then change directory as desired with Function 3b, and finally reestablish the current drive with Function e. Functions 39 and 3a are used to create and remove a directory. The Turbo C Library routines **chdir**, **getcurdir**, **mkdir** and **rmdir** are based on functions mentioned in this paragraph.

Function 56 can be used to *rename* a directory or a file, and can move a file (but not a subdirectory) from one directory to another on the same medium. Its function is thus identical to the Turbo C Library routine **rename**.

Functions 4e and 4f are used for *wild card searches* for directories and/ or files; they underlie Turbo C Library routines **findfirst** and **findnext**. To invoke Function 4e, you point DS:DX to the file specification. It returns AX = 2 if there is no such file; otherwise it records in the current DTA (Disk Transfer Area) information about the first file matching the specification. Function 4f uses the DTA data to continue the search. It returns AX = hex 12 if no more files match the specification; otherwise it updates the data in the DTA. Header file **DOS.H** defines a C structure **struct ffblk** that reflects the DTA organization. Used for the **findfirst** and **findnext** parameters, it was discussed in detail in Section 6.4.

This technique clearly requires that the DTA remain undisturbed between Function 4e and 4f calls. Since *any* disk input/output may alter the current DTA, you must be able to change DTAs to prevent interference. Thus, you need to set and ascertain the current DTA location. The default DTA is a 128-byte area starting at offset hex 80 in your program's PSP (Program Segment Prefix). To change or ascertain the current DTA location, use Functions 1a and 2f. All this detail is taken care of automatically by the Library routines **findfirst**, **findnext**, **getdta**, and **setdta**.

You can invoke Functions 43 and 57 to set or ascertain the *attributes and date and time stamps* of a directory or file. AL = 0,1 indicates whether the functions return this information or establish new values. With Function 43 you identify the directory or file by pointing DS:DX to an ASCII Z-string specifying its name; it underlies Turbo C Library function **chmod**. Function 57 works only with files, and requires the file handle in BX. Registers CX and DX are used for the attribute and time, and for the date. The attribute format is described in Section 6.1. The time and date formats are shown in Figure 8.5.5. These formats are reflected in a Turbo C structure defined in header file **IO.H**:

```
struct ftime {
    unsigned ft_tsec  : 5;     /* Two-second interval*/
    unsigned ft_min   : 6;     /* Minutes           */
    unsigned ft_hour  : 5;     /* Hours             */
    unsigned ft_day   : 5;     /* Days              */
    unsigned ft_month : 4;     /* Months            */
    unsigned ft_year  : 7; }   /* Year              */
```

Turbo C Library functions **getftime** and **setftime** use parameters of this type to ascertain and set the file time and date, given a file handle **F**:

int getftime(int F, struct ftime *T)
int setftime(int F, struct ftime *T)

You can use Function 3c, 5a, or 5b to *create* a file. You specify the desired file attribute by setting register CX. In each case DS:DX must point to an ASCII Z-string specifying the file name. Function 3c is the

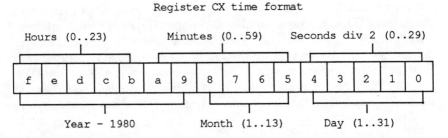

Figure 8.5.5 DOS Function 57 file time and date formats

standard way to create a file; it erases any existing file with the same name. Function 5a requires that the specified name end with \; this is really a directory name. DOS supplies a file name guaranteed to differ from all others in that directory, and returns with DS:DX pointed to it. You can then use this file for temporary storage. Function 5b merely fails if a file already exists with the specified name. If successful, each function returns the corresponding file handle in AX, and opens the file for reading and/or writing according to the specified attribute. With Function 41 you can *erase* a file. Again, you must point DS:DX to its name. You may erase an open file; closing it then has no effect. To indicate an error, each of these functions sets the Carry Flag CF and returns an error code in AX. These functions underlie Turbo C Library routines **creat**, **_creat**, **creattemp**, **creatnew**, and **unlink**.

Functions 3d and 3e *open* or *close* an existing file. The former again requires DS:DX to point to the file name, and returns a handle in AX. The latter requires merely the handle in BX. When opening a file, you must request access rights by setting AL; you may be denied access if the file was created as read-only. If your user has executed DOS utility **Share.Exe**, the complete file sharing access system is implemented, as mentioned in Section 6.2. Function 5c can be used in a file sharing system to lock or unlock portions of a file to prevent access by others while it is being updated. These three functions report errors like those in the previous paragraph. They form the basis for Turbo C Library routines **_open**, **_close**, **lock**, and **unlock**.

You can *move a file pointer* by using Function 42. Register BX is used for the file handle and CS:DX for a 32-bit integer indicating the length of the move. AL = 0,1,2 indicates whether the move is relative to the beginning, current pointer location, or end of the file. If successful, the function returns the new pointer location in DX:AX. Thus, you can ascertain the current pointer location by moving zero bytes relative to the current location. Functions 3f and 40 read or write from a file. Each uses BX for the file handle, DS:DX to point to the memory area to or from which the data is transmitted, and CX for the number of bytes to transfer. If successful, the number of bytes transferred is returned in AX. These three functions report errors like those in the previous paragraphs. They form the basis for Turbo C Library functions **lseek**, **_read**, and **_write**.

Function 44 provides several services collectively called *I/O Control*. You specify the service number in AL. Turbo C Library function **ioctl** enables you to obtain these services from a C program. Since the various

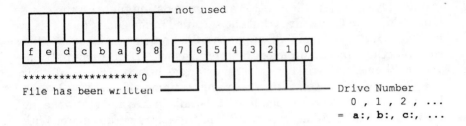

Figure 8.5.6 DOS Function hex 44 Service 0 file information in DL

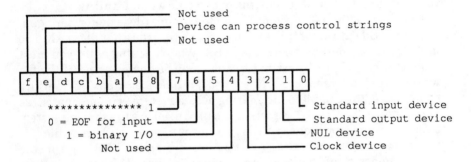

Figure 8.5.7 DOS Function hex 44 Service 0 device information in DL

options require different calling sequences, and most are very low level, concerned with device drivers, only a few **ioctl** services will be described further. Some of the Function 44 services, however, are noteworthy.

To obtain Function 44 Service 0 or 1 place a file handle in BX. Service 0 then returns a code in DX, whose format, shown in Figures 8.5.6 and 8.5.7, depends on whether the handle refers to an ordinary file or a device. As noted, bit 7 distinguishes the two cases. For ordinary files, only the drive number and file written condition (for input) is returned. For devices, bit 5 tells whether characters are processed in binary (raw) or ASCII (cooked) mode. In ASCII mode,

- control characters are output as two characters starting with ^;
- Ctrl-S, Ctrl-P, and Ctrl-C are detected, and may trigger special services;
- Ctrl-Z terminates output;

- during output, tabs are expanded to spaces;
- input is echoed to standard output;
- output may be echoed to **PRN**;
- input is buffered and the user may edit it with the backspace and function keys.

In binary mode, none of these statements hold. Moreover, control characters are output as one-byte ASCII codes—for example, the code for ^A is 01. Service 1 lets you *set* all these attributes. Setting them individually can probably produce inconsistent combinations and unpredictable results: take care!

Bit 7 provides the only means for telling whether standard input/output has been redirected from the console device to an ordinary file. This strategy is implemented in Turbo C Library function

int isatty(int Handle)

This routine, whose prototype is in header file **IO.H**, returns a nonzero value just when the specified handle is associated with a device, not a file. If your programs must handle both standard and redirected input/output robustly, you may want to use **isatty** to choose methods. (For example, you can ask whether an input file is at the end of file, but this hardly makes sense for the keyboard device.)

I/O Control Function 44 Services 2 to 5 are used to read and write control strings from and to devices that produce or accept them. Services 6 and 7 return AX = ff if the file handle in BX is ready for input or output, and AX = 0 if not. Service b lets you set the number of times DOS will attempt to access a shared file before giving up.

Function 44 Service 8 returns AX = 0 if the drive specified in BL has a removable medium, 1 if it is fixed. AX = f indicates an invalid device number. You might use this, for example, in writing a backup routine that asks the user to insert a new diskette, provided that's possible.

Functions 45 and 46 cause one file handle to duplicate the behavior of another in all respects. That is, any command to the first handle is obeyed as well by the second. The former function actually creates a new handle as a duplicate; the latter uses an existing handle. These functions underlie Turbo C Library routines **dup** and **dup2** used for redirecting input/output.

Memory management and program execution services

All the DOS memory management and program execution services have already been considered in Chapter 7 in the guise of their Turbo C Library implementations, except for those specifically designed for installing custom interrupt service routines. The latter are designated with ISR in Figures 8.5.2 and 8.5.3 and described separately in Chapter 9. It is tedious and awkward to use this type of DOS service directly, because of the many technical parameters involved. Therefore, the various interrupts and functions are merely catalogued here and correlated with the appropriate Library routines. Some of the DOS features in this category have been supplanted by more recent techniques. In particular, Function 26 is obsolete; other obsolete features are noted in passing.

DOS Functions 48 to 4a allocate a memory block to the current program, release it to DOS for reallocation, or alter its size. They form the basis of Turbo C Library routines **allocmem, freemem**, and **setblock**.

Interrupt 20 was formerly the standard way to terminate a program and return control to DOS. It was used in Section 8.3 because it is so simple. In more recent versions of DOS it was supplanted first by Function 0, then by Function 4c. The last method, used by the Turbo C Library routine **_exit** to terminate all programs, sets the DOS **ErrorLevel** variable. DOS uses Interrupt Vector 22 to store the address to which it will jump after terminating your program.

You will recall that important information is stored in the Program Segment Prefix (PSP), described in Section 3.5. DOS Function 62 returns the PSP address in register BX. Currently, when a Turbo C program starts, the DS and ES registers both contain the PSP segment address, and the Turbo C startup code places a copy of that in global variable **_psp** (defined in header file **StdLib.H**), so there is no need for Function 62. Some later versions, however, might use a different scheme.

DOS Function 4b underlies the Turbo C Library routines that load and execute other programs. It's impossible to obtain this service directly through the Turbo C functions that execute interrupts, because they don't preserve and restore the original values of the Stack Segment and Pointer registers SS and SP, which a child program will almost certainly change. The **spawn..** Library functions, however, do save and restore those registers. Function 4b has another option, which the **exec..** Library routines use to load a program overlay. Since overlays are not executed independently, **exec..** takes no special pains with SS and SP.

Once your program has used Function 4b to spawn a child, and your child has terminated via Function 4c, setting the **ErrorLevel** variable, you can read that value by invoking Function 4d: **ErrorLevel** is returned in AL. **spawn** invokes that service, then passes **ErrorLevel** back to its calling program as return value. Actually, Function 4d returns more information than **spawn** uses:

AH	Previous program's termination
00	Normal;
01	<Ctrl-C> or <Ctrl-Break>;
02	**Abort** response to the **Abort, Retry, Fail?** critical error prompt (see Section 8.9);
03	Stayed resident in memory (see Chapter 9).

Unfortunately, you can't use Function 4b to obtain this further information, because the first invocation of the 4b service routine always destroys the termination data from the previous program.

One final DOS service in this category governs some aspects of program execution: you can use Function 33 with AL = 0 or 1 to ascertain or set the DOS Break switch. Register DL transmits the switch setting. This function is the basis of Turbo C Library routines

int getcbrk(void)
int setcbrk(int Value)

The former returns a zero value just when the switch is *off*. The latter uses a zero or nonzero **Value** to set the switch off or on. These functions have the same effect as the DOS **Break** command or the corresponding line in a **Config.Sys** file.

8.6 Printer services

> **Concepts**
>
> BIOS printer services
> DOS printer services
> Controlling the DOS **Print** utility
> Turbo C TOOLS **Print** utility routines

For routine work, your programs ordinarily do not need low-level printer control. Output via the file system is usually sufficient. However, the BIOS and DOS do provide some low-level printer services, described in this section. High-level program control of the DOS **Print** utility was introduced with DOS 3.0; this is made available to Turbo C programs by several Turbo C TOOLS routines, also described here. These are demonstrated and extended by a new tool to suspend printing and record what was left unprinted.

BIOS printer services

Through software Interrupt 17 the BIOS provides your programs low level printer access. Three services are available, obtained by placing the service number in AH. Moreover, you can select parallel port LPT1:, LPT2:, or LPT3: by setting DX = 0, 1, or 2. Services 1 and 2 initialize a port and read its status. These are based on output to or input from a CPU port connected to the printer adapter. For their exact meaning, you must consult the adapter manual, and perhaps your printer manual. Service 0 sends to the port the character in AL. If it fails, it retries until a time limit expires. The time limit is a value in the BIOS data area set during the boot process; it can be changed.

The Turbo C Library makes the BIOS printer services accessible to Turbo C programs via function

int biosprint(int Service, int Byte, int Port)

This is not much of an improvement over the straight BIOS code: you simply indicate the desired BIOS service, the byte to transmit (if that makes sense), and the port to use; **biosprint** just sets up the appropriate registers and executes Interrupt 17. The **biosprint** prototype is in header file **BIOS.H**. Not missing an opportunity for clarification, Turbo C TOOLS provides three functions with more memorable names for the three **biosprint** services:

int prchar(int Port, char Byte)
int prinit(int Port)
int prstatus(int Port)

These are implemented in Turbo C TOOLS header file **BPrint.H** as rather simple macros that call **biosprint**.

On detecting the <Shift-PrtSc> keystroke, the BIOS keyboard Interrupt 9 service routine executes software Interrupt 5. The BIOS itself provides an Interrupt 5 service routine that sends to LPT1: the contents of the active (visible) display page. This only works for text modes. To print a Color/Graphics Adapter graphics mode display, DOS provides **Graphics.Com,** a memory resident utility to which Vector 5 is redirected. The EGA BIOS has a poorly documented alternative text mode print screen routine that adjusts for the number of screen rows. The PC BIOS routine will only print the first 25 lines of a 43 line EGA screen. Another PrtSc elaboration—to send formatted screen hardcopy to a file—is considered in detail in Sections 9.3 and 9.4 as an example ISR or intervention routine written with Turbo C TOOLS.

DOS printer services

DOS provides a simple service via Interrupt 21 Function 5: send the character in DL to the standard printer device PRN:. Since you can do the same thing by outputting to file **Prn,** you shouldn't have much need for this. Incidentally, the common errors associated with printers—off line and out of paper—result in DOS *critical error* interrupts. These are discussed in Section 8.9. Also, DOS interprets the <Ctrl-PrtSc> keystroke as a toggle switch for printing standard output. When it is active, all output to the standard output file handle is echoed on PRN:.

Controlling the DOS Print utility

Much more interesting services are provided via Interrupt 2f and the DOS print spool utility **Print.Com**. Actually, the corresponding ISR specifications are designed to work with *any* print spooler. You can obtain six services by placing a service number in register AL and device number 1 in AH before executing **Int 2f**. Four Turbo C TOOLS routines make these all easily accessible from Turbo C programs. A new tool demonstrating their use is described later.

Service 0 returns a code in AL. Code ff indicates that the **Print** utility has been installed and is ready for use. Code 0 says that you can install it by executing **Print.Com** with appropriate parameters. Any other value indicates that something is wrong. Using this service, Turbo C TOOLS function

int prinstld()

returns a nonzero value to indicate that the **Print** utility is ready. All other results, including the discovery that the DOS version is too early, result in a zero value.

Interrupt 2f Service 1 submits a file to the print queue. You must set DS:DX to point to a memory buffer containing a zero byte (purpose unknown) followed by an ASCII Z-string giving the complete file name. No wildcards are permitted. This service, like the others described below, reports various error conditions by setting CF = 1 and placing an error code in AX. The corresponding Turbo C TOOLS routine is function

int prspool(char *File)

You set the name of the file to be submitted, and **prspool** returns the error code.

To cancel a file from the print queue, invoke Service 2 with DS:DX pointing to an ASCII Z-string giving the complete file name. Wildcards are permitted here. To cancel all files, invoke Service 3. Errors are reported as indicated for Service 1. The single Turbo C TOOLS function

int prcancel(char *File)

implements both services. You specify the empty string or a null pointer to cancel all files.

You may use Service 4 to inspect the print queue. It returns in DS:SI a pointer to the print queue, a sequence of file names up to 64 characters long. These are really ASCII Z-strings. A null byte terminates the sequence. Invocation of this service freezes the print queue until some other Interrupt 2f service is invoked. Service 5 does nothing except thaw it. Turbo C TOOLS function

int prgetq(int EntryNumber, int *QLength, char *File)

returns the name of the specified entry in the queue, as well as the queue length and the usual error code. The currently printing file is entry number 0. If you specify an **EntryNumber** beyond the extent of the queue, the function returns an empty string, but nevertheless reports the queue length. Perhaps unwisely, it invokes Service 5 to thaw the queue. Turbo C TOOLS provides mnemonic constants for error codes signifying these conditions:

PR_OK	No error.
PR_INSTAL	**Print** not installed.
PR_EMPTY	Queue is empty.
PR_RANGE	There is no queue entry with that number.
PR_BUSY	**Print** is busy—try again later.

(The **PR_EMPTY** error code takes precedence over **PR_RANGE**.)

Figure 8.6.1 displays a function **HoldPrnt** that demonstrates Turbo C TOOLS functions **prgetq** and **prcancel**. (In turn, they call **prinstld** to ensure that the **Print** utility is available.) **HoldPrnt** cancels all print queue entries except the one currently in process, and records and returns to the caller the names of the unprinted files. It then delays while the current file is printed. You could use this tool to suspend printing for an emergency job. You could pass the unprinted file names to another routine to resume printing. Function **HoldPrnt** is rather inefficient: it reassembles the Interrupt 2f Service 4 output after **prgetq** has disassembled it. However, the point is to show how to use the Turbo C TOOLS functions, and, in particular, their error codes.

The DOS **Print** utility operation is highly dependent on concurrent activity. It tends to start and stop at every excuse. (Try decreasing the **Delay** constant in **HoldPrnt.Dem**!) The documentation states that it is incompatible with networking. Of course, a print spooler for a multiuser system serves a rather different purpose from one for a personal

```
/*******************************************************************/
/* HoldPrnt.Dem    Demonstrate function HoldPrnt. Before   */
/*                 executing this, use the DOS Print util-*/
/* ity to set up and start printing a queue of files. This */
/* program will terminate the queue after the current one is */
/* printed, and output a list of the unprinted files.      */
/*                                                         */
/* Function HoldPrnt terminates the DOS Print utility      */
/* queue after the current file is printed, and returns a  */
/*********************************** pointer to a concatena- */
                                 /* tion  Q  of the names of */
#include <General.H>             /* the unprinted files—each */
#include  <BPrint.H>             /* with a terminal zero—    */
                                 /* followed by a final zero.*/
char *HoldPrnt() {               /* It allocates memory for  */
  int   M,N,FLength;             /* Q  as necessary.         */
  char  File[65];                /***************************/
  char *R;
  char *Q        = NULL;         /* Concatenation & length,  */
  int   QLength = 0;             /* not including last  0.    */
while (PR_OK ==                  /* Get first file in queue. */
         prgetq(1,&M,File)) {    /* M  parameter is not used.*/
  FLength = strlen(File);        /* Make room for the concat-*/
  N = QLength + FLength + 1;     /* enation + this file name */
  R = (char *) malloc(N+1);      /* + the final  0.          */
  memcpy(R,Q,QLength);           /* Copy them into the new   */
  strcpy(R+QLength,File);        /* concatenation and free   */
  R[N] = 0;                      /* the old one.             */
  free(Q);                       /* New QLength doesn't in-*/
  prcancel(File); }              /* Shorten the queue.       */
while (PR_EMPTY !=               /* Delay while the current  */
    prgetq(0,&M,File))          /* file is printed.         */
  delay(2000);
return Q; }
void main() {
  char *Q = HoldPrnt();
printf("Files remaining to print:\n");
if (Q == NULL)
   printf("None");
  else
    for (; Q[0] != 0; Q += strlen(Q)+1)
      printf("%s\n",Q); }
```

Figure 8.6.1 Program **HoldPrnt.Dem**

computer. You should exercise caution when trying anything fancy with
Print.Com.

8.7 Clock/calendar services

Concepts

PC clock/calendar features
BIOS services
Turbo C functions **sleep** and **delay** are misleading
Turbo C TOOLS timer functions
DOS services
Turbo C Library clock/calendar routines
Additional PC/AT BIOS services
Generating sound

The clock/calendar features of the original IBM PC did not meet user
requirements. DOS provided a few additional services, but the most
obvious omission, a nonvolatile clock, was available only as a component
on various manufacturers' enhancement boards. There are no standards
for the PC in this area. Timing features provided by the BIOS, DOS, and
other subsystems usually have incompatible data formats. There is no
standard nonvolatile clock interface at all. The PC/AT presents a
considerable improvement: it has a nonvolatile clock, and its BIOS
makes that device available to serve your programs. Even in the PC/AT,
however, the problem of incompatible formats persists. This section will
consider first the organization of the original PC clock system, then the
PC BIOS services, and some corresponding Turbo C Library and Turbo
C TOOLS functions. Next several DOS services are described and
correlated with Turbo C Library routines. The section concludes with an
overview of the newer PC/AT features.

The underlying event that drives the PC clock system occurs about
18.2 times each second. That frequency corresponds to the period 1/18.2
$\approx 2^{16}/1193182$, which is called one tick. The tick length is an exact
multiple of the period of the clock chip oscillation that governs the
operation of the entire computer. The 8253 timer chip counts oscilla-
tions, and after each tick interval requests interrupt service via the

highest priority maskable interrupt line IRQ0. Sensing this, the interrupt controller chip requests the CPU to execute hardware Interrupt 8.

The PC BIOS Interrupt 8 service routine performs just three tasks. First, it increments a double word tick counter in the BIOS Data Area. The counter is initialized to zero during booting, and the service routine restarts it every 24 hours, recording that action. Second, it turns off a diskette drive motor if no diskette access has occurred in a certain interval. Third, it executes software Interrupt 1c.

The BIOS provides only a dummy 1c ISR. If you want to perform some task at each tick, you must supply your own custom ISR and redirect Interrupt Vector 1c to it. Techniques for using this feature are described in Chapter 9.

When you boot DOS, it ordinarily asks you to enter the current date and time. However, if you use an **AutoExec** program, it assumes that this includes a command to execute software to obtain the same information from a nonvolatile clock/calendar via some CPU ports. This kind of software isn't standard. It's supplied with the clock hardware, and can vary in port utilization and data format. The DOS clock setting process must correlate the BIOS tick counter value with the current time. After that, DOS clock services like the **Time** command can inspect the counter and determine the corresponding time. If you disturb the counter, you will, of course, cause DOS to report the time incorrectly.

The original PC BIOS provides your programs only two timer services via software Interrupt 1a. You can ascertain the tick counter value or set it by placing service number 0 or 1 in register AH before executing the interrupt. In each case CX and DX are used for the high- and low-order counter words. Service 0 returns AL = 1 or 0 to indicate whether or not the counter has passed the 24-hour mark since this service was last performed. You can use Service 0 to delay for a certain number of ticks, or to determine the execution times of parts of your programs. The timing technique is demonstrated later. The Turbo C Library makes both services available to your programs through function

long biostime(int Service, long Ticks)

You set the service number and **biostime** either returns the tick count as function value or sets it according to parameter **Ticks**. Unfortunately this function disregards the 24 hour flag. That oversight is remedied dby Turbo C TOOLS function

int utgetclk(long *Ticks)

This places the tick count in *Ticks and returns 1 or 0 to indicate whether the 24-hour mark has passed. Instead of executing Interrupt 1a, utgetclk just accesses the locations where the BIOS 1a ISR stores the information. This is faster but less portable. The function turns off maskable interrupts during access so that the data is guaranteed consistent.

With the BIOS services you cannot obtain a resolution finer than one tick, approximately 0.055 second. If you need better resolution, you probably should resort to assembly language techniques, because the Turbo C overhead might be comparable to the interval that you're trying to time. The PC/AT BIOS provides timing service with finer resolution, described later. It is also possible to program the PC's 8253 timer chip via the CPU ports to provide high resolution timer services. For this technique, you may consult References [11,33].

The Turbo C Library provides two delay services, and Turbo C TOOLS provides one: functions

void sleep(unsigned Seconds)
void delay(unsigned Milliseconds)
unsigned utsleep(unsigned Ticks)

In each case, the parameter is a requested delay time. The first two are amateurishly implemented, and very misleading. Their prototypes are in header file **DOS.H**. The *Reference guide* documentation for **sleep** points out that it is accurate to one tick. But its parameter is an integral number of seconds, not ticks, so one wonders what's the point. It can't be used for a precise delay of a period shorter than one second. The **delay** documentation warns that its accuracy varies from system to system; the units of its parameter suggest that it may provide a resolution finer than one tick. However, experimentation with program **Delay.Dem** in Figure 8.7.1 reveals that this is not true. The program allows you to execute a specified delay a number of times, and uses Interrupt 1a Service 0 to time the result. The observed delay is always an integral number of ticks. Similar experimentation with Turbo C TOOLS function **utsleep** shows that it performs exactly the way you would expect, delaying a specified number of ticks. Since it could be interrupted during the delay, and consequently fail to resume on time, it returns as function value the actual number of ticks delayed. The **utsleep** source code was shown earlier, in Figure 1.5.1, as an example of Turbo C TOOLS programming style.

```
/****************************************************************/
/* Delay.Dem    Analyze function  delay:  delay a specified   */
/*              number of milliseconds for a specified number*/
/* of trials.  Read the  BIOS  clock before and after to get  */
/* the elapsed number of ticks, then report the average delay */
/* in tick units.  From the source code it appears that the   */
/*****************************************  first execution of  */
                                        /* delay  is used for  */
                                        /* calibration, so exe-*/
#include <General.H>                    /* cute it once before */
                                        /* the experiment.     */
void main() {                           /***********************/
  unsigned MSec,N,I,_DX0;
  float    Average;
delay(1000);                            /* For calibration.    */
for (;;) {
  printf("Delay time (MSec)     : ");
  scanf ("%u",&MSec);
  printf("Number of trials    : ");
  scanf ("%u",&N);
  _AH = 0;                              /* Request  Int 1a     */
  geninterrupt(0x1a);                   /* Service 0 :  time is */
  _DX0 = _DX;                           /* in  DX.             */
  for (I = 1; I <= N; ++I)              /* Nothing irrelevant  */
    delay(MSec);                        /* between time checks. */
  _AH = 0;                              /* Look at the clock:  */
  geninterrupt(0x1a);                   /* time is in  DX.     */
  Average = (_DX - _DX0)/N;
  printf("Average delay (Ticks) :  %5.2f\n", Average); }}
```

Output

```
Delay time (MSec)     : 838
Number of trials      : 10
Average delay (Ticks) : 16.00
Delay time (MSec)     : 839
Number of trials      : 10
Average delay (Ticks) : 17.00
```

Figure 8.7.1 Program **Delay.Dem**

The 8253 Timer Chip is connected to the PC speaker, and you can program it via certain CPU output ports to output a square wave (on/off oscillation) to produce a given pitch. No BIOS or DOS services are provided for this kind of programming, so it requires knowledge of the 8253 beyond the scope of this book. See References [11,33] for further information. The source code for Turbo C Library functions

void sound(int Hz)
void nosound(void)

is also helpful. The first turns on the speaker at the given frequency, the second turns it off. Prototypes for these functions are in header file **DOS.H**.

Interactive user interfaces frequently use a sound of specified pitch and duration as a prompt or alarm. The Turbo C Library provides the means for two such features. One is employed by the macro **Beep** found in the header file **General.H** for this book:

#define Beep putchar('\a')

The sound is produced by DOS' driver for the **CON:** device when **putchar** asks it to display the ASCII 7 **'\a'** BEEP character. You can produce a more general signal this way:

sound(Hz);
delay(MSec);
nosound();

Unfortunately, functions **sleep, delay,** and the delay mechanism used by the **CON:** device driver cause problems when called by some memory resident software; the exact reason isn't clear. In place of the conventional **Beep,** some Chapter 9 ISRs use function **Peep,** based on the Turbo C TOOLS timer routine **utsleep.** It's shown in Figure 8.7.2.

The four DOS clock/calendar Functions 2a through 2d form the basis of Turbo C Library routines as follows:

Int 21	Function	Turbo C Library Function
2a	Ascertain date	**void getdate(struct date *Date)**
2b	Set date	**void setdate(struct date *Date)**
2c	Ascertain time	**void gettime(struct time *Time)**
2d	Set time	**void settime(struct time *Time)**

Using either technique is straightforward. The Library routines use C structure parameters as shown; they were described earlier in Section 3.8. Here is the corresponding register format for the DOS functions:

DOS	Function	AL	CX=CH/CL	DH	DL
2a	Ascertain date	Weekday	Year	Month	Day
2b	Set date	Valid	Year	Month	Day
2c	Ascertain time		Hr/Min	Sec	.01 Sec
2d	Set time	Valid	Hr/Min	Sec	.01 Sec

The weekday numbers are 0..6 for Sun..Sat; years are numbered 1980..2099, months 1..12, days 1..31, hours 0..23, minutes and seconds 0..59, and .01 sec 0..99. The date/time setting functions return AL = 0 or ff to indicate input validity or error.

The PC/AT nonvolatile clock is a component of its battery-powered Motorola MC146818 CMOS chip. It has two main features: a clock/calendar that gives DOS the time and date during booting, and a timer

```
/**********************************************************/
/* Peep.C     Function Peep : sound Concert  A  for half a  */
/*            second.                                     */
/**********************************************************/

#include   <DOS.H>
#include <BUtil.H>

#define  HalfSecond    9        /* 0.5 sec  in ticks.  */
#define  ConcertA     440       /* 440  Hz.            */

void Peep(void) {
sound(ConcertA);
utsleep(HalfSecond);
nosound(); }
```

Figure 8.7.2 Function **Peep**

and alarm with resolution of about one millisecond. To support these features, the PC/AT BIOS provides several services beyond those described earlier for the PC.

You can still use the original Interrupt 1a Services 0 and 1 to read and set the BIOS tick counter. Services 2, 3 and 4, 5 let you read and set the CMOS clock and calendar. The time and date information are transmitted via registers CX and DX, but the format is different from that used by the corresponding DOS Functions 2c, 2d and 2a, 2b. DOS automatically uses Services 2 and 4 to set its own clock during booting.

PC/AT Interrupt 1a Service 6 sets an alarm for a time specified in hours, minutes, and seconds by setting CX and DX. At the appropriate time, the CMOS chip requests the interrupt controller to execute hardware Interrupt 4a. You must provide your own custom 4a ISR to do whatever you want when this alarm occurs. The complementary BIOS Interrupt 1a Service 7 lets you cancel an alarm that you previously set.

More precise timing, with one millisecond resolution, is provided by PC/AT Interrupt 15 Services 83 and 86. To use the former, you place in registers CX and DX a 32-bit count in microseconds, and in ES:BX the address of an alarm byte. Executing **Int 15** with AH,AL = 83,00 then causes the high order bit of the alarm byte to be set after the specified number of microseconds. You must clear the alarm bit before setting the alarm, and inspect it periodically to determine when it changes. It seems impossible to cancel this alarm, though you can change it. Service 86 provides an analogous delay: specify the duration in microseconds in CX and DX as before. These two PC/AT services operate by causing its CMOS chip to request hardware Interrupt 70 service about one thousand times per second; the BIOS ISR 70 simply decrements a counter and sets a bit when it reaches zero.

You can find more detail about the PC/AT timer services, with demonstration programs, in the author's earlier book, Reference [34, Section 10.3].

8.8 Serial communications services

Concepts

General principles of serial communication
Universal Asynchronous Receiver Transmitter (UART) chip
BIOS and DOS services
Turbo C Library serial communication function
Polling vs. interrupt driven serial communications
Further references

The PC BIOS provides some serial communications support for your programs; DOS provides a subset of those, so small that it is useless. To obtain sophisticated support, you need custom software. The goal of this section is to give you enough information to understand and use these services, then suggest what others are possible and indicate sources of software and information.

Serial communication with the PC

In *serial* communication, bits are sent sequentially via a single data line. (In contrast, *parallel* communication systems send all bits of a byte or word simultaneously over separate lines.) Figure 8.8.1 illustrates transmission of a single character. Before it is transmitted, the communica-

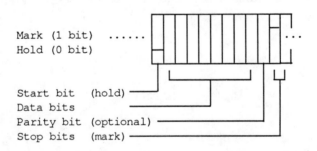

Figure 8.8.1 Sending one character

tion line voltage is in what is called a *mark* state. The start of the character is signalled by a *start* bit in the complementary, or *hold* state. Then follow the character's data bits, with mark and hold states representing ones and zeroes. All bits have the same duration; the reciprocal of this bit transmission time is called the *Baud* rate (indecently named after the French engineer Baudot). After the data bits follow an optional *parity* bit that can be used for error detection, and some mark state stop bits, as required for the receiving device to reset itself for receiving the next character.

The optional parity checking can be set for *even* or *odd* parity: the total number of ones among the data and parity bits should be either always even or always odd. (If the parity bit is wrong, the receiver knows that it received at least one data bit or the parity bit incorrectly.)

A *break* signal, commonly used to abort a communication, consists of a hold state maintained on the data line at least as long as a character transmission time.

In order to communicate using this scheme, transmitter and receiver must agree on these *communication parameters:*

- Baud rate,
- Number of data bits,
- Parity checking, and
- Minimum number of stop bits.

In the PC family, devices that support serial communication are called *serial ports*. Each is controlled through a bank of eight CPU ports. The number of serial ports is essentially unlimited, but the BIOS and DOS support only two, called COM1: and COM2:. DOS designates one of these as the *standard auxiliary device* AUX:. Normally this is COM1:, but you can use DOS command **Mode** to change that. DOS assigns to this device *standard auxiliary file handle* 3. A port's interface to the outside world is usually a 9- or 25-pin connector on the back of the PC. The port is implemented on an expansion board by a Universal Asynchronous Receiver/Transmitter (UART), usually a National Semiconductor INS 8250 chip. This is connected to the CPU ports mentioned earlier. Jumpers or switches on the board permit you to set the port as COM1: or COM2:. The rest of the material under this subheading tells you what you need to know about the UART in order to understand and use the rudimentary BIOS and DOS services. You will need more information for more sophisticated use.

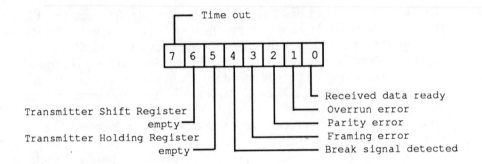

Figure 8.8.2 UART Line Status register

To transmit, the BIOS sends a character via a CPU port to the UART *Transmitter Holding Register.* The UART then moves it to the *Transmitter Shift Register.* From there, it's shifted onto the data line one bit at a time, framed by start, parity, and stop bits. Receiving a character is essentially the reverse process. Bits are shifted from the data line one at a time into the *Receiver Shift Register,* stripped of their framing start, parity, and stop bits, and the assembled character is moved to the *Receiver Holding Register,* ready for the BIOS to remove.

The UART has an 8-bit *Line Status Register,* in which it records what's happening, as shown in Figure 8.8.2. The UART reports time out if a requested transmission or anticipated reception doesn't occur within a

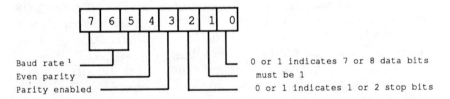

[1] The numerical value of this three bit field selects the Baud rate as follows:

Value	Baud	Value	Baud	Value	Baud	Value	Baud
0	110	2	300	4	1200	6	4800
1	130	3	600	5	2400	7	9600

Figure 8.8.3 BIOS Interrupt 14 Service 0 register AL communications parameter settings

preset time limit. Usually this means that the port wasn't connected or the device at the other end of the communications line has quit transmitting. The UART maintains the Transmitter Shift and Holding bits so that you won't ask it to transmit a character before it has finished sending a previous one. The remaining status port bits are concerned with data reception. One bit tells you to remove a character from the Receiver Holding Register. If you don't do that fast enough, the next character received will overwrite it. In that case, the UART sets the Overrun Error bit. Its parity checking and break signal detection circuitry set corresponding bits as appropriate. Finally, if the UART doesn't sense the mark state stop bits when the communication parameters indicate that it should, it will set the Framing Error bit. This usually indicates data line noise or a disagreement concerning parameters.

The UART also monitors several other lines that may be connected to the serial port. These are often used to control a *modulator/demodulator,* or *modem*—a device that converts digital UART to analog telephone signals. The status of these lines is reflected in the bits of the UART *Line Status Register.*

BIOS services

The BIOS offers serial communication services via the Interrupt 14 service routine. You specify service number in AH and port number in DL before executing the interrupt. Only ports COM1: and COM2: are supported: DL = 0, 1.

Service 0 allows you to specify serial port communication parameters, using AL bits as shown in Figure 8.8.3. The service routine returns the UART Line and Modem Status Registers in AH and AL. (The definitions of the Modem Status Register bits are regarded as beyond the scope of this book. You may want to consult one of the references suggested at the end of this section, as well as the manual for your modem.)

Service AH = 1 requests the UART to transmit the character in AL. It returns the UART Line Status Register bits in AH, except that bit 7 indicates failure in general—not specifically time out. Service AH = 2 moves to AL the byte in the UART Receiver Holding Register, and sets AH bits 7,4,3,2,1 to reflect the corresponding Line Status Register bits. Other AH bits are cleared, so that AH ≠ 0 just when the UART is indicating an error condition. Finally, service AH = 3 returns the UART Line Status and Modem Status register values in registers AH and AL.

The Turbo C Library provides meager access to the BIOS serial communications services via function

int bioscom(int Service, char Byte, int Port)

This merely places the **Service** number in AH, **Byte** in AL, and the **Port** number in DX, then executes **Int 14**. It returns the value that the BIOS places in AX. The function prototype is in header file **BIOS.H**.

DOS services

During booting, DOS initializes device AUX = COM1:, and if it is actually installed, selects 2400 Baud, eight data bits, no parity, and one stop bit. You can change these settings with the **Mode** command.

DOS offers only two program services, via Interrupt 21. Function 4 requests the UART to transmit the character in register DL. Function 3 reads a character from the UART Receiver Holding Register if one is ready, waiting if necessary. Neither service reports any status or error information, hence they are really useless. Use the corresponding BIOS services.

Polling vs. interrupt driven communications; references

To use the BIOS or DOS services just described, you must adopt a *polling* strategy. At intervals less than the time between successive received bytes, you must inspect the Line Status register to see if you must remove a character from the Receiver Holding Register, and to monitor error conditions. Thus, you have to devote a significant portion of your computing resource to this one repeated inquiry.

A much more efficient and reliable method is to use *interrupt driven* communications software. Such a system initializes the UART interrupt circuitry, so that it will request a maskable interrupt whenever one or more of the following conditions is met:

- a character has been received,
- a character has been transmitted,
- an error has been detected, or
- certain Modem Status Register bits are set.

You can select which interrupt conditions to activate. Jumpers or switches on the serial port expansion board govern which interrupt request line to use. The conventional selections for COM1: and COM2: are IRQ4 and IRQ3. (Since the former has lower priority, COM1: is apparently intended for routine activity like telephone communication, while COM2: is for some higher-priority serial device like a printer or mouse.)

An example custom interrupt driven serial communications package for use with Turbo C is *Asynch Manager,* by Blaise Computing Inc., Reference [2]. Structured much like the Turbo C TOOLS package, it sets up data transmission and reception queues; its serial communications interrupt service routines move characters between UART registers and queues as demanded by the UART. Your program can then output to and input from the queues at its own speed, without risking loss of data or devoting resources to frequent polling. This package also includes file transmission routines using the popular XMODEM protocol.

For additional information about the UART and serial communication in general, you may consult the introduction to the *Asynch Manager* manual, the section on the serial communications adapter in your PC *Technical Reference* manual, Reference [20 or 21], or material on data communications in References [11, 27,33].

8.9 Error handling

Concepts

DOS function errors
Turbo C Library error reporting features
Critical errors
Abort, Retry, Fail?
User breaks

This section considers some related questions concerning error handling:

- How DOS functions report error conditions,
- How this information and other error data can be reported via Turbo C Library functions,

- How DOS handles critical errors like diskette drive door open,
- How DOS handles user break keystrokes.

Error handling specific to particular programming techniques has been discussed in earlier sections as appropriate.

DOS function errors

In early versions, DOS functions reported errors in various ways. Some—mostly those designated FCB in Figure 8.5.2—returned AL = ff. Others—mostly those introduced with DOS 2.0—set the Carry Flag CF. In each case, an error description code was available in some register. With DOS 3.0 a unified error reporting and diagnosing system became available. Once you have detected an error as just noted, invoke Function 59. It will return in AX an *extended error* code, referring to a long list of possible errors. Further, BH will contain an *error class* code, BL a *suggested action* code, and CH an approximate *error location* code. Appendix E lists these codes. You should not take them too seriously, because DOS clearly cannot anticipate all situations. Nevertheless, they can provide very useful information.

Turbo C Library error reporting features

When a Turbo C Library function invokes a DOS function and the latter reports an error condition, the Library function sets global variable **_doserrno** accordingly. These and other Library functions also set **errno**, an analogous variable for an independent error reporting system derived from UNIX. The Turbo C *Reference guide,* Reference [7], lists the **errno** codes. The Library provides three functions for manipulating **errno**:

char *strerror(int N)
char *_strerror(char *S)
void perror(char *S)

The definitions of the first two functions changed significantly with the introduction of Turbo C Version 1.5. **strerror** returns a string consisting of an interpretation of error code **N** followed by a newline character. **_strerror** returns a string consisting of **S** followed by a colon, a space, an interpretation of the current value of **errno**, and a newline. (The colon and space are omitted if **S** is null or empty.) The first two functions have prototypes in header file **String.H**. Function **perror**, with prototype in **StdIO.H**, outputs to the standard error file handle a string almost like that of **_strerror**. You may use **S** for your own custom error message; its length mustn't exceed 94 characters. The functions construct the full error message in a static buffer that is overwritten on every call.

You may customize the Turbo C error messages as well: they are contained in the global array

char *sys_errlist[]

Global variable **int sys_nerr** must always contain the array length. These variables, as well as **_doserrno** and **errno**, are declared **extern** in header file **StdLib.H**.

A program demonstrating the **errno** features is shown in Figure 8.9.1. The vertical spacing shows that the newlines were output.

Critical errors

A *critical error* occurs when a DOS function attempts an input/output operation and meets a condition like a diskette drive door open or printer out of paper. Usually it's appropriate to inform you of such a condition, to give you a chance to correct it. When DOS encounters a situation like this, it loads various registers with codes identifying the condition, then executes **Int 24**.

The rudimentary DOS Interrupt 24 ISR ordinarily handles this situation: it writes a brief message describing the error and asks whether you want to

Abort, Retry, Fail?

If you opt to *retry*, DOS will attempt again to execute the function that encountered the error: perhaps you have corrected the situation. If you opt to *fail*, the function will terminate, returning an error code. If the programmer was careful in interpreting the function's error codes and

```
/****************************************************************/
/* ErrNo.Dem    Demonstrate functions  strerror,           */
/*              _strerror,  and  perror,  and global varia- */
/*              bles  errno  and  sys_errlist.              */
/****************************************************************/

#include <General.H>
#define  Call_perror   printf("%27c",Blank);  perror(S)

void main() {
  char *S;
  errno = 3;
  printf("errno          = %d\n",errno            );
  printf("strerror(errno) = %s\n",strerror(errno)  );
  printf("S    _strerror(S)        perror(S)\n\n");
  S = NULL;       printf("Null   %s",_strerror(S));  Call_perror;
  S = EmptyStr;   printf("Empty  %s",_strerror(S));  Call_perror;
  S = "SS";       printf("SS     %s",_strerror(S));  Call_perror;
                  sys_errlist[errno] = "New message";
                  perror("sys_errlist[errno] altered"); }
```

Output

```
errno           = 3
strerror(errno) = Path not found

S     _strerror(S)        perror(S)

Null   Path not found
                        (null): Path not found
Empty  Path not found
                        : Path not found
SS     SS: Path not found
                        SS: Path not found
sys_errlist[errno] altered: New message
```

Figure 8.9.1 Program **Error.Dem**

acting accordingly, failure may lead to proper software behavior; if not, the software may crash, or—sometimes worse—produce incorrect results while seeming to operate correctly. Finally, if you opt to *abort*, DOS will terminate the program ungracefully, without even closing open files. Abortion can be disastrous, particularly if the program in question was involved in file input/output or had placed the interrupt vectors or some other aspect of the system in a state inappropriate for software that must use it later. Moreover, even if graceful termination would result from an option for failure, you can't trust your user not to press <A> for **Abort**. Thus, the DOS critical error ISR is inappropriate for building robust software systems.

Programmers are invited to replace the DOS Interrupt 24 service routine with a custom ISR tailored to the individual program. That would create a problem if the program terminated but left installed a custom critical error handler inappropriate for use with its parent. Therefore, when DOS executes any program, it places a copy of the parent's interrupt vector 24 in the child's PSP; when it terminates the child, DOS restores the interrupt vector from the PSP. A custom critical error handler might enhance software robustness by identifying the error more precisely, limiting the user's options, and terminating the program as gracefully as possible if the user opts for abortion.

In DOS versions before 3.3, the third critical error option was *ignore* instead of fail. If you opted for ignoring a critical situation, DOS would let the program proceed even though the input/output operation involved had not been completed. That nearly always led to disaster.

User breaks

You are certainly familiar with PC behavior following a *user break* <Ctrl-Break> keystroke, and perhaps after <Ctrl-C> as well. The latter is the older feature, developed for using DOS on machines with limited keyboard.

When the BIOS keyboard Interrupt 9 ISR detects <Ctrl- C> or <Alt-(keypad) 3> it places ^C = ASCII 3 in the keyboard buffer and takes no further action. These keystrokes have no special meaning for the BIOS. However, when it detects <Ctrl-Break>, the BIOS executes **Int 1b** then places ASCII 0 in the buffer. The BIOS itself provides a dummy 1b ISR—just an **IRet** instruction—but interrupt vector 1b is redirected to a DOS ISR during booting. The DOS ISR raises a <Ctrl-Break> flag.

DOS inspects the <Ctrl-Break> flag and checks the keyboard buffer for ^C = ASCII 3 when one of two situations occurs:

- when it's executing certain character I/O functions,
- when it's executing certain other functions *and* its Break switch is ON.

The Break switch is controlled by DOS or **Config.Sys** command **Break**, or DOS Function 33: you have some control over how often DOS checks for a user break signal. When DOS detects a user break signal, it executes **Int 23**.

The rudimentary DOS Interrupt 23 ISR ordinarily handles this situation. It closes files opened with handles (not with FCBs), and terminates the currently executing program. This may cause a crash if that program leaves the machine in a state inappropriate for software that must use it later. Thus, the DOS user break ISR is inappropriate for building robust software systems.

Programmers are invited to replace the DOS Interrupt 23 service routine with a custom ISR tailored to the individual program. As with the critical error ISR, that would create a problem if the program terminated but left installed a custom user break handler inappropriate for use with its parent. Therefore, when DOS executes any program, it places a copy of the parent's interrupt vector 23 in the child's PSP; when it terminates the child, DOS restores the interrupt vector from the PSP. A custom user break Interrupt 23 handler might enhance software robustness by terminating the program as gracefully as possible, or by taking some other action altogether. For reasons discussed in Section 9.1, programmers are cautioned to use an Interrupt 1b service routine like DOS: only for limited actions.

Interrupt Service Routines

In Chapter 8 you considered the interrupt mechanism in general, and saw how you can use it to obtain services for your Turbo C programs, either directly or via Turbo C Library and Turbo C TOOLS routines. The present chapter shows how to write custom interrupt service routines (ISRs) in Turbo C to provide such services to your software, or to software supplied by other developers. Some aspects of this problem require elaborate organization and assembly language techniques. The Turbo C TOOLS package provides routines that satisfy these needs. With it you can write ISRs entirely in Turbo C. The Turbo C TOOLS ISR features let you avoid the tedious lower-level language detail, but you cannot avoid the requirement for knowledge of the interrupt system and its intricate relationships with DOS and the BIOS. Chapter 8 was largely devoted to that material, but the examples given there involved few of the complications that you commonly encounter in *writing* ISRs. The present chapter must face these directly.

Section 9.1 presents a general overview of the problems of writing ISRs in any higher-level language. Then Section 9.2 shows how Turbo C TOOLS attacks these problems. It introduces the most important routines, and presents in a simplified example the framework used later to organize more realistic demonstrations.

Section 9.3 is devoted to three demonstrations. The first example is a custom user tick interrupt service routine that beeps periodically. The ISR itself is very simple, but you must provide the means for it to interrupt itself recursively while it's beeping. The second example, a keyboard ISR that detects and reacts to simultaneous <P> and <Q> keystrokes, is simpler in this respect—it can't interrupt itself. But its service is surprisingly complicated—almost too complex for inclusion in a book like this. However, it is included to demonstrate programming techniques concerned with the keyboard buffer that could not be considered earlier in Chapter 5. The final example in Section 9.3 is a PrtSc service routine that sends formatted screen hardcopy to a file. This encounters some severe problems due to unsatisfactory DOS design aspects. Some interesting techniques are introduced to circumvent some of the difficulty, but the solution is not entirely satisfactory.

The final section, Section 9.4, describes the Turbo C TOOLS *intervention* techniques for scheduling interrupt services to respond to various keystrokes and timing conditions. Intervention routines systematically use some of the methods introduced earlier for the PrtSc ISR. That example is recast as an intervention routine to circumvent the earlier difficulty.

9.1 General concepts

Concepts

What interrupts might you need to serve?
ISR organization
Interrupt filtering
Implementation problems

Surveying the most common needs for custom interrupt services may help you grasp some of the underlying concepts and the difficulties with their implementation. For which interrupts might you need to provide services? There are several categories, which sometimes overlap:

1. Interrupts that request real time service for some equipment.
2. Interrupts generated by system software to give you the opportunity to perform some service.
3. Hardware and software interrupts that request error diagnosis and recovery or termination.
4. BIOS or DOS interrupts whose services you might want to modify.
5. Software interrupts that you might use to extend DOS and BIOS program services.

A Category 1 example is hardware Interrupt c, requested by the interrupt controller in response to a signal issued by serial port COM1 on the IRQ4 interrupt request line. Efficiency is usually a major design criterion for this kind of ISR. The PC BIOS provides two such ISRs, for the timer and keyboard Interrupts 8 and 9. Timer Interrupt 8 is executed at each tick of the system clock, about 18.2 times per second. The BIOS ISR updates the BIOS tick counter and in turn executes Interrupt 1c, which belongs to Category 2. The BIOS Interrupt 1c service routine is a dummy—a single **IRet** instruction. You are invited to redirect the corresponding interrupt vector to a custom ISR for any service that is needed at a certain clock time. Efficiency is likely to be a major design criterion for this kind of ISR, too.

Some similar BIOS and DOS interrupts are better placed in Category 3. For example, when BIOS ISR 9, executed in response to every keyboard event, detects a <Ctrl-Break> keystroke, it executes Interrupt 1b. If you redirect that vector from the dummy BIOS 1b ISR, you can tailor your own response to a user break signal.

Another example of Category 3 is the DOS *critical error* Interrupt 24. This occurs in response to a number of situations that ordinarily require user intervention, such as printer out of paper, or an attempt to write on a write protected diskette. The DOS ISR issues the familiar prompt

Abort, Retry, Fail

and acts according to your response. You may want to substitute your own routine to tailor the prompt to your own circumstances and disable the **Abort** and **Fail** responses. The MS-DOS *Encyclopedia*, Reference [28], Article 12, provides detailed information on the steps your ISR should follow to diagnose the error and react so that DOS can carry on properly.

The first two examples can be regarded simply as modifications of existing dummy BIOS ISRs. Category 4 includes more general situations where you might want to modify an existing service. For example, if you know that a program always obtains keyboard input through the standard BIOS Interrupt 16, you could change its behavior by modifying the corresponding BIOS ISR to alter the information it passes on about certain keystrokes. As a second example, on the author's system, DOS always reports, in response to a Function 44 I/O Control Service 8 request, that high-capacity diskette drive **e:** has a nonremovable medium. That causes the **Backup** utility to terminate whenever a diskette in **e:** is full, rather than to request a fresh diskette. This problem could be corrected by modifying the behavior of the DOS function call Interrupt 21 service routine in that one case.

Finally, there are many opportunities for extending the DOS and BIOS program services. One way to organize such an extension consistent with existing services is to use an otherwise unclaimed interrupt vector to obtain the new services from a memory resident program. This approach is now common. For example, the Blaise Computing Inc. interrupt driven serial communication package *Asynch Manager* and the Digital Research Inc. *Gem* screen interface are organized this way— see References [2,9].

Now, knowing how interrupts operate at the hardware level, and familiar with many situations that invite their use, consider the overall ISR installation and execution scheme depicted in Figure 9.1.1. This organization is simplified and idealized. The three entries correspond to three separate functions: ISR installation, execution, and removal. Installation consists of initializing the data area and terminating, remaining resident in memory. The data area is termed global, because it might serve more than one ISR installed by the same program, or more than one invocation of a reentrant ISR. Ideally, only the global data and the ISR code should remain resident, along with enough information to remove it. ISR removal is sometimes neglected, though it is polite, and often necessary, to provide for removal of memory resident software without rebooting the system. The service entry represents execution of the ISR itself via the interrupt vector. The ISR has access to the global data, and that data remains available until the whole system is removed.

What major problems will you encounter writing ISRs? Most can be classified under the headings

- filtering,
- prioritization,
- reentrancy, and
- high-level language.

The first of these is the simplest. Often you want to *modify or supplement, but not replace,* the action of an existing ISR. Thus your routine should be able to invoke the one to which the corresponding interrupt vector was formerly directed. This is easy enough—simply save the former value of the vector and use that to invoke the former ISR as appropriate.

You must be familiar with the interrupt prioritization scheme: which interrupts can preempt others, and when maskable interrupts are enabled or disabled. For example, you should remember that interrupt instructions themselves disable maskable interrupts; you must turn them on again or risk disrupting timer, communications, and keyboard

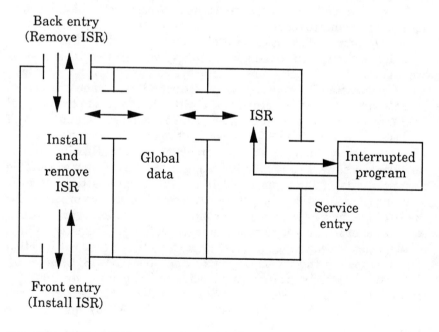

Figure 9.1.1 ISR installation, execution, and removal

services, for example. Moreover, you must send an end of interrupt (EOI) signal telling the interrupt controller to reenable interrupts of equal and lower priority when you have finished serving a maskable interrupt. On the other hand, you must protect your ISR from interruption by disabling maskable interrupts when time is critical or you are placing the interrupt system momentarily in an inconsistent state.

The most severe problems fall under the heading of reentrancy, or recursion. A timer Interrupt 1c must be able to interrupt its own service routine whenever that performs a task—such as an alarm triggered input/output operation—that requires more than one tick. More generally, various interrupts must be able to interrupt each other's service routines. Thus, your ISR often requires stack space sufficient for recursion. You can't assume that stacks set up by interrupted programs have enough free space to accommodate you; you must set up your own. On the other hand, you may want to *inhibit* an interrupt from reentering its own ISR. The BIOS Interrupt 5 PrtSc routine does this. As another example, you may have to prevent your custom keyboard handler from reinterpreting keystrokes while you let your user define a new keyboard macro.

The worst reentrancy problems stem from the fact that DOS isn't designed to facilitate recursion. When a DOS routine is invoked, it often stores necessary information in a global DOS variable. If it is interrupted, and the ISR itself calls for a DOS service, this variable may be overwritten. That usually causes a crash, sooner or later. For example, if the overwritten information was a return address, then the nested DOS service routine will return to the ISR, and the ISR to the original DOS routine (perhaps an hour later, in an extreme case), but that will get lost. Sections 9.2 and 9.3 discuss ways to avoid this trap.

Finally, you will encounter some problems writing ISRs in Turbo C that would occur with any high-level language. The common executable program units are programs and functions. Programs terminate by invoking DOS; functions, by a **Ret** instruction. There is no provision for the **IRet** instruction required to terminate an ISR. Moreover, parameters are generally passed to and from ISRs via the CPU registers. These problems are surmounted, at least in part, by the **interrupt** function type described in the Turbo C *User's guide,* Reference [8, Chapter 9]. However, the documentation is sketchy, and it's not clear that this feature fills all your needs. It will not be considered further. The Turbo C TOOLS ISR techniques discussed in Section 9.2 do meet all the requirements for a general ISR facility.

One remaining high-level language problem is speed. If you cannot make a Turbo C ISR fast enough, you will have to resort to in-line machine language code, or perhaps to an assembly language external procedure. Both techniques are used in Turbo C TOOLS.

9.2 Writing ISRs with Turbo C TOOLS

Concepts

ISR dispatcher and control blocks
ISR installation
Interrupt filtering
Sensing a custom ISR
Removing a memory resident program

In Section 9.1 you encountered a number of obstacles in the way of writing interrupt service routines in Turbo C. Several of these are surmounted by features of the Turbo C TOOLS package. This section describes its methods for installing, executing, and removing Turbo C ISRs. These techniques also support interrupt filtering, and provide stack support for reentrant ISRs. However, they do not directly attack the DOS reentrancy problems. A simplified demonstration program in this section presents the framework on which more realistic examples are constructed in the next.

ISR dispatcher and control blocks

Consider first two problems that must be solved to write a custom ISR in any higher-level language:

- It must have access to the CPU registers that may be used to transmit ISR parameters.
- The routine should return with an **IRet** instruction.

Turbo C provides a function type—**interrupt**—that seems to meet these needs. However, Turbo C TOOLS uses a different device, probably because its intricate ISR features were developed through several years' work with various compilers, whereas the **interrupt** type is peculiar to Turbo C. A Turbo C TOOLS ISR is declared like this:

void ISR(ALLREG *Register, ISRCTRL *ISRBlk, ISRMSG *S)

ALLREG is a data type defined in Figure 9.2.1, reproduced from Turbo C TOOLS header file **BUtil.H**. It combines all the features of the Turbo C Library header file **DOS.H** structures **REGS**, **SREGS**, and **REGPACK**. The **ISRCTRL** and **ISRMSG** data types are described in detail later.

Besides these structures, the Turbo C TOOLS ISR technique also involves the *ISR dispatcher:*

extern void isdispat(void)

This routine is an intermediary between the interrupted program and function **ISR**. To install **ISR**, you incorporate it in an ISR installation program along with the dispatcher and an *ISR control block* data structure of type **ISRCTRL**. Such a program can install service routines for several interrupts by using corresponding control blocks with a single dispatcher. The installation program terminates but remains memory resident after initializing some global data, as suggested by Figure 9.1.1. The dispatcher is written entirely in assembly language, assembled to an **.Obj** module, and included in the appropriate Turbo C TOOLS library file. The control block stores information for use in executing and

```
typedef struct {                    typedef union {
    unsigned char l;                    HALFREGS hl;
    unsigned char h; }                  unsigned x; }
  HALFREGS;                           DOUBLREG;

typedef struct {
    DOUBLREG ax,bx,cx,dx;           /* General registers. */
    unsigned si,di;                 /* Index    registers. */
    unsigned ds,es,ss,cs;           /* Segment registers. */
    unsigned flags,bp,sp,ip; }      /* Other    registers. */
  ALLREG;
```

Figure 9.2.1 Turbo C TOOLS data structure **ALLREG**

removing the custom ISR, including its address. The very first control block item consists of two machine language instructions: a **NoOp** and a far call to the dispatcher. The first is a harmless way to assure word alignment of the structure. The second consists of a far call opcode followed by the **isdispat** address. The installation program sets the appropriate interrupt vector to point to the control block. When the interrupt in question occurs, it pushes onto the stack then in use the flags register and return address for the interrupted program. The next instruction executed is the far call just mentioned, which pushes onto the same stack the address of the next item in the control block, then jumps to the dispatcher.

When the dispatcher begins execution, it knows the flags register and return address for the interrupted program, as well as the location of the control block, hence that of function **ISR**. Since its intermediary role requires complex stack and segment register manipulations, the dispatcher must store the interrupted program's register values and transmit them later to **ISR** via the **ALLREG** parameter. It must secure proper storage for that parameter again when **ISR** is finished, and use it to reset the registers just before returning to the interrupted program.

Thus, the dispatcher's first task is to stack all the registers. Next, it alters the stack slightly so that it will return not to the control block, but to the appropriate address in the interrupted program. That address was stacked earlier by the interrupt. The dispatcher sets up a new stack for function **ISR** to use; it can't assume that the interrupted program's is large enough to meet the **ISR** stack storage needs. Now reconsider the **ISR** calling sequence:

void ISR(ALLREG *Register, ISRCTRL *ISRBlk, ISRMSG *S)

Before calling **ISR** the dispatcher must build the **ALLREG** and **ISRMSG** structures **Register** and **S**, and modify the ISR control block **ISRBlk** if necessary. (It obtains the initial version of the control block from the installation program.) Then it must place addresses of these structures on the **ISR** stack. The dispatcher secures the interrupt service simply by calling **ISR**, emulating the Turbo C function call

ISR(&Register,&ISRBlk,&S)

When **ISR** returns, the dispatcher must process the parameters, discard the **ISR** stack, give the registers the values specified by the **ALLREG** structure, and return to the interrupted program.

The general ISR installation, execution, and removal scheme of Figure 9.1.1 is modified and redisplayed in Figure 9.2.2 to show the Turbo C TOOLS ISR control block and dispatcher technique. The main entry is for ISR installation only; removal is a separate process. During installation, the illustrated program sets up the control block and dispatcher and other global data as needed. ISR execution requires separate service entry and exit. Entry is via the control block and dispatcher; exit bypasses the control block.

Details of the Turbo C TOOLS function that constructs an ISR control block are discussed later, with a demonstration program. Before that, consider just what *must* be recorded there, for the dispatcher and the ISR to function as just outlined. You've seen already that the control block includes the far call to the dispatcher, hence the dispatcher address, and the address of the ISR function itself. The machine language used by the ISR to access the global data area assumes that the DS and ES registers have been set to the appropriate segments for the ISR. This would not ordinarily be the case after the interrupt: these registers would still be set to whatever values they had in the interrupted program. Therefore, the installation program must store register values **_DS** and **_ES** in the

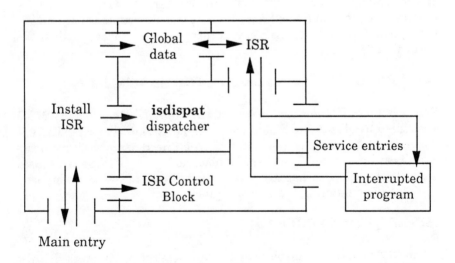

Figure 9.2.2 Turbo C TOOLS ISR installation and execution

control block, and the dispatcher must set those registers before calling the ISR. Also, in order to filter interrupts—i.e., execute the routine to which the interrupt vector was directed before your custom ISR installation—your ISR must have access to the previous vector. The installation program keeps that in the control block as well. It is thus accessible to your ISR, because the control block is itself part of the global data area. Of course, the previous vector value must also be used when you remove your custom ISR.

Three items are included in the cntrol block to facilitate recognizing it. First is a Blaise Computing Inc. signature of type **unsigned**. Second is its ones complement (produced with the ~ operator). Third is a string of sixteen characters that identifies this particular custom ISR. A program that knows the Turbo C TOOLS ISR technique can thus ascertain whether an interrupt vector points to an ISR control block, and if so, inspect its identification string. Thus, you can avoid installing a second copy of an ISR that is already present, and insure that a custom ISR that you're about to remove is really the one you intend.

Figure 9.2.3 is the complete ISR control block type definition from header file **BIntrupt.H**. Comments of the form /* >> ... << */ identify items that have not yet been discussed. Several of these—**iret_opcode**, **control**, **status**, and **scratch**—seem to be relics from earlier versions. The ISR installation functions initialize them, but they are not used. The installation program PSP segment address is stored in **isrpsp** for use when you remove the ISR, and for updating DOS' record of the currently executing process (see the last paragraph of this section). The remaining items are concerned with stack provisions for reentrant ISRs; they are described later.

The greatest difficulty that the ISR dispatcher must overcome is recursion. Since a hardware interrupt may well interrupt its own service routine, several ISR invocations may be active at once. Actually, only one copy of the ISR code is ever loaded (by the installation program), but the dispatcher creates a separate stack for each invocation. The installation program must choose a stack size and a limit to the number of nested invocations: ISR control block items **isrstksize** and **limit**. Further, it must allocate for these stacks a memory block of **isrstksize * limit** bytes, and set ISR control block item **isrstk** to point to it. Items **level** and **isrsp** keep track of the number of invocations currently active, and the bottom (highest address) of the stack for the current invocation. Roughly,

isrsp = isrstk + level*isrstksize.

```
#define ISRCTRL struct isr_control        /* ISR control block */
struct isr_control {
    unsigned fcall_opcode;       /* NoOp & far call  opcodes.     */
    void (far *isrdisp)();       /* ISR  dispatcher address.      */
    unsigned iret_opcode;        /* >> IRet  &  RetF opcodes.  << */
    char far *isrstk;            /* >> Beginning, size of  ISR  << */
    unsigned isrstksize;         /* >> stacks.  Pointer to stack << */
    unsigned isrsp;              /* >> for current invocation.  << */
    unsigned isrds;              /* DS  value for  ISR.           */
    unsigned isres;              /* ES  value for  ISR.           */
    void (far *isr)(ALLREG *,    /* ISR  address.                 */
        ISRCTRL *, ISRMSG *);
    unsigned isrpsp;             /* >> Installing program PSP. << */
    void far *prev_vec;          /* Previous interrupt vector.    */
    unsigned level;              /* >> Current recursion depth. << */
    unsigned limit;              /* >> Maximum recursion depth. << */
    unsigned signature;          /* Signature of this structure.  */
    unsigned sign2;              /* Ones complement of signature. */
    char      ident[16];         /* Identification string.        */
    unsigned control;            /* Not used.                     */
    unsigned status;             /* Not used.                     */
    char      scratch[10]; }     /* Not used.                     */
```

Figure 9.2.3 Turbo C TOOLS data structure **ISRCTRL**

(The exact interpretation of this equation depends on how **isrstk** was allocated and the memory model in use. In any case, **isrsp** is redundant, hence a likely source of misunderstanding.) The installation program initializes **level** to zero and **isrsp** accordingly.

Before invoking an ISR the dispatcher asks whether

level < limit.

If not, there is no ISR stack space left, and the dispatcher returns gracefully to the interrupted program, but provides no service. (This may cause a crash later anyway, particularly if the interrupt was generated by the 8259 and required an EOI signal from the service routine.) If there is stack space remaining, the dispatcher increments **level** and **isrsp** and loads new stack segment and pointer register values SS:SP computed from **isrstk** and **isrsp**. At this point, the new ISR stack is active. (According to the Turbo C TOOLS source code, the Turbo C stack overflow detection mechanism is adjusted to reflect the new stack size. Since that Turbo C feature is inadequately documented, this coup is difficult to verify.)

Each time one of its interrupts occurs, the ISR dispatcher is invoked. How does Turbo C TOOLS provide reentrancy for the dispatcher? The values of its local variables are always associated with particular ISR invocations, and are kept on the appropriate ISR stack. When the dispatcher is invoked, it stores the interrupted program's registers on the stack then active, saves a pointer to them in register BX, generates the ISR stack, and switches stacks as described in the previous paragraph. Using BX as a pointer, the dispatcher copies the stored information to an **ALLREG** structure on the new stack, builds the required **ISRMSG** structure (described later), and stacks any other variables and register values local to this ISR invocation. Next, it loads registers DS and ES with the appropriate values for the ISR, stored in ISR control block items **isrds** and **isres** by the installation program. Finally, the dispatcher stacks pointers to the **ISRMSG** structure, the ISR control block, and the **ALLREG** structure—the ISR calling sequence—and calls the ISR.

When the ISR returns, the dispatcher pops from the ISR stack all the information it saved there, restoring required values of registers and local variables, including the contents of **ISRMSG** structure. Using the addresses in various restored registers, it pops the **ALLREG** values, perhaps modified by the ISR, back into their original locations in the stack that was active when the dispatcher was originally invoked, then restores SS:SP to the values they had just before it switched to the ISR stack. At this point that original stack is active again; the dispatcher discards the ISR stack by decrementing ISR control block items **level** and **isrsp**. Finally, the interrupted program's registers are restored by popping the stack, which restores SS:SP to the values they had just after the original interrupt. The dispatcher executes an **IRet** instruction to return to the interrupted program.

The **ISRMSG** data structure is defined in header file **BIntrupt.H**:

```
typedef struct {             /* Structure for    */
     int    exit_style;      /* ISR/dispatcher   */
       unsigned working_flags; }   /* messages.   */
ISRMSG;
```

Before calling an ISR, the dispatcher sets **exit_style** = 0 and places in **working_flags** a copy of the flags register as it appeared when the dispatcher was invoked—i.e., the interrupted program's flags. The ISR may set **exit_style** = 1 and change **working_flags**. In that event, the dispatcher will restore the interrupted program's flags register from **working_flags** and return via a far return instead of an **IRet**. (The latter instruction would restore the flags from a copy of the interrupted program's original flags, which is still on the stack; the far return leaves that copy on the stack.) This Turbo C TOOLS feature implements a suggestion in the DOS *Technical reference* manual, Reference [18], concerning ISRs for the User Break and Critical Error Interrupts 23 and 24.

ISR installation

Turbo C TOOLS provides a function that does most of the work for your custom ISR installation program:

```
int isinstal(int N,
        void (*ISR)(ALLREG *Register,
                ISRCTRL *ISRBlk,
                ISRMSG *S),
        char *ID,
    ISRCTRL *ControlBlock,
        char *Stacks,
        int   StackSize,
        int   MaxDepth)
```

You must allocate memory for **ControlBlock** and **Stacks**. The latter must accommodate **MaxDepth** stacks of **StackSize** bytes each. **MaxDepth** is the maximum recursion depth—the maximum number of stacks that need be active at once. The **ID** string identifies your custom service routine **ISR** for Interrupt **N**: it must be exactly sixteen characters long, including any terminal zero. **isinstal** also sets the interrupt vector to point to the far call instruction in the control block, and returns its former value. The dispatcher **isdispat** is declared as an external function in **isprep**, a function called by **isinstal**. Thus, when your program terminates, remaining resident in memory, the dispatcher is loaded. Your ISR is loaded as well, since it is a function in the installation program.

Figure 9.2.4 shows a prototype custom ISR function **ISR** with an installation program **ISInstal.Dem**. This ISR merely beeps to announce its execution. Use command line parameters to specify the interrupt number and the identification string: for example, enter

ISInstal 5 ThomasIsPeeping

```
/*****************************************************************/
/* ISInstal.Dem    Demonstrate functions  isinstal  and     */
/*                 isresext:  install a   Turbo C TOOLS  ISR */
/*                 function.  Use the interrupt and  ID      */
/***************************************** specified on the   */
                                        /* command line. Allo-*/
#include <BIntrupt.H>                   /* cate a  1K  stack. */
#include  <General.H>                   /***********************/

void ISR(ALLREG  *Registers,            /* Turbo C TOOLS  cus- */
         ISRCTRL *ISRBlk,               /* tom  ISR:  it       */
         ISRMSG  *S) {                  /* beeps.  Beep  is in */
 Beep; }                                /* General.H.          */

#define StackSize 1024                  /* This routine is not */
#define MaxDepth     1                  /* reentrant.  Don't   */
char    Stacks[StackSize*MaxDepth];     /* press  <Shift-PrtSc>*/
 ISRCTRL ControlBlock;                  /* during a beep!      */

void main(int    ParamCount,
          char *ParamStr[]) {
int N = strtol(ParamStr[1],            /* Get interrupt number*/
          (char **) NULL,16);          /* from command line.  */
printf("Touch  <CR>  to install"
  "  ISR  %d,  or  <Ctrl-Break>"       /* Second thoughts?    */
  "  to terminate.",N);
getch();                               /* Wait for keystroke. */
isinstal(N,ISR,ParamStr[2],           /* Install ISR.        */
  &ControlBlock,Stacks,StackSize,      /* Terminate, remaining*/
    MaxDepth);                         /* resident, setting   */
isresext(0); }                         /* ErrorLevel = 0.     */
```

Figure 9.2.4 Program **ISInstal.Dem**

to install **ISR** to serve PrtSc Interrupt 5, with a memorable ID string. Enter the interrupt number in hex: the installation program calls Turbo C Library function **strtol** to convert a hex numeral to the required **int** value.

To return and set interrupt vectors, **isinstal** uses Turbo C TOOLS routines

void far *isgetvec(int N)
void isputvec(int N, void far *V)

These are defined as macros in header file **BIntrupt.H**, using type casting and the Turbo C TOOLS functions **getvect** and **putvect** already mentioned in Section 8.5. Because they don't involve the Turbo C **interrupt** type, the Turbo C TOOLS macros are easier to use.

To terminate a program but keep it memory resident, you may use Turbo C Library function

void keep(int ErrorLevel, int Size)

This frees the memory allocated to the resident program, except for the first **Size** bytes. It sets the DOS **ErrorLevel** variable as specified, and terminates, remaining resident. This function is implemented as a call to DOS Function 31. Usually, as in program **ISInstal.Dem**, you'll want to retain all memory, perhaps after you free whatever's no longer necessary. The program uses Turbo C TOOLS function

void isresext(int ErrorLevel)

for this purpose. This routine is implemented as a macro in header file **BIntrupt.H**, using **keep** and the Turbo C TOOLS function **mmsize** discussed earlier in Section 7.2.

To test the installation process, enter the command suggested earlier to install **ISR** to serve PrtSc Interrupt 5. Now, when you touch <Shift-PrtSc>, you get no screen hardcopy, just a beep. *Warning!* At this point, you have no way to restore the original PrtSc service, or the original value of any interrupt vector altered by **isinstal**, short of rebooting. You will see later how to construct a program to restore the previous vector.

Interrupt filtering

Many ISRs *filter* interrupts: when they gain control, they handle some special situations themselves, but invoke the previously installed ISR to process ordinary events. The Turbo C TOOLS installation process just described preserves the address of the previous ISR in ISR control block item **prev_vec**. Using that to invoke the previous ISR presents a minor problem: the ISR expects to be invoked by an interrupt, not called by a Turbo C program. You could store **prev_vec** in a temporary interrupt vector and use that with Turbo C Library function **geninterrupt** to invoke the ISR. This solution doesn't work, however, if that vector is needed by other software, particularly before your program can regain control to restore its original value.

Turbo C TOOLS function

int iscall(void far *ISR, ALLREG *R)

provides a cleaner solution. This assembly language routine copies into the registers the values stored in the **ALLREG** structure, then executes the specified **ISR** via a far call instruction. You can test this by making a slight alteration to function **ISR** in Figure 9.2.4. Invoke **iscall** before **Beep**, as follows:

```
void ISR(ALLREG *R,
         ISRCTRL *ISRBlk,
         ISRMSG *S) {
iscall(ISRBlk->prev_vec,Registers);
Beep; }
```

If you use **ISInstal.Dem** to install this routine as a PrtSc Interrupt 5 service, then touching <Shift-PrtSc> will give you a beep as well as a hardcopy.

Sensing a custom ISR

The **ident** field in the ISR control block makes it possible to detect whether your custom ISR is in fact installed to serve a specific interrupt vector. You can use that knowledge to avoid installing multiple copies of the same ISR. Moreover, you can extract from the control block sufficient information to remove your ISR and restore the previous service for that vector. Part of this task is performed by Turbo C TOOLS function **issense**:

ISRCTRL far *issense(void far *P, char *ID)

If **P** points to an ISR control block whose **ident** item agrees with **ID**, this function returns **P**, recast to the indicated type. Otherwise, it returns a far null pointer.

Removing a memory resident program

You can remove a memory resident program with specified PSP segment address via Turbo C TOOLS function

int isremove(unsigned PSPSeg)

This returns zero to indicate success, or else a DOS error code. This function follows the chain of DOS memory control blocks upward from the indicated PSP, its associated environment block, or the block of the current program, releasing all blocks that belong to the indicated PSP. (See Section 7.2.)

Function **RstorISR**, shown in Figure 9.2.5, uses **issense** and **isremove** to remove a Turbo C TOOLS custom ISR and restore the corresponding vector to its former state; it returns a code indicating success or failure. You may want to construct a demonstration program that uses it to remove ISRs installed by program **ISInstal.Dem**, as noted earlier. *Warning!* You may install several custom ISRs with a single installation program somewhat like **ISInstal.Dem**. **RstorISR** will remove all of them—not just the one you specify with its **Interrupt** and **ID** parameters!

Changing the current PSP

Certain DOS services, like opening a file and allocating a memory block, affect the *currently executing program*. DOS records its PSP segment

```
/****************************************************************/
/* RstorISR.C    Function RstorISR: Remove a Turbo C       */
/*              TOOLS ISR for a specified interrupt, pro- */
/* vided its control block has a specified ident field. Re-*/
/* store the interrupt vector to its previous value. Return */
/*******************************************  values:       */
                                           /*               */
#include  <General.H>                      /* 0  Success    */
#include <BIntrupt.H>                      /* 2  No such ISR */
                                           /* 7  MCB destroyed */
int RstorISR(int N, char *ID) {            /* 9  Invalid MCB */
  ISRCTRL far *ISRBlk;                      /********************/
ISRBlk = issense(isgetvec(N),ID);
if (FARNULL == ISRBlk) return 2;           /* FARNULL  is a far */
isputvec(N,ISRBlk->prev_vec);              /* null pointer.     */
return isremove(ISRBlk->isrpsp); }
```

Figure 9.2.5 Function **RstorISR**

address, and updates that record when it terminates or executes a program. This record does not change, however, when a program is interrupted and a memory resident ISR begins executing. In order to use such DOS services reliably, an ISR must

- copy and remember the current PSP address,
- substitute its own PSP address,
- obtain and use the DOS services, and
- restore the current PSP address,

before returning to the interrupted program. To help perform these tasks, Turbo C TOOLS includes function

unsigned iscurprc(int Option, unsigned NewPSP)

You set **Option = IS_SETPROC** or **IS_RETPROC** to set or ascertain the current PSP. The function returns the current PSP, then, if required, changes the recorded address to **NewPSP**. The prototype and macro constants for **Option** are in header file **BIntrupt.H**. The function is implemented via DOS functions 50 and 51, neither of which is documented.

9.3 Example custom ISRs

Concepts

User tick routine **TimerISR** that beeps periodically
Sending EOI signal
Keyboard routine **KBDISR** that detects <P-Q> keystroke
PrtSc routine that sends formatted hardcopy to a file
DOS critical sections
Ascertaining whether DOS services are available

This section is devoted to three custom interrupt service routines: one for the user tick Interrupt 1c, one for keyboard Interrupt 9, and one for the PrtSc Interrupt 5. Together, they illustrate most of the problems you will encounter while writing ISRs with Turbo C and Turbo C TOOLS. (You won't meet one type of problem here, though: the efficiency of Turbo C itself. If speed is of paramount importance, you may have to resort to assembly language.) The keyboard ISR also demonstrates some advanced keyboard handling techniques beyond the scope of Chapter 5. Because the custom PrtSc ISR requires DOS file manipulation, it meets obstacles that are insurmountable with the techniques described here. Those are handled by the *intervention routine* methods discussed in Section 9.4.

User tick ISR that beeps periodically

The first example ISR in this section is a service routine **TimerISR** for the user tick Interrupt 1c. The BIOS tick Interrupt 8 service routine executes Interrupt 1c just after it updates the tick counter. You are invited to provide a custom service routine to replace the dummy BIOS 1c ISR. Your ISR will thus be executed at each tick, or about 18.2 times per second. In this example, **TimerISR** decrements a tick **Countdown** variable. If the resulting value is zero, the ISR resets **Countdown** to ten seconds (182 ticks) then beeps for half a second. Therefore, when **TimerISR** is installed, you hear a beep every ten seconds. The source code is shown in Figure 9.3.1. It's quite simple—this example was chosen for that quality. **TimerISR** is an interrupt filter—its first action invokes whatever routine previously served the user tick interrupt. Therefore, previously installed tick services—on the author's system, a screen clock—will continue to function even after **TimerISR** is installed. The Section 8.7 function **Peep** is used here; the usual **putchar('\a')** doesn't work—probably because it calls DOS.

There is one complication. Since the timer tick, hence the countdown, must continue during the beep, **TimerISR** must be interruptible by **Int 8**. Since **TimerISR** was invoked by the Interrupt 8 ISR, that ISR must be interruptible by its own interrupt. The interrupt controller will not allow that unless you send it an EOI signal. Therefore, just before the beep, **TimerISR** sends **EOI** = hex 20 to port **IntA00** = hex 20. (This terminology stems from an identifier used in the PC BIOS code.) Because the Interrupt 8 ISR has essentially completed its work by this time, its code presents no reentrancy problem. However, when installing **TimerISR**, you must provide stack space for two simultaneous invocations.

Program **TimerISR.Dem**, that installs and removes **TimerISR**, is also shown in Figure 9.3.1. It uses the framework introduced with program **ISInstal.Dem** in Figure 9.2.4. Its first action, however, is to use function **RStorISR**, described in the previous section, to remove **TimerISR** if it is installed. If it was not, **RStorISR** returns code 2 and **TimerISR.Dem** proceeds to initialize the countdown and install the custom ISR with Turbo C TOOLS function **isinstal**. **TimerISR.Dem** also allocates space for two 1K ISR stacks.

Detecting simultaneous <P> and <Q> keystrokes

The next example is a custom keyboard Interrupt 9 service routine **KBDISR**. Demonstration program **KBDISR.Dem** installs it, then accepts and echoes keyboard input so that you can observe the ISR in action. **KBDISR** is typical in reacting to a certain combination of keyboard events—in this case simultaneous <P> and <Q> keystrokes— but processing all other keyboard events as usual. Thus, like **TimerISR**, it is an interrupt filter. It handles all keyboard input, takes special action if necessary, then executes the BIOS keyboard ISR to process ordinary keystrokes. The special <P-Q> keystroke simply causes it to beep. Of course, you could apply the same technique to invoke a more complex reaction. This example was chosen for several reasons:

```
/*****************************************************************/
/* TimerISR.Dem     Install and remove a custom user tick  ISR*/
/*                  to beep for half a second every ten sec-  */
/* onds.  The  ISR  must interrupt itself to count time during*/
/* a beep, so allocate two  1K  ISR  stacks.  TimerISR  tog-  */
/****************************************** gles the custom  ISR*/
                                         /* on and off.        */
                                         /************************/
#include <BIntrupt.H>
#include  <General.H>

int       Countdown;                     /* Global variable.   */
#define   TenSeconds   182               /* 10 sec  in ticks.  */
#define   IntA00       0x20              /* Interrupt control  */
#define   EOI          0x20              /* port and  EOI  code.*/

void TimerISR(ALLREG  *Registers,        /* Custom  ISR.       */
              ISRCTRL *ISRBlk,
              ISRMSG  *S) {              /* Call previous  ISR. */
iscall(ISRBlk->prev_vec,Registers);      /* When  Countdown  ex-*/
if (--Countdown) return;                 /* pires, restart it,  */
Countdown = TenSeconds;                  /* tell  8259  to let  */
outportb(IntA00,EOI);                    /* timer tick interrupt*/
Peep(); }                                /* sound, then beep.   */

iscall(ISRBlk->prev_vec,Registers);      /* Call previous  ISR. */
if (--Countdown) return;                 /* When  Countdown  ex-*/
Countdown = TenSeconds;                  /* pires, restart it,  */
outportb(IntA00,EOI);                    /* tell the  8259  to  */
sound(440);                              /* let the timer tick  */
delay(1000);                             /* interrupt the sound,*/
nosound(); }                             /* then beep.          */

#define UserTickInterrupt   0x1c         /* Interrupt number.   */
#define ID    "10 Sec  Sounder"          /* ISR  identification.*/
#define StackSize          1024          /* 2nd  stack for ser- */
#define MaxDepth              2          /* vice during sound.  */
char    Stacks[StackSize*MaxDepth];
ISRCTRL ControlBlock;

void main() {                            /* Remove the  ISR if */
if (RstorISR(UserTickInterrupt,ID)       /* it's present.  Oth- */
    == 2) {                              /* erwise, start count-*/
```

Figure 9.3.1 Program **TimerISR.Dem** (*Continued on next page*)

```
Countdown = TenSeconds;              /* down and install      */
isinstal(UserTickInterrupt,          /* TimerISR  with spec-  */
    TimerISR,ID,&ControlBlock,       /* ified  ID  & stacks;  */
        Stacks,StackSize,MaxDepth);  /* terminate,  staying   */
isresext(0); }}                      /* memory resident.      */
```

Figure 9.3.1 *(Continued)* Program **TimerISR.Dem**

- It displays realistically several Turbo C TOOLS ISR features.
- It isn't complicated by timing considerations.
- It uses very sophisticated keyboard handling methods, complementing those discussed in Chapter 5.

Demonstration program **PQ.Dem**, shown in Figure 9.3.2, contains global variables, installation code, the keyboard input test loop, and code to remove the ISR and restore the original BIOS Interrupt 9 service. Since **KBDISR** serves a maskable interrupt, the interrupt controller will not allow it to interrupt itself: space for only one ISR stack is required. **KBDISR** uses three global variables: **PDown, QDown,** and **FirstKey**. The first two are **Boolean** variables that record the status of the warm keys <P> and <Q>. (**Boolean** variables have values 0,1 = **False,True**; the type is defined in this book's header file **General.H**.) When **KBDISR** detects a warm keystroke, it must remember the full keystroke code—ASCII as well as scan code—in order to interpret it properly later if it's not the first of a hot <P-Q> pair. **FirstKey** stores this code. Its initial value zero indicates that no code is stored.

The **PQ.Dem** keyboard input test loop simply reads and writes one character at a time until you touch <CR>. You'll notice that all keystrokes are processed normally except that

- <P> and <Q> are echoed only after they're released;
- the <P-Q> combination (in either order) produces a beep but no echo.

There are also some minor differences in behavior when you hold down one of the warm keys and strike others, and when you type fast enough to fill the buffer.

After every keyboard event—keystroke or release—the keyboard controller requests service with a signal on interrupt request line IRQ1.

```
/*****************************************************************/
/* PQ.Dem    Install and demonstrate a custom keyboard In-    */
/*           terrupt 9 service routine KBDISR, that beeps */
/* when you press  P  and  Q  simultaneously, but processes   */
/* other keyboard events as usual.  The demonstration reads   */
/******************************************** and echoes key-   */
                                     /* strokes until you      */
#include <BIntrupt.H>                /* press  <CR>.           */
#include  <General.H>                /************************/

Boolean  PDown     = False;          /* Are  P,Q  down?        */
Boolean  QDown     = False;          /* FirstKey is 1st        */
unsigned FirstKey = 0;               /* of possible <P-Q>.     */

#define  KBD_Int    9                /* Interrupt number.      */
#define  ID         "Watch  Ps & Qs!" /* ISR  identification.*/
#define  StackSize  1024             /* This  ISR  isn't       */
#define  MaxDepth   1                /* reentrant, so one      */
char     Stack[StackSize*MaxDepth];  /* stack suffices.        */
ISRCTRL  ControlBlock;

void KBDISR(ALLREG *Registers,       /* Prototype.             */
            ISRCTRL *ISRBlk,
            ISRMSG *S);

void main() {
  char Ch;
printf("KBDISR  test:   ");
isinstal(KBD_Int,KBDISR,ID,          /* Install  KBDISR        */
  &ControlBlock,Stack,StackSize,     /* with specified  ID     */
    MaxDepth);                       /* and stack.             */
do Ch = getche();                    /* Process keystrokes     */
  while (Ch != CR);                  /* until  <CR>.           */
RstorISR(KBD_Int,ID); }              /* Restore  BIOS  ISR.    */
```

Figure 9.3.2 Program **PQ.Dem**

Simultaneously it places in CPU port **KB_Data** = hex 60 an event code. For a keystroke, that's just the scan code; for a release, add 128. The interrupt controller responds with a request for Interrupt 9. This invokes the custom ISR function **KBDISR** via the Turbo C TOOLS interrupt dispatcher **isdispat** as described in Section 9.2. Although **KBDISR** is an interrupt filter, which lets the BIOS Interrupt 9 service routine process most keyboard events as usual, it mustn't invoke the BIOS ISR immediately, because the BIOS doesn't preserve enough information about the event. To detect simultaneous depression of two keys, you must monitor both the keystrokes and corresponding releases. The BIOS ISR enters keystrokes <P> and <Q> into the keyboard buffer, but ignores the releases. Therefore, **KBDISR** must first inspect port **KB_Data** to detect these events. You may follow its source code, shown in Figure 9.3.3.

Imitating the BIOS ISR, **KBDISR** reads the **Event** code from **KB_Data** and another byte simply called **Code** from port **KB_Ctrl** = hex 61. The latter is a read/write port used for sending control codes to the keyboard. **KBDISR** needs to ascertain its current setting, to restore it after informing the keyboard that the event has been processed.

If the **Event** code indicates a warm keystroke, then **KBDISR** records that in global variable **PDown** or **QDown**. The <P-Q> keystroke is betrayed by the condition **PDown = QDown = True**. When this holds, **KBDISR** beeps, reinitializes these variables and **FirstKey**, and prepares to return. So far, according to this description, it has not seemed necessary for **KBDISR** to invoke the BIOS—or the previous ISR—to process warm keys. (Sometimes, though, you may want to pass on a special hot keystroke combination for routine processing after your custom ISR has done its job.) However, a major problem occurs if the BIOS doesn't process a warm keystroke that is not, in fact, part of a hot <P-Q> combination. This difficulty is described later; global variable **FirstKey** is part of the solution of the problem.

The BIOS ISR normally performs some housekeeping tasks before it returns. Because it does not always invoke the BIOS, **KBDISR** calls procedure **CleanUp** to do the same job. Its source code is at the end of Figure 9.3.3. **CleanUp** sets one bit of the control byte saved in variable **Code**, and sends the resulting byte to port **KB_Ctrl** to inform the keyboard controller that the current event has been processed, so that a new one can be signalled. Next, the original value of **Code** is output to restore the original status. Finally, the end of interrupt EOI code is sent to port **IntA00** to inform the interrupt controller that the current maskable interrupt service is complete. (This allows the controller to honor interrupts of equal or lower priority.)

A major difficulty arises when **KBDISR** detects a warm keystroke that is *unmatched*—not the second of a <P-Q> pair. It may be the first of such

```
/****************************************************************/
/* KBDISR.C      Custom  Turbo C TOOLS  keyboard  Interrupt 9  */
/*                service routine  KBDISR,  that beeps when you */
/*******************************press  P  and  Q  simulta-*/
                               /* but processes other key-   */
#include <BIntrupt.H>          /* board events as usual.      */
#include <General.H>           /****************************/

extern Boolean  PDown,QDown;
extern unsigned FirstKey;

void PutFirstKey(void);                    /* Prototypes.     */
void GetFirstKey(void);


#define  KB_Data      0x60      /* KBD  scan code and con-     */
#define  KB_Ctrl      0x61      /* trol ports,  <P>,<Q>  scan*/
#define  P            25        /* codes, and some  BIOS      */
#define  Q            16        /* data segment variables.    */
#define  BIOSData     0x0040
#define  BufferHead   (unsigned far *) MK_FP(BIOSData,0x001a)
#define  BufferTail   (unsigned far *) MK_FP(BIOSData,0x001c)

void CleanUp(int Code) {            /* Imitate the  BIOS:  reset  */
outportb(KB_Ctrl,Code|0x80);       /* keyboard and send  EOI  to */
outportb(KB_Ctrl,Code);            /* the  8259.  Code  was input*/
outportb(IntA00,EOI); }            /* earlier from  KB_Ctrl port.*/

void KBDISR(ALLREG  *Registers,        /* Custom  ISR  that    */
            ISRCTRL *ISRBlk,           /* beeps when  P,Q  are*/
            ISRMSG  *S) {              /* pressed together.    */
  unsigned FormerTail;
  char     Code  = inportb(KB_Ctrl);   /* Input keyboard con-  */
  char     Event = inportb(KB_Data);   /* trol, event codes.   */

 if ((Event == P) || (Event == Q)) {   /* If event is  <P> or */
     if (Event == P) PDown = True;      /* <Q>,  note that the  */
     else            QDown = True;      /* key's down.          */
     if (PDown && QDown) {              /* If both are down,    */
         Beep;                          /* then beep,           */
         PDown = QDown = False;         /* forget any depressed */
         FirstKey = 0;                  /* keys,                */
         CleanUp(Code); }               /* and clean up.        */
```

Figure 9.3.3 Custom ISR function **KBDISR** (*Continued on next page*)

```
      else {                            /* If only one's down,  */
        FormerTail = *BufferTail;       /* call  BIOS,  so you  */
        iscall(ISRBlk->prev_vec,        /* can buffer the key   */
        iscall(ISRBlk->prev_vec,        /* can buffer the key   */
          Registers);                   /* later if it's not    */
        if (*BufferTail != FormerTail)  /* hot.  Store buffered */
          GetFirstKey(); }}             /* code in FirstKey.    */
  else {                                /* BIOS  cleans up.     */
    Event -= 128;
    if ((Event==P) || (Event==Q)) {     /* If  P  or  Q  was    */
      if (Event == P) PDown = False;    /* released, note that. */
        else          QDown = False;    /* Buffer the corre-    */
      PutFirstKey();                    /* sponding keystroke.  */
      CleanUp(Code); }                  /* Clean up—the  BIOS   */
    else                                /* hasn't.              */
      iscall(ISRBlk->prev_vec,          /* Let  BIOS  handle    */
        Registers); }}                  /* other events.        */
if ((Event == P) || (Event == Q)) {     /* If event is  <P>  or*/
  if (Event == P) PDown = True;         /* <Q>,  note that the  */
    else          QDown = True;         /* key's down.          */
  if (PDown && QDown) {                 /* If both are down,    */
    Beep;                               /* then beep,           */
    PDown = QDown = False;              /* forget any depressed */
    FirstKey = 0;                       /* keys,                */
    CleanUp(Code); }                    /* and clean up.        */
  else {                                /* If only one's down,  */
    FormerTail = *BufferTail;           /* call  BIOS,  so you  */
    iscall(ISRBlk->prev_vec,            /* can buffer the key   */
      Registers);                       /* later if it's not    */
    if (*BufferTail != FormerTail)      /* hot.  Store buffered */
      GetFirstKey(); }}                 /* code in FirstKey.    */
  else {                                /* BIOS  cleans up.     */
    Event -= 128;
    if ((Event==P) || (Event==Q)) {     /* If  P  or  Q  was    */
      if (Event == P) PDown = False;    /* released, note that. */
        else          QDown = False;    /* Buffer the corre-    */
      PutFirstKey();                    /* sponding keystroke.  */
      CleanUp(Code); }                  /* Clean up—the  BIOS   */
    else                                /* hasn't.              */
      iscall(ISRBlk->prev_vec,          /* Let  BIOS  handle    */
        Registers); }}                  /* other events.        */
```

Figure 9.3.3 *(Continued)* Custom ISR function **KBDISR**

a pair, or an ordinary keystroke. These alternatives are distinguished by which of two later events occurs first: depressing the complementary warm key, or releasing the first one. You have already seen that in the first event, neither warm keystroke should be buffered. However, in the second, the unmatched warm keystroke should be. This means that an unmatched warm keystroke should be remembered, in case it must be buffered later.

At first thought, remembering seems simple; then you realize that you must check all shift and toggle keys to discover the ASCII/IBM code to place in the buffer later with the event code. (Does keystroke <P> represent P, p, ^P, or is it part of <Alt-P>?) The foolproof way to find that code is to let the BIOS process the keystroke. This is possible, because the data that the BIOS must read from ports **KB_Data** and **KB_Ctrl** is still there. (Reading from a port is nondestructive.) Therefore, at this point, **KBDISR** uses Turbo C TOOLS routine **iscall** to invoke the BIOS ISR; its address is available in the ISR control block, saved when **KBDISR** was installed. The BIOS interprets the keystroke and buffers the event and ASCII/IBM code—unless the buffer is full. That outcome can be detected *a fortiori* by checking whether the BIOS changed the value of its **BufferTail** variable: entering data at the tail of a circular queue always changes the tail pointer. If **BufferTail** indicated that the buffer was full, **KBDISR** gives up—it's too hard to remember the unmatched warm keystroke. However, **BufferTail** usually does change, and in that case you must *remove* from the buffer the information that the BIOS just put there. You can't use the standard BIOS Interrupt 16 keyboard input service, because that removes data from the *head* of the queue, not the tail. **KBDISR** calls its own routine **GetFirstKey** to move an entry from the buffer tail to global variable **FirstKey**. **KBDISR** can now return, and it need not call procedure **CleanUp**, because the BIOS just did the required housekeeping.

When **KBDISR** detects release of a warm key, it updates **Boolean** variable **PDown** or **QDown** accordingly. If it was remembering this keystroke for later buffering, it must do that now, using function **PutFirstKey**, the complement to **GetFirstKey**, to move an item from global variable **FirstKey** to the buffer tail. **KBDISR** must now call **CleanUp** for housekeeping before it returns, because it did not invoke the BIOS.

Finally, when **KBDISR** detects an unmonitored keystroke, it simply invokes the BIOS ISR and returns.

Functions **PutFirstKey** and **GetFirstKey**, with some related decla-

```
/****************************************************************/
/* FirstKey.C    Functions PutFirstKey and GetFirstKey.    */
/*               These are required for function  KBDISR.    */
/****************************************************************/

#include <General.H>

#define   KBBuffer       0x001e      /* First buffer cell offset.*/
#define   KBBufferEnd    0x003c      /* Last  buffer cell offset.*/
#define   BIOSData       0x0040
#define   BufferHead     (unsigned far *) MK_FP(BIOSData,0x001a)
#define   BufferTail     (unsigned far *) MK_FP(BIOSData,0x001c)

extern unsigned FirstKey;

void PutFirstKey(void) {        /* Put  FirstKey  code in key-  */
  unsigned Next;                /* board buffer, if possible.   */
if (!FirstKey) return;          /* Do nothing if no  FirstKey.  */
Next = *BufferTail + 2;                /* Find next buffer      */
if (Next > KBBufferEnd)                /* cell, allowing for    */
Next = KBBuffer;                       /* wraparound.           */
if (Next == *BufferHead)               /* If queue is full,     */
   Beep;                               /* report failure.       */
   else {
     disable();                        /* Otherwise, with in-   */
     *(unsigned far *)                 /* terrupts off, place   */
       MK_FP(BIOSData,*BufferTail)     /* FirstKey  in next     */
         = FirstKey;                   /* cell and update tail  */
     *BufferTail = Next;               /* pointer.              */
     enable(); }
FirstKey = 0; }                        /* Forget  FirstKey.     */

void GetFirstKey(void) {        /* Get  FirstKey  code from tail */
  unsigned Previous;            /* of keyboard buffer.           */
Previous = *BufferTail - 2;             /* Find previous buffer  */
if (Previous < KBBuffer)                /* cell, allowing for    */
  Previous = KBBufferEnd;               /* wraparound.           */
disable();                              /* With interrupts off,  */
FirstKey = *(unsigned far *)            /* get FirstKey  from    */
  MK_FP(BIOSData,Previous);             /* previous cell and     */
*BufferTail = Previous;                 /* update tail pointer.  */
enable(); }
```

Figure 9.3.4 Procedures **PutFirstKey** and **GetFirstKey**

separate file was used simply to make the program more comprehensible. You can use the program comments to follow the circular queue manipulations. Each of these routines uses Turbo C Library functions **disable** and **enable**, described in Section 8.1 to disable and reenable maskable interrupts. This is necessary because the keyboard buffer and the BIOS **BufferTail** variable are temporarily in an inconsistent state. No timer interrupt, for example, should be allowed to access the buffer during that brief period. The assembly language Turbo C TOOLS function **kbplace**, discussed in Section 5.3, could have been used here instead of **PutFirstKey**. However, since that package doesn't provide the functionality of **GetFirstKey**, the author decided to write a comparable routine in C, displaying the complementarity of the two algorithms.

Sending formatted PrtSc hardcopy to a file

The final example ISR in this section is an enhancement of the familiar BIOS PrtSc service. You may have been irritated at times with that feature: it starts printing at the perforation instead of leaving a top margin, and stops without ejecting the page. Moreover, if your paper is only as wide as the screen—usually the case—the output fills it, and you lose data when you punch it for your binder. The enhanced ISR, called **PrtSc1**, remedies all these evils. It selects a 17 char/in font, centers the screen image, and ejects the page.

The point of the example is not printer control, but the author had to choose *some* printer. The following control strings, specific to the venerable Epson MX-100, appear in program file **PrtSc.C**, shown in Figure 9.3.5:

Reset = "\x1b\x40"   Compressed = "\xf"

The first resets the printer; the second selects the font. If these are not appropriate to your printer, change them. File **PrtSc.C** contains some declarations and function **PrtSc** that form the core of the enhanced ISR. The code is unremarkable, except for a few minor points. First, it sets a global **Busy** flag that the ISR checks to ensure that no **PrtSc** invocation interrupts another. Turbo C TOOLS function **virdrect** is used to copy the screen instantly to a buffer in memory, (without snow, even if you

```
/************************************************************/
/* PrtSc.C    Function PrtSc:  Core code for custom  PrtSc */
/*             interrupt service and intervention routines   */
/*********************************** that append format- */
                                    /* ted screen hardcopy */
#include   <FCntl.H>               /* to a file.          */
#include   <IO.H>                  /************************/
#include <General.H>
#include   <BVideo.H>

#define Exists(F)  (access((F),0) == 0)     /* ≠ 0  <-> file */
                                            /* F  exists.    */
#define EscAt        "\x1b\x40"    /* ASCII 27 64 = Esc@.    */
#define SI           "\xf"         /* ASCII 15 = SI = Shift in.*/
#define FF           "\xc"         /* ASCII 12 = Form feed.  */
#define CRLF         "\r\n"
#define Reset           EscAt      /* Esc@  resets Epson.    */
#define Compressed      SI         /* SI  selects  17  pitch. */
#define RowsPerPage     66         /* 8.5x11  paper:  17  col- */
#define ColumnsPerPage  136        /* umns,  6  lines per inch.*/
#define MaxRows         43         /* Number of screen rows.  */
#define MaxColumns      80         /* Number of screen columns.*/

extern   Boolean  Busy;               /* These two variables */
extern   char     *FileName;          /* must be global.     */
                                      /* Make other variables*/
int   Rows,Columns;                   /* global to keep the  */
int   TopMargin,LeftMargin;           /* ISR  stack short.   */
int   Ignore;                         /* For useless info.   */
int   File;                           /* File handle.        */
int   Row;                            /* Loop index.         */

char Buffer[MaxRows*MaxColumns];      /* Copy of screen.     */
char Blanks[MaxColumns/2];            /* For left margin.    */

void PrtSc(void) {
Busy  = True;                         /* Set the  Busy  flag.*/
Rows  = scrows();                     /* Get screen informa- */
Ignore = scmode(&Ignore,&Columns,     /* tion (ignoring some */
  &Ignore);                           /* data).              */
virdrect(0,0,Rows-1,Columns-1,        /* Screen to character */
  Buffer,CHARS_ONLY);                 /* buffer, no snow.    */
```

Figure 9.3.5 ISR function **PrtSc** (*Continued on next page*)

```
File = (!Exists(FileName) ?            /* Create or open hard-*/
  _creat(FileName,0)       :           /* copy file.          */
  open (FileName,O_WRONLY|O_APPEND));
write(File,Reset      ,2);             /* Send Epson   MX-100 */
write(File,Compressed,1);              /* reset, pitch codes. */

TopMargin  = (RowsPerPage    -Rows  ) / 2;
LeftMargin = (ColumnsPerPage-Columns) / 2;
memset(Blanks,Blank,LeftMargin);       /* Build left margin.  */
for (Row = 0; Row < TopMargin; ++Row)  /* Print blank lines   */
  write(File,"\r\n",2);                /* for top margin.     */
for (Row = 0; Row < Rows; ++Row) {     /* For each row,       */
  write(File,Blanks,LeftMargin);       /* print left margin,  */
  write(File,&Buffer[Row*Columns],     /* screen characters,  */
    Columns);
  write(File,CRLF,2); }                /* and   CR,LF.        */
write(File,FF,1);                      /* Eject page with  FF.*/
write(File,Reset,2);                   /* Reset the printer.  */
close(File);                           /* Close the file.     */
Busy = False; }                        /* Reset  Busy  flag.  */
```

Figure 9.3.5 *(Continued)* ISR function **PrtSc**

rations, are included in file **FirstKey.C**, shown in Figure 9.3.4. A have a Color/Graphics Adapter). Functions **scrows** and **scmode** are called just before that to ascertain the current screen dimensions. Function **access**, described in Section 6.2, is used to ascertain whether the hardcopy file exists or not; accordingly, it's opened for appending or created. After outputting enough blank lines for a top margin, the character codes are output from the buffer, a line at a time. After the page is ejected, the printer is reset. (Otherwise it will remain in 17 char/in mode.) Finally, the **Busy** flag is turned off.

The ISR **PrtSc1** itself is a very short procedure, included with the installation code in file **PrtSc1.Dem**, shown in Figure 9.3.6. **PrtSc1** either executes **PrtSc** or just peeps, depending on the **Busy** flag. Before either alternative, it turns on interrupts. (These were turned off by the **Int 5** instruction itself, but shouldn't remain so—**PrtSc** is a long, high-level procedure. The Section 8.7 function **Peep** is used here: the more usual **putchar('\a')** doesn't work in this context—that is probably because it calls DOS. When it peeps, **PrtSc1** has interrupted itself. It seems

```
/****************************************************************/
/* PrtSc1.Dem    Install and remove a custom  PrtSc  Inter-  */
/*               rupt 5  service routine that appends format-*/
/* ted screen hardcopy to the file specified on this program's*/
/* command line, defaulting to the printer file  PRN.  Speci- */
/* fy parameter  /  to remove the custom  ISR  and restore    */
/* previous service.  PrtSc1  sets a  Busy  semaphore when in */
/* operation.  If you request  PrtSc  service while it is set,*/
/***************************************** PrtSc1  just beeps. */
                                       /* Thus, it can inter- */
#include    <FCntl.H>                  /* rupt itself.  PrtSc1*/
#include    <IO.H>                     /* fails if invoked    */
#include  <General.H>                  /* during some   DOS   */
#include <BIntrupt.H>                  /* operations.         */
#include    <BVideo.H>                 /***********************/

Boolean  Busy = False;                 /* Busy  semaphore.    */
char     *FileName;

void PrtSc1(ALLREG  *Registers,        /* Turbo C TOOLS  cus- */
            ISRCTRL *ISRBlk,           /* tom  PrtSc  hardcopy*/
            ISRMSG  *S) {              /* ISR.                */
enable();                              /* Enable interrupts.  */
if (Busy)                              /* Semaphore.          */
   Peep();                             /* Just peep if  PrtSc */
  else                                 /* is underway, else   */
    PrtSc(); }                         /* execute core code.  */

#define PrtScInterrupt 5                  /* Interrupt no.  */
#define ID             "Screen Hardcopy"  /* ISR  ident.    */
#define StackSize      1024               /* A semaphore    */
#define MaxDepth       2                  /* prevents deeper*/
char     Stacks[StackSize*MaxDepth];      /* recursion.     */
ISRCTRL ControlBlock;

void main(int   ParamCount,         /* Command line specifies  */
          char *ParamStr[]) {       /* file, or  /  for removal.*/
RstorISR(PrtScInterrupt,ID);        /* Restore previous  ISR.  */
if (ParamCount < 2)                 /* Use standard printer file*/
   FileName = "PRN";                /* if no file is specified. */
  else if (ParamStr[1][0] == '/') {
```

Figure 9.3.6 Program **PrtSc1.Dem** (*Continued on next page*)

```
      printf("Custom  PrtSc  is no "    /* Only removal was    */
         "longer installed.");         /* requested.          */
       return; }                        /* Ordinary exit.      */
    else
      FileName = ParamStr[1];
isinstal(PrtScInterrupt,PrtSc1,ID,     /* Install  PrtSc1     */
    &ControlBlock,Stacks,StackSize,     /* ISR.                */
      MaxDepth);
printf("PrtSc  outputs to file  %s.",
  FileName);                           /* Terminate, remaining */
isresext(0); }                         /* resident in memory.  */
```

Figure 9.3.6 (*Continued*) Program **PrtSc1.Dem**

safe to assume that this recursion will go no deeper, so two ISR stacks should suffice. (You might want to guard against agitated abuse of the <PrtSc> key during the peep—that might crash **PrtSc1**.)

The **PrtSc1.Dem** installation code uses function **RstorISR**, described in Section 9.2, to remove any existing **PrtSc1** code before installing code for a new hardcopy file. You specify the file name via the command line when you execute **PrtSc1.Dem**. The default file is the standard DOS printer file **PRN**. Thus, command lines **PrtSc1** and **PrtSc1 PRN** are equivalent. Executing **PrtSc1 /** merely removes existing code and restores the previous **PrtSc** interrupt service.

You should test the enhanced **PrtSc1** ISR in several ways. First, install it to send hardcopy to a disk file—or better, a virtual disk file. Then invoke it after the DOS prompt by touching <Shift-PrtSc>. Second, invoke it via a one-line program that merely executes Interrupt 5. Finally, execute another one-liner that invokes Turbo C Library function **getch** to wait for keyboard input. Touch <Shift-PrtSc>, then a key for **getch**. Check that **PrtSc1** creates a new hardcopy file after you erase the old one, and appends to an existing one. Although a hardcopy file prints attractively, its screen image produced by the DOS **Type** command is messy, because its lines are longer than eighty columns. Finally, try these experiments over, sending the hardcopy directly to the printer. You might want to try the experiments with and without a print buffer.

The author *hopes* that **PrtSc1** performs as well on your system as on his. It is not flawless, however! For example, after saving any valuable data on a virtual disk, test **PrtSc1** by executing a command that spends a lot of time doing DOS disk operations: for example, the **ChkDsk** utility or the DOS **Dir** command to produce and redirect a long directory to a disk file. While the program is running, touch <Shift-PrtSc>. *CRASH!* What's happening now?

DOS critical sections

The **PrtSc1** ISR failure just noted is a symptom of DOS non-reentrancy. At some stages of execution—in fact, most of the time—DOS stores important information in global variables. When it's interrupted by **PrtSc1**, and that routine in turn invokes DOS for file input/output, this information is overwritten. The nested invocation of DOS returns to **PrtSc1**, and **PrtSc1** returns to the interrupted program, but DOS then gets lost. DOS was interrupted in what's called a *critical section*.

This situation occurs frequently. The example with file operations was chosen simply because it's easy to reproduce. Here are some other cases where an ISR might need DOS services while DOS is in a critical section:

- The ISR handles a *critical error,* like a diskette drive door open, during DOS input/output.
- The ISR wishes to respond to an alarm, but the triggering user tick interrupt occurred during DOS file input/output.

These examples show that it is essential to understand the problem and find a solution.

DOS sets a *critical section* flag whenever it enters such an unstable state. If an ISR can find this flag, and inspect it before invoking DOS, it can avoid such a crash. (Of course, it might not be able to do its intended job, either, if it *requires* a DOS service at just that instant.) The tool for this purpose is DOS Interrupt 21 Function 34, which returns in registers ES:BX a pointer to the critical section flag. Simple logic underlies the strategy to return a flag *pointer*, rather than the flag *value:* if you are indeed in a critical section, Function 34 might itself cause a crash, whereas if you had previously determined the flag location, you need only inspect it.

Turbo C TOOLS functions

void utcrit(void)
int utdosrdy(void)

make the flag accessible to your programs. The first stores the flag address in Turbo C TOOLS global variable **b_critadd**; the second inspects the flag and returns 1 or 0 to indicate whether you can safely request DOS services—i.e. DOS is *not* in a critical section. Execute **utcrit** at least once before invoking **utdosrdy**. You'll find the **utcrit** prototype, **utdosrdy** macro, and **b_critadd** declaration in Turbo C TOOLS header file **BUtil.H**.

The following variant of Figure 9.2.4 interrupt service routine **ISR** illustrates use of the critical section flag:

```
void ISR(ALLREG *Registers,        /* Turbo C TOOLS */
         ISRCTRL *ISRBlk,          /* custom ISR.    */
         ISRMSG *S) {              /* ConIO function */
cputs("Are DOS services available? ");   /* cputs doesn't  */
cputs((utdosrdy() ? "YES!" : "NO!"));  }  /* invoke DOS.    */
```

Test this by using function **isinstal** to install it as a **PrtSc** Interrupt 5 service routine. Your installation program must call **utcrit** before **isinstal**. You can then invoke this version of **ISR** several ways. First, use a one-line program like **ROMBASIC** in Figure 8.3.4 to execute Interrupt 5: **ISR** should report that DOS services are available. Second, execute a one-line program that simply waits for a keystroke. While it's waiting, touch <Shift-PrtSc>: the **ISR** response depends on which keyboard input routine you used. If it was BIOS Interrupt 16, or Turbo C TOOLS function **kbgetkey**, you will see that DOS is available. However, if you used a DOS function or any of the Turbo C Library functions, DOS will be in a critical section and unavailable. Next, touch <Shift-PrtSc> after the DOS prompt: **ISR** reports that DOS is unavailable. Finally, after securing any valuable data stored in a virtual disk, execute the program that earlier caused the custom **PrtSc1** ISR to crash, and touch <Shift-PrtSc> during its output. You should see that DOS is again in a critical section.

These test results partially explain the behavior of the **PrtSc1** ISR. Whenever DOS was *not* in a critical section, **PrtSc1** succeeded. When it failed, DOS *was* in a critical section. However, in two cases—when you touched <Shift-PrtSc> while waiting for **getch** input, and after the DOS prompt—**PrtSc1** succeeded even though DOS was in a critical section. Thus the critical section flag seems to be a conservative safeguard.

Before leaving the subject of the critical section flag, you should realize that according to the *MS-DOS Encyclopedia*, Reference [28, Article 11],

Microsoft may change the flag's function at any time. Nevertheless, other DOS features and other Microsoft products use the flag, so it seems unlikely to blow away.

In these last paragraphs, you have seen an explanation of the **PrtSc1** ISR failure, but no way to repair it. The next section describes the Turbo C TOOLS *intervention routine* technique for constructing robust ISRs that work regardless of DOS critical sections.

9.4 Turbo C TOOLS intervention routines

> **Concepts**
>
> Intervention strategy
> DOS Idle Interrupt 28
> Installing and removing intervention functions
> Example intervention function for sending formatted screen
>   hardcopy to a file

At the end of the last section, you encountered a major problem concerning interrupt service routines. An apparently well-crafted routine crashed because it used DOS services and was invoked at a point where DOS is not reentrant. How can you avoid this situation, if your routine absolutely needs DOS services and you cannot control precisely when it is executed? The Turbo C TOOLS *intervention* technique works if execution can be delayed for a short period until DOS regains reentrancy. Fortunately, this does not mean that you have to handle the required timing details. Turbo C TOOLS takes care of that for you. The goal is to let you write service routine code without regard to the DOS reentrancy problem.

Since the strategy is to postpone reentrant DOS calls to appropriate times, intervention involves *scheduling*. The Turbo C TOOLS technique extends beyond the timing considerations just mentioned, to include scheduling three kinds of events:

- preset alarms,
- expiration of specific time intervals,
- monitored *hot* keystrokes.

In addition, intervention code servicing these kinds of events can interact with conventional Turbo C TOOLS ISRs like those described in Sections 9.2 and 9.3.

The principal routine in the intervention system is a *scheduler*, which is invoked at each timer tick. It checks whether any alarm or specified time interval countdown has expired, and compares any intervention requests generated by these events and by hot keystrokes against the DOS resources available. When it's possible to honor such a request, the scheduler executes your custom *intervention routine,* which calls the appropriate service routine. The scheduler is supported by ISRs that filter Interrupts 8, 9, 13, 21, and 28. The overall organization of the installed scheduler and filters is shown in Figure 9.4.1. These routines are supplied with Turbo C TOOLS; they are written in assembly language. The filters are customized: they are not conventional Turbo C TOOLS ISRs. The only code you must write is for the intervention routine and service routines shown underlined in the upper right corner. These do not have to be separate routines. However, if you want to provide services for several events—for example, an alarm and some hot keystrokes—then you probably want to isolate the separate services, and use the intervention routine as a dispatcher to interpret the scheduler's signals and select the appropriate service.

To find your way through Figure 9.4.1, it's perhaps best to begin by tracing execution following a keyboard event. A keystroke or release triggers Interrupt 9, which is served by the Turbo C TOOLS keyboard filter. The filter immediately executes the previously installed ISR— probably the BIOS service routine—then uses BIOS Interrupt 16 Service 1 to inspect the keystroke. A monitored hot keystroke is recorded so that the scheduler can intervene and service it as soon as possible. If the previous keyboard event is still being processed, or an intervention request from a previous hot keystroke is still pending, the filter merely returns to the interrupted program, without even checking the keystroke. Thus, the keyboard filter is reentrant, and at most one hot key intervention request can remain pending.

The keyboard intervention filter design has two unfortunate consequences. First, the BIOS service inspects the keystroke at the head of the keystroke queue, not the tail, so a hot keystroke will go undetected unless the queue is empty. Second, the hot keystrokes must be among those that the BIOS recognizes and places in the queue. For example, you cannot use <P-Q> or even <Shift-PrtSc> as a hot keystroke. The latter causes a problem for program **PrtSc2.Dem** considered later.

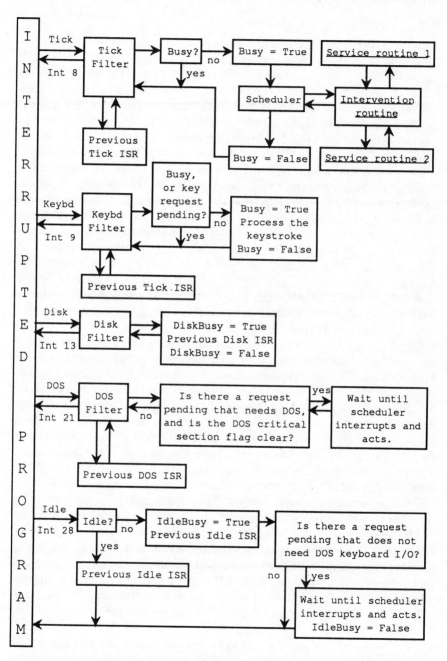

Figure 9.4.1 Turbo C TOOLS Intervention Strategy

The intervention system filters Interrupt 13 to avoid interrupting the BIOS disk ISR. The filter activates a **DiskBusy** flag while the BIOS ISR executes. The scheduler honors no intervention requests while that flag is set. (If all custom intervention routines used only DOS disk services, this would be unnecessary, since DOS protects itself. This Turbo C TOOLS feature merely prevents a custom disk service routine from interrupting the BIOS ISR and possibly corrupting the disk as a result.)

In many situations, DOS is executing most of the time, and most timer ticks invoke the scheduler during a critical section. A technique is needed to prevent a routine that requires DOS services from remaining pending indefinitely. The DOS Interrupt 21 intervention filter is a device for "catching" DOS in a noncritical section and allowing the scheduler to intervene. After executing the requested DOS Interrupt 21 function, the filter checks whether DOS is available and an intervention request pending that needs DOS. If so, the filter enters a wait loop before returning to the interrupted program. That is, it sets a "waiting" flag and repeatedly checks whether the flag is still set. This loop will continue until the scheduler is invoked by the timer tick interrupt, services the request, and deactivates the flag.

The DOS *idle* Interrupt 28, mentioned briefly in Section 8.5, is executed whenever DOS is waiting for keyboard input and can provide disk services. This provides another opportunity for the intervention system to "catch" DOS when it's available for some tasks, and thus avoid indefinite postponement of intervention service. The intervention filter executes the previously installed ISR, then enters a wait loop if an intervention request is pending that does not require DOS Interrupt 21 Functions 0 through c. (These cause reentrancy problems.) At the next timer tick, the scheduler will intervene to service the request. This filter also uses an **IdleBusy** flag to avoid its own reentrancy problems.

Finally, you can trace execution following a timer tick Interrupt 8. Its intervention filter immediately executes the previous tick ISR (probably the BIOS routine), then invokes the scheduler, provided it's not still busy reacting to a previous tick. The scheduler records any requests triggered by time signals. Now, if there is a request pending, any required DOS resources are available, and the BIOS disk ISR is not executing, the scheduler calls your custom intervention routine, passing a parameter to identify the triggering event. Before calling your intervention routine, the scheduler checks whether you require DOS services. If so, it disables <Ctrl-Break> and <Ctrl-C> and uses function **iscurprc** to make itself the currently executing process, so that you can open files and allocate memory reliably. Your intervention routine probably calls one of several service routines to handle the request. When the intervention routine returns to the scheduler, the latter performs some housekeeping, then returns to the tick filter, and ultimately to the interrupted program.

Turbo C TOOLS header file **BInterv.H** defines several data structures that organize communication among your intervention routine and the Turbo C TOOLS functions that make up the intervention system. These must be considered before the function calling sequences can be described. The first two structures describe hot keystrokes and timer events:

```
typedef struct {
      char ch;         /* Low  byte    keystroke        */
      char keycode;    /* High byte    code.            */
      int  action; }   /* Intended action.              */
   IV_KEY;
typedef struct {
      long ticks;      /* Alarm time or event interval.  */
      int  action; }   /* Type of event.                 */
   IV_TIME;
```

The **action** fields can have values

IVKEY action
0 .. not set
1 .. invoke intervention routine
2 .. disable it temporarily
3 .. reenable it

IVTIME action
0 .. not set
1 .. interval
2 .. alarm

IV_KEY action options 2,3 permit you to use a hot key to deactivate your intervention routine temporarily, then reactivate it. This is necessary, for example, if one of its functions is to redefine the hot keys. Option 0 permits one event service routine to selectively deactivate others. Installing the intervention routine, you will create two arrays that describe the events that will trigger intervention:

IV_KEY KeyTable [Keys]
IV_TIME TimeTable[Times]

The next structure describes a triggering event:

```
typedef struct {
    IV_KEY key;              /* Hot key description.    */
    int   time_action;       /* Type of timer event.    */
    int   time_index;        /* Index in  TimeTable.    */
    long  time; }            /* Current time in ticks.  */
IV_EVENT;
```

An intervention function **Interv** must be declared like this:

void Interv(IV_EVENT *E)

Turbo C TOOLS provides this function to install an intervention routine **Interv**:

```
int ivinstal( void  (*Interv)(IV_EVENT *E),
            char   *ID,
            char   *Stack, int StackSize,
          IV_KEY   *KeyTable, int Keys,
         IV_TIME   *TimeTable, int Times,
            int    Option)
```

You must supply an array **ID** of exactly sixteen characters to use in identifying **Interv**, in case you want to deactivate or remove it. As for ISRs, the installation program must allocate a global variable

char Stack[StackSize]

for the intervention routine's stack. This is simpler than for ISRs, however, since intervention routines are never called recursively, and needn't be reentrant. Turbo C TOOLS documentation indicates that the stack must be at least 256 bytes long, and suggests a length of 2K. As mentioned earlier, parameters **KeyTable** and **TimeTable** list the hot keystrokes, alarms, and time intervals, with the kinds of responses they should evoke. The scheduler will intervene at appropriate times and invoke your routine, sending it a signal to identify the triggering event. Your routine must then decide which custom service to provide.

The last **ivinstal** parameter **Option** is the disjunction of three bits, for which Turbo C TOOLS provides mnemonic macros reminiscent of South C pidgin:

1 : **IV_DOS_NEED**
2 : **IV_DKEY_NEED**
4 : **IV_FLOAT_NEED**

These let you specify whether the intervention routine needs DOS functions in general, Functions 0 through c, or uses the Turbo C floating point emulation library. The first two options tell the scheduler when it must wait for DOS to idle or enter a non-critical section. If you include the last option, the scheduler will always load a set of interrupt vectors for the emulation routines before invoking the intervention routine. (Other software may have reset them since the intervention routine was installed.)

Before considering an example intervention routine installation program, you must see how to remove an installed routine and restore the services previously invoked by the filtered interrupts. Part of this task is performed by Turbo C TOOLS functions

int ivvecs(int Option, IV_VECTORS far *Vectors)
IV_CTRL far *ivsense(IV_VECTORS *Vectors, char *ID)
int ivdisabl(IV_CTRL far *IVBlock)

The first function ascertains or sets the values of the interrupt vectors corresponding to the filters, according as **Option** is 0 or 1. It returns 0 to indicate success. A data structure of type **IV_VECTORS** is used to transmit the vectors. **IV_VECTORS** is defined in header file **BInterv.H**. There's no need to describe it here, since it's used only as a parameter for function **ivsense**, which ascertains whether an intervention function with specified **ID** string and **IV_VECTORS** structure is installed. If not, **ivsense** returns a far null pointer. If the function is, in fact, installed, **ivsense** returns a far pointer to the corresponding **IV_CTRL** structure **IVBlock**. Also defined in **BInterv.H**, this *intervention control block* structure plays a role similar to that of the ISR control block for Turbo C TOOLS interrupt service routines. Only one item of an **IV_CTRL** structure is used separately here: **IVBlock.psp** is a far pointer to the corresponding intervention function installation program's PSP. You can pass this to Section 9.2 function **isremove** to remove that memory resident program. Otherwise, the intervention control block is used only as a parameter for function **ivdisabl**, so there's no need to describe all its features here, either. This last function disables an intervention routine with the specified control block by replacing the current values of the filtered interrupt vectors with their previous values, obtained from the control block. (They were stored there by the installation program.)

Function **RstorInt**, shown in Figure 9.4.2, uses **ivvecs, ivsense, ivdisabl**, and the function **isremove** described in Section 9.2 to remove an intervention routine with a specified ID string. It works just like function **RstorISR**, also described there, and needs no further explanation. *Warning!* **RstorInt** will return to DOS *all* memory allocated to the program that installed the specified intervention routine. If you used it to install any other memory resident routines, they will be disabled as well.

Program **PrtSc2.Dem** in Figure 9.4.3 demonstrates installation and removal of intervention routine **PrtSc2**, a version of the Section 9.3 routine **PrtSc1** that will not crash if called during a DOS service.

```
/**************************************************************/
/* RstorInt.C    Function RstorInt: remove a  Turbo C      */
/*              TOOLS  intervention routine, provided its   */
/* control block has a given  ident  field. Restore filtered */
/* interrupt vectors to their previous values.  Return values:*/
/*********************************************/            */
                                          /* 0   Success       */
#include  <General.H>                     /* 1      ivdisabl   */
#include <BIntrupt.H>                      /* 2       error     */
#include  <BInterv.H>                      /* 3       codes     */
                                          /* 4  No such routine*/
int RstorInt(char *ID) {                   /* 7      isremove   */
  IV_VECTORS    Vectors;                   /* 9      error codes */
  IV_CTRL far *IVBlock;                    /*********************/
  int          Code;
ivvecs(IV_RETVEC,&Vectors);                /* Get filtered vecs.*/
IVBlock = ivsense(&Vectors,ID);            /* Look for control  */
if (IVBlock == FARNULL)                    /* block.            */
    return 4;                              /* Couldn't find one.*/
  else if (Code = ivdisabl(IVBlock))       /* Restore previous  */
    return Code;                           /* services;  return */
  else                                     /* if impossible.    */
    return isremove(IVBlock->psp); }       /* Remove interven-  */
                                          /* tion program.     */
```

Figure 9.4.2 Function **RstorInt**

```
/**************************************************************/
/* PrtSc2.Dem    Install and remove an intervention routine  */
/*                PrtSc2 that uses function PrtSc like the    */
/* custom  ISR  PrtSc1  did.  The command line specifies the */
/* PrtSc  file name or service removal just like program     */
/* PrtSc1.Dem. Since intervention routines can't detect       */
/***********************************  <Shift-PrtSc>, an  ISR  */
                                    /* called PrtScISR is used*/
#include      <FCntl.H>             /* to set a service  Wanted */
#include      <IO.H>                /* flag;  but it just beeps */
#include   <General.H>             /* if  PrtSc  service is al-*/
#include  <BIntrupt.H>             /* ready underway.  PrtScISR*/
#include  <BInterv.H>              /* thus interrupt itself.   */
                                    /**************************/
Boolean Busy   = False;
Boolean Wanted = False;

void PrtScISR(ALLREG  *Registers,       /* Turbo C TOOLS  PrtSc*/
              ISRCTRL *ISRBlk,          /* ISR.  Beep if       */
              ISRMSG  *S) {             /* PrtSc2 is busy,     */
enable();
if (Busy)                               /* else set the  Wanted*/
   Peep();                              /* flag.  PrtSc2  will */
  else                                  /* provide service as  */
    Wanted = True; }                    /* as possible.        */

void PrtSc2(IV_EVENT *E) {              /* Intervention rou-   */
if (!Wanted)                            /* tine.  If service is*/
   return;                              /* requested, execute  */
  else {                                /* core  PrtSc  code,  */
    PrtSc();                            /* PrtSc  code and     */
    Wanted = False; }}                  /* reset the flag.     */

#define  PrtScInterrupt 5              /* Interrupt no.  */
#define  ID              "Screen hardcopy"  /* Identification.*/
char     *FileName;                     /* PrtSc  file.  */
ISRCTRL  ControlBlock;
#define  ISRStackSize    256           /* A semaphore     */
#define  MaxDepth        2             /* prevents deeper*/
char     ISRStacks[ISRStackSize*MaxDepth];  /* recursion.     */
#define  IVStackSize     2048          /* Intervention    */
char     IVStack[IVStackSize];         /* system stack.  */
```

Figure 9.4.3 Program **PrtSc2.Dem** (*Continued on next page*)

```c
#define  Times           1            /* Only one event:*/
IV_TIME  TimeTable[Times] =           /* check  Wanted  */
         {{1L,IV_TM_INTERVAL}};       /* flag each tick.*/
                                      /* Command line speci- */
void main(int   ParamCount,           /* fies file, or  /    */
          char *ParamStr[]) {         /* for removal.        */
RstorISR(PrtScInterrupt,ID);          /* Restore previous    */
RstorInt(ID);                         /* PrtSc  service.     */
if (ParamCount < 2)                   /* Use printer if no   */
    FileName = "PRN";                 /* file is specified.  */
  else if (ParamStr[1][0] == '/') {
    printf("Custom  PrtSc  is no "    /* Only removal was    */
      "longer installed.");           /* requested.          */
    return; }                         /* Ordinary exit.      */
  else
    FileName = ParamStr[1];
isinstal(PrtScInterrupt,PrtScISR,     /* Install  PrtScISR   */
  ID,&ControlBlock,ISRStacks,         /* with prescribed  ID */
    ISRStackSize,MaxDepth);           /* & allocated stacks. */
ivinstal(PrtSc2,ID,
  IVStack,IVStackSize,
    (IV_KEY *)NULL,0,
      TimeTable,Times,
        IV_DOS_NEED);
printf("PrtSc  outputs to file  %s.",
  FileName);                          /* Terminate, remaining*/
isresext(0); }                        /* resident in memory. */
```

Figure 9.4.3 *(Continued)* Program **PrtSc2.Dem**

Invoked like demonstration program **PrtSc1.Dem**, this program first uses functions **RstorISR** and **RstorInt** to remove any previously installed memory resident code with the appropriate ID, then interprets the command line. If the command line parameter was merely /, requesting code removal, the program terminates. Otherwise, it installs the code, reports its action, and terminates, remaining resident in memory.

As mentioned earlier, **PrtSc2.Dem** must install two memory resident routines: intervention function **PrtSc2** and a conventional Turbo C TOOLS ISR **PrtScISR** to process PrtSc Interrupt 5. The latter is needed because the intervention system keyboard interrupt filter executes the BIOS keyboard Interrupt 9 service routine *before* checking for a hot keystroke. The BIOS routine executes Interrupt 5 as soon as it detects the <Shift-PrtSc> keystroke, and does not record that keystroke in the keyboard buffer. Thus, the intervention system keyboard filter can never detect it: <Shift-PrtSc> *cannot* be a hot key. If **PrtSc** service is currently busy, then **PrtScISR** just beeps, like the Section 9.3 ISR **PrtSc1**. Otherwise, it sets a **Wanted** flag to tell the intervention function **PrtSc2** to declare itself busy and execute function **PrtSc**, already described in Section 9.3, to produce the formatted screen hardcopy file.

Section 8.7 function **Peep** produces the beep instead of the more conventional **putchar('\a')**. In fact, the latter causes **Prtsc2** to crash, even if several precautions are taken beyond those described here. The author conjectures that the problem is caused by the delay mechanism invoked when DOS sends '\a' to the console; unfortunately, that DOS feature isn't documented.

PrtSc2.Dem invokes **isinstal** as usual to install **PrtScISR**, then **ivinstal** to install the intervention routine **PrtSc2**. The **ivinstal** calling sequence includes parameter **IV_DOS_NEED**, to indicate that **PrtSc2** uses DOS services (when it calls function **PrtSc**). The **KeyTable** pointer is initialized as a far null pointer, and **Keys** set equal to zero, indicating that there are no hot keys. Parameter **Times** is set equal to 1, and **TimeTable[1]** initialized with a record instructing the scheduler to invoke the intervention routine **PrtSc2** at each tick. **PrtSc2** checks the **Wanted** flag, and calls function **PrtSc** for service only when the flag is set. Since suggested earlier, a 2K character array **IVSTack** is allocated for the intervention routine stack, and its address and size passed to **ivinstal**.

You should test **PrtSc2** exactly like **PrtSc1** in Section 9.3. It should perform similarly, but should *not* crash if you invoke it by touching <Shift-PrtSc> during a program that uses DOS file input/output intensively.

Turbo C TOOLS includes two more examples of intervention routines: **IVClock**, a utility that places a real time clock in a corner of the screen and allows you to set alarms; and **CMKey**, a general keyboard macro utility.

A

Diskette Directory

On the next page is a list of the files on the diskette with volume label **AP&ATC** accompanying this book. The **.Bat** file is a DOS batch program. C source code is in **.C** and **.Dem** files. In file **All.Prj** you'll find copies of all **.Prj** files used in making the programs. You can compile and link the programs that use only Turbo C and its Library. For the programs that use Turbo C TOOLS , as many **.Exe** files were included as space permitted.

```
\                   \Chapter3           \Chapter4           \Chapter8
  Read      .Me       ErrorLvl.Bat        CharSet .Dem        CtryInfo.C
  General .H          Strings .C          Cursor  .Dem        ExtMem  .C
  All       .Prj      CharIO  .Dem        MonoAttr.Dem        Peep    .C
                      ChrConst.Dem        PutText .Dem        Delay   .Dem
\Chapter2             ComLine .Dem        Speed   .Dem        ErrNo   .Dem
  X         .C        Country .Dem        TTyCtrl .Dem        GenInter.Dem
  Y         .C        Environ .Dem        ViSc    .Dem        HoldPrnt.Dem
  Z         .C        FN      .Dem        Whirlwin.Dem        IV      .Dem
  Z1        .C        G       .Dem        Window  .Dem        ROMBASIC.Dem
  Z2        .C        Gregory .Dem        ViSc    .Exe        To_D    .Dem
  BIOSMem .Dem        IntCvt1 .Dem        Whirlwin.Exe
  CharCast.Dem        IntCvt2 .Dem                          \Chapter9
  FarHeap .Dem        Main    .Dem      \Chapter5             FirstKey.C
  Heap    .Dem        RealCvt .Dem        ASCIIBM.Dem         KbdISR  .C
  HugePtr .Dem        RealCvt2.Dem        KbReady .Dem        PrtSc   .C
  MiscFunc.Dem        StPCpy  .Dem        KbStuff .Dem        RstorInt.C
  Model   .Dem        StPJust .Dem        LeftOver.Dem        RstorISR.C
  PokeStar.Dem        StPTabfy.Dem        Menu1   .Dem        ISInstal.Dem
  PtrCast .Dem        StPXlate.Dem        Menu2   .Dem        PQ      .Dem
                      StrAlloc.Dem        Shft&Num.Dem        PrtSc1  .Dem
                      StrChr  .Dem        ^ZSticks.Dem        PrtSc2  .Dem
                      StrDay  .Dem        Menu2   .Exe        TimerISR.Dem
                      StrEqual.Dem                           UtDOSRdy.Dem
                      StrIndex.Dem      \Chapter6             PQ      .Exe
                      StrIns  .Dem        DiskInfo.Dem        PrtSc2  .Exe
                      StrNCpy .Dem        FileCas1.Dem
                      StrNDel .Dem        FileCas2.Dem
                      StrPBrk .Dem        GetDFree.Dem
                      StrRev  .Dem        NewName .Dem
                      StrShrtE.Dem        Sharing .Dem
                      StrStr  .Dem        Wildcard.Dem
                      StrSubst.Dem
                      StrTime .Dem      \Chapter7
                      StrTok  .Dem        Env&Prog.C
                      StoToMon.Dem        MemryMap.C
                      StrULToE.Dem        Child   .Dem
                      Telephon.Dem        Dup     .Dem
                      ToUpper .Dem        FReopen .Dem
                                          Malaysia.Dem
                                          MapTest1.Dem
                                          MapTest2.Dem
                                          Mem     .Dem
                                          Spawn   .Dem
                                          System1 .Dem
                                          System2 .Dem
```

General.H

```
/**************************************************************/
/* General.H    This header file contains declarations and   */
/*              definitions used throughout the book, as well*/
/***************************************** as prototypes of all*/
                                          /* functions for gener-*/
#include    <ConIO.H>                     /* al use written for   */
#include      <DOS.H>                      /* the book.          */
#include    <StdIO.H>                     /*********************** /
#include   <StdLib.H>
#include   <String.H>
#include     <Time.H>


#define    Boolean      int
#define    True         1
#define    False        0


#define    Blank        ' '
#define    CR           13
#define    Beep         putchar('\a')
#define    NewLine      putchar('\n')
#define    EmptyStr     ""


#define    FARNULL      (void far *) NULL


#define    IntA00       0x20        /* Interrupt control port.  */
#define    EOI          0x20        /* End-of-interrupt code.   */
```

```
#define   StrEmpty(S)  (*(S) == 0)

Boolean   StrEqualsF  (char *S,
                       char *T,
                       char **PS,
                       char **PT);

Boolean   StrEqualsB  (   char *S,
                          char *T,
                       unsigned *PM,
                       unsigned *PN);

#define   StrChrF      strchr

char      *StrChrB    (char *S,
                       char *P,
                       char  C);

#define   StrPBrkF     strpbrk

char      *StrStrF    (char *S,
                       char *T);

char      *StrStrB    (char *S,
                       char *T);

char      *StrAlloc   (   char Ch,
                       unsigned N);

char      *StrSubst   (char *S,
                       char *A,
                       char *B);

char      *StrLtoA    (long N,
                       char *S,
                        int Radix);

char      *StrShrtE   (double X,
                          char *S);

char      *StrULtoE   (unsigned long N);

char      *StrToMoney (double X,
                          int Code);
```

```
char      *StrTime   (            char *TimeStr,
                      const struct tm *T,
                             Boolean TwentyFourHours,
                             char  Separator);

char      *StrDay    (            char *DateStr,
                      const struct tm *T,
                             int Format,
                             char Separator);

#define   Leap(Year) ( (Year) % 4   == 0 && \
                       ( (Year) % 100 != 0 || \
                         (Year) % 400 == 0   ))

int       DayOfYear  (int Day,
                       int Month,
                       int LeapYear);

long      Gregorian  (int Day,
                       int Month,
                       int Year);

#define   WeekDay    (Day,    \
                       Month,  \
                       Year)   (Gregorian(Day,Month,Year)+5)%7

unsigned  EnvSeg     (unsigned PSP);

char      *ProgName  (unsigned PSP);

void      MemryMap   (void);

unsigned  ExtMem     (void);

void      CtryInfo   (unsigned       Code,
                       struct country *C);

void      Peep       (void);
int       RstorISR   (int  N,
                       char *ID);

int       RstorInt   (char *ID);
```

ASCII/IBM Codes

In Turbo C, data of type **char** are stored as bytes, usually representing text characters. The code that defines this correspondence is known as ASCII/IBM. Codes 0..127, known as ASCII (American Standard Code for Information Interchange), were standardized once, to represent the digits, upper and lower case letters, some punctuation marks and special symbols, and some commands commonly used for teletype control. These standards are still respected, although some of the control codes are obsolete and used now for other purposes. Some ASCII control codes have familiar names of the form "Control-x" where x can be an upper case letter or one of several special symbols. The word "Control-" is often abbreviated by the symbol ^. Use of codes #128..#255 varies widely among different input/output equipment. All codes represent distinctive characters on PC displays according to a defacto standard established by the IBM Monochrome Display Adapter. Codes #0, #32, #255 all correspond to the blank screen character; these are the only instances of non-uniqueness in the code. Here is a complete description of the codes and corresponding characters.

Key for table	
n	– ASCII code in decimal
#n	– Character displayed
Comment	– Interpretation of the code

n	#n	Comment		n	#n	Comment
0		^2 = NUL = Null		41	)	Right parenthesis
1	☺	^A = SOH = StartHead		42	*	Asterisk
2	☻	^B = STX = StartText		43	+	Plus
3	♥	^C = ETX = EndText		44	,	Comma
4	♦	^D = EOT = EndTrans		45	-	Hyphen = Minus sign
5	♣	^E = ENQ = Enquire		46	.	Period
6	♠	^F = ACK = Acknowledge		47	/	Slash
7	●	^G = BEL = Beep		48	0	
8	◘	^H = BS = Backspace		49	1	
9	○	^I = HT = HorizTab		50	2	
10	◙	^J = LF = LineFeed		51	3	
11	♂	^K = VT = VertTab		52	4	
12	♀	^L = FF = FormFeed		53	5	
13	♪	^M = CR = Return		54	6	
14	♫	^N = SO = ShiftOut		55	7	
15	☼	^O = SI = ShiftIn		56	8	
16	►	^P = DLE = DLinkEsc		57	9	
17	◄	^Q = DC1 = DevCtrl1		58	:	Colon
18	↕	^R = DC2 = DevCtrl2		59	;	Semicolon
19	‼	^S = DC3 = DevCtrl3		60	<	Less
20	¶	^T = DC4 = DevCtrl4		61	=	Equal
21	§	^U = NAK = NegAcknlg		62	>	Greater
22	▬	^V = SYN = Synch		63	?	Question
23	↨	^W = ETB = EndTxtBlk		64	@	At
24	↑	^X = CAN = Cancel		65	A	
25	↓	^Y = EM = EndMedium		66	B	
26	→	^Z = SUB = Substitut		67	C	
27	←	^[= ESC = Escape		68	D	
28	∟	^\ = FS = FileSepar		69	E	
29	↔	^] = GS = GroupSepar		70	F	
30	▲	^6 = RS = RecordSepar		71	G	
31	▼	^- = US = UnitSepar		72	H	
32		Blank		73	I	
33	!	Exclamation		74	J	
34	"	Double quote		75	K	
35	#	Number, sharp		76	L	
36	$	Dollars		77	M	
37	%	Percent		78	N	
38	&	And		79	O	
39	'	Right single quote		80	P	
40	(	Left parenthesis		81	Q	

n	#n	Comment	n	#n	Comment
82	R		123	{	Left brace
83	S		124	¦	Two vertical marks
84	T		125	}	Right brace
85	U		126	~	Tilde
86	V		127	⌂	House
87	W		128	Ç	
88	X		129	ü	
89	Y		130	é	
90	Z		131	â	
91	[	Left bracket	132	ä	
92	\	Back slash	133	à	
93	]	Right bracket	134	å	
94	^	Carat	135	ç	
95	_	Underscore	136	ê	
96	`	Left single quote	137	ë	
97	a		138	è	#128..#154 are
98	b		139	ï	for various Eu-
99	c		140	î	ropean languages.
100	d		141	ì	
101	e		142	Ä	
102	f		143	Å	
103	g		144	É	
104	h		145	æ	
105	i		146	Æ	
106	j		147	ô	
107	k		148	ö	
108	l		149	ò	
109	m		150	û	
110	n		151	ù	
111	o		152	ÿ	
112	p		153	Ö	
113	q		154	Ü	
114	r		155	¢	Cents
115	s		156	£	Pounds
116	t		157	¥	Yen
117	u		158	Pt	Pesetas
118	v		159	ƒ	Groschen
119	w		160	á	
120	x		161	í	#160..#165 are
121	y		162	ó	for various Eu-
122	z		163	ú	ropean languages.

n	#n	Comment
164	ñ	
165	Ñ	
166	a	As in prima
167	o	and primo.
168	¿	Spanish punctuation
169	⌐	Corner
170	¬	Corner
171	½	
172	¼	
173	¡	Spanish punctuation
174	«	Much less than
175	»	Much greater than
176		Lightly shaded block
177	▒	Medium shaded block
178	▓	Heavily shaded block
179	│	
180	┤	
181	╡	
182	╢	
183	╖	
184	╕	
185	╣	
186	║	
187	╗	
188	╝	
189	╜	#179..#218 are
190	╛	for drawing
191	┐	single and
192	└	double line
193	┴	boxes.
194	┬	
195	├	
196	─	
197	┼	
198	╞	
199	╟	
200	╚	
201	╔	
202	╩	
203	╦	
204	╠	
205	═	
206	╬	
207	╧	
208	╨	
209	╤	

n	#n	Comment
210	╥	
211	╙	
212	╘	
213	╒	
214	╓	
215	╫	
216	╪	
217	┘	Corner
218	┌	Corner
219	█	#219..#223 are
220	▄	solid blocks
221	▌	for drawing
222	▐	pictures
223	▀	
224	α	
225	β	
226	Γ	
227	π	
228	Σ	#224..#235,#237
229	σ	are Greek
230	μ	letters
231	τ	
232	Φ	
233	Θ	
234	Ω	
235	δ	
236	∞	Infinity
237	∅	
238	∈	Membership
239	∩	Intersection
240	≡	Congruent
241	±	Plus or minus
242	≥	Greater or equal
243	≤	Less or equal
244	⌠	Top of integral sign
245	⌡	Bottom of integral
246	÷	Division
247	≈	Approximately equal
248	°	Degrees
249	•	Dot for product
250	·	Almost invisible dot
251	√	Radical
252	ⁿ	Superscript n
253	²	Superscript 2
254	■	Small solid block
255		Blank

Keyboard Codes

This appendix lists the PC keyboard buffer codes corresponding to various keystrokes. They are arranged by key number and keytop label. The PC's Intel 8048 keyboard processor handles all keyboard events—keystrokes and releases—equivalently. It sends to a CPU port a *keyboard event code*, consisting of the key number and a bit to distinguish between a keystroke and a release. Since there are fewer than 128 keys, the key number requires six bits. Bit seven is set to signal a key release.

The keyboard processor also executes the *typematic* key repetition when you hold a key down long enough. That is not relevant for the considerations in this appendix.

Keyboard event codes are interpreted by the PC BIOS Interrupt 9 service routine, unless a custom keyboard handler is installed. In the PC *Technical reference* manual BIOS listing, this routine is labeled **KB_INT**. It ignores most key releases. Most keystrokes cause it to enter a corresponding keystroke code into the keyboard buffer for later processing. A few keystrokes receive immediate special handling.

KB_INT ignores all key releases *except* the <Shift>, <Ctrl>, and <Alt> keys. It records the current status of each of these. Several keys—for example <CapsLock> and <NumLock>—are regarded as *toggles*: corresponding status bits are initialized inactive during booting; keystrokes activate or deactivate them. **KB_INT** refers to the shift and toggle key status to interpret other keystrokes. For example, the upper and lower case <P>, <Ctrl-P>, and <Alt-P> keystrokes are characterized by distinctive codes in the keyboard buffer.

Keystroke codes consist of two bytes. There are three types of codes:

Code Type	Low order byte (*Even* buffer address)	High order byte (*Odd* buffer address)
Ordinary	ASCII/IBM code	Key number
Alt-Keypad	ASCII/IBM code	0
Extended ASCII	0	Extended ASCII code

Ordinary keystrokes correspond to some of the ASCII/IBM codes listed in Appendix C. Some of these codes have no corresponding key, so you must use the <Alt> key and the numeric keypad. The high order byte of the keystroke code distinguishes these two types of keystroke (there is no key numbered 0). It also distinguishes between codes entered via the numeric keypad and the top line of keys. The Extended ASCII codes are used for function keys, etc.

The following tables list the keyboard buffer codes for all interpreted keystrokes. The letter x identifies Extended ASCII keystrokes. Only a few codes are affected by the <NumLock> status; these are listed in the last table. Vacant spots in the tables indicate that the BIOS keystroke processing routine **KB_INT** places no code in the buffer. (It processes several other keystrokes specially: shift and toggle keystrokes are used to update the keyboard status bits; <Shift-PrtSc> triggers Interrupt 5, which normally prints the screen; <Ctrl-Alt-Del> triggers Interrupt 19, which reboots. <Ctrl-Break>, besides being buffered, triggers Interrupt 1b, for which you are invited to install a custom routine to handle user break signals.)

Key # = scan code	Key Label	ASCII/IBM or Extended ASCII (x) keystroke codes			
		Base case	Shift case	Ctrl case	Alt case
1	Esc	27	27	27	
2	1 !	49	33		x120
3	2 @	50	64	0	x121
4	3 #	51	35		x122
5	4 $	52	36		x123
6	5 %	53	37		x124
7	6 ^	54	94	30	x125
8	7 &	55	38		x126
9	8 *	56	42		x127
10	9 (	57	40		x128
11	0)	48	41		x129
12	- _	45	95	31	x130
13	= +	61	43		x131
14	←	8	8	127	Backspace
15	⇒ ⇐	9	x15		Tab

Key # = scan code	Key Label	ASCII/IBM or Extended ASCII (x) keystroke codes			
		Base case	Shift case	Ctrl case	Alt case
16	Q	113	81	17	x 16
17	W	119	87	23	x 17
18	E	101	69	5	x 18
19	R	114	82	18	x 19
20	T	116	84	20	x 20
21	Y	121	89	25	x 21
22	U	117	85	21	x 22
23	I	105	73	9	x 23
24	O	111	79	15	x 24
25	P	112	80	16	x 25
26	[{	91	123	27	
27	] }	93	125	29	
28	↵	13	13	10	
29	Ctrl				
30	A	97	65	1	x 30
31	S	115	83	19	x 31
32	D	100	68	4	x 32
33	F	102	70	6	x 33
34	G	103	71	7	x 34
35	H	104	72	8	x 35
36	J	106	74	10	x 36
37	K	107	75	11	x 37
38	L	108	76	12	x 38
39	; :	59	58		
40	' "	39	34		
41	` ~	96	126		
42	⇑				Left Shift
43	\ ¦	92	124	28	
44	Z	122	90	26	x44
45	X	120	88	24	x45

Key # = scan code	Key Label	ASCII/IBM or Extended ASCII (x) keystroke codes			
		Base case	Shift case	Ctrl case	Alt case
46	C	99	67	3	x46
47	V	118	86	22	x47
48	B	98	66	2	x48
49	N	110	78	14	x49
50	M	109	77	13	x50
51	, <	44	60		
52	. >	46	62		
53	/ ?	47	63		
54	⇑				Right Shift
55	* PrtSc	42		x114	
56	Alt				
57	Space	32	32	32	32
58	Caps Lock				
59	F1	xa9	x84	x94	x104
60	F2	x60	x85	x95	x105
61	F3	x61	x86	x96	x106
62	F4	x62	x87	x97	x107
63	F5	x63	x88	x98	x108
64	F6	x64	x89	x99	x109
65	F7	x65	x90	x100	x110
66	F8	x66	x91	x101	x111
67	F9	x67	x92	x102	x112
68	F10	x68	x93	x103	x113
69	NumLock				
70	Break			0	ScrollLock
71	Home 7	x71	55	x119	7
72	↑ 8	x72	56		8
73	PgUp 9	x73	57	x132	9
74	-	45	45		
75	← 4	x75	52	x115	4

Key # = scan code	Key Label	ASCII/IBM or Extended ASCII (x) keystroke codes			
		Base case	Shift case	Ctrl case	Alt case
76	5		53		5
77	→ 6	x77	54	x116	6
78	+	43	43		
79	End 1	x79	49	x117	1
80	↓ 2	x80	50		2
81	PgDn 3	x81	51	x118	3
82	Ins 0	x82	48		
83	Del .	x83	46		

Key # scan code	Key Label	ASCII/IBM NumLock case
71	Home 7	55
72	↑ 8	56
73	PgUp 9	57
74	-	45
75	← 4	52
76	5	53
77	→ 6	54
78	+	43
79	End 1	49
80	↓ 2	50
81	PgDn 3	51
82	Ins 0	48
83	Del .	46

DOS Error Codes
and Information

The following error codes are returned by many DOS 3.3 function calls and Turbo C Library functions.

Error Codes

0 No error encountered
1 Invalid function number
2 File not found
3 Path not found
4 Too many open files (no handles)
5 Access denied
6 Invalid handle number
7 Memory control block destroyed
8 Insufficient memory
9 Invalid memory block address
10 Invalid environment
11 Invalid format
12 Invalid access code
13 Invalid data
14 Internal error - reserved
15 Invalid drive number specified
16 Cannot remove current directory
17 Device names are different
18 No more matching files found
19 Diskette is write-protected
20 Unknown unit
21 Drive not ready

22 Unknown command
23 Data error (CRC error)
24 Bad request structure length
25 Seek error
26 Unknown media type
27 Sector not found
28 Printer out of paper
29 Write fault
30 Read fault
31 General failure
32 Sharing violation
33 Lock violation
34 Invalid disk change
35 No more file control blocks left
36
   :   Reserved
70
80 File exists
81 Reserved
82 Cannot make
83 Fail on Int 24

For the error codes listed above, the DOS *Get extended error* Function 59 returns the appropriate one of the following *error class numbers*:

Error Classes

1 Out of resource
2 Temporary situation
3 Authorization
4 Internal
5 Hardware failure
6 System failure
7 Application program error

8 Not found
9 Bad format
10 Locked
11 Media
12 Already exists
13 Unknown

Also, for each of these codes, Function 59 returns a suggested *action code*, as follows. (These are merely suggestions, and may be inappropriate in certain situations.)

Suggested Action Codes

1 Retry
2 Delay retry
3 User
4 Abort

5 Immediate exit
6 Ignore
7 Retry after user intervention

Finally, the function returns the following *location codes*:

Error Location Codes

1 Unknown
2 Block device
3 Reserved

4 Serial device
5 Memory

Bibliography

[1]   AST Research, Inc., *RAMpage!™ Expanded memory card for the IBM personal computer, IBM PC-XT, and IBM-compatible machines: User's manual*, Publication 000295-001 B, 1985.

[2]   Blaise Computing Inc., *ASYNCH MANAGER Serial communications support: User reference manual*, 1987.

[3]   Blaise Computing Inc., *POWER SCREEN: User reference manual*, Version 1.00, 1987.

[4]   Blaise Computing Inc., *Turbo C TOOLS Function support for Turbo C: Reference manual*, Version 5.00, 1987.

[5]   Borland International Inc., *Turbo C 1.5 run-time library support*, 1988.

[6]   Borland International Inc., *Turbo C Addendum: Version 1.5 additions and enhancements*, 1987.

[7]   Borland International Inc., *Turbo C Reference guide*, Version 1.0, 1987.

[8]   Borland International Inc., *Turbo C User's guide*, Version 1.0, 1987.

[9]   Digital Research Inc., *GEM™ programmer's guide*, 2 Vols., 1985.

[10] Ray Duncan, *Advanced MS-DOS*, Microsoft Press, 1986.

[11] Lewis C. Eggebrecht, *Interfacing to the IBM personal computer*, Howard W. Sams, 1983.

[12] Samuel P. Harbison & Guy L. Steele Jr., *C: A reference manual*, 2nd ed., Prentice-Hall, 1987.

[13] *IBM Personal Computer Seminar Proceedings*, (II, No. 11, Nov. 1984). This issue of IBM's "Publication for Independent Developers of Products for IBM Personal Computers" is devoted to the IBM Enhanced Graphics Adapter.

[14] Institute of Electronic and Electronics Engineers, Inc., *IEEE standard for binary floating-point arithmetic*, IEEE, 1985.

[15] Intel Corporation, *iAPX 86,88,186 and 188 User's Manual: Programmer's Reference*, 1985.

[16] Intel Corporation, *iAPX 286 programmer's reference manual including the iAPX 287 numeric supplement*, 1984.

[17] Intel Corporation, *Microsystem components handbook*, 2 Vols., 1985. This is a huge compendium of the technical reference manuals for many different chips.

[18] International Business Machines Corporation, *Disk Operating System Version 3.00 Technical Reference*, 1985.

[19] International Business Machines Corporation, *Disk Operating System Version 3.30 Reference*, 1987.

[20] International Business Machines Corporation, *IBM Personal Computer hardware personal reference library technical reference*, 1982. There's a different manual for each PC model.

[21] International Business Machines Corporation, *IBM Personal Computer hardware personal reference library technical reference: Options and adapters*, 1984 ... This huge work includes technical reference manuals for many IBM PC products.

[22] Brian W. Kernighan & Dennis M. Ritchie, *The C programming language*, Prentice-Hall, 1978.

[23] Bradley Dyck Kliewer, *EGA/VGA: A programmer's reference guide*, Intertext/McGraw-Hill, 1988.

[24] Donald E. Knuth, *The art of computer programming, Vol. 3: Sorting and searching*, Addison-Wesley, 1973.

[25] Lotus Development Corporation, Intel Corporation, and Microsoft Corporation, *The Lotus®/Intel®/Microsoft® expanded memory specification*, Version 3.20, Part No. 300275-003, Intel Corporation, 1985.

[26] Lotus Development Corporation, Intel Corporation, and Microsoft Corporation, *Lotus®/Intel®/Microsoft® expanded memory specification*, Version 4.00, Part No. 300275-005, Intel Corporation, 1987.

[27] John E. McNamara, *Technical aspects of data communication*, Digital Equipment Corporation, 1977.

[28] Microsoft Corporation, *The MS-DOS encyclopedia*, Ed. Ray Duncan, 1988.

[29] Morgan Computing Co., Inc., *Advanced Trace86™: Assembly language debugging tool and assembler interpreter/compiler*, Version 2.2, 1986.

[30] Peter Norton, *Inside the IBM PC*, Rev. & enl. ed., Brady, 1986.

[31] Peter Norton, *Programmer's Guide to the IBM PC*, Microsoft Press, 1985.

[32] Charles Petzold, "Exploring the EGA," *PC magazine*, August, September, 1986.

[33] Murray Sargent III & Richard L. Shoemaker, *The IBM personal computer from the inside out*, Addison-Wesley, 1984.

[34] James T. Smith, *Programmer's guide to the IBM PC AT*, Prentice-Hall, 1986.

[35] James T. Smith, *Getting the most from Turbo Pascal*, MicroText, 1987.

[36] Mitchell Waite and Christopher L. Morgan, *Graphics primer for the IBM PC*, Osborne/McGraw-Hill, 1983.

Index

A diskette containing programs for the book *Advanced Turbo C* is available directly from the author. It includes all source code, as well as executable code for programs demonstrating screen handling with windows, keyboard input with menus, and interrupt service routines for hot key recognition and enhanced PrtSc hardcopy. To order your copy of this non-copy-protected diskette, fill out and mail this card.

Yes, please send me a copy of the diskette accompanying *Advanced Turbo C*, by James T. Smith. I enclose a check or money order for $15 plus 6.5% sales tax in California BART counties, 6% elsewhere in California.

Name _____

Firm _____

Address _____

City _____ State _____ ZIP _____

This offer is good only in the United States. We are sorry that we cannot accept credit card orders.

James T. Smith
Mathematics Department
San Francisco State University
1600 Holloway Street
San Francisco, CA 94132